Wind in the Wires

and

An Escaper's Log

And there was somewhere in me the thought: 'By Jove! This is the deuce of an adventure – something you read about.'

Joseph Conrad, *Youth*

Wind in the Wires
and
An Escaper's Log

Two Classic Memoirs of the Great War

Duncan Grinnell-Milne

Pen & Sword
AVIATION

Wind in the Wires first published in 1933
An Escaper's Log first published in 1926
This edition combined first published in Great Britain in 2016 by
Pen & Sword Aviation
an imprint of
Pen & Sword Books Ltd
47 Church Street
Barnsley
South Yorkshire
S70 2AS

ISBN 978 1 47382 268 9

Typeset in Ehrhardt by
Mac Style Ltd, Bridlington, East Yorkshire
Printed and bound in the UK by CPI Group (UK) Ltd, Croydon,
CRO 4YY

Pen & Sword Books Ltd incorporates the imprints of Pen & Sword
Archaeology, Atlas, Aviation, Battleground, Discovery, Family
History, History, Maritime, Military, Naval, Politics, Railways, Select,
Transport, True Crime, and Fiction, Frontline Books, Leo Cooper,
Praetorian Press, Seaforth Publishing and Wharncliffe.

For a complete list of Pen & Sword titles please contact
PEN & SWORD BOOKS LIMITED
47 Church Street, Barnsley, South Yorkshire, S70 2AS, England
E-mail: enquiries@pen-and-sword.co.uk
Website: www.pen-and-sword.co.uk

Contents

List of Plates

Foreword

Have you ever wondered, dear reader, who was the man behind the war hero, the real person? What was he like in normal life? Was he an everyday hero helping grandmothers and children across the street or did he have his faults like you and me?

Being Duncan's grandson, this question has always been of importance to me. I am very pleased that *Wind in the Wires* and *An Escaper's Log* are back in print. Since I never met my grandfather, they give me an insight into his life. Both books are very important from a personal and family point of view as part of our family history and both are very interesting as they are a record of wartime flying and captivity.

Duncan married my grandmother, Frances de La Lanne, in 1923 while he was posted as attaché in the Air Section of the British embassy in Paris. My grandmother was from a wealthy French family which left their plantations in Haiti and later in France shortly after the French Revolution. In Philadelphia, USA, they made their new home. After the First World War, Frances and her elder sister Mimi, who had lost both parents rather suddenly, left Philadelphia and settled in Paris.

I can imagine Duncan seemed like a dashing officer in Paris during the roaring twenties. My grandparents must have led an exciting life in the city during the period of Josephine Baker, jazz and scandal. But maybe Frances became disillusioned, for in 1927 their marriage broke up. My father Robin was a 2-year-old boy at the time. Frances went on to marry W.H.B. 'Reay' Mirrlees, one-time colonel of 3 Royal Horse Artillery who fought against Rommel in Northern Africa and was later promoted to major general serving with the Royal Artillery in India. Duncan married three times in all.

When I started studying law at the University of Freiburg, Germany, I found out that Duncan had also studied there before the First World War. At that time, in about 1981, I discovered a recording of Duncan broadcasting the news for BBC before the Second World War. The amazing thing was that he was broadcasting in faultless German, French and Italian. I wondered whether his excellent German was one of the reasons why he managed to escape from a German POW camp disguised as a German officer during the First World War.

Only when my father Robin de La Lanne-Mirrlees died in 2012 did I come across an unpublished manuscript written by Duncan's brother Douglas. Douglas Grinnell-Milne is sometimes mixed up with my grandfather Duncan since they shared the same initial 'D' and both were pilots in the First World War.

Douglas was ten years older than Duncan. Douglas's account starts in the family's home in Ennismore Gardens, London. Their father owned a bank. The Milne family originated from Banff, Aberdeenshire, Scotland, and their ancestors lived at Inchdrewer Castle. Douglas attended Harrow public school.

At the start of the First World War Douglas joined the 7th Fusiliers and, after a year, was seconded to the Royal Flying Corps, just like Duncan. With typically British understatement, he very briefly mentions his war exploits in his manuscript, but he must have been a remarkable fighter pilot, good enough to be included in *Pusher Aces of World War I* by Jon Guttman. Douglas was eventually shot down and he ended up in the same German POW camp as my grandfather Duncan. This how Douglas reports their encounter:

In a month we all go to Friedberg, and as I walk, I meet my brother Duncan, who has also just walked in from another camp – also a pilot in the R.F.C., also shot down, but six months earlier. We get into a room together, dig a magnificent tunnel together – with others, forty-six feet long – which is discovered by an unlucky chance, then in the end escape together, and in the most amusing way. For this act he and Fairweather and I become quick-change artists, and have four layers. Next to our skin, bandoliers of sausages and biscuit. On top of this civilian clothes. On top of this D. and F. the smartest German uniforms, made out of Russian cloth by the French tailor. On top of this English uniform, i.e. greatcoat and slacks. We can walk – breathing is the difficulty, for the sausages are very tight. We have three accomplices and walk with them into the hornet's nest – a small lobby with three swing doors, through which German clerks come and go continually – right in the middle of the German Kommandantur. The trained accomplices tear off our khaki strips of trouser, pull off our khaki coats, hand us new hats, and in two seconds D. and F. and I are transformed into Germans, turn right outside the building, an old sentry rushes for the keys – salutes – and we sail slowly – we can't sail fast – out of a side gate.

What happened next I will not give away in this foreword, but Douglas's narrative continues: 'The brothers are separated, and I go to Ingolstadt ...'.

In the Second World War both brothers joined the Royal Air Force again. Douglas, although he was a captain and a highly decorated one and in his late forties, was commissioned as a lowly pilot officer and was in charge of fire fighters at various air fields. One day he met my grandfather Duncan, and this is how he describes the episode in his manuscript:

One morning a large Army Staff car rolls through the Station gates, and pulls up in front of our H.Q. Inside is General de Gaulle, and sitting next to him, the only other occupant, is his first English Liaison Officer – a Wing Commander . . . my younger brother. Yes, it is true! My younger brother, ten years younger, is a Wing Commander, while I am just a humble, rather mould, and extremely irritable P.O. Actually I keep on getting letters from rude friends saying – 'What impertinence Duncan being a W.C. when you are only a P.O.!!!'

In the last war, Duncan, also a pilot in the R.F.C. – also shot down – also a prisoner – escaped and escaped, till he got back to England – then worried and wangled till he got back to France – got the M.C., D.F.C. and bar – commanded his squadron – and my younger brother was one of the boys!

He is also one of the lads – in love at sixteen with an infant dancing prodigy – engaged at eighteen to a well-known dancer – engaged at twenty-two to a notorious actress (with a lovely romantic name) – chronically entangled and disentangled through prosperous years of wild oat bumper crops – yet no can accuse him of being – to use the old expression – not 'a marrying man', and for why, because he is now going very strong and very happily in harness with his third most charming wife.

I often meet people who say to me: 'Your brother is the most amusing man I have ever met!' He is the most amusing man I have ever met, and that's why from quite early on, despite our disparity in years, we have gone about, and real rollicking times together.

I have heard him called a sort of genius, I think he is a genius in some ways – but like so many of that ilk there is something defective with his steering, a sort of wheel wobble, which sometimes results in getting him – instead of where he oughter – where he oughtn't. But socially he is a great acquisition, and has a most charming gift – a trick – I don't know what to call it – which works like this.

When you tell somebody a funny story or something funny, some laugh – some don't, some listen, most are thinking of the story they're going to tell you when you've finished. Some don't even wait for you to finish.

Not so my dear old younger brother, he not only listens, he not only laughs with keen enjoyment, but he takes your joke such as it is – however poor – and plays with it, twists it about, tosses it up, adds a bit on, and then roaring with laughter (at your joke), hands it back to you, rather better than before. This is most pleasant, and much appreciated by everyone he meets.

Though Duncan is a most remarkable chap, and I am very fond – and proud of him, the fact – odd – sad – and at the moment really very awkward – is that we aren't on speaking terms – haven't been since just before the war. A family row, childish but spirited. You've guessed it! – Money! – as usual – my fault perhaps as much as his. Still the fact remains, we don't know each other, don't bow when we meet – not that we have met – yet, or lately.

While de Gaulle is doing his rounds various busybodies are being extra busy sending signals: 'Your brother's here!' to me, as I am moving stealthily about the camp. As for Duncan he doesn't even know, when he arrives, that I am in the R.A.F. again, let alone at Odiham. But in the end the messages prevail. I produce myself in front of Station H.Q. – salute the Wing Commander – shake hands. We say less than half a dozen words – but de Gaulle is already sitting in the car and can't be kept waiting – my brother joins him – the car moves off – then stops again. Like all genii my brother being absent-minded – he has left his respirator behind. Willing hands hunt for it – the General waits – it is found – off goes the car, and I don't see brother Duncan again for nearly two years – for he goes with de Gaulle to Dakar, then off to Greece and places.

What an extraordinary encounter this must have been. Just imagine how differently the two brothers, who hadn't seen each other for years, would have behaved if their meeting had taken place generations before among their more emotional and talkative forefathers in southern France.

I hope this foreword has shed some light into who Duncan Grinnell-Milne really was. I admire the courage and determination he showed throughout his life, but most especially during the First World War as a fighter pilot and then as a prisoner of war trying again and again to escape from captivity. I am extremely proud of my British ancestors and grandfather in particular.

Patrick de La Lanne-Mirrlees
Mayor (retired)
Bremen-Delmenhorst, Germany

Wind in the Wires

Part I

Principal Officers in Wind in the Wires Identified from Nicknames

16 Squadron

The Starched Shirt – Major H. C. T. (Stuffy) Dowding, RA (later Air Chief Marshal Lord Dowding, RAF)
Growl – Captain C. Wigram, RFC
Wilhelm or Little Willie – Lieutenant H. S. Ward, RFC
Dante – (Observer) Captain C. Strong, TA

56 Squadron

Gilly – Major E. J. L. W. Gilchrist, 9th Lancers and RFC O.C. 56 Squadron
Shutters – Lieutenant R. F. Shutes, RFC and RAF
Johnny – Captain John Speaks, RFC and RAF (American)
Larry – Lieutenant Laurence G. Bowen, RFC and RAF (American). Killed in action, 15 September 1918
The Newt – Lieutenant D. S. C. Newton, RAF
The acting-adjutant – Lieutenant W. E. Clarkson, RAF

Chapter 1

The Wings Start to Grow

In July, 1915, I left the infantry regiment to which I belonged to be attached to the Royal Flying Corps. The meaning behind the word 'attached' was that the employment should be purely conditional. Like a defendant in a breach of promise case, I might claim to be attached but not definitely engaged. My status remained that of an infantry officer; if I were found to be unsuitable as a pilot, or if once in the air I discovered an unconquerable dislike for aviation, then I could return without let or hindrance to my battalion. There was no binding engagement to metamorphose me into an airman or, failing that, to use me in any capacity at all in the flying branch of the Army. It so happened, however, that my temporary posting became permanent and lasted for more than a dozen years of war and peace. This is, in part, the record of the first four of those years.

I

I arrived at Shoreham-on-Sea after dark. On the way from London, or rather during the change of trains at Brighton, I met an officer bound for the same destination. His name was on his luggage-labels, together with the address of the particular Reserve Air Squadron which I myself was to join. As he was a subaltern and as I saw no signs of his being a qualified aviator, I was not more than usually awed by the fact that he was a gunner. I had hoped that in aviation he would be as much of a novice as I was, but in the course of conversation he informed me that he had been at Shoreham quite a long time, that he was in fact just returning from leave which, I knew, was not usually granted until one had fully qualified. My respect for him increased.

I asked him about the squadron. He was very willing to talk and the first impression he gave me was encouraging: few parades, no unnecessary drill, no compulsory church on Sundays, rather more liberty than in an infantry regiment – provided, of course, that one 'got on well'. That, to me, meant showing promise as a pilot; my head was, so to speak, already in the air. And my companion must, I thought, be something of an expert, spending most of each day off the ground, for he told me that he 'simply loved the work'.

But a little later he let fall that he was struggling to qualify as a squadron adjutant and had practically given up the idea of becoming an active service pilot. Also he told me that no one did much flying at Shoreham and that after a few days' trial many officers returned to their regiments. I was not quite so sure that I was going to 'love the work'.

At Shoreham station a Crossley tender[1] met us – that, at any rate, was a step up from the infantry! – and took us over to the Mess in a bungalow near the sea. There, in addition to an air of comfortable informality, I found cheese, biscuits and beer.

II

The next day was Saturday, no parades but attendance at the aerodrome. From the Mess to the aerodrome was perhaps as much as a mile; we were driven there in a Crossley tender.

In the sheds was a collection of aircraft, most of them interesting museum pieces in which we were to be instructed, and two dangerous-looking single-seaters (said to be capable of ninety miles an hour!) with which, I was glad to hear, we were to have no dealings whatsoever. There were about half a dozen of us novices and the same number of older pupils. The instructors were pre-war regular officers, of the rank of Captain; they had flown in France, had actually been fired at in the air, had survived engine failures, forced landings, rifle fire and thunderstorms. We regarded them as living evidence that the Age of Heroes had come again.

During the morning one of the museum pieces was wheeled from its shed and set down upon the edge of the turf. With much pushing and pulling it was carefully arranged so as to face the wind, although to us laymen the

---

1. Crossley Motors supplied all the RFC's transport from 'workshop lorries' to the squadron 'touring car'. The 'tender' was a light personnel-carrier.

manoeuvre was a little obscure, since the bows of the aeroplane were almost identical with its stern. It had an elevator – or stabilising surface – stuck out in front upon curving outriggers of wood, and a double set of stabilisers – or elevators – fixed to wooden spars at the stern. But for the propeller which drove the machine inexorably forward and the arrangement of the pilot's seat and controls, it might have been designed to travel in either direction. Officially it was called after its inventor: a Maurice Farman biplane; but it was better known as a 'Longhorn', because of the outriggers to the forward elevator. A slightly more modern sister-ship was called the 'Shorthorn', because the inventor had, rather rashly we thought, done away with the outriggers and elevator; and taking them all round the *vaches mécaniques* of Monsieur Farman's breeding were pleasant beasts. But except for slowness and docility the resemblance to cows ended with the horns. To the uninitiated eye the Longhorn presented a forest of struts and spars, with floppy white fabric drooped over all, and enough piano wire to provide an impenetrable entanglement. At the sight of the craft before us, we put our heads on one side like puzzled terriers.

Presently the Longhorn's engine was started up. It was a Renault of uncertain strength, eight-cylindered, air-cooled, small but wonderfully reliable. When running slowly it made a noise suggesting a pair of alarm-clocks ticking upon a marble mantelpiece.

One of the instructors and a senior pupil picked their way through the wire entanglements, stepped over the wooden horns where they curved to the ground to become skids, mounted upon the wheels and clambered with a good deal of difficulty into the *nacelle*. No, it was not a body, nor a fuselage, nor yet a cockpit; it was a *nacelle*. The same name is used for the baskets that hang beneath balloons, but this *nacelle* was not of wicker. It was smooth and fairly solid-looking. It recalled the bath in which Marat was murdered. Doubtless to remove this ominous impression it had been painted a nice cheerful blue … The pilot and his passenger settled down into their elevated seats, adjusted goggles, helmets, and took a long look round as though it might be their last. After listening awhile to the engine, the pilot waved hands, attendant mechanics removed wooden blocks from beneath the wheels, and the machine moved forward slowly, lurching slightly over the uneven ground like a cow going out to pasture. The alarm-clocks ticked much louder; the forest of struts, the network of piano-wire, the *nacelle* with its occupants, all hanging rather mysteriously together, moved away at increasing speed. The draught from the propeller rippled the grass, rushing back to make us duck and clutch at our caps.

When I looked again the Longhorn was scurrying across the aerodrome at the most alarming speed. It seemed incredible that the various parts should still be holding together. The machine hugged the ground; the curving horns, the wheels and skids, the tail-booms were all buried in the uncut grass through which the propeller seemed to be blazing a trail, and that and the noise of the receding engine made me think of nothing so much as a lawnmower running amok. I watched, holding my breath. And – lo! – it began to unstick from the earth. It rose a few inches; higher; it flew! O wondrous contrivance: 'Hail to thee, blithe spirit, bird thou never wert!' Shelley should have been a pilot.

III

Nowadays such a machine in flight would seem ridiculous even to a child; but to us it was impressive enough. It was flying: that alone was sufficient. There in the sky was an aeroplane in which we could take a personal interest, in which presently we too would ascend, not as passengers but as pupils. It was very thrilling.

We watched that antiquated cage of a machine as if it were our own property. We noted the manner of its leaving the ground, followed its course in the distance, observed how it banked at the turns, held our breath as it glided in to land as gently as any thistledown. We forbore from criticism, we did not even remark to each other how, flying into the wind, this Longhorn appeared to have solved the problem of hovering like a helicopter, so low against the breeze was its forward speed. Nor did we discuss the value of such a craft in war. No matter what its limitations, this machine was to give up to us its one priceless secret, the mystery of how to fly. With luck we might some day progress to swifter, more deadly aircraft, but in this one we would first learn to grow our wings. She (*it* for such a venerable machine is not nearly enough) – she would foster the fledgelings. And out of a hundred craft, her we should never forget …

We crowded round when she came to rest in front of the sheds. The instructor got down from the *nacelle*, gave orders for the machine to be put away and strode forward with an expressionless face. A pupil braver than the rest of us made so bold as to ask: 'Will there be any flying today? Instructional flying?'

The instructor chewed a piece of grass.

'No,' he said curtly, 'it's not good enough.'

There was a wisp of cloud at about a thousand feet from the ground; the wind speed was perhaps as much as ten miles an hour. Out to sea it was a little misty. No, it was clearly not good enough.

'You didn't get very high during your flight,' another pupil remarked to the lucky one who had been passenger, a grave individual who seldom spoke to the novices because he had been a motor salesman before the war and had then taken a few lessons in piloting which placed him upon a higher level than the rest of us. He pushed his way through our crowd, looking rather grim and haughty.

'Of course we didn't get high!' he answered, and there was a rebuke in his tone. 'We could hardly get off the ground. No lift in the air.'

He seemed very wise as I watched him stroll away. Here, thought I, was another complexity added to the puzzling business of aviation. One had to study the air. The wind must be of a certain strength, the clouds at a given height and of known density. In addition there was something of which I as yet knew nothing. I must learn to sniff the air like an old hound, a flying hound; to judge the quality of the atmosphere from the wind upon my cheeks; to feel its nature between finger and thumb. Otherwise I might some day embark upon a flight only to find that there was 'no lift in the air' – whatever that might mean.

IV

'In aviation,' a friend of mine was wont to say, 'there is as much art as science.' And there is more in this remark than is at first apparent. Pursuits there are and professions that demand science and nothing else; for instance one may suppose that putting a man on the moon calls for a great deal of science but for very little art. On the other hand certain arts have scant need of science to bring them to fruition. A poet is not necessarily a scientist, not even as much of a chemist as Keats; and with aeronautics, in its earlier stages, art often seemed to be marching ahead of a science that was in its infancy and waiting for the pilots whose progressive discoveries, be it said, were frequently the result of accident.

I began to glean information concerning my new calling.

To be successful, I gathered, a pilot must learn to steer a steady course between the Charybdis of 'spinning', the remedy for which was not yet known, and the Scylla of diving into the hard, hard ground. 'Stalling' – that was a word I heard on everyone's lips: to lose flying-speed and, in consequence, all control of the machine. There were other minor difficulties to be reckoned with, mainly those connected with the strength – or rather the weakness – of the aeroplanes of those days. At all points one encountered either the unknown, or the more or less certain structural dangers. It was, they told me, courting death to dive the majority of machines at any appreciable angle, the speed and increased strain would pull the wings off. To bank too steeply might involve a sideslip or loss of flying-speed, either of which might quickly develop into the irremediable spin. 'Looping' had, of course, been done and overdone before the war, but only on machines strong enough to stand the strain. Had anyone attempted to loop a Longhorn, the poor thing would have tied herself into knots. And since looping was of no value by itself it was neither taught nor encouraged on any type of machine.

Before coming to Shoreham I had been taken up as a passenger several times, so that I had a rudimentary knowledge of flying. But now I perceived what innumerable lessons there were to be learned, anxiously, attentively, before one could hope to become an artist worthy of the name of Air Pilot. The whole business was unpleasantly suggestive of tight-rope walking, the margins of safety were so narrow. A Longhorn – and a good many other machines for that matter – would leave the ground at well under forty miles an hour, and I doubt if her top speed ever exceeded forty-six or seven whatever may have been calculated on paper. This gave one a variation of some ten miles an hour; if you went too fast something fell off or snapped; if any slower you stalled, spun, dived, slipped one way or another and ended for a certainty by breaking your neck. And then there was the question of the engine. At full power it was just enough to get one safely off the ground and to climb high enough for turning, but if you ran it at too great a speed the engine would overheat, and at the slightest loss of power the nose of the machine had to be pushed well down to maintain flying-speed. A tricky business!

In the Mess we talked a great deal of shop.

V

Eighteen is an impressionable age, especially for a budding pilot, so that it is not surprising that the first real lessons – roughly, horribly taught – should have been driven into me with such force that I never afterwards forgot them. It happened on a Sunday, the very first Sunday at Shoreham.

The day of the week did not make much difference to the routine of a Flying Corps squadron. If it were fine and there were machines available and pupils to be taught, instruction took place as usual, save that early flying was cancelled, we got up later and spent more time over breakfast. A stiff breeze came off the sea and the large masses of damp cloud everywhere would have made it far too bumpy for Longhorn work. But we strolled down to the sheds because we were all young enough to enjoy stroking our cows in the byre, even if we could not have them brought out for exercise.

At the aerodrome a treat was in store for us. A brand-new aeroplane of the most modern type had just arrived on a visit. It was being flown around the country upon a series of test flights by a well-known pilot from the Royal Aircraft Factory at Farnborough, accompanied by a civilian expert. We gathered about it in silent wonder, mindful of the pilot's request that we should not touch anything.

It was sheer joy to examine such a machine at close quarters. Those of us who had flown as passengers before coming to Shoreham had seen a good many sorts of ancient aircraft; all the greater now was our interest and admiration. The engine of this biplane was in front (like some German machines I had seen before the war), whereas most of those we knew by sight had it astern – 'pushers' – and the body was long, narrow, neatly shaped. The wings were thicker than those of Maurice Farman machines; they looked solid, strong. The bracing wires were no longer cable or piano, they were of a new design: 'streamline'. In the pilot's cockpit was a neat dashboard with instruments. The controls were operated by a straight 'stick', not 'handlebars' as in the Longhorn; there was a rudder bar instead of pedals. The tanks were said to contain fuel for more than four hours' flying and it was evident that in addition to the passenger this aeroplane would be capable of carrying a machine-gun or bombs. An improvement upon older models of the same type, it was believed to attain no less than seventy-six miles an hour at full speed. It was known as the B.E.2c; its engine was the 90 horse-power 'R.A.F.' – the letters standing for Royal Aircraft Factory, the home of those expert minds whose latest conception now stood before us.

I gazed at the pilot with envy while imagination soared faster than the swiftest biplane. Some day I too would wear Flying Corps 'Wings' upon the left breast of my tunic, I too would steer a wonderful B.E.2c and learn to manoeuvre it with graceful ease. I would fly such a machine in France; my wings would darken the skies above the expectant battlefront, the enemy's secrets would be disclosed to me. At my approach Zeppelins would hurry home, their huge sheds leap up in flames beneath my deadly rain of bombs, Berlin would pass sleepless nights. And at the end I would make a perfect landing before the assembled heads of the Flying Corps …

At lunch in the Mess that day we were very quiet, listening in awed silence to the instructors and the pilot from Farnborough discussing technicalities almost entirely over our heads. It was thrilling to hear the names of famous airmen bandied familiarly about, to hear of all the different types of aeroplanes with exaggerated speeds which we might hope to fly, and particularly to hear this so experienced pilot (a test pilot!) give his views on how to do this and that, how to turn quickly and with almost vertical banking, how to do a spiral glide, how to deal with the ever-mysterious 'spinning' and so on. It was rumoured that this pilot had frequently looped, and had even looped a B.E.2c! We listened attentively, trying to pick up what crumbs we might from his learned conversation.

There had been talk of the test-pilot staying the night at Shoreham; he had landed because of the bad weather. But during the afternoon it cleared up considerably and the wind, although still strong, showed signs of abating. He decided to leave. We hurried down to the aerodrome to watch him go.

The beautiful machine was wheeled forward, her engine started, warmed up. The test-pilot and his civilian passenger donned much leather flying clothing, climbed into their seats. The engine having been run up and found satisfactory, the wooden chocks were removed, the machine turned and taxied out to the far side of the aerodrome. A short pause, and the pilot gave the engine full throttle, taking off obliquely towards the sheds.

Against the wind the machine rose at once and began to climb steeply. The pilot waved farewell as he passed us by, heading west into the sunlight. Against the bright sky the machine was silhouetted, hard to see beyond the end of the sheds. But, as we watched, shading our eyes, there came to us suddenly the spluttering of a starved engine. The steady roar of the exhaust died down, the nose of the machine dropped. And now this expert pilot made his great mistake.

In the course of the short flight, he had attained a height of about one hundred and fifty feet and had crossed the boundary of the aerodrome. A road, a line of telegraph wires were beneath him, ahead a series of small meadows intersected by ditches. Rough ground, but possible in an emergency, especially as the strong wind against him would make the run on landing exceptionally short. There was, strictly speaking, no alternative for a safe pilot. But this pilot was more than commonly skilful, and he wanted to save his new machine from damage. Not that it would have suffered anything worse than a broken undercarriage, possibly a smashed propeller, from the forced landing; he wished to avoid even that much. And so he tried something which, in this instance, he had not one chance in a thousand of bringing off. He turned back to the aerodrome.

In the very few seconds that followed I remember feeling, in spite of my ignorance of piloting, an intense admiration for the brilliant way in which he handled the machine. Without a moment's hesitation he turned down wind as quickly and as flatly as possible so as not to lose the little height he had, held a straight course for an instant, then over the sheds began another sharp turn that, when completed, would bring him into wind with a space of fifty or sixty yards of smooth ground on which to land. Actually it was just possible of achievement, although as I see it now he was taking a terrible risk; the whole performance was cut too fine.

As he came towards the sheds his speed down wind seemed terrific, yet in trying to maintain his height he had in fact lost the essential flying speed. He was stalling even as he banked over the sheds. The nose went down with a jerk in the first turn of a spin. He missed the roof by a miracle but within a second of the machine's disappearance behind the end shed we were horrified to hear an appalling crash.

Naturally we rushed forward in spite of the first-shouted order that all pupils should stand back – the sight of a probably fatal crash, it was rightly thought, might upset some of us – we *had* to see; we ran for it. Beyond the end shed the new aeroplane lay flat on the ground, a mass of wreckage. Both men sat in their smashed cockpits motionless. Unconscious or dead? We were not long in doubt for worse was to follow. As we came nearer the wreck about which mechanics were already trying to extricate the pilot and passenger, there was a flicker of fire from beneath the fuselage. And all at once the mechanics sprang back as with a roar a great flame shot up from the burst petrol tank. It swept back over the passenger; when it reached the pilot he moved uneasily, seemed to shake himself, fumbled with his safety-belt, then jumped out just in time, his clothing alight.

There were cries for extinguishers, for axes to hack through the broken wings, for help to pull away the wreckage, for the ambulance – for anything and everything to save the passenger. He was still in the machine and still alive. Mercifully he did not recover consciousness – afterwards it was found that his skull had been fractured in the crash – but he kept on moving. And we were powerless. The extinguishers had no effect upon thirty gallons of blazing petrol. The strong wind blew the flames into his face. Before our very eyes he was burnt to death, roasted. It took a long time; it was ghastly …

The fire died down, smouldered awhile, went out. The wind dropped; the sun set and the sky glowed with rare beauty. But we pupils walked back to the mess in glum silence.

VI

Upon the following morning all attached officers were summoned to the Squadron Office. We expected the summons, although I don't quite know what we expected to hear. I suppose that, amongst other things, we thought to be given news of the pilot in hospital, possibly to be complimented upon the vain efforts we had made to penetrate the barrier of fire and upon the *sang-froid* we had shown afterwards. Perhaps more than anything we hoped to hear that the fire had not been so intense as our eyes had led us to believe, that the unfortunate passenger had in some way been protected – by his goggles, by his flying helmet or by his leather clothing – from the devouring fury of the flames, so that there might be a chance of his recovery. Or did we hope to be told that something very strange had gone wrong with this new aeroplane, something very startling and unusual which could not occur again, that flying was not like this, horrible, cruel?

The squadron-commander strode into the Office, flung his cap upon the table, drew a cane chair forward. Placing one foot upon the seat he rested an elbow on his knee.

'With regard to this unfortunate and unnecessary happening,' he began harshly, 'the first and only thing to do is to find out the causes of the accident, to see where the pilot was to blame so as to learn what lessons we may. Now in this particularly stupid case ...'

I thought him terribly callous.

* * *

'A pilot must never turn down wind at a low altitude when faced with the possibility of a forced landing.

'A pilot in difficulties after leaving the ground must keep straight on and not attempt to turn back.

'A pilot must save himself and his passengers first, not the aeroplane. It is better to smash wheels and propeller than burn a man to death.

'A pilot must take particular care to maintain flying-speed after engine failure.'

Those were the lessons. If the manner of their teaching was hard, it was also effective.

VII

It was a long time between this accident and the start of my regular training in the air. After one preliminary flight many days passed before I was again taken up. Bad weather, too few machines and instructors, too many pupils, were the real causes of delay; but I began to fret and to wonder if discrimination rather than luck was not responsible for my name so seldom being called when the Longhorns stood in fantastic array upon the turf. I remembered the words heard on the evening of my arrival from the would-be adjutant; that little flying was done at Shoreham and that many pupils returned in disgust to their regiments. I had no intention of leaving the Flying Corps until I had had a fair chance of becoming a proficient pilot, but the slowness of the commencement was discouraging.

Nearly two weeks had gone by when one evening I was noticed as I stood disconsolate in front of the sheds. An instructor saw me and beckoned. We embarked in a Longhorn; I was given a flight lasting nearly half an hour. And after that things moved more quickly. Several days in succession were marked by flights either in the stillness of very early morning or in the calm of late afternoon. I began to know my way about a Longhorn. The forest of struts did not grow any thinner, but meaning and order came to it. It no longer took me minutes to thread an anxious path through the wires; I learnt to scramble quickly into my seat in the *nacelle* where the controls were at last becoming familiar. I was allowed to feel those controls while flying. After half a dozen flights I was even permitted to land and take off with only slight assistance from the instructor. In the air I could sense some connection, however vague, between the harmonium pedals working the rudder and the handlebars shaped like a pair of spectacles which gave lateral control. Presently I felt sure that I was making steady progress.

VIII

One cold grey morning a few of us were gathered upon the stretch of tarmac in front of the sheds expecting to enjoy that most exquisite of amusements, the sight of another's embarrassment, agony and discomfiture. One of our number, a man who had come to Shoreham before me and who had done considerably more flying, was to go for his first solo flight. He had been warned the night before, after half an hour in the air with the senior instructor.

'You'll go solo at dawn tomorrow,' he had been told briefly. And if for 'go solo' the words 'be shot' had been substituted he could not have been more upset.

Anxious though we were to be taken up for instruction, we hoped that first of all we should be permitted to witness the unfortunate man's departure. Secretly, I think we rather hoped that he would crash – not badly, we wished him no harm, but just enough to provide us with real entertainment. Before one's own turn comes, one is apt to be merciless – not only in aviation.

We were discussing the prospects of this little quiet fun at another's expense, when the instructors came from the office. One of them marched up to our group; as he passed I caught his eye. He stopped. Ah-ha, I thought, this is where I put in some more instructional flying. But the Winged Hero was regarding me thoughtfully with something in his eye that reminded me of a hungry tiger looking at his meat.

'How much dual control have you done?' he asked.

'Three hours and twenty minutes,' I answered, hopeful that so small an amount would induce him to give me more at once.

'H'm …' he muttered, still looking at me fixedly. 'Do you think you could go solo?'

The question staggered me. All my past lies flashed before me, whirled in my head and merged into one huge thumping fib.

'Yes,' I answered, and at once regretted it.

'Very well then …' The instructor's voice was kind now, like that of a surgeon about to announce the necessity for a major operation. 'Very well, take up Longhorn Number 2965.'

Behind me there was titter of mirth, but it evoked no response on my part. My hour had struck before I was prepared. I knew nothing whatever about flying, and it was far too early in the morning and it was cold and I hadn't had breakfast. I was doomed and I knew it. I felt like asking for a priest … Walking blindly forward, I put on my flying cap.

Against the wings and struts of Longhorn Number 2965 mechanics were idly leaning. They made no move as I approached, gave me no more than a quick glance. They knew well enough that I was a pupil, that unless I came to a machine with an instructor there was nothing doing. But when I began to clamber into the *nacelle* they stopped talking and looked at one another uneasily.

'I am taking this machine up, Flight-Sergeant,' I announced boldly.

There was a nasty sort of silence during which I felt that behind my back signs were being made indicating doubt of my sanity. At length I heard a subdued voice say, 'Very good, sir. Switch off?'

'Switch off,' I replied, nervously settling into the front seat of that *nacelle* which now seemed as lonely as an autocrat's throne. At my back whispering mechanics turned the propeller. 'Contact?' came a voice like that of an undertaker.

For a moment I gave myself up to the wild and wonderful hope that the engine was not going to start. They had to pull it round twice. And then it clitter-clattered into life and I knew that I was 'for it'. Adjusting the throttle to slowest running, I stared round fearfully at the collection of struts, tail-booms and spars that had once again resolved itself into a dense forest in which I would presently be as lost as any Babe in the Wood. Through wire entanglements I caught sight of two mechanics grinning at me. Horrible ghouls, gloating over my forthcoming demise! Was there no way out? I turned my face to the morning sky where the light was still growing. Like the tenor in Tosca I had never loved life so much. Not a breath of wind anywhere, save the slight draught of the slowly revolving propeller. I sniffed the air, and inspiration came to me. Perhaps if I got out of the *nacelle* and strolled nonchalantly over to the sheds murmuring, 'No lift in the air,' I should be granted a reprieve. I looked hopefully over the side. Below stood the instructor.

'Get well out across the aerodrome before you take off,' he said. 'And don't taxi too fast.'

I nodded, speechless, and buckled up the safety-belt.

IX

In those days the newspapers still occasionally referred to an aeroplane pilot as 'the intrepid rider', and upon the instant when Longhorn and I rose gently into the air I came to know that the expression referred to me. I was intrepid whether I liked it or not. And I was certainly a rider. I squatted rigidly upright upon the edge of my elevated seat, holding the handlebars delicately between forefinger and thumb, treading the rudder pedals as though I were walking upon unbroken eggs. Behind me the alarm-clocks ticked relentlessly; ahead that tea-tray of an elevator held not only my gaze but all my hopes of surviving the adventure.

Ah, that forward elevator, what a blessing it was! It gave one something to look at, something to guide one in keeping the nose of the machine at the right level. If you kept it on or just below the horizon you were safe – until the time came to make a turn. Then you put the nose down lower still. Never make a level turn, still less a climbing one – that was bound to be fatal. Before putting on any bank push the stick forward a little to increase the speed ... I was remembering my lessons, anxiety was diminishing. I looked quickly about me. Everything seemed to be all right. But it would not last unless I continued to be very, very careful. I glued my eyes to the front elevator.

Presently, without daring to move my head, I rolled my eyes towards the instruments. The altimeter was recording something. I was indeed off the ground: nearly four hundred feet! It was exhilarating at this altitude. But only momentarily so; I had to get back. My wrist-watch showed that I had been in the air for no less than three minutes. Underneath the elevator, Worthing pier was beginning to come close. Yes, I had to get back! Without great skill this first turn would be my last ...

Nose down; a slight movement of the handlebars; the machine banked slowly. Softest pressure of the foot; she began to turn. I repeated my lessons over the sea. 'Beware of stalling. Beware of spinning. Don't push the nose down too far, or you'll strain the engine or pull the wings off or something. Gently does it!' The bungalows of Shoreham came in sight. 'Now – off rudder, off bank – steady! Level up, watching the elevator. And watch the speed-gauge too. Fifty-three miles an hour? Oh, that's far too much! Up with the nose – gently – just a ve-ry lee-tle. There!' I had completed my first turn.

The aerodrome came towards me again, passed by directly underneath. I risked a glance over the side. There was quite a crowd of pupils on the tarmac. They were staring up, watching me; I was on my first solo and it was proving to be successful! But I was not home yet and pride comes before a fall ... The speed indicator showed thirty-eight. Too slow! Down with the nose – but *gently*. Unless I was gentle as a nursing mother something dreadful would happen. I would spin into the ground and wake up to find, at the best, wings very different from those I coveted sprouting from between my shoulder-blades.

Not far from Brighton I made my second turn and headed back into wind. Then over Shoreham town I pushed the nose firmly down and pulled back the throttle. Longhorn commenced to glide towards the aerodrome. The air-speed settled down to a steady forty-two. I had entered the last phase.

In the very early days machines used to be flown down with the engine almost full out, a procedure considered necessary to maintain flying-speed. Of course the majority of the early aviators never had to come down from any very great height or they would have found it a tiresome business, but the first time that a pilot (whose engine, it so happened, had failed at a considerable altitude) *glided* down to his landing something new and wonderful was discovered. The French called it a *vol plané*, the British Press a 'Death Dive'. It was that morbid expression which I remembered as the Longhorn bore me earthwards.

Not that I found gliding unpleasant, far from it. It was the prospect of landing that I dreaded. All had gone well so far. Longhorn was still intact, making a happy rustling sound as she sailed slowly through the calm air. On the green surface of the aerodrome the sun shone, the wind rippled the long grass. But what was going to happen when these two met, the aeroplane and the aerodrome? I was sure I could never bring myself – alone, unaided – to 'flatten out' at just the right moment. There would not be much noise, I thought; a heavy crunch and then struts, spars, wires, white fabric would all collapse and fold themselves about me. I would remain sitting in the crushed *nacelle* until they sent a party from the sheds to liberate me; and their laughter would be restrained only if I were seriously hurt.

Meanwhile the ground seemed to be coming up in normal fashion. The broad river curving towards the sea glinted darkly, momentous as the Rubicon. But Longhorn did not falter; she crossed it, and was at just the right height on passing the tall bank at the eastern side of the aerodrome. The sun still shone. I could see the daisies in the grass beneath me. Time to flatten out. With the utmost gentleness I pulled back the handlebars, treading nervously on the harmonium pedals to bring the nose dead into wind. The front elevator rose, the noise of the wind in the wires died away. I stared ahead like a hypnotised rabbit. From directly underneath there came a hollow rumble, from further astern a scraping sound; the machine shook, gave a gentle lurch. My heart rose to my throat with alarm. What was happening? Still keeping my head rigidly to the front I squinted down at the speed indicator. Nothing! At the altimeter – Zero ... I looked boldly over the side. The grass was very near, almost motionless. I could see each blade. Fuzz from a dandelion blew slowly past the lower plane. I had landed.

As I taxied back to the sheds two mechanics came out to guide the machine in. They were still grinning. Never have I seen smiles of such seraphic beauty.

'How did you get on?' a fellow pupil asked.

'Oh, all right,' I answered carelessly. 'But – not much lift in the air.'

X

Not many days later a number of us were transferred at short notice to Gosport, to complete our training and to be attached to a new squadron then being formed. The transfer was something of a move up, but to me it was also very alarming. I had got the hang of things at Shoreham; I had done some half a dozen solo flights, I knew the instructors and their ways, I was at home in two different Longhorns, and I had learnt to find my way about the country within a radius of as much as three miles in the air. What was going to happen at Gosport? Would the new instructors understand me or I them? Would they fly in the same manner? Would their machines be the same? There were many different types at Gosport; would I be expected to fly them all? If I were not taken up again soon I might forget the little I had learnt. The very air might be different; it might not have as much lift as at Shoreham. It was all very disquieting.

And indeed for the first few days at the new station I was not altogether happy. The quarters were uncomfortable, my kit had not arrived, the place was overcrowded, and overcrowded not only with pupils but with a lot of people who already had their 'Wings' and would scarcely speak to the novices. Worst of all when I arrived there was only one Longhorn available for training; a queue waited to fly her.

There were also, it is true, a couple of Shorthorns, but my log-book showed that I had not yet been up in one and the shortage of instructors prevented my being given the necessary dual-control flights. The trouble with a Shorthorn was that it had no nice tea-tray elevator in front with which to judge the correct flying angle, and thus the first impression to a Longhorn pilot was quite frightening, as if he were hanging out recklessly over a balcony. I stationed myself close to the only Longhorn and pestered everyone who came by to let me take her up.

In this way I managed to get in an occasional flight, accomplished safe landings, broke nothing. But progress was distressingly slow. I began to think that perhaps I was fated to remain a Longhorn pilot all my days; at times I even hoped so, for some of the other machines at Gosport were rather terrifying. There were B.E.s of various categories – and the last B.E. I had seen had been the burning wreck at Shoreham – there were Caudrons with powerful 80 horsepower 'Gnome' engines, Blériot monoplanes, Martinsyde scouts and many others. All seemed wonderfully fast, modern, powerful, and all a trifle dangerous to the eye of a novice.

One fine evening after I had completed a practice flight in the Longhorn, a friendly young instructor took me over to look at a Caudron from close quarters. She was a nice little machine with engine and propeller in front, a small boat-shaped body for two people, and wooden tail-booms running back to the elevator and rudders. She could do about sixty miles an hour when hard pressed.

The instructor climbed up, inviting me into the passenger seat in front of him. It was a bit cramped and I did not at all like the way a piece of cowling, removed to let me enter, was bolted down behind me to prevent my falling out. I was afraid that if the machine crashed that front seat would become a death trap. But I said nothing and a moment later the engine was started.

I held my breath as we took off, but except for the engine smelling abominably and making a great deal of noise (it was the first time I had flown behind a rotary engine) I enjoyed the flight thoroughly. I was with an excellent pilot and I felt quite safe after all in the front seat. This was, for me, a new type of aeroplane, a new experience about which I would be able to talk in the Mess. All too soon it was over. I was rather surprised when we landed in the middle of the aerodrome and when, turning round, I saw the pilot getting out of his seat although the engine was still running. I unbolted the cowling at my back and started to get out too, thinking that perhaps something had gone wrong and that I could help. But by now the pilot was standing on the grass, buzzing the engine on and off by means of a switch at the side of the body. He signed to me not to get down but to climb into the pilot's seat.

'Try the controls,' he said between buzzes.

I tried them. They seemed all right. Lateral control was by 'warping' the wing instead of by aileron; it seemed rather stiff, but I supposed that very little would be necessary for normal bank. The rudder control was much lighter.

'She needs a bit of left rudder in the air,' the pilot remarked. 'And you can leave the throttle control there' – he indicated the position – 'all the time you're flying, but hold on to it. Cut it down a little when you want to glide, and use your thumb-switch. Understand?'

I nodded intelligently, thinking it all over and trying to remember some of it for future reference.

'All right,' he went on, 'don't stay up for more than twenty minutes. Off you go!'

'Off I go?' I repeated, unable to believe my ears.

He wagged his head cheerfully and let go of the switch. The machine began to move forward.

I cried out anxiously.

'But – I say …' The engine was making a horrible noise and I had forgotten where the switch was. The pilot did not hear me.

'Don't forget,' he shouted as he skipped out of the way of the tail-booms, 'don't forget that she stalls at forty-two!'

I stared forward helplessly, hopelessly. The machine was bumping about over a stretch of uneven ground, swinging wildly from side to side. Which rudder had he told me to use? Left or right? I tried each in turn, gradually discovering how to keep the nose straight while fumbling around with my left hand to find the switch. My fingers encountered the throttle lever; more by less or chance I pushed it forward to the very position the instructor had indicated. The engine roared with satisfaction. The tail came off the ground, I felt myself being lifted in my seat. Instinctively – already it was becoming an instinct! – I eased back the control stick to prevent the machine from falling on her nose. The bumping and bounding suddenly ceased – merciful heavens, I was off the ground!

My immediate reaction was one of far greater apprehension than I had experienced upon my first solo. Then, for all my ignorance, I had really been quite comfortable in a Longhorn seat. Now everything was unfamiliar. I could not see ahead; there was a flame-spitting, whirling mass of cylinders and propeller in front of the frail boat in which I squirmed. And wherever I looked there seemed to be struts or wings to obscure the view – except of the departing earth. I held the stick firmly in what I judged to be a neutral position and watched the speed gauge.

I found the switch at last, but now I deemed it wiser to go on. I had very little spare flying-speed. If I tried to land I should come down like a cast-iron pancake, smashing the machine to match-wood. Besides, there was a line of trees ahead – about the only thing I *could* see – somehow I would have to get over them before finding safety. No use getting upset, I had to make a circuit of the aerodrome if I wanted to live to tell that young instructor what I thought of him. Clutching desperately at the throttle and stick I was borne aloft, thinking upon Elijah.

Compared to a Longhorn this Caudron was speedy and climbed remarkably fast. In no more than ten minutes I had reached a height of one thousand feet. She seemed to be climbing too fast. I peered hastily at the speed gauge. It was very hard to see, for the cockpit was dark and my eyes were half blinded by the sunset (probably my last) over the Solent towards which I was being unwillingly carried. At what speed, I wondered, had that man told me she would stall? Was it forty-two? Anyway, I was taking no risks. Well above forty-five for me. I pushed the stick farther forward – *Trial by Jury* was then playing in Portsmouth, a line slightly parodied came into my head in tune with the engine's beat:

> 'She might very well stall at forty-five,
> In the dusk with the light behind her.'

The light was certainly behind the instruments; I had to guess my speed by the feel of the machine, a lesson it was just as well I should learn then and there. Dusk? Yes, that was coming; unless I hurried the light would be bad for landing. I should bounce like a tennis ball. I tried a turn. It succeeded better than I had hoped. And of a sudden I felt a new confidence coming to me.

This was fine, this was real flying, better than a Longhorn. I made another turn. The light was on the instruments now, I felt much happier. Height two thousand feet, speed fifty-one, revolutions per minute, one thousand and fifty; everything smooth and comfortable. I looked out of the boat and down.

Fort Grange was directly underneath; the aerodrome a little to my left. Ahead the houses of Gosport; in the distant Portsmouth lights were already beginning to twinkle in the streets. I throttled down, buzzing the engine to keep the propeller turning. The machine glided slowly but extraordinarily steeply, I found; it was so nearly a dive that I watched the ground over the top plane. The summer air grew pleasantly warmer as I came lower, and greatly daring I essayed a turn on the glide. It was easier than I had thought, for there was not a bump or a pocket in the air on this quiet August evening.

Above the sheds, still a good fifty feet up, I straightened out, began calculating my landing point. A sidelong glance at the tarmac showed me the young instructor looking up from among a group of other pilots. He was very tall and therefore known as 'Tiny'. I hoped that he was proud of his pupil. I felt angry no more. Rather I wanted to laugh and shake him by the hand. I was glad that he had had confidence enough in my abilities to send me off upon this delightful machine ...

The landing held all my thoughts. Shakily I buzzed the engine as though sending out an SOS, drew the stick back gently, gradually, guessing the distance to the ground. The rush of wind died away; the nose came up steadily; the tail sank. I looked at the air-speed: dangerously near to the fatal forty-two mark, then just under. The machine sank a little, slowing down. And but for the rumbling of the wheels and the scratch of the tail-booms over stones beneath the grass, I should not have known that I had landed.

XI

There followed a spell of exceptionally fine weather, during which I was sent up two or three times every day for short flights on the Caudron, the Longhorn, or occasionally on one of the Shorthorns. But in spite of my new confidence I was still very cautious in the air, and on the ground I found myself always listening for useful hints that might be dropped by those Winged Heroes, the fully-fledged pilots. There were plenty of minor crashes, but none so ghastly or so close to me as that first one at Shoreham, and I fancy that those of us who had survived the moral effect of that disaster were no longer much disturbed by other people's misfortunes. And yet some of the mysterious happenings to experienced aviators filled me every now and then with anxiety for the future. There was a limit it seemed to the wisdom of even the best pilots; what on earth – or in the air – could I be expected to do in circumstances with which they themselves did not know how to deal?

The newly forming squadron at Gosport was to be equipped with B.E.2c aeroplanes. A pilot whom I knew and liked was sent to bring one from a depot near London. When he landed he became at once the centre of an admiring crowd, for the B.E. with its latest improvements and its 90 horse-power engine was a novelty and highly thought of. The pilot gave a half-humorous account of his flight.

'It was very bumpy over Winchester,' he announced, 'and the dirty beast tried to spin on me!'

Exclamations of interest were followed by many questions. How had it started? What was it like, how serious had it been, what had he done to correct it? His answers were calmly given, but they were not very clear. I at least could gather nothing from them; a spin remained something mysterious and deadly, a danger from which there was no salvation, which attacked one suddenly and for no reason in mid-air. I must watch for signs of that spin as a traveller through unexplored country might watch for a savage ambush.

The little Caudron, however, was perfectly safe; she had never been known to spin. Providing one did not stall her, she would give no trouble. She was strong, had a low landing-speed, required a comparatively short run for taking off and was more or less fool-proof in the air. Her one weakness was that whirling incinerator of an engine. But in spite of occasional trouble, I developed a great affection for the little machine. In her I made my first long cross-country flights and enjoyed my first two forced landings. I say 'enjoyed' retrospectively, because I managed to bring them both off successfully, not because I was at all happy at the time they occurred.

XII

It happened one day that, when I was about to leave on a cross-country flight in the Caudron, a letter had to be delivered urgently to a senior officer at that moment inspecting the reserve squadron at Shoreham. With some formality and many cautions not to tarry on the way, I was entrusted with the despatch.

To say that I was pleased to revisit in so smart a machine the scene of my first trembling solo would be far short of the truth. It mattered not to me that the despatch was of no real importance and that a copy was being sent by post; at being selected to perform this mission I was elated as if I had been promoted two steps in rank. It was a glorious morning, the engine sang a crackling paean of triumph; I flew via Fareham, Chichester, Arundel and Lancing. After much climbing, the Caudron reached a height of four thousand feet; below me small puffs of cloud drifted slowly astern. I felt rather reckless in thus flying above them, they gave such an impression of altitude; but I was beginning to know the look of the country from the air. I could distinguish between a railway and a river, between forests and factory chimneys.

Everything went well on the way out and I reached Shoreham in good time, looking down proudly before commencing the glide. Some of the less fortunate pupils of my day were still being taught here. I fancied I could discern one or two of them in the drooping Longhorns slowly circling the aerodrome. I switched off and dived earthwards – dived, because gliding in a Caudron, except that it was delightfully slow, resembled in angle of descent the 'Death Dive' of the newspapers. Over the sheds I buzzed the engine a good deal and did one gentle turn of a spiral so as to make sure of having an audience, then straightening out, came lower and – glory be! – made a very decent landing.

To complete the impression of efficiency I taxied in very fast, and in a Caudron that meant with the tail off the ground to avoid the braking effect of the tail-booms in the grass. More by luck than by good judgment, I switched off in the nick of time, fetching up on the edge of the tarmac, my propeller almost touching a Longhorn's rudder. A few yards away a group of officers stood watching; I spied my senior officer amongst them. Wishing to complete my performance as smartly as possible, I sprang lightly from the pilot's seat, forgot the control wires which ran aft to the tail, and tripping over a cable fell flat on my face. I began to regret that all the pupils were now assembled in front of the sheds; I could see wide grins on several familiar faces. However, picking myself up I limped clear of the Caudron with a barked shin, and hastened to deliver my despatch to the senior officer. He smiled, thanked me warmly; and when he added that I had made a very nice landing and that he hoped I had not hurt myself, I felt as proud as though I were the dying patriot reporting to the Emperor at Ratisbon.

In the Mess they treated me as if I already had my Wings. Even the No-lift-in-the-air motor salesman (*still* there) deigned talk with me. I told him the Caudron was very apt to spin.

XIII

But upon the return journey I paid for the pride and joy of the morning. I had had a swim and an excellent lunch; had I been my own master I should also have had a short *siesta*. When at length I soared into the air, watched by a crowd of envious pupils, and set course for Gosport I felt – for the first time in my life in an aeroplane – really happy, almost drowsy. The engine no longer seemed to emit a menacing roar, but rather to hum a regular, slightly monotonous lullaby. The air had all the requisite 'lift' in it, there were no bumps, it was warm even at two thousand five hundred feet and the sky was cloudless all the way to Gosport. I leaned back, very nearly at my ease.

On the way home I followed the seashore to see from the air a coast I had long known on the ground. Ahead, Hayling Island came gradually into my ken. I had done a course in machine-gunnery there before joining the Flying Corps and I thought that I would like to look more closely at so familiar a locality. After passing over it I should, of course, have to turn inland to avoid the prohibited area of Portsmouth; that would involve quite a long detour by Fareham. But there was plenty of time before sunset; the evening was calm, clear, and of such beauty as to make the temptation to stay up a little longer irresistible to a young airman.

Presently I was above marshes and mudflats and the arms of the quiet sea encircling the island. I began to recognise roads, lanes, cottages, clumps of trees, to see paths down which I had so often marched, open stretches across which I had rushed perspiring with weighty pieces of Vickers or Lewis guns. I smiled contentedly from the superior position to which I had advanced … Perhaps it was over-confidence that did it. I don't know. At all events there was a sudden change of note in the engine's steady music, then a slowing down and much vibration. From rhythmical roaring the explosions dwindled until they were like nothing more than a faint crackling of ice in a cocktail-shaker. Then they ceased altogether. The silence seemed immense. And with it came a nasty pain in the pit of my stomach: alone, two thousand feet up, an amateur pilot, and no engine! This must be the end. I fumbled around desperately; wiggled the throttle lever, tried the switch, buried my head in the cockpit to see if the petrol was properly turned on, fumbled some more.

When I took my head out of the cockpit I found that the noise of wind in the wings and wires had unaccountably died away. The rudder bar and control stick seemed strangely easy to move. And the nose of the machine was dropping heavily, uncontrollably … Heavens, I had lost flying-speed! I was stalling – about to spin? Without thinking I pushed the stick hard forward. The Caudron gathered speed; and within two seconds I was sighing my relief, wind had come back to the wires, feeling to the controls. I flattened to a more normal glide and began to do some quick thinking.

What were my lessons? 'Keep straight on, don't lose flying-speed.' Well, after a moment's panic I was doing that all right. The next step? 'Make sure of the direction of the wind.' At Shoreham I had been heading directly into it, how was it here? I gazed earthwards. There was a ripple of air over the cornfields, too erratic to be a sure guide. A herd of cows was obstinately refusing to obey the laws of bovine nature, for not two faced the same way. No sailing craft at sea, no flags on the houses. Ah, smoke from a cottage chimney! I had never seen household smoke as friendly. Country people should always let their chimneys smoke to help poor airmen in distress. I took the wind's bearing with precision, turned into it at once. Now? 'Choose the field in which you intend to land, and choose it as early as you can.' A glance at the altimeter – less than fifteen hundred feet – in alarm I hung over the side, goggling at the earth. Choose? Not so easy. There were innumerable fields, but only a few large enough. I examined those few attentively. Marshes! Or else green mud from which the tide had receded … Under a thousand feet now. No time to lose.

At last, just in time, I found it. The only smooth bit of pasture, it seemed, for miles, but not so very smooth at that. A sort of paddock, small, enclosed on three sides by trees, with a tall hedge upon my side. 'Aim at the hedge on the near side,' I had been taught. I did so and found that I was too high. Another lesson came back to me: 'If you think you are going to overshoot make "S"-turns so as to lose height.' I did so. In the middle of the second turn the engine all at once started again. If it had happened any higher up I might have tried to continue the flight, with unfortunate results for a second later it stopped for good. However, low down it only served to remind me of one more lesson: 'Always switch off before a forced landing, to minimise the risk of fire.' I knocked up the switch immediately. Fire? The field was small and the trees very close; I might crash and crash badly, but I refused to burn. I could remember no more lessons, there was no time to think of anything else. The machine hopped over the hedge; I commenced shakily to flatten out.

The landing was not too bad, although rather fast – a better fault than stalling! – and all would have been well but for a partly filled in drainage ditch concealed by the grass. I was staring ahead, wondering whether I should be able to stop before hitting the trees on the far side of the field, when there came a heavy bump beneath the wheels. The machine swerved, listed to port, and came to a sudden stop.

It took me a few moments to recover my wits in the surprising stillness of the summer's evening here on the ground. It seemed very wrong of me to have thus brusquely disturbed the dignified quiet of this sweet-smelling field. Then I scrambled out to inspect the damage. It was nothing much. A wheel had been broken in the ditch, a steel undercarriage strut twisted. It could all easily be repaired on the spot …

Solicitous inhabitants crowded round, offering help, advice, congratulations, food and drink, shelter for the night, a guard for the machine. I asked for a telephone. This was the first time I had broken anything since starting to fly, and now that the anguish of the descent was past I wondered ruefully whether the breaking of a wheel would not put a black mark against my name. From the nearest house I 'phoned through to Gosport.

The orderly-officer to whom I spoke was non-committal, he told me to stay where I was and that perhaps help would be forthcoming on the morrow. Then he rang off. I passed an uneasy night despite hospitable surroundings ...

But upon the next day, back at Gosport with the repaired Caudron, they said I had not managed so badly for a beginner – although they refused to believe that I had not got a girl hidden away on Hayling Island. No one, they said, would land there for less than that.

XIV

These ugly rumours were soon dispelled. Another and much longer cross-country flight in the same Caudron resulted in a second forced landing, this time near Winchester. And not only was it generally agreed by the pilots of Gosport that, with Portsmouth so close, it would be silly to have a girl in Winchester, but the condition of the 'Gnome' engine revealed on examination that I could not have flown another yard in any direction.

I had broken nothing on this landing and I was now considered advanced enough to pilot the famous B.E.2c. As a matter of fact I am not quite sure whether the machine I flew at Gosport was a '2c' or some other earlier category. It had a less powerful engine – an 80 horse-power Renault – cables instead of streamline wires, and wooden skids on the undercarriage. Altogether a less modern craft than the ill-fated machine I had seen burned at Shoreham, which had been of the type just coming into fashion.

But despite some preliminary nervousness due to the rumours of spinning, I soon began to like the B.E. as much and more than the other types I had flown. She was stable, easily manageable if a bit heavy on the controls, strongly built. One of the more experienced of the Gosport pilots had been known to loop his B.E. several times and no harm done, although he had not been allowed to repeat the performance in front of the novices lest we should be tempted to emulate him, which, frankly, was not very likely. After a few practice flights in this type of machine I was allowed to take up my first passengers, luckless young men who little knew into what trembling hands they had trusted their lives. Also I was allowed to fly in windy, bumpy weather that hitherto had been the signal for machines to be securely locked in their sheds for the day ... I flew over the New Forest, circling above lonely heaths and dark glades and gypsy encampments, retracing a hundred boyhood rides. I flew over the Solent and peered into the secret places of that shallow sea whose waters roll over my early dreams. I learned to fly a straight course by compass and to make allowances for the wind; I learned how to bank at 45 degrees, and how to do a spiral glide from a height of several thousand feet. The war? It seemed far away, but I would be in it soon enough.

XV

On the ground, during all this time, instruction in rigging and engine fitting went steadily on; occasionally we were given vaguely scientific lectures upon aerodynamics. And at length the great day arrived. A few of us who were deemed worthy were driven off in a Crossley tender to the Central Flying School at Upavon to be examined in our knowledge of aeronautics.

That the tests were not entirely easy was a matter of common knowledge. If we passed we would be qualified pilots, if we failed we would be set back many weeks, perhaps months. Failure was by no means unknown. In my own case it happened that I was a little ahead of the customary time, but there were only two things I had cause to dread: that I might not yet have enough flying hours to my credit or – much worse – that I should not have sufficiently mastered the Morse code, a thing which for years had tried my patience. We were required to read messages at a fair speed, so many words a minute. My average rate was so many minutes per word. All the way to Upavon I practised with a portable buzzer.

The examination started as soon as we had disembarked, and I quickly found that it was less terrifying than I had been led to expect. I was conducted round the sheds by a venerable naval airman – anything over thirty with pre-war flying experience was considered venerable – who asked all the hard questions of which I had had warning and who seemed surprised that I could also answer the easy ones. Another old gentleman – his hair was grey at the temples – took me to the repair shops and asked me what most generally went wrong with 'Gnome' engines. From personal experience with the Caudron I was able to tell him quite a lot of things in the manner of an expert, and I gathered from his friendly smile that I had scored a good mark. Then came the Morse. In a darkened shed a nasty little lamp flashed irritatingly before my dazed eyes. Pencil and paper were handed to me; I made a pretence of scrawling. And to my amazement the dots and dashes assembled themselves in the correct order. The letters, even the words came out right. But I must have been helped by some guardian angel, for never again was I able to repeat the performance.

The dreaded business was over. In the cool of the evening we motored home, singing and occasionally stopping at a wayside pub to drink to our own success.

XVI

Before leaving Upavon I had made fairly sure that I had qualified, but the official result was not announced at Gosport until a day or two later. At length the news came through. I was summoned to the squadron office to hear it. The squadron-commander beamed, offered congratulations. I was no more a fledgeling, he said, I was a pilot, a member of the Corps, entitled to wear the badge and uniform, *sic itur ad astra* and so on. But to me it meant even more than that. I felt that I was no longer temporarily 'attached' to the Flying Corps; I was permanently devoted.

In a momentarily serious frame of mind I hurried from the office and across the sunlit barrack square of Fort Grange. Barely six weeks previously, at Shoreham, I had seen a man burnt to death because of a pilot's error. Since then I had learned to fly. I had made no fatal errors so far, I must see to it that I made none in the future. I had been taught all the essential lessons. Now to apply them.

In the tailor's shop I watched a man sew the Wings to my tunic. When it was done I went to the sheds and had the old training machine brought out. By my orders and upon my responsibility she was started up. As soon as she was ready I took her into the air. For half an hour I flew steadily and, in a Longhorn, for the last time.

Chapter 2

The Wings are Spread

I

I had hoped to fly out to France as a member of one of the new squadrons, but it was not to be. At short notice a number of us were ordered overseas by boat and train. In the dawn of a September morning we came to St Omer.

At the railway station no one knew anything; elsewhere in the town men slept. There were five of us in the party, all pilots; we routed round the nearby offices together. From a sleepy N.C.O. we gathered the information that there was nothing doing until after nine o'clock, but he told us of a café that would be open, to which we repaired and ate omelettes uneasily, disturbed by a distant rumbling of guns that seemed to be calling us forward away from this strange inactivity.

St Omer was headquarters of the Flying Corps as well of the Army in France. The fact was known to the world, yet in the town itself the secret was closely guarded and we could find no one to guide us. At length we tried the telephone; to good purpose, but it was nearly ten o'clock before we reported to the Flying Corps' château. Then things went a little more rapidly. Too many pilots had collected during the past few days, there was no room in the château, no room at the aerodrome or anywhere else in the vicinity. Rather regretfully we were informed that we should have to be sent on at once to squadrons at the front. We sighed our polite relief and bundled into the inevitable Crossley.

A couple of hours later we were in the town of Aire, reporting to wing headquarters. More delay. The wing château was a place of dingy refinement. We were shown into a little *salon* that had all the feel of a dentist's waiting-room, including the month-old papers. The doors were firmly closed behind us – I was afraid that they were locked until I tried them – and for a while there was silence, save for that mutter of gunfire grown closer.

Unconsciously we talked in whispers, starting guiltily whenever some stern-visaged staff officer peeped in to glance at us as though we were exhibits in a morgue. There were a few books apart from the papers; I dipped into a life of Wellington (left about for the guidance of young officers?), wondering what he would have done or said. Here, nobody seemed to want any of us.

We lunched in the same *salon*, the wing transport-officer honouring us with his presence. Of the wing-commander we saw nothing. There were Indian troops in the neighbourhood, perhaps he had adopted their caste system. Towards four o'clock however there was a slight stir in an adjoining office; we were summoned forth and released from the sunbaked stuffiness of the house. In silence we re-embarked in the Crossley. The transport-officer, smiling mysteriously, saw us off. The driver alone seemed to know of our destination.

It was hot, motoring. The dusty roads slipped by beneath shady avenues or between the gently undulating fields of northern France. Two pilots were dropped off at a drowsy village near which was said to be an aerodrome. We could see no signs of it and they set out to find it for themselves. A little further on two more pilots departed; I was left alone on the front seat with the taciturn driver.

Heading north-east, we passed through Merville, alive as on a peace-time market day. The voice of the guns was like thunder now, but the countryside was heavy with peace. Hindus bathed and washed in a stream by the roadside. A great wagon laden with forage came towards us and, although the men beside it wore khaki, the stout hairy-heeled draught-horses might have been cut from a print after Morland, and the sweet scent of hay lingered long after our passage. I grew sleepy from the quiet drive; my head was nodding when we turned from the main road to bump over a deeply rutted track.

I rubbed my eyes and sat up straight. By the side of a russet farmhouse a line of motor lorries was drawn up. Beyond canvas tents, poplars cast long shadows across a reed-grown canal. The Crossley came to a stop. In the farmhouse I found the offices of my new squadron.

II

The Flying Corps seemed to have a knack of finding varied, even picturesque, quarters. At Shoreham we had lived in railway carriages more or less artistically converted into bungalows; at Gosport I had occupied a dugout in a dismantled fort; here the Mess and accommodation for more than half the squadron was in a barge floating upon the canalised River Lys.

From the farmhouse I found my own way to the barge past workshop lorries, stores tents, transport lines. There were very few officers about and the one or two I met were strangely distant, offhand, unwilling or unable to speak. Near the river I met one who so far broke the ice as to ask me to which Flight I had been posted. I told him, and in reply he nodded down the river-bank to a line of canvas hangars. 'There's your flight-commander,' he said.

Glad to know of someone to whom I had a legitimate right to speak, I hurried off.

'Come from Gosport have you?' he remarked when I had explained my presence. 'H'm – how much flying have you done?'

'Thirty-three and a half hours.'

'How much?' he exclaimed, but he meant 'how little'. And he went on to declare violently that it was a disgrace to send pilots to a squadron on active service who did not have fifty, no, a hundred hours to their credit. What types had I flown? Longhorn? Of course, but that was no damn' use! Caudron? Good Lord – that was worse than nothing! Ah, so I had flown a B.E., had I? What sort of a B.E.? Not the latest type, with the new undercarriage and the 90 horse-power 'R.A.F.' engine? No? Well then – no good. A Shorthorn? So I had actually had the goodness to fly a Shorthorn. Well, I should fly more of them here. 'And stand to attention when I'm speaking to you,' he concluded sharply. 'And salute when you wish to address me and call me "sir", and put your cap on straight!' – or words very much to that effect.

I slunk wretchedly away, wishing myself dead and decently buried. No wonder people spoke of the horrors of war, this flight-commander must be one of them. Later on I discovered that he was not such a bad fellow as he made himself out to be, although addicted to the three 'R's' – Raving, Ranting and Remorse. But at the time I was thoroughly crestfallen; joining this squadron was worse than being a new boy at school. Boarding the barge, I went to hide my shame in the little cabin which had been allotted to me.

After seeing to the disposal of my kit I sallied forth boldly to look at the sheds and aerodrome, or rather to look *for* the aerodrome; I had seen nothing so far that could be given so large a name. Walking along the river-bank I encountered near the canvas sheds a pilot and an observer. They stared at me and passed on without a word. I looked into one of the sheds. It contained a Shorthorn, a rather tired-looking machine with the extensions of the upper plane folded downwards for want of space. Some mechanics were working on her, in silence. I went on to the next shed; another Shorthorn and my flight-commander were in it alone. I backed out hurriedly, saluting. The flight-commander gazed at me thoughtfully, chewing a piece of straw, but he said nothing. People in England did not know all the truth; the navy was not the only Silent Service. I began to wonder whether I had not by some chance strayed into a colony of Trappists.

But whereas until then I had been willing to talk to anyone about anything, the aerodrome – so called – left me speechless. Roughly it was shaped like the letter L, but the upright stroke was barely one hundred yards long by twenty wide, while the horizontal stroke following the curve of the Lys was perhaps two hundred and fifty yards in length and varied in width from about a hundred feet at the far end to no more than forty in front of the sheds. The angle where the two strokes met was rough ground sloping down to the riverside at the barge's mooring-place. On the far side of the river stood a line of tall poplars, elsewhere there were hedges, ditches, farm buildings and aeroplane hangars. The short stroke of the L could plainly not be used unless there happened to be a strong and favourable wind; the main stretch seemed scarcely better. As a temporary and concealed landing-ground the place had little enough in its favour, but as the permanent base of a busy squadron I have still not the slightest doubt that it was one of the least suitable spots for an aerodrome in all the flat country of north-eastern France.

On the other hand, there was no denying that from the officers' latrines, which I next visited, the view of plough-land, lush grass meadows, reeds bending over still water, slender poplars, high red-tiled farm gables, the whole scene backed by a wooden horizon and cloud-flecked sky, was perfect in the best manner of the old Dutch masters. Whoever selected that aerodrome may very well have been an artist, he was certainly not a pilot.

On my way back to the barge I fell in with the flight-commander. He had an unpleasant way of materialising like some grotesque character from *Alice*. I was not quite sure which one, but it was not the Cheshire Cat for I missed the reassuring grin. 'Growl,' I thought, would be an appropriate name for him.

'Did you say that you *had* flown Shorthorns?' he asked in a more kindly tone than he had previously used. I told him respectfully that I had indeed had that pleasure.

'Lucky for you,' he answered gloomily, 'that's all I've got in my Flight at present. You'll have to hang around and watch. There's no machine for you. I've too many pilots as it is.'

That seemed to me the last straw. I hid in my cabin until it was time for dinner. *Que diable allais-je faire dans cette galère?* That was the right name for this vessel – a galley. What on earth had I been sent here for?

III

At dinner that night there was some effort at conversation, but it was not sustained. Almost everyone seemed afflicted with unnatural reserve. Alone the two flight-commanders spoke with any freedom, seated one on either side of an empty chair in which, I supposed, the squadron-commander would presently take his place. Only one other pilot spoke much above a whisper and he was a man who had recently been awarded a Military Cross for bringing down a German machine. He was not much older than I, very little senior in the Flying Corps; I would have liked to talk with him, to listen to his account of the fight. But he was very sullen, with a perpetual scowl on his face emphasised by a peak of hair growing low over his forehead almost to the bridge of his nose. He spoke only to the senior flight-commander, who gave him a patronising smile every now and then.

Half-way through the meal, the squadron-commander entered and made for the empty chair, murmuring faintly, 'Don't get up, don't get up,' as everyone rose to his feet. When all were seated again, Growl, my flight-commander, suddenly remembered me and I had to walk round the table to shake hands while the entire company stared in open-mouthed silence as though I were some newly discovered disease. The major gave me a limp hand together with a tired smile, and if I had not been so nervous myself I should have seen at once that, amongst other things, he was cursed with shyness. After I had returned to my place dead silence reigned which he attempted to break by speaking to everyone in turn. But it was always with that same tired smile, in a quiet, rather nasal voice, his eyes half-veiled like a coy maiden's, ready to turn hastily away from embarrassing talkativeness. He seemed satisfied at rarely eliciting anything more than a 'Yes, sir,' or 'No, Sir,' by way of response. Conversation dwindled gradually to a sort of timid squeaking of mice in the wainscot when the cat is near. It was plain that he was not popular in the squadron.

And yet he was in many ways a good man. In the long run I came to esteem him as much as any member of that peculiar squadron. But he was too reserved and aloof from his juniors. He had been a gunner before the war, and what in those palmy days had persuaded him to exchange the dignified security of his regiment for the risky unconventionality of the Flying Corps is more than I shall ever know. Perhaps, being like most gunners brainy and fond of maths, he thought to find those attributes useful in the air. But he was not a good pilot, seldom flew, and had none of that fire which I then believed and later knew to be essential in the leader of a good squadron. Nevertheless my heart warmed to him when one day, in the course of a rare conversation, he confided to me that he thought Surtees in some ways superior to Dickens.

Naturally upon the evening of my arrival I knew nothing of all this; yet I did receive a first and definite impression not so much of him alone as of all the men sitting about the gloomy table. They were bored. Bored with one another, bored with the war, bored even with flying. And the boredom seemed to be working from the head down to the feet. I don't go so far as to suggest that the major himself was bored with his command, but whatever enthusiasm he may have felt was stifled by his own reserve. The flight-commanders could hardly be inspired by his leadership, and the junior pilots had little or no incentive to strike out on their own. Joy was not the only thing lacking. The very life seemed, to my first ignorant glance, to be ebbing from the Mess in the barge as though we were the doomed crew of a derelict ship.

Towards the end of dinner my neighbour at the table jogged my elbow.

'Pass the bread, please,' he said in a hoarse whisper.

I had been spoken to.

IV

When we had risen from table I went up alone on deck and made my way to the bows of the barge. It was a gloriously fine night, starlit, windless and warm. Leaning my arms upon the rail, I looked down over the side. Upon the towpath along the opposite bank a man and a girl strolled, arms about each other's shoulders linking them so closely that in the dusk they seemed to be one very broad person with two voices. The man talked in low tones; at every pause the girl's laughter rang out clearly. As they came abreast of where I stood, there was a scurrying in the bank beneath them, the plop of a small body falling into the water, and the darkly shining surface of the river showed for a moment the arrowhead wash of a water-rat. There were few flowers nearby, but from the farm came a blend of warm, homely odours, of cattle and of straw. Close at hand it was very peaceful.

I leaned back against a deck-house, raising my eyes to the tall poplars sweeping the sky. Beyond them to the east the horizon flickered with intermittent fire, alternating from orange-yellow to greenish white. An incessant racket shook the air. Every few seconds calcium flares rocketed to the heavens, hesitated, then parachuted slowly earthwards, silhouetting the poplars and rimming their leaves with frozen light as though with hoar-frost. For an instant the countryside would be silent beneath the garish light, the trees motionless as if afraid, and then as darkness fell again distant machine-guns clattered anxiously at some unseen foe. Ragged bursts of rifle fire broke out suddenly like the angry barking of a disturbed pack of hounds. A shell sighed heavily over, settled down wearily; its explosion silenced the barking as if a door had been slammed in the kennels. Far to the south countless guns drummed with monotonous insistence the prelude to the battle of Loos.

From where I stood the nearest point of the firing line was under four miles distant. The noise made it seem even less, and yet viewed from the peaceful countryside it did not seem like war. Without stretching the imagination I could fancy myself watching the grand finale of fireworks at a big local fair. The surprising thing was that I should be watching alone. The only two possible spectators in the vicinity, the man and the girl on the towpath, were heedless of both the menacing gunfire and the display of coloured lights. It was as though they had tired of the noise and grim fun of that fair to the east and had sought the solitude of the river-bank to do their courting in the dark shadow of the poplars. They did not see me and I turned away from them to gaze at the unintended beauty of the battle scene.

All at once, from some room beneath my feet, a gramophone blared. It played the Foxtrot, latest of London dances; but its screeching was like an insult; a mockery of the night's tragedy. A voice from a cabin near the stern yelled furiously: 'Stop that bloody row!' The squeaky record came to an abrupt stop. A mile away a heavy shell burst impressively ...

When I went below to the Mess the senior flight-commander and his sulky friend with the Military Cross were drinking whisky together, in silence and without any apparent enjoyment. Another couple were playing chess. All four looked up in surprise at my muttered 'Good night.'

V

I had dreaded the morning and its threat of further encounters with the silent members of the squadron, its lack of anything to do except, as Growl had put it, to 'hang around'. But I was immensely cheered when after breakfast I was ordered to jump into a Crossley about to leave for St Omer. At the headquarters aerodrome, it appeared, I should find an aeroplane waiting to be flown back to the squadron ... For the organisation which wasted two days and two cars on moving one small pilot I was deeply grateful, since had I been told on the previous day to fly direct to the squadron I should never have found it even with the most accurate of maps. As for landing, I would certainly have crashed had I not been able to walk over the ground first to note the position of treacherous ditches and rough ground.

The drive itself was pleasant enough, but, as I might have expected, when I reached the aerodrome it was to discover that nothing was known of any aeroplane to be delivered to the squadron. In an office hut a polite but argumentative young man informed me that he had plenty of aeroplanes to dispose of – at a price. The price being a paper of written instructions, an official document or a signed order of some sort – a bond, in fact, by way of payment. I had nothing except my own word and Growl's command which

I repeated but which did not seem to carry much weight. We spent all the morning and part of the afternoon haggling, as it might have been over the price of a rug in an Oriental *souk*. At length when the young man saw that he could not get rid of me because I did not know where else to go, he took pity and ordered an aeroplane to be brought from the sheds.

The machine was only a Shorthorn and not very smart at that, but to me she was more precious than gold. She was to be my own aeroplane, the machine in which I was, to all intents and purposes, going to win the war single-handed – that is, if ever I managed to get her safely back to the squadron. I inspected her with the utmost care, examined her log-books, warmed up her engine slowly; too slowly for the attendant mechanics, as soon as I was settled in the *nacelle* they whisked away the wheel chocks and departed. I was left alone with my machine. No one took any further interest; St Omer aerodrome was deserted. I took off unnoticed.

In contrast to the previous day the weather had turned cold and damp; the wind was against me and there were banks of cloud below two thousand feet. I flew beneath them, anxious not to miss the aerodrome. The Forêt de Nieppe was a sure guide to the neighbourhood and after that the River Lys, but it was necessary to be cautious. Flanders is a patchwork quilt from the air, and the aerodrome lay close to the lines. I found it at last, the smallest of all the surrounding fields, and when I had landed and taxied the Shorthorn up to the hangars by the riverside I felt that a good day's work had been done.

Even Growl deigned to unbend a little. He exclaimed tersely that he was glad I had not crashed. Profiting from this favourable reception I asked if I could do a job of work on the morrow; I was keen to start, there were important operations afoot. Perhaps he was a little embarrassed by my persistence, or else he was suffering from remorse after his first unnecessarily severe treatment of me (for now I was flinging salutes at him upon the slightest provocation); at any rate after staring in silence for a few moments he told me grumpily that I could take the Shorthorn up in the morning. An experienced observer would be sent with me to show me the lines and to see that I did not get lost. I saluted again, but I could have jumped for joy.

VI

The members of the Mess were rather more lively at dinner that night. The great attack at Loos was in full blast; rumours of success were current. The squadron had done much good work during the day, mainly artillery observation; even the major showed that he was pleased by loosening up a little. At the end of the meal he sent the Mess-servants out of the room, had the doors carefully closed and read us the latest official *communiqués*, together with a vaguely humorous Intelligence Report generally known as 'Comic Cuts'. At the time it was thrilling to listen to the reading of events that might be more decisive than any since Waterloo.

It appeared that our infantry had overrun the enemy trench system, taking huge numbers of prisoners and guns. A break-through had almost been achieved, was expected within twenty-four hours. The cavalry were ready! Far away to the south the French had attacked on an even larger scale in Champagne, a wide sector of the German line had been pierced, cavalry were beginning to advance. The enemy, demoralised at the two simultaneous offensives, would probably retire all along the front to avoid being caught in the pincer-like concentration of the victorious Allies … And so on and so forth.

The duties of the Royal Flying Corps were announced in a secret document accompanied by a very secret map. The map was handed round to be seen and initialled by each officer. It showed the general scheme of the forthcoming campaign, the points to be attacked after the success of the first blow at Loos. The time and date of each further advance were marked, the distances of the objectives growing once the trench lines had been passed. And after the trenches – open warfare! Red lines and arrows showed the roads by which our transport would advance. The red lines ran eastward for miles before meeting a vertical black stroke south of Lille, representing the first position at which the enemy might hope to make a stand against our terrific onslaught. Thence dotted red lines with smaller arrows, dates with question marks in brackets showed that the great advance was to be pressed still farther. The roads to Brussels were shown. 'Brussels by Christmas,' it was said.

VII

It was so bright and sunny in the morning that, with victory flying on the wings of rumour, I would have been very unhappy had I been condemned to stay on the ground. But Growl was as good as his word. The Shorthorn was ready at the appointed hour; waiting near her I found the observer who was to accompany me. We took off from the aerodrome without delay.

Guided by the observer, I began by steering a northerly course, following the Lys towards Armentières. The map was consulted frequently so that I should get to know the few outstanding landmarks, but aside from the river itself and the distant hill of Cassel there was little enough of importance or interest. Innumerable strips of cultivated land made a good natural camouflage, rendering observation difficult. I saw a man and two horses ploughing, a farm cart being driven down a narrow track, a toy train puffing along a thread-like railway. But there were no large-scale movements and, save to the east, no signs of war. The Lys, winding like a snake, made me think of d'Artagnan and Milady ...

We reached Armentières and started to turn. The town had been a good deal knocked about by gunfire, the streets were deserted; but the railway station, or a portion of it, was evidently in use. Close by were an engine with steam up and a large number of trucks. Eastwards the double track ran straight towards Lille; it was pockmarked with shell-holes, overgrown with weeds. My eyes followed it over the nose of the machine as we turned. There was a point where the railway lines and their beds were cut by a trench; a short, uninterrupted stretch of rails, and then another trench. The shell-holes were more numerous. I was above the firing line.

Turning south, I stared down intently at the battle-front. And my first impression was of its immensity. It was incredibly vast. It did not seem possible that men had made all this mess within one short year. From the North Sea to the Alps! But surely there must be some other way in which the war could be waged. Loos? Ah, yes, that was the way to do it. It was strangely exciting to think that in the south we were actually breaking through the whole system, that we should soon be out in the open again, guns limbering up and galloping forward, cavalry reconnoitring and charging, infantry marching along dusty roads, deploying in fresh country, taking cover to fire from hedges instead of from holes in the ground. Scarcely worth my while to 'learn' this old trench-line so carefully; we should soon be flying east.

It was while my attention was concentrated upon the ground, where I was trying to locate a village shown upon the map but which seemed to have been obliterated in the extraordinary welter of digging, that I received a nerve-racking shock. Something – much more than the worst air bump I had ever felt – struck the machine. She quivered and vibrated violently. I started in alarm, uncertain whether the engine was breaking up or if something even more serious had befallen. Momentarily I was afraid that one of the wings had snapped off – a thought which frequently came to me in a Shorthorn. But over my shoulder I could see nothing unusual, the wings were in place, the propeller revolved, the alarm-clocks ticked ... Again the machine shook, seemed to hesitate in her flight, rocked uncontrollably. Fear swung my head round; beyond the wing tip I saw blue-grey vapour drifting by. Fire? The paralysing thought had scarcely come into my head before a third jolt, greater than the first two put together, almost unseated me. Like an explosion – and it came from beneath my feet, jarring the floor of the *nacelle* as though some unseen giant had kicked it. I turned to look forward, mystified as much as scared. And there in front of the machine's nose I saw unrolling, like a ball of soft wool, a puff of yellowish smoke. I looked back; astern were two more puffs, already less dense, dissipating slowly. I was being shelled.

The likelihood of such an occurrence was something I had entirely forgotten. Growl had said nothing to me about anti-aircraft fire, but then he had not expected me to be so foolish as to sit passively over the German lines on my first visit to them. And for an opening salvo the shooting seemed dangerously accurate; I felt uncomfortable even now that the surprise was past. Furiously I trod upon the harmonium pedals, waggling the bespectacled handlebars as nervously as on my first solo. A tap on the shoulder made me twist my head in renewed alarm.

'It's all right,' the observer yelled in my ear. 'Better turn away from the lines.'

The shelling went on, but the machine shook less after each explosion, until only a slight air-bump lifted one wing or the other some time after a shell had burst. Eventually the firing became an entertainment at which I could afford to smile, a harmless spectacle like that I had witnessed from the deck of the barge. A few minutes later, steadying the machine on a southerly course, I looked back to the east. Three, six, nine – a dozen fading puffs dotted the sky. More than a dozen high-explosive shells at one inoffensive Shorthorn and no damage done! It seemed too much. A waste of valuable ammunition, and therefore well worth the trouble of being fired at if only to annoy the enemy and make him wear out his guns.

The thought warmed me. I wanted more of the entertainment, also I wanted to get used to it without getting hurt. When at length the firing ceased altogether, to have turned away did not strike me as being a very noble action. I was already some three miles from the front lines whence I had departed at nearly sixty miles an hour. I felt rather ashamed. And of a sudden a silly feeling of bravado came over me. Without consulting the observer, I banked and steered due east.

The intricate diggings of the British passed underneath the *nacelle*. No movement was to be seen anywhere. Across No Man's Land the inside of the enemy trenches became distinct. The positions appeared to be unoccupied. Not a sign of life nor of death; not a sound audible above the clatter of the engine, not a shell burst upon the invaders' front. Hard to believe that even one man was alive down there; none at least to take notice of me.

The machine travelled steadily east; the enemy lines began to thin out. Soon I was over open country in occupied territory. I had, so to speak, thrown down the gauntlet – although Heaven preserve me from throwing out even a glove with a wooden propeller behind my head! – and I had disobeyed orders. That seemed to be enough for one morning's work. Not a solitary German to be seen either on the ground or in the sky, and the anti-aircraft gunners had apparently gone off to lunch. It was becoming rather dull.

And then it came down like a hailstorm – or rather it came up. There were a couple of explosions as though lightning had struck close to my head, and a moment later the whole sky crackled into life. On either side and straight in front were yellow flashes; black walls of angry-looking smoke unrolled themselves from nothing like a conjuring trick. I could see pieces of metal flying through the air that had become as rough as a choppy sea in a tideway. It did not seem credible that all this stuff could be coming up from the quiet earth, but more as if a host of malignant spirits had materialised in mid-air. It made me accomplish the quickest about-turn I had so far attempted in an aeroplane. With the throttle hard open and the nose pushed well down, I fled westwards.

The air-speed rose to sixty-five. Things shook and vibrated, the engine rattled, the wind whistled in the wires. Over my shoulder I saw the observer, his jaw set, clinging rigidly to the sides of the *nacelle*. But we got through the storm. The bursting shells became less frequent, less startlingly loud as No Man's Land was left behind. The silent British lines received us into their quiet atmosphere. And the enemy's last shot sounded no more harmful than a husky, deprecating cough.

Pulling out the map, I laid off a straight course for home. Far ahead the shining water of the Lys winked through a familiar row of poplars.

After a successful landing I got out and looked under the wings of the Shorthorn to see what scars she might bear of the tremendous bombardment to which she had been subjected. For a long time I hunted high and low. I was disappointed. Near one of the wing tips I discovered two small holes ...

In the afternoon we read headlines in an English daily paper: *'Two Real Victories At Last!'* Champagne and Loos – September, 1915. 'At last' – it sounded more like a sigh of relief than a cry of triumph. 'Real?' – by nightfall we learned that the attacks had been held up.

VIII

'You had your first look at the lines today, didn't you?' a young pilot asked me at dinner. I stared dumbly, unable to credit the fact that I was being spoken to in a normal tone of voice. When the truth had sunk in I nodded, still unable to find my tongue. He went on in a manner of polite enquiry, smiling a little. 'How did you like it?'

I pulled myself together, forced an answer and mentioned that there had been a certain amount of 'Archie' (the name invariably used for anti-aircraft fire and derived from a pre-war comic song: *'Archibald – certainly not!* '). From the other side of the table Growl looked up quickly.

'What? You were "Archied"? You must have been damn' scared, weren't you?'

I admitted that I had been very scared; but I added that, once I got used to it, it had not seemed so terrible after all. I imagined that it could never be so unpleasant as heavy shelling on the ground.

This, the longest speech I had yet made in the squadron, was greeted with a look of severe displeasure from Growl. His tone in reply was as nasty as any he had yet used to me.

'Don't talk nonsense!' he said cuttingly. 'Just wait, young fellow, until you've had a bit more experience before you talk lightly about Archie.'

From farther down the table the other flight-commander blinked, as though he were seeing me for the first time and did not much appreciate what he saw. He had thin, rather demure lips, sly red-rimmed eyes and a long nose. He looked something like a fair-haired fox.

'Who says he doesn't mind Archie?' he demanded staring at me. 'Good God, just because you've seen a couple of shells in the distance you think you know a lot, don't you? The first time you really get fired at you'll go all "goosey" and try to run like a hare. Hot air that's what you're suffering from!'

At the end he suddenly smiled at me in quite a friendly fashion as if implying that we had now been introduced. The Military Cross pilot by his side laughed silently, looking down at his soup as though anxious to avoid my gaze and pretended that he was not laughing at me. I had nothing to say in answer, for I was quite ready to admit that I knew less than anyone in the world about aerial warfare. But I could not fathom the reasons for so much fierceness. Could it be that Archie was really so fearsome, or were they trying to scare me? If so, why?

After dinner I stayed on for some time talking to the friendly young pilot beside me and thus I learned the names of the others, also some belated information about the squadron and its work. The members of the third Flight, I heard, lived 'ashore' in a farmhouse half a mile away. They messed separately and were in other ways almost independent of the squadron. They had a flight-commander who was, it appeared, a wonderful man, exceptionally good at artillery observation, experienced at bombing and photography, keen on fighting in the air and a jolly good fellow to boot. From the way he was described to me I pictured him as someone midway between Napoleon and God. He was obviously too good for this squadron and I was not surprised to hear that he was soon leaving it to command one of his own.

My new friend was known as 'Wilhelm', or 'Little Willie', because he bore a faint facial resemblance to the war-time caricature of the German Crown Prince. He was never allowed to forget the fact, but he took his daily dose of chaff in good part.

Presently we found ourselves listening to the conversation of the only two remaining men in the Mess, the foxy flight-commander and his Military Cross friend. 'Foxy' could be very funny at times, but his sense of humour was of a sort that wisdom should have counselled him to hide. He had a perpetual if comical sneer for everything and everyone. He scoffed at the major, derided Growl, laughed at pilots who had met with misfortune in peace or war, and ridiculed the better known members of the Flying Corps in France. The conversation ran something like this:

MILITARY CROSS (politely and in a low voice): What has become of that fellow – who used to fly at Hendon before the war?

FOXY (vehemently): That damn' fool? Why, he crashed months ago in England and was completely *carboneezay* – tee-hee!

M.C. (laughing): *What* was that word?

FOXY: *Carboneezay?* That's what the French papers always say when a fellow is burnt to death, it means carbonised. Before the war it was the usual thing in France, after every flight. The papers just put in a paragraph saying: 'Mr Smith took his machine up last week. He was *complète-mong carboneezay*; his widow looks very pretty in black.' Tee-hee-hee!

Not knowing the late pilot personally I ventured a mild laugh which drew from Foxy a smile of gratification, but from M.C. a scowl of annoyance. It was plain that the direct way to Foxy's heart was to laugh at his jokes; that, however, was something M.C. regarded as his privilege and monopoly. I noticed that he went on hurriedly to other topics so as to prevent the conversation from becoming general.

'I wonder what has happened to young G –?' he asked Foxy. G – was a pilot who had been missing from the squadron for a day or two, having failed to return from a reconnaissance.[2]

'Oh, he's all right,' Foxy replied cheerfully. 'He has "gone west" sure enough. He's probably having the time of his life dining with the Kaiser in Potsdam!'

At this sally M.C. was unable to contain his mirth and choked, red in the face. Foxy smilingly patted him on the back and ordered a round of drinks. Conversation came gradually back again to the subject of G – .

'He *was* a silly young lad,' Foxy went on. 'What the devil did he want to go so far over the lines for? He had rotten weather as an excuse for not going at all. But it's the major's fault really, he could easily have handed the job on to another squadron. Still, young G – ought to have had the sense to back out. That's the worst of a lot of the pilots in this squadron, they're so beastly keen to go chasing over the lines – think they're going to get covered with honour and glory, I suppose. And all they achieve is either to get shot down and *carboneezay* or join the Kaiser for a meal in Potsdam. Makes me go all "goosey" to think of it!'

M.C. was still chuckling as I left.

IX

After another preliminary flight to study the topography of the trenches and the country from Armentières to Lens, I began to follow a regular routine of patrolling the lines, generally at dawn, on the watch for enemy aircraft. The other Shorthorns of the Flight had similar work to do at different periods of the day, while the remaining Flights now re-equipped with the new B.E.2cs performed the more important tasks of reconnaissance and artillery observation. The B.E. pilots got most of the hard knocks and, therefore, most of the credit.

Patrolling was dull work to pilots of greater experience provided with more efficient machines, but for me those early morning flights never lost

---

2. Some days later we heard that he had been killed and his observer taken prisoner.

their thrill, nor the spice of adventure its flavour. Flying itself was always interesting, apart from the war, even if you had to do it in a staid old Shorthorn; and although for a long time very few German aeroplanes were visible on our sector of the front there were plenty of sideshows to keep one wide awake. There were anti-aircraft batteries to spot and report so that they might be dealt with by our own guns, enemy artillery positions to be noted and any change reported, unusual movements in the trenches (such as saps being pushed forward) to be observed. Since the patrol took place above the lines careful observation would also reveal activity of troops or transport in the areas immediately behind the front. And although much of this was of minor importance, a good observer would as a rule bring back a list of small facts useful in compiling the Intelligence Report.

But the fact remained that the principal object of these defensive patrols was to prevent German aircraft from crossing the lines to reconnoitre, bomb or take photographs. On our section of the front there was not, after the failure of the Loos battle, much activity of any sort, in the air practically none. German aeroplanes did come over the front occasionally, but it was not their policy, as it was ours, to carry out numerous daily offensive flights. In the air they were on the defensive whereas the Flying Corps believed in maintaining as many machines as possible over the enemy's territory. Whether this policy of ours was wholly wise or not is a matter of opinion; it was certainly in keeping with the spirit of the majority of our pilots; but there can be no doubt that we lost many more machines than the Germans and that engine failure – a fairly common thing – cost us many prisoners. From my personal point of view the safer policy of the enemy made patrolling the front very uneventful. The heavens are immense and a Shorthorn slow; even admitting that the sky, within an aeroplane's range of action, is not limitless it is big enough to restrict the utility of a low-powered craft. From two thousand feet, the lowest height at which an enemy would be likely to come over, up to ten thousand, which was the Shorthorn's ceiling, along a front of twenty miles was a vast area. If at the northern end of the beat one sighted a suspicious aircraft to the south – a mere dot in the sky – it was all very well opening the throttle wide and pushing the machine's nose down in pursuit; unless the two aeroplanes happened to be travelling towards each other, the twain, like East and

West, would assuredly never meet. The Shorthorn having less speed than most British and far less than any German aeroplane, could not hope to overtake. Pursuit from any distance was such a hopeless business that the best course open to us was to cruise up and down the front, trying to look important so as to scare away German machines, making meanwhile all possible observations of the ground on the enemy's side. Then at the end of each flight we would generally descend to within a thousand feet or so of the lines for the observer to practise with his Lewis gun and teach the enemy in the trenches to keep their heads down.

X

Early in October I attacked an enemy kite-balloon. I note the occurrence because it was my first experience of an aerial engagement, and not because the performance was either remarkable or very successful.

The patrol started just after dawn that day. The morning was dark, cloudy, strips of angry orange light to the east emphasised the sombre aspect of the battle scene. There was no wind and a heavy dew made the fabric droop slackly over the planes of the Shorthorn. There was an autumn dampness in the cool air; I was inclined to think that there was very little 'lift' in it.

But we took off easily enough; the clattering of the engine smashed the quiet of the new day while the propeller's draught bent the poplars as we sailed narrowly over them. Upon the deck of the barge Growl stood gazing upwards. I imagined his feelings: relief at seeing me off so punctually, gruff ill-humour at being disturbed from his slumbers. It was a joy to be in the air. I headed for Armentières.

As usual there was nothing much doing in the northern part of our sector. Most of the activity was confined to the areas from La Bassée to Lens where the aftermath of the Loos battle still dragged on – desultory but fierce fighting for the possession of broken trenches and disputed shell-holes, local attacks and counter-attacks about mounds exalted in this flat country to the war-time importance of 'hills'. The quiet line to the north had to be watched, naturally, but if the Shorthorn was ever to score any points worth the marking it was to the south that her efforts would have to be concentrated.

From Armentières I turned to follow a zig-zag course over Fleurbaix, Laventie, Neuve-Chapelle, and Festubert. All along this stretch the trenches lay silent, clearly defined, almost respectable in their tidiness. But south of La Bassée a thin yellow fog hung ominously over the chaos of devastated land as though to hide its shame from the watchful heavens. Smoke rose from burning ruins, through the haze the flashes of guns flickered balefully, puffs of smoke and dust rose from the chalky soil. It was an evil sight, yet since it was also the scene of the tragedy which held our hopes and our hearts, there was something in it that stirred a desire to share in the adventure.

A mile inside the German lines at a height of five thousand feet there floated something like an elephant's appendix much inflamed. On calm sunny days, from a safe distance behind the front, I have seen observation balloons looking graceful, creamy yellow, bright with the red, white and blue circles of our national markings, toy-like with the little *nacelle* dangling and the string holding it, one must suppose, to some excited lad playing in a field below. But on this day, above a grim battlefield there was no charm or beauty in that sinister German intestine. Rather it seemed to be the genius presiding over the evil deeds of men on the ground, the eye searching for blood. I took a sudden dislike to that balloon, it disgraced the morning sky. It was grey-green with a black cross upon its ugly side. It must be destroyed or at least made to go down. I banked and pointed the Shorthorn viciously at it.

Many people used to think that a balloon was a harmless sort of thing, unable to defend itself, but nothing was harmless against a Shorthorn. And although the balloon itself was not armed it had powerful allies on earth; at least one battery of anti-aircraft guns near its mooring place, another a short distance away. For aeroplanes that ventured to descend below two or three thousand feet there were groups of machine-guns to be reckoned with and, since the attendants of these weapons had nothing to do but to watch the balloon whose height they already knew, when an aeroplane began the attack they all let fly. Sometimes a long line of observation balloons might, owing to the scarcity of guns and to the very length of the line, be less efficiently guarded; a single balloon had the attention of the whole neighbourhood.

As we hastened – I use the word with care, in relation to a Shorthorn – towards the balloon there came a scattered volley of Archie shells. The bursts were very unevenly spaced, some of them so far off that I could barely hear their apologetic coughing. I pointed to the balloon, yelling back at the observer when and where he was to open fire. He had the machine-gun, a Lewis, and he had to be careful how he used it. In the Shorthorn there was only the most primitive form of gun-mounting which limited the field of fire to a very small arc. He could not fire straight ahead because I was in the way, and he could not fire astern or indeed anywhere abaft the beam because of the engine, the propeller and the forest of struts braced with piano-wire. Only on either bow could he get a clear shot.

I put the balloon on my port bow and dived towards it. (A dive which in these days would be considered a flat glide.) The engine rattled and shook; the air-speed indicator showed nearly seventy, which was, I think, about as much as this particular craft could stand. The balloon came rapidly nearer. But so did the Archie shells. Their explosions now contained an unpleasantly sharp menace; once or twice I heard a sudden click and thud as when a penny is pushed into a slot-machine: the wings were being hit. We were still between two and three hundred yards from the balloon when I waved my arm for the observer to open fire.

The loud clatter of the machine-gun close to my left ear was rather inspiring. At last, I thought, we are engaging an aerial target, an enemy! But the effect was disappointing. With memories, I suppose, of toy balloons, I had expected this one to go pop at the first prick of a bullet's impact; now with growing annoyance I realised that the low pressure in the bag would only let the gas escape by slow degrees. We could do no more than puncture it; we could not even set it on fire for we had no special incendiary ammunition. Short of flying so close as to be able to dig our teeth into it, there were no means of destroying the hateful thing. It was infuriating. Here we were in a powerful (*sic*) aeroplane, armed with a deadly machine-gun, yet we could do nothing to a mere sausage.

And then I noticed something very odd. I had brought the Shorthorn quite near to the balloon, so that Archie, for fear of hitting his own side, was easing off, and having banked the machine to port I was circling round to give the observer the best chance of firing. He had put in several bursts, unable to miss so big a target, when I found that I was being compelled to push the nose further and further down in order to keep the balloon in the

same favourable position. The truth only gradually penetrated my mind.
The balloon was being hauled in.

The observer had finished a drum of ammunition, the balloon was going
down fast, and Archie was becoming troublesome. We had done all that we
could for the time being. I turned back to the lines. In less than a minute we
had crossed them and Archie faded away. Much relieved, I throttled down
the engine to give it a rest.

Looking astern I could not find the balloon where I expected it to be. I
searched the sky, or as much of it as I could see, but no balloon. Had we
then, by some fortunate chance, destroyed it utterly? Banking the machine,
I stared down – then up … It was still there, large as life and actually higher
than before! Turning the machine about, swiftly I headed back to the east,
balloon-murder in my heart.

It was above us at the start, I wondered whether we should be able to
climb steeply enough if they went on letting out the string. But as soon as
they saw us coming they began pulling it in, evidently anxious to have no
more trouble. It did not go down very fast and was at about our own level
when we came within reasonably close range. This time I made directly for
it, the observer pointing the gun from close beside my head.

At the very instant when he opened fire, Archie came crashing up with
renewed energy and fair accuracy. I began wishing myself somewhere else.
The situation was distinctly alarming because I was once more a long way
over the lines, heading for Germany at under three thousand feet; if the
engine were hit I might not be able to get home … The balloon was going
down faster now, faster than I could follow without risking trouble with the
Shorthorn. At two thousand feet I levelled off and the observer ceased fire.
For a moment I thought of going still lower to start again, but as I throttled
down to glide there came to me above the rush of wind, the sound of fire from
the ground, the faint *crack-crack* of passing bullets from well-aimed rifle fire.
It was plain that things were getting much too hot; opening wide the throttle
I turned homewards. The balloon was well down and I felt convinced that
we had made it leak sufficiently to keep it on the ground for a day or two.
But I no longer cared much, for I was not sure if we should get back safely.

There were moments as I zig-zagged towards the English trenches,
which, for all their devastation, now seemed peaceful and friendly, there

were moments when I was sure the flight would end in disaster. Archie was continuous, close and fierce. One shell sent a multitude of fragments to rattle a sonata upon the piano-wires, two of which snapped. If many more of them went, then according to all the rules the wings would fall off. I made another wild zig-zag, only to bring us closer to a shell whose wide flash glowed angrily through the smoke. I saw a large fragment fly past. There was a crash behind me, and twisting round I saw that in the top plane, immediately above the observer, a hole had opened as big as your fist. Banking in the opposite direction I drove the nose down for increased speed, my only remedy ...

But the worst was over. In a short time Archie lost the range and the shell explosions dwindled again to harmless coughs. A few seconds more and we were well over the British lines where the battle seemed to have stopped – 'to watch us', I supposed proudly in my joy at being safe.

Turning to the north-west, reducing speed and following the front at a respectful distance, we finished the patrol. We were out of ammunition, almost out of fuel. Now for breakfast. Presently the River Lys and a tall line of poplars came in sight. From three thousand feet I began a slow straight glide, mindful of the advice that it is not wise to stunt an aeroplane after she has been fired at.

Before landing I took a long look back to the east. Clouds there were, and autumn haze, and fading Archie puffs. But no longer were the heavens marred by a German kite-balloon.

XI

'So you attacked a sausage and forced him down, did you?' Growl's voice, still gruff and fierce, was softer than I had ever heard it. He was pleased, and that was something I had almost ceased to hope for. My observer having left the sheds first had evidently given him some of the details. I went on to explain more fully what we had done. Growl's face darkened.

'To get as close as that you must have been a long way over the lines,' he grumbled.

I explained hastily.

'Not so very far. You see, the balloon was quite near the front and ...'

'Nonsense!' he interrupted. 'I've seen that balloon myself and it's a long way back. I thought you had orders not to cross the lines? You're looking for trouble, young fellow-me-lad!'

I tried to protest that I had taken no unnecessary risks, that the sausage had tempted me. Growl turned his back and disappeared down the barge's companion ladder.

Later in the morning I encountered the major. He smiled distantly at the vibrating salute I gave in an attempt to mollify the wrath to come, and then murmured something about a 'good show – under heavy fire – machine quite badly hit'. And without another word he strolled off, looking about him and moving his thin sandy-coloured head like a melancholy bird. A lonely, austere figure, I thought him.

In the Mess I was wise enough to hold my tongue. Any remarks on the subject of my morning's adventure would, I felt sure, be greeted with biting sarcasm by the more senior pilots. Alone to Wilhelm, who had been the first to converse with me and with whom I was fast becoming acquainted, did I announce the facts of the affair. I spoke quietly so as not to draw attention to myself, but I could see by the glance I got from M.C. and the sidelong look of suspicion from Foxy that the less I said the better. It was something approaching impertinence for a Shorthorn pilot to attempt a combat in the air.

The real trouble with me in this squadron was that I did not in the least understand the others. If I did anything good they seemed to regard it as impudence, if I did nothing they did not speak to me or so much as acknowledge my existence. It would, I think, have pleased them most had I been sent away in disgrace. That would have given them something to talk about.

One of the pilots had developed piles. He was very shy and ashamed about it himself. But it became the standing joke of the squadron. Everyone sniggered whenever he came near, and coarse innuendoes were continually made in his hearing. My own troubles seemed much smaller by comparison. I was glad that I had not got piles.

XII

Days of bad weather followed, during which scarcely any work could be done in the air, and a great deal of ping-pong was played in the Mess; then the Shorthorn, her wounds patched and repaired, was up again on patrol. Upon alternate days I was on duty in the afternoon, watching the line during the hours of artillery spotting. But it was less interesting then than in the early mornings; what activity there might have been seemed always to have died down after lunch. The line was quiet, the sky deserted.

One day in search of enemy aircraft I went up through a ragged bank of clouds, climbing persistently until we came out in glorious sunshine above a limitless white plain of motionless, frozen mountains. 'Another world' – how often that has been said of the space above the clouds, when the earth is hidden and one is alone with the sun and the wind. It is more than a mere expression; it is indeed the first stage of that journey to the stars …

An hour's steady climbing brought the Shorthorn to over ten thousand feet (the aneroid showed eleven thousand eight hundred). It was the highest I had yet been in the air and, beyond that the machine resolutely refused to go. I looked around to see what advantage might be drawn from this great altitude. To the east I caught sight of a black speck. Was it one of our machines on reconnaissance or an enemy? Probably the latter, but I was unable to find out for certain, since although I turned towards it at once to investigate I could get no closer. The speck maintained its distance, heading north. At this height the Shorthorn's air-speed was down to well under fifty, and I had difficulty in keeping her level; the nose had a tendency to sink earthwards. To seek a fight under such conditions was worse than useless; it was asking for trouble.

Giving up the attempt to close the suspected enemy I throttled down, and with only the wind in the wires and a soft ticking from the engine we sailed down through the clouds into the mists of the war zone. Over the enemy lines we went low to fire a few score rounds into their trenches, while Archie flashed sporadically but did no damage. The Shorthorn was not easy to control in really bumpy weather; in the disturbed air beneath the clouds we rolled and pitched uncomfortably on the way home.

Next day we were out on patrol again, but not then nor on succeeding flights could I get her to fly so high. She was getting tired.

XIII

The days of the Shorthorn were numbered. A regular supply of the new aeroplanes was now available; machines of the older type were being sent back to the depot. Eventually there were only two left in the squadron. Mine was the last to go.

A few patrol flights, mostly uneventful, and then warned for a practice flight on a B.E. I was forced to desert the Shorthorn for good. Poor old lady, she was too slow and antiquated to be of any further use. She could never hope to catch up with an enemy, or fight him successfully if she herself were caught up. On artillery observation she was an easy prey for Archie or a German scout, and it was hard to understand why, on patrol, I had so long been left unmolested. During those short but frequent crossings of the lines any of the newer opposing machines could, in spite of my hopeful optimism, have had her entirely at their mercy. But perhaps the German aviators did not think it worth their while, or did they respect the dignity of her age?

I took her off the ground for the last time with a feeling of sorrow. She had served her purpose, she had worked nobly; she had proved herself reliable, trustworthy, incapable of vicious or underhand tricks. She bore the marks of her patience under fire, her endurance was witnessed by honourable scars: a dozen patches on her white wings, new wires here and there, a bound strut, a patch of darker paint on her *nacelle*.

She was, in a sense, too much of a lady, not 'fast' enough to be efficient for the demands of an increasingly sophisticated war; and, since for training purposes there were plenty of her kind in England, she herself was to be taken away and dismantled, reduced to her component parts. A few, a very few of those parts might eventually find their way as useful scrap to some aircraft factory, but as an individual her life was finished, her identity destroyed when her number was erased from the books. Yet to me she will remain as I used so often to see her in the uncertain light of daybreak. In memory I can see her still, from the deck of the barge where half-dressed I have come to sip hastily from a steaming-hot cup of tea. She stands before her canvas hangar, her large yet frail-looking wings outspread, glistening with dew. Her *nacelle* points towards the east whence come the stealthy rays of the hidden sun, and towards which she will presently fly in search of adventure if not glorious at least not unworthy. Her engine warms slowly, emitting a sharp, regular tick like that of a cheap but sturdy clock. By her side two sleepy mechanics await my coming ... She is gone now, but her memory brings back a zest of youth. *Ave atque vale.*

XIV

However sorry I might be to abandon the faithful Shorthorn, the new machines soon made me appreciate the change. For a few days there was no particular craft I could call my own; I was compelled to make my first flights on one belonging to Growl. And nervous work it was, for a bad landing would have brought down upon my head a torrent of abuse. Several weeks with the Shorthorn had made it hard to judge distance in a machine with the engine in front and with the pilot's seat much closer to the ground. Also the B.E.'s gliding and landing speeds were slightly greater than those to which I had become accustomed. What with the difficult aerodrome and my fear of hurting the machine I had an anxious time, making some very poor landings at too high a speed.

When, however, I had got the knack of it the machine became, in comparison to older types, a joy to fly. I had not altogether forgotten the B.E.s at Gosport, so that I could relish the increased speed due to the bigger engine as well as to the improvements in streamline. The engine was nominally of 90 horse-power, but upon the boss of the four-bladed propeller was stamped '100 H.P. R.A.F.', which gave it in my eyes an added importance: it was the highest-powered engine behind which I had yet flown. And for her power she ran extraordinarily smoothly and quietly; or at least it seemed so from the pilot's seat, although I dare say that the propeller's draught silenced many a startling rattle which would have been audible had the engine been behind as in the Shorthorn. Moreover, the exhaust noise was reduced by two long pipes leading vertically up from the engine to point like diminutive funnels above the top plane.

In the air the machine was easy to handle, stable, and, once used to her ways, I found her very manoeuvrable. She was capable of making vertically banked turns and, I recalled, was strong enough to be looped with safety – inspiring thought! Another, less pleasant thought, was what the pilots at Gosport had said: that she might spin at any moment. But that fatal and mysterious eventuality was, according to Wilhelm and others, unlikely to occur, and as time went on I found out for myself that it was not really to be feared.

The practice flights over, I was sent off again on patrol. Soon I should be wanted for more important work, reconnaissances far over the lines, photography, perhaps even bombing raids, all of which might be productive of much adventure. The one thing I really dreaded was spotting for the artillery; since coming to France I had forgotten the Morse code.

XV

Almost at once Adventure came my way. It seemed indeed that she had been lurking in the clouds, waiting only for me to appear in something more suitable than a Shorthorn. Upon a dawn patrol, I had my first taste of combat with enemy aeroplanes.

It happened towards the end of the morning's work. I had been visiting the northernmost points of the beat when, turning south for the last lap, I noticed some ten miles away a cluster of Archie bursts. With insufficient experience it was hard for me to distinguish our own shell smoke from the enemy's, but it did seem that the firing came from much farther to the west than was usual. It was certainly worth investigating.

Flying south I aimed for a point just ahead of the most recent bursts, rejoicing in the speed of my B.E.2c. At full throttle flying level she made seventy miles an hour; with the nose down but losing only a very little height she would do nearly eighty, whilst in a steady dive she could be counted on for something not far from eighty-five. A fine and fast machine! The only fault to find being that the German machines were considerably faster.

As we sped southwards I pointed out the shell bursts to the observer, indicating the black speck of an aeroplane and making signs that he should get the machine-gun ready for action. The aeroplane I had sighted was turning to the east; I turned still farther to head it off from the lines if it should prove to be an enemy. Ten minutes at full speed brought us close enough to make out the type and national markings. It was British: a B.E. Disappointed I made a turn to the west, slowing down with the intention of cruising around for a little longer before going home.

Below us Archie shells were bursting. I could not make out why. We were some distance from the lines; it could not be at us the guns were firing, nor as far as I could make out at the other B.E. I stared over the side of the fuselage, puzzled.

And then suddenly I saw them. Two German aeroplanes, beneath us, astern and a little to the east. They were almost stationary in relation to us, travelling in the same direction. They looked like venomous insects, the black crosses like the markings on a moth's wing, five hundred feet below. But in front of me the observer still sat facing forward. He had seen nothing. Forgetting that he could not possibly hear, I shouted at the top of my voice: 'Hey! There they are! Fire that bloody gun!' He still faced forward. I banged the top of the fuselage between our two seats, slapped it hard with my open hand. No good. Then I waggled the control stick backwards and forwards to make him move; but I jerked it too fast, the machine did not respond, and I saw those two German machines coming up closer and closer behind us. A nightmare!

At length the observer turned. He was a big man and the violence of his move shook the whole machine; yet he did not turn because he had heard me, but because he heard, as I did too, an ominous *crack-crack* of passing machine-gun bullets.[3] The machines below were firing at us. I looked down fascinated. The nearest German was about to pass beneath. Over his top plane I could see an observer in the back seat aiming a machine-gun. I could see the flashes.

The immediate and most urgent problem was to get our own gun in action, for it was in the wrong place, on the forward mounting for use in pursuit. Now that we were the ones pursued it had to be changed to the rear. My signals to the observer were needless, he was already struggling manfully with the unwieldy gun, hampered by the propeller's slipstream, whilst I held to my westerly course, passing right over the first German and only turning a little to let my observer fire a short burst as soon as his gun was ready. Then for a moment the German disappeared under our stern.

---

3. It was many years before I appreciated that, with a muzzle-velocity of something over Mach 2, the sound made by passing bullets was a miniature sonic boom.

What was to be done next? I supposed that if the enemy came on after us my observer could deal with him with the gun in the same position. But if I were to circle round and try to attack him the gun would have to be changed again, a tiresome business. Which was it to be?

I hesitated. Not for long, not for more than ten seconds at the outside. And yet when, having decided to hold my course, I looked out over the far side of the fuselage expecting to see the enemy bobbing up alongside I was amazed to find that he had turned back towards the lines. Already he was quite a long way off, and he had stopped firing.

The feeling of mild panic of a few moments previously gave way to an absurd desire for a fight at all costs. Seeing the enemy so close, his murderous-looking gun pointed, shots passing by our heads, I had expected serious trouble. Yet after a score of contemptuous rounds to scare us away he had calmly made off, heading home for his own part of the world. He had done his morning's work, reconnaissance or photography, and now he was going back to tell his friends that he had met a British machine which had turned tail after the first few shots … I had done the wrong thing evidently. I had made a fool of myself by having the gun placed on the rear mounting, by not having turned to attack on first sighting the enemy. My mistake must be remedied and at once. Banking vertically, throttle wide open we started in pursuit.

South of us the second enemy craft was being engaged and chased by the other B.E.; ahead, to the east, our own particular foe was hurrying off in the direction of Lille. I put the nose down, using up the little advantage in height that still remained to us in an attempt to overhaul the enemy. For a few moments he seemed to be rising and moving slowly backwards, the range was decreasing; and while the observer pulled and pushed the Lewis gun into the forward mounting I heard again the *crack-crack* of enemy bullets … At last we were close enough, the Lewis was ready; I started ahead, elated with a wild hope of victory.

But another great difficulty became at once apparent. In a B.E. it was impossible to fire straight forward because of the propeller. The forward gun-mounting gave an arc on either bow, above and below, but to fire straight ahead would be to send shots into the propeller, possibly smashing a blade and consequently bringing the machine down. To hit our enemy we had to turn slightly away from him, put in a burst or two and turn back quickly so as not to open the range.

Accordingly I signalled the observer, and turned off course while he hastily fired off half a drum of ammunition. Then we turned back, nose down to try to close the enemy. But we had no longer any superiority of height from which to dive and gain speed, and on the level the German had an advantage over us of at least ten miles an hour. The range which had been increased by my enforced half turn for firing did not grow less when I turned back in pursuit. On the contrary it began to open up rapidly as the German made for home. The distance between us had never been really short, soon from two hundred yards it lengthened to three hundred, three-fifty, four hundred. The enemy gun ceased fire. We were out of effective range.

Beneath us the open countryside of occupied territory showed that we had come far over the lines. The time for the patrol to end was long past. From fifteen miles away I fancied that I could smell eggs and bacon. And with that I turned the B.E. sharply, setting course for the barge and breakfast.

XVI

Trivial though this fight had been, I discovered shortly after landing that some mystery was connected with it. An uneasy feeling that I had done something wrong came to me; although, thinking the matter over, I believed that I had done everything possible considering my inexperience, yet I was not at all satisfied with the result. Neither, it seemed, was Growl. He said nothing definite, not even as much as on the morning of the balloon attack. But he knew all about the fight before I had a chance to give him my version.

'Where did you first see them?' he asked, meeting me on the way to the barge. 'Did they fire at you? Which way did you turn? Did you see the other two B.E.s?'

I gave him the details as I remembered them – the whole affair was still rather confused in my mind – adding that I had only seen one B.E.

'Only one? You're sure of that?' he insisted.

'As sure as I can be under the circumstances.'

'What circumstances?'

'Well, meeting enemy aircraft for the first time, the excitement of being fired at and of not knowing quite which way to turn or how to get the gun to bear.'

Growl nodded and turned away.

'All right, young fellow. You'll learn in time.'

His tone showed that he was not displeased with what I had done, but he did not choose to enlighten me any further either as to air-fighting or as to the reasons for the questions he had asked. Nor, apparently, was it a subject to be discussed in the Mess. I was greeted with an uncomfortable silence when I attempted to raise the matter at breakfast.

Wilhelm told me all about it later. He had not been off the ground that morning and so had been able to listen to the gossip. The trouble about the fight was that there had been two of the squadron's B.E.s close to the enemy when they had first crossed to our side of the lines, long before I had appeared on the scene. One of them, the B.E. I had seen, had attacked immediately, although there had been no need for him to do so since he was on artillery duty. Sticking closely to his enemy he had chased him back over the lines and forced him down. But the rumour was this, that the other B.E. on patrol at the time had taken no notice of the fight, had kept well out of range and had eventually turned right away to steer a straight course back to the squadron. The major was furious, for it was alleged that the pilot of the B.E. which had 'run away' was one of the flight-commanders.

As Hilaire Belloc once sang: 'Due east the foe, due west he steered ...'

XVII

It was at about this time that Wilhelm and I, aided by another pilot, started discussing and devising new gun-mountings for our machines.

The B.E., good in her day for so many purposes, was really rather hopeless when it came to aerial combat. The observer, sitting in the front seat, was enclosed by a cage of struts and wires which made it extremely hard not only to handle the gun but also to obtain a clear field of fire. Different mountings for various angles of fire were suggested by the pilots of several squadrons, including our own, and in the majority of machines four of these mountings were adopted as standard. To the underside of the Lewis gun was fitted a blunt spike that could be slipped into a number of different sockets attached to the sides of the observer's cockpit. One of these sockets, like a candlestick, was fixed just behind the engine, allowing the observer to fire over the top of the propeller; two more, one on either side of the fuselage, gave a small arc on each bow; and, at the back of the front seat, another at the end of a swinging arm afforded protection from the stern. This last mounting was without doubt the best. The observer knelt on his seat with his back to the wind and obtained a good view, the swinging arm gave him a wide arc without him having to move. But it was purely a defensive mounting; its use presupposed that the enemy was in pursuit which, except on artillery spotting or during the return from a long reconnaissance, was not a very usual occurrence.

If we intended to attack, pursue and bring down enemy craft we would have to use the forward gun positions, and these were inevitably restricted by wires, struts and, most of all, by the propeller. Only a fortunate chance could give us the victory we so desired, yet short of reconstructing the entire machine there was nothing we could do.

As far as protection was concerned it would plainly have been better to have put the observer in the back seat, as the Germans had already done, with a revolving mounting; but as regards attack the only thing for which we could hope was that someone in England would speedily invent a means of firing through the propeller. Both the French and the Germans were reported to be developing different methods; others were slowly bringing out inventions of their own; meanwhile the Flying Corps had nothing. Nothing except ideas for new mountings, guns on the wings, guns on the top plane, new schemes of attack, new aeroplanes – everything save the solution of the real problem to which, it seemed, our scientists refused to apply themselves. With characteristic British skill at compromise, our designers went so far as to produce an extraordinary craft which in their fertile brains did away with the problem altogether. It was called the B.E.9, but the reason for its unofficial name – 'The Pulpit' – was all too obvious. A little three-ply box projected from the front of the machine, a box supported upon ball-bearings running on an extension of the propeller shaft and prevented from rotating by cables to the wingtips. The wretched man in this box had indeed an unrestricted forward view, but just behind his head revolved the four deadly blades of the propeller. There was no communication possible between front and back seat; if anything happened, if the pilot were wounded, or even if nothing more serious occurred than a bad landing in which the machine tipped over on its nose, the man in the box could but say his prayers: he would inevitably be crushed by the engine behind him.

One of these machines was attached to the squadron in which I served; but by the merciful dispensation of providence it never succeeded in defeating an enemy craft. Had it done so I have no doubt that the brains of the Farnborough factory would have rejoiced in their war-winning discovery, hundreds of Pulpits would have been produced and in a short while we should not have had a living observer in France to tell the experts what it was like in that little box. However, even in 1915 when almost every new machine was looked at with delighted wonder, it was recognised that in the B.E.9 unsuitability of design had reached its acme. The Pulpit was soon returned to the depot.

To the faults of the B.E.2c we resolutely shut our eyes, determined with the blind and absurd optimism of youth to make the best of the only aeroplane at our disposal. The more we studied our gun-mountings the more unreasonably hopeful we felt. At nights, after a drink or two in the Mess, we grew positively certain of our chances in any fight that might come our way. The omens of the year were favourable: 1415–1915. The fifth centenary of Agincourt! The feast of Crispian was not so far away, and Crispin-Crispian should ne'er go by from this day unto the ending of the world but B.E.s and Lewis guns in it should be remembered ... Waiter, another beer!

XVIII

By a fortunate succession of accidents my own role in the squadron became gradually more that of a fighting pilot than of an artillery spotter or photographer. The first accident occurred when much to my annoyance I was sent off one foggy afternoon to observe for a battery down near La Bassée. Wireless had been fitted to my machine and I had spent a sleepless night trying to remember the Morse code. As soon as we had left the ground I let down the aerial and started nervously to send out my call sign. I went on sending it out at intervals for half an hour whilst cruising around the battery position, wondering why they did not start shooting, until at length I noticed a white strip on the ground informing me that they were not getting my signals. Thinking that probably my poor sending of Morse was responsible for the failure I returned to the squadron in fear and trembling. But there I learnt, much to my relief, that it was the battery's wireless set which had broken down.

The following day was fine, artillery activity was violently renewed, experienced observers were required. I was not wanted. Instead I was sent off with a special observer in Growl's highly polished aeroplane to take a few very dull photographs of the area behind the Bois de Biez. Photography was uninteresting from my point of view because there was so little to do; one had to fly slowly over a straight and clearly defined course taking no notice of Archie or of enemy aircraft. Of course if one was attacked one defended oneself, but one did not go off in pursuit – which was what I most wanted to do.

As a matter of fact there was not a German in the sky when I went out to take photographs, and Archie was much more distant than usual. Only one gun seemed to be in operation; every time we reached the end of our beat he fired three shells. We took little notice of them.

When we returned to the squadron it was discovered that all the photographic plates had been put in the wrong way round. Not a single picture was any good. Had they all come out it might have been argued that such a steady and reliable pilot should always be employed upon this particular job. My career might have been altered, I might have become a professional photographer. As it was, the machine was Growl's, the observer (who was to blame) was Growl's. The job had to be done again, Growl did it. And the next time I went into the air it was to go upon a reconnaissance from Lens to Lille.

XIX

I remember that reconnaissance because it was so uneventful that I had all the time necessary to examine the world spread out beneath me and gain a lasting if superficial impression of the war as it then was in the west.

We were Archied when we crossed the lines near Lens, but after that there were no interruptions as we headed north over the enemy's back areas. There were no aircraft, hostile or friendly, to be seen. The sun shone, and the country below was so peaceful that a momentary fear of my own wakefulness shook me. I must be asleep, dreaming. The war was an illusion of my own. Surely the immense and placid world upon which I gazed could not be troubled by human storms such as I had been imagining. In that quiet land a million human beings could never have become so furiously enraged that they must fly at each other's throats … At ten thousand feet on a sunny afternoon, with only the keen wind upon one's face and the hum of an aero-engine in one's ears, it is hard not to feel godlike and judicial.

We passed over Lille. The great town, marked out by the angular lines of its old fortifications which had not saved it from easy capture, looked oddly deserted, dead. What were they doing down there, those unfortunate French? Of what were they thinking? What an intolerable nuisance the war must be for them; not even the more hideous nuisance of active warfare with its compensating hopes and fears and adventures, just plain unalleviated ennui whilst their masters walked about proudly, strong in their conquest, dealing with them as they willed. From that great French city there came up a dozen noisy shells to show us whose it was. Upon the Ronchin aerodrome stood three aircraft, small as miniature models from our elevation, but they did not come up. The German held his prize firmly; there was no need for him to be unnecessarily aggressive. Circling slowly we turned to the west, leaving the sad town to bask inactive in the melancholy autumn sunlight.

Over the Messines Ridge we flew, to recross the lines near Wytshaete; but before turning homewards it struck me that here was a good opportunity to learn the line as far as the coast. We headed north following the curve of the Ypres salient, and at once Archie reopened, accompanying us on either side. Far below, at some two or three thousand feet from the ground, another avenue of Archie puffs was growing. I found the machine at which he was firing, just distinguishable as a B.E. twisting and dodging to avoid the shells. At our level the fire became heavier as we approached the neighbourhood of Ypres, but on the ground, save for a rare flash, a puff of dust or smoke, nothing seemed to be happening. Our own artillery, of course, was always said to be short of ammunition, yet now the Germans were not firing either. Were *they* running short of ammunition or were they merely bored? Nothing to fire at on the ground so they amused themselves by wasting their precious shells in the air. I tried to count those that had been fired since we left Lille. It was impossible. There were too many. The sky behind us was mottled with fading puffs. A score, two, three score? One might be nearer the truth if one estimated more than a hundred. And not half a dozen had come within the range where a chance splinter would have strength enough to do serious damage. Once or twice I had turned to one side or the other, had changed altitude a little to make sure that the gunners should have no time to improve their aim; but never, during this flight at least, had the bursting shells given me cause for alarm; from the objectives of the reconnaissance they had not forced us to deviate by so much as a hair's breadth. In the air a futile bombardment; in the trenches nothing more than occasional gun-fire.

In front of Ypres the sector was a little more active than other parts of the line, but still strangely silent. The opposing armies faced each other motionless in the disarray of their diggings as though puzzled, now that they had levelled everything within sight, as to how they could work further mischief. Again I was struck by the immensity, the colossal size not merely of the war (of which one could judge at home by adding up the totals of the armed men engaged), but of these ruinous digging operations. I stared back along the route we had been following. For league upon league and from either side the zig-zag trails rushed forward, branching, rejoining, intersecting one another like forked lightning. The turned soil was pale upon the brown surface of the earth, so that the vast disturbance showed up plainly, even in the haze of distance, like the breaking waves of a frozen sea, the two fronts facing each other like rival oceans beating vainly upon an interminable isthmus. That narrow strip of land between the foaming waves of trenches resisted staunchly, its shores bound with wire, its surface only a little marked by the splashes of shell-fire. No Man's Land – the name took on a new significance. For only where no man could live was the earth permitted, in a measure, to survive.

To the north were flooded fields, covered with shallow water, dark brown, stagnant ... Stagnant? The whole line was that, the whole Western Front, the whole war! The hard-pressed line around tragic Ypres told a simple story. We held it because we had made a stand there, because it was the last town in Belgium, because of the moral effect. Yes, but from my aeroplane seat I saw the Channel ports. So close! There lay the sea. But I saw no ships. The long lines of ripples advancing slowly to break in foam upon the sandy coast were as deserted as the lines of trenches, almost as motionless. Would we ever attack that bleak coast? I wondered. Or had we had enough of such landings after the experience of the Dardanelles? Even there it seemed the war had come to a standstill.

XX

I encountered the major that evening after I had landed. There was no avoiding him.

'I saw you do a spiral glide,' he said in a melancholy voice. 'You were making quite a steep bank too. You must remember that towards forty-five degrees the rudder tends to become the elevator and helps you to keep the nose up. Your glide was quite nice to watch. But you really must take more care over your landings.'

At the first words of unexpected appreciation a novel feeling of friendliness had come to me, but his final remark took away all pleasure. I had made an abominable landing. He went on to tell me what I should do in order to make a good one. As if I didn't know! If he had laughed or rated me soundly for a clumsy pilot, a second-rate artist, I should have understood it. It was the toneless pedantry of voice and the reserve of manner that awoke my faint resentment. He made no comment on the flight from which I had just returned, but proffered with a frozen tongue some general observations on not landing too fast, on not landing too slow, on gliding in straight and on judging the distance accurately. And then he turned away, walking off with long, rather high-stepping strides, turning his head inquisitively from side to side, more like a lonely bird than ever.

I sat on the ground to remove my leather flying-kit. The officer with the distressing complaint passed by.

'What was that old Starched Shirt talking to you about?' he wanted to know.

'Oh, nothing much. Just complaining about my bad landing.'

'Well, I like his impudence! The last time he made a landing he almost broke his neck!'

He went on to state that in his opinion the Starched Shirt was a blot on our horizon. And not only in his opinion, but in that of the squadron as well. Smarting under criticism of my flying, I thought – with youthful bumptiousness and pride – that the squadron was probably not far wrong.

XXI

In the barge Wilhelm grabbed my arm and drew me into his cabin.

'I've done it!' he exclaimed in an excited whisper.

'Done what?' I asked, catching some of his excitement.

'Looped! This afternoon – well away from the lines, behind Armentières.'

'Good work – what was it like?'

'Frightful! I was scared stiff. But it wasn't really so difficult. I've forgotten exactly what I did, but I'll tell you about it later when I've had time to think it out. For Heaven's sake don't tell anyone else!'

'Of course not,' I replied emphatically. 'If Growl got to know he'd throw a fit. And the major would probably send you home under arrest.'

From looping we went on to talk and argue about the intricacies of flying as we knew them. Apart from the mysteries of spinning there was still much that was unexplored, and we young pilots could still improve our art by discussing all that we had seen and heard, by evolving our own theories, and by practising in the air manoeuvres that were neither taught nor encouraged. What of looping? Would it help us fight? Would it tend to improve our ability in the air?

The Germans had brought out a new fighting craft: a Fokker monoplane with a rotary engine. It was fast, very manoeuvrable, with a gun firing through the propeller by means of a mechanism captured, it was said, from the French. For these good reasons the machine was proving almost certain death to our B.E.s, particularly when it was flown by a German pilot named Immelmann. Very vaguely it was being rumoured that this young officer (who had already brought down the incredible number of six machines) had invented a new method of turning. As a matter of fact I believe he never did any such thing, but he certainly had a remarkably clever way of throwing his machine around so as to appear suddenly, almost sitting on his enemy's tail, with his machine-gun banging away straight through the propeller. The 'Immelmann Turn' it was beginning to be called, and it opened up a new set of problems in aerial fighting.

It was not so long since machines of the Longhorn type had sidled gingerly past one another firing with rifles at a safe range of half a mile or more. Some of us still carried rifles for there was a shortage of guns, but the principle of machine-guns for all aircraft had long been recognised. A few machines were occasionally allowed to carry two guns, although one would have been just as good had we been able to fire through the propeller. The Fokker announced the first phase of a new era. Through-propeller firing was an accomplished fact, and, coupled with the type of aeroplane in which it was being used, was forcing upon us new ideas, new tactics. To bring down an enemy machine of any type required luck, persistence, a fast aeroplane, and a well-aimed machine-gun; but to bring down the Fokker or even to defend oneself successfully against it required something much more. It required from the scientist a better war machine.

Sometimes we would talk far into the night, waiting hopefully for the fine morning when we might start practising these new ideas that were to guard us against the menace of the Fokker.

XXII

But now again for several days of appalling weather there was no flying. No machines of any sort, let alone enemies to test our prowess, were to be seen in the damp and foggy skies. The days passed in dull wanderings about the aerodrome, in lengthy and fruitless visits to the hangars where our aeroplanes stood silent in the clammy darkness from which it seemed that they would never emerge. Games other than ping-pong were seldom played in that squadron; horses were difficult to obtain. A long walk in the rain followed by a long drink in the Mess would often form the sole recreation of an entire day.

After one dreary evening I remember how Wilhelm leaned back with a sigh: 'Oh dear, oh dear – what a bloody life this is, anyway!'

I agreed, but asked him what constituted the particular 'bloodiness' he had in mind.

'Oh – the uselessness and flatness of it all,' he answered, frowning at not being able to express his feelings more eloquently.

I agreed again, remarking that we hadn't been in the air for three days and that it didn't seem to matter to anyone if we stayed on the ground for three days more.

'The trouble is,' I added, 'that no one gives us anything to do.'

'What do you expect?' retorted Wilhelm. 'Since the Loos offensive failed, no one has done anything anywhere. Hundreds of unfortunate men die in trenches every day – uselessly and almost accidentally – but otherwise we might just as well be at peace. And now this damned weather stops even our flying.'

'I wonder,' I put in, 'if anyone in this squadron really cares if we bring down an enemy or not?'

Wilhelm grunted scornfully.

'Foxy and one or two others would sooner we didn't – they have their own reputations to think of.'

I remarked gloomily that for the sake of something to do I would almost prefer to return to the infantry. But the remark was made in exasperation; I did not really mean it, and Wilhelm was quick to protest.

'The infantry are having a rotten time, but they're not doing any more good in the trenches than we are in the air. I tell you fighting, serious fighting, is over until next spring. And the only thing for us to do is to go on looking for trouble until we get shot down or spin into the ground. Foxy is right – we shall probably end by being *carbonee-zay* ...'

Everyone, I suppose, groused in that way at some time or another. It did not mean very much and it made no difference to the length of the war.

XXIII

A few dull flights in bad weather, a few patrols productive of nothing more exciting than a little inaccurate Archie, and then the tedium was unexpectedly broken. In surprisingly rapid succession several aerial combats came my way.

They are no longer of any account, those fights whose importance, small enough at the time, has faded altogether with the years. Their very similarity makes them monotonous to relate, robs them of the last vestiges of specious glamour with which we then surrounded them as with a halo of glory. Today there can be but one reason for describing such fights in any detail, the mild excuse of historical interest. Aerial fighting as it was in those days will never be seen again. The machines in which we fought are as antiquated as the three-deckers of Nelson's day, the methods and conditions of fighting so primitive as to seem unreal, even ridiculous. Of all that time not much is left other than a few memories of adventure, zestful enough to stimulate even now a quicker beat of the pulse.

And it does not add to the story of these occasions to have to admit that in the course of my next three fights I failed to bring down a single enemy. Each combat began as a pursuit above the trenches, was continued beyond the lines, and ended by the enemy descending to take refuge upon the territory of his own aerodrome. It could scarcely be otherwise. At this period of the war the German two-seaters had orders to leave fighting to the fighting craft (Fokkers and such) and not to become involved in scraps which formed no part of their work of reconnaissance or photography. They were very wise. Their missions accomplished, it was their duty to return safely with the information they had gathered and not to waste time bandying bullets with marauding British craft. They had in any case to run the gauntlet of our machines which, save on special occasions, were expected to engage any hostile aeroplane sighted. The German tactic of turning away formed a sound policy which often lured our machines to their doom.

One day on patrol I decided to climb my B.E. up to her maximum altitude. In the squadron, M.C. had been much admired a week or so previously for having taken his machine to a height of twelve thousand feet, and at the time it had indeed seemed a remarkable performance. Nevertheless, having passed the ten thousand mark in the Shorthorn, I felt confident of getting a good deal higher. For an hour I dragged my aeroplane skywards and, after passing through a layer of scattered clouds, at length emerged in sunshine at a height – according to the untrustworthy aneroid – of fourteen thousand feet. But here it was so bitterly cold that it was plainly useless to dally unless something in the nature of an enemy turned up pretty swiftly.

Far to the east and considerably below us a diminutive white wing gleamed in the sunlight, turned and became an indistinct speck. An enemy? Mighty far away whatever he was, hardly worth while investigating. I tilted the machine backwards and forwards to attract the observer's attention. He turned to face me; and I got a shock. Both cheeks and the tip of his nose were dead white, frozen. His eyes, too, were rimmed with ice; he kept rubbing them but they seemed to freeze over again immediately, and he had such difficulty in moving that it took no more than a glance to see that he was in a bad way. I throttled down at once and began to glide.

At fourteen thousand feet over northern France in November one realised how very exposed were the seats of a B.E. I was thoroughly chilled myself and I had a windscreen, whereas the observer's had been removed to make room for the forward gun-mounting. With the engine running slowly it was possible to make oneself heard, I shouted to ask how he felt. He turned, trying to grin; but his face was stiff, he could barely move his jaw enough to shout something back at me. I only got the one word: 'Awful'; sufficient to make me push the stick forward for a faster descent.

One of the disadvantages of flying so high was that it seemed to take such a long time to come down, especially as I had to run the engine every now and then to make sure that it was not getting too cold. Had we met an enemy during that glide we would have had to run for it; the observer could never have handled the gun with frozen fingers. It did not begin to be noticeably warmer until we were below six thousand feet, but I went on down and did not flatten out until we were at three thousand. In contrast with the height at which we had been the machine now seemed to be dangerously low, almost on the ground, but the air was like summer. And a little later when Archie opened fire the air became warmer still.

The long glide had taken us to the southern sector of the line; we were over the La Bassée Canal, where in the greenish water of the dock basin a string of barges were moored – when straight ahead, near the disturbed area of the Loos battlefield, an aeroplane materialised as if by magic. Unmistakably an enemy, and an unusual one at that: it was Two Tails himself.[4]

---

4. Later identified as the 'Ago CIII'.

As far as I know he had not been seen more than two or three times, had been fought (indecisively) only once. In general appearance he bore a slight resemblance to a Shorthorn, much improved and modernised. Instead of a bare framework of tail-booms he had two neat streamline fuselages supporting the rudders and tail-plane. He was reputed to carry at least three machine-guns and, according to Foxy, 'half a dozen gentlemen in top-hats' (meaning crash-helmets) by way of crew. At all events he was fast, with a Mercedes engine giving probably double the power of the 'R.A.F.', and therefore with a much better climb than the B.E. On the only occasion when he had been seriously engaged there had been terrific descriptions in the British press, and a full-page drawing in an illustrated paper of this new and fearsome strong-man of the skies. At the sight of him, glinting in the pale yellow sunlight that illuminated the hazy battlefield, banking to dodge a cluster of British Archie shells, I felt the sort of alarming thrill that might run through the crew of a merchantman on encountering an enemy battle-cruiser.

The observer, now completely thawed out, had seen him too and turned to point, an anxious question in his eyes. I waved frantically, the gun was transferred to the forward mounting, and we started off in pursuit like ornithologists after a little-known specimen. At the start our courses converged so that almost immediately I began to hear a quick *crack-crack, crack-crack* as of two machine-guns. Then, as we came within range, our own gun began to clatter and – the observer's aim must have been good – Two Tails made a violent swerve, turning almost at right-angles to head north-east across the lines.

Conforming to his movement I made the mistake of trying to climb up to his height (he was about five hundred feet higher) and this, together with a turn aside for the observer to fire again, deprived us of any chance we might have had of bringing him down near the lines. As we climbed the range opened out, changing in a few minutes, during which my observer could not put in a single shot, from two to five hundred yards. After that it increased still more rapidly, for Two Tails was no longer climbing. On the contrary, finding himself safely over his own territory he was pushing his nose down to gain speed and outdistance us. Our only possibly reply was to do likewise even at the risk of losing a safe height over enemy country. We had gained about a thousand feet since the beginning of the engagement; now we commenced to descend again, pushing on at full throttle at a speed approaching eighty miles an hour. To all appearance Two Tails became stationary, then began to move slowly backwards; the range was shortening.

But the chase lasted a long time and at the swift pace we were travelling I could see a dark and misty patch of buildings. We were coming close to Lille. It was essential to do something quickly for we were being drawn much too far over the enemy's territory. I pointed, waved to the observer, making signs for him to shoot. He must have been expecting my suggestion, for he nodded and opened fire at once – through the propeller.

It was not quite such a foolish thing to do as might be imagined. What the exact odds were against smashing the propeller I cannot say; they depended a great deal upon the engine speed and its relation to the gun's rate of fire. I seemed to remember having heard that the number of shots likely to hit one of the blades was in the neighbourhood of four per cent, and as my observer would not be able to fire more than about thirty rounds I believed that we could get away with it, particularly since there was no certainty that the propeller would break if hit. Cases had been known of enemy bullets piercing the blades neatly and without splintering the wood.

As it happened I think my observer got off some twenty-five rounds before I felt a faint shock and slightly increased vibration of the engine, indicating that he had hit the propeller. Then, quickly turning off course to prevent any further damage from our own fire, I watched the enemy. Two Tails had also turned, but away from us. Evidently our fire had been accurate and he did not like it. He was going down.

There seemed to be nothing wrong with his manner of descent, save that it was too fast for me to follow; the range was opening out once more and he did not appear to be bothering about us at all, his guns were silent. Looking ahead I soon perceived the reason: the Ronchin aerodrome was less than two miles off, he was gliding home to lunch; if I did not take care we would be his unwilling guests, for our height was under three thousand and Ronchin was full of waiting aircraft. Someone might be sent up to invite us to the meal. The place was the reputed home of the fabled Immelmann.

The very thought of that dangerous young man's nearness made me crane my neck to search the heavens for possible foes, guiltily remembering that I should have looked sooner had I not been so intent on the chase. And then I caught my breath. Three or four thousand feet above us, hovering – so it seemed – hawklike in the sky was a swart monoplane. A Fokker!

My observer was still hanging half out of his seat, his eyes glued upon Two Tails; the sharpness of my turn almost flung him out altogether. Bumping heavily back into the cockpit he gave me a reproachful glance, whilst I jerked my hand upwards over my head. He stared for a moment and I saw the look on his face change from surprise to anxiety. Then without further ado he began to wrestle with the gun, tugging it clear of wires and struts and dumping it upon the rear, defensive mounting. He was a sharp lad and knew what was wanted.

Fortunately for us the Fokker was a long way up and dived neither very fast nor very steeply, whereas with the throttle hard open, nose well down, we were rattling home at a really tremendous speed – over eighty five – straight for the nearest point of the lines. The observer watched anxiously astern, occasionally loosing off a few rounds as a warning that we were not to be caught napping. Perhaps some of those shots came close enough to annoy him. At all events, a mile or so from the lines he turned away to climb back towards the east, leaving us at only two thousand feet to be escorted over the trenches by a lengthening trail of Archie bursts.

XXIV

'Hm …' murmured the major, smiling whimsically as though at a mild but rather subtle joke. 'And so you met Two Tails, did you? What was he like?' So might an awkward child have recited: '*And hast thou slain the Jabber-wock?*' But there was no '*Come to my arms*' in his tone. He continued, 'I hear you followed him across the lines? Was he much faster than your machine? Why didn't you follow him to Lille?'

The questions were put calmly, but with slightly more than the usual amount of interest. I answered his last by explaining the proximity of a dangerous enemy.

'Saw a Fokker, eh? Ah, then I suppose you did right to come back. But all this must have taken place very low down. You should be careful never to cross the lines at less than six thousand feet.' (Heavens! thought I, having crossed them twice that morning at under three.) 'You had better make out a report of your fight …'.

He sauntered off, pleased but absent.

* * *

'Hullo! Had a scrap?' Wilhelm came towards me, grinning cheerfully. 'What – with Two Tails? You're lucky to be alive! How many machine-guns did he have?'

'I don't know,' I told him truthfully. 'I never had a clear view of him. The propeller was in the way all the time.'

'Then how did you see to fire at him?'

'Ah – you must ask my observer that!'

* * *

From behind me heavy footsteps drew near.

'Now then, young fellow,' Growl exclaimed truculently, 'how the devil did you manage to get two bullets through that propeller of yours?'

His voice was menacing, he looked as if he might bite.

'I had a scrap.'

'Damn it, I know you did. But where did those bullets come from? The enemy?'

'Er – yes, I think so.'

'Nonsense! Don't try to tell *me* that story. Those shots came from your own gun! You'll have to get a new propeller, and these things cost money. Don't you know that? How would you like it if the Government said that *you* had to fork out forty pounds?' I kept quiet while he scowled angrily at me for a second or two, then slowly his features relaxed into a tolerant smile. 'Well, all right. Go and make out your report.'

* * *

On the way to the barge I passed M.C. He was whistling and slashing the heads of thistles with a cane made from the propeller of the German aeroplane he had brought down in the summer. Except to answer my 'good morning', he said nothing. I wanted very much to tell him that I had beaten his height record, but I felt too shy to break down his stony reserve. In this squadron taciturnity was the best policy.

XXV

No more than three days later I had the luck to run into another fight in the air. But this time the engagement was very brief and uneventful, and it was Archie who played the major part with almost fatal consequences.

An observer was sent with me who was no novice and needed no practice flights to get the hang of things. In the earlier days of the war his machine had been brought down in Holland; he had only recently escaped from internment, all the keener for his enforced rest. On the early patrol we went straight across the lines in the neighbourhood of the Bois de Biez.

For once there were quite a few machines about and it was hard to know which of the many specks to investigate first. At least it seemed certain that over British territory there was as yet nothing doing, it was too early; no Archie bursts signalled the presence of enemy aircraft. At length, however, above the Aubers Ridge we sighted a grey two-seater of foreign design heading towards our lines, and we were nearing eight thousand feet, with the other a little higher, when I first made out the black crosses on the underside of his wings. Not that I had for a moment believed him to be British, but in the days before national markings were clearly and prominently displayed, Frenchmen in new and unfamiliar types of craft had sometimes been fired at ...

As soon as we were sure of his identity I turned away, hoping to inveigle him across our lines before attacking. By that time I should have gained height and if we could outfight him we stood a chance of bringing him down upon our side of the trenches. But we had no luck. I suppose he must have seen us and suspected our motives from the start, for he made a sharp turn, came straight towards us and opened fire, putting his first few shots through the wings. Our gun was on the rear mounting at the time, and, as he circled almost over our heads, the observer gave him a long burst. This seemed to decide him for he straightened out of the turn and made for home. On the same level we exchanged shots, then he dived away to the east. My observer switched the gun to the forward mounting and once again a pursuit commenced.

On this as on other occasions the chase led to Ronchin. It seemed indeed as though the enemy had planned to lure any and every attacking aeroplane to Lille and I watched the sky anxiously, blinking at the rising sun, thinking it likely that a Fokker might be waiting for us. The eastern heavens appeared to be empty, but Archie was wide awake, warning anyone who happened to be about and giving us a foretaste of what we must expect on the return journey. On the way out we scarcely fired a shot. The range was excessive and, with Growl's admonition in mind we could not risk firing through the propeller. Only once did I hear bullets coming close to us, but they did no damage; our pursuit continued at greater speed as the German airman increased the angle of his descent.

At length it became apparent that, short of landing at Ronchin and fighting it out with our fists, we should never catch up. As I flattened out and started to turn, the observer put in one more burst of fire to make sure that the enemy did not return to bother us, and then transferred the gun to the rear mounting. A last glance when we had settled on the homeward course showed us the German throttling down and making as if to land. The fight was over, Lille was alongside, now we had Archie to contend with.

He was certainly lively and uncommonly accurate that morning. So much so that after only a few rounds had been fired I realised that we should have to start dodging in earnest. Chasing to the east had reduced our altitude considerably, in fact we were now at the right height for Archie to do his dirtiest work, but I could not for the life of me remember what procedure was recommended as the best means of fooling the gunners. How often did one turn? How long did one wait after turning? Did one alter one's height just after a shell had burst or just before? 'After', might be too late; but how did one know when it was just 'before'?

A succession of shells banged out on either hand. Cast iron splinters flew from yellow smoke balls. Small clicking vibrations in the body of the machine told that she was being hit. Two more bursts. I looked forward. There was a dent in the engine cowling, a tear in the fabric of one wing. Nothing serious as yet, but we had to get away from this. Abruptly I turned, at right-angles, away from the lines; held the new course for half a minute, turned back at right-angles; throttled down to dive several hundred feet off our altitude. The next salvo of shells exploded at a more generous distance. I was reassured, but we were not safe yet and I kept the engine at half throttle to lose still more height.

And then, above the roaring of the wind, I heard a strange hooting noise, rising to an alarming shriek. I stared forward uneasily. What the deuce was happening? Had the observer been wounded? He was leaning back, his knees drawn up to allow his feet to rest upon the forward gun-mounting; with one of his hands he waved his flying-cap over his head. He was singing – no, I beg his pardon; he was a cavalry officer and he was making huntin' noises. At every Archie shot he waved his cap again and gave a terrific view-halloo! I don't know how he had the nerve. Personally I was feeling cold and ill …

Archie got the new range. A shell burst sickeningly close, sending a big jagged fragment to smash against an inter-plane strut. A foot-long wooden splinter chipped off, the strut vibrated like a rope drawn suddenly taut. If it gave we were finished … In front of me I caught sight of a grinning face. 'Yoicks!' yelled the observer.

XXVI

Going aboard the barge I ran into Foxy. I was carrying the damaged strut from my machine, intending to hang it up in my cabin as a reminder of what Archie might sometimes do. He eyed it grimly, then smiled and chuckled with a little shake of the head that implied a hopeless view of my case.

'Fire-eating again? Oh, you make me go all "goosey" – you're too hot for me, altogether too hot. You won't last long at this rate, you'll soon "go west", see if you don't – *tee-hee*!'

His manner of speaking, shivering with mock terror, was really very comical, and he was a very senior flight-commander so of course I laughed heartily. But I hid my strut and waited until the Mess was nearly empty before going in.

I found Wilhelm alone at the breakfast table.

'You lucky beggar!' he muttered. 'Another fight? You'll be getting ahead of me, if I'm not careful. What does the major think of it?'

'How do you expect *me* to know?' I answered. 'He doesn't say anything much. He seemed particularly listless this morning.'

'Listless? Ah, that's because of the King.'

'Why? What about the King?'

'Well, he's in France, inspecting and visiting troops and trenches.'

'Yes, I know – but he doesn't want to see the major, does he?'

Wilhelm grinned and shook his head.

'I'm sure he doesn't. But the point is that H.M. is due somewhere in this vicinity tomorrow afternoon and we have to be in the air patrolling. You and I go up after lunch.'

XXVII

With romantic thoughts of the fierce combats we might have to endure in the course of protecting the King, we worked ourselves into a state of considerable excitement, and had some luckless enemy wandered across the lines that day the quality of our mercy would not have been strained, for we would have shown him none. But it was the weather that kept the peace in the air. From early morning it grew steadily worse. Heavy layers of grey cloud sank momentarily lower as they drifted by like partially deflated balloons, just high enough to clear the upper branches of the poplars, whilst over the farm and down the Lys there rolled slowly from the north a yellowish mist. English fog had escorted His Majesty across the Channel. At noon thin rain commenced to fall.

Upon all normal occasions such weather would have been labelled totally unfit for flying, but on this day not only were we expected to fly, we were keen to do so. I confess without shame that, as my machine rushed down that curving strip of an aerodrome towards a barely visible row of trees I felt a pang of very real anxiety. What would happen when I was off the ground if already I could not so much as see the treetops? And what should I do when the mists closed in about me, obscuring all view of the earth? Blind flying was not a thing any young pilot cared to undertake in those days; there was too great a likelihood of a turn developing into a spin. And I could not imagine how I was to find my way back to the squadron, or indeed to any other safe landing-ground.

But no sooner were we away, clear of all immediate obstructions, than I began to regain confidence. True, at five hundred feet we encountered the first cloudbank, but it was quite thin and through many large gaps I could see the darkened earth streaked with familiar fields and streams. Circling the aerodrome, we climbed rapidly to the second layer. It was not more than a few hundred feet above the first, yet the black clouds were thick and closely knit together, so that I had much difficulty in finding a space through which to fly.

My orders were to patrol at a height of roughly eight to ten thousand feet, but as it appeared unlikely that we should ever get so high I should have been justified in returning after a short flight to report that the weather was hopeless. Yet now, at a comparatively safe altitude, I was lured on to explore the mystery of those lowering clouds. No more perhaps than a wish for adventure, a need to get away from the tedium of the small world below; but there was also in me a desire to seek a fight on this of all days. Of course the fact that M.C. was already flying somewhere in the mists spurred me on, too; I had no intention of being outflown by him. But there was no time to waste in puzzling out the reasons for wanting to go on, steering the B.E. through the unfrequent cloud gaps held all my attention.

Dodging the larger masses, driving through the smaller ones when it was inevitable, we climbed steadily and at length reached a vast grey space between two main layers of seemingly impenetrable vapour. Shut off from the sky as well as from the earth it seemed now as if the world had passed forever from our ken, as if, over some endless desolate plain of Inferno, I, the Virgil-guide, were conducting to a scene of eternal sorrow my observer Dante. A glimpse of his profile reassured me: stolid, unimaginative, beefy, unmistakably British. Yet the illusion persisted. I climbed higher to seek others.

Only once during the ascent did we get any prolonged sight of the ground. From five thousand feet I peered through a gap in the several layers, and with the help of the map made out that we were over a clearing in the Foret de Nieppe, the very point from which the patrol was to radiate. Ten minutes to the north and south of this clearing, with a few minutes extra one way to allow for the wind, that was to be the limit of our flying for two hours. I began hurriedly comparing watch, air-speed and compass, setting the throttle to obtain an exact number of revolutions while climbing. The gap passed astern, the damp mists closed in about us. Heavy rain drove by, soaking Dante.

There were no more gaps either up or down and it soon became apparent that we were involved in the main bank. I was uneasy, for this mass of clouds might well extend to fifteen or twenty thousand feet, far above the utmost ceiling of the B.E. Should I continue to climb with the unpleasant prospect of having to return through the same mass, or should I throttle down and terminate the patrol at once? Whilst I yet hesitated, time went by. The first ten-minute period was almost up, I had to make a turn. Easier said than done. It was quite possible to steer a fairly straight course for a while by watching the instruments and by keeping the control stick steady in the position which I knew would give the best climb. But in these dense clouds the slightest bump tended to alter the course unnoticeably by putting on a small amount of bank, starting a turn. And then it became difficult to judge the amount of pressure required on the rudder-bar; the turn might increase, or it might develop in the other direction. A sudden raising of the speed might denote that the nose was down; it might also be caused by a sharp downward turn. To pull the stick back then might bring on a spin.

Fortunately at exactly the end of ten minutes the clouds thinned out before us, we flew on into a large irregularly shaped cavity. Jagged grey walls, massive in their imposing thickness, surrounded us; a little sickly yellow light came from the roof, but the gloom was awe-inspiring. We were at nearly eight thousand feet and there was no sign of the end, of the beginning of blue sky. Carefully, I turned the machine round and drove back into the wall of vapour.

A violent bump lifted my right wing. I corrected it slowly. A wave of air rolled beneath the other wing and I felt a forward tilt as though the tail were lifting. The air-speed went up. Very gently I eased back the stick, steadying the machine until I judged that she was once more on an even keel and a straight course. Minutes passed whilst I strained my eyes through the fog. And all at once I perceived a dim white shape just above us: faintly luminous, circling swiftly, hovering as though about to dive. Another machine? An enemy? Or some unknown horror of the air, something that could see through the clouds, that had the advantage of us in speed?

Giddiness and tremendous relief came to me at one and the same time. The sun! We were coming through the clouds; and we were turning. Turning – the circle was so narrow that had I pulled the stick back another inch we must at once have gone into a spin. We were turning at speed, yet before sighting that livid disc neither I nor my observer had noticed anything wrong … Cloud-flying, before the days of turn-indicators, was a mystifying business.

Hastily I straightened up, grinning at Dante, and a minute or two later we came out into bright sunlight at a height of nine thousand feet. All about and above us lay huge tumbled mountains of cumulus, not snow-white today, for at an immensely greater height a final layer of misty cirrus was stretched like a golden veil across the sun, but rose-tinted where the light struck them, orange-brown in the shadow, dark blue in the clefts and hollows. Upon the greatest of the towering clouds our own shadow was cast, encircled by a wide halo of rainbow hues. The summit of that nebulous mountain was rounded, sculptured with perfect symmetry – vast as Coleridge's 'stately pleasure dome'. The analogy was easy to follow … At its foot nestled the white houses of Xanadu. Southward, across a level brown plain, drifted the dust of Kublai Khan's horsemen. And beside me, in a black and terrifying canyon with walls five thousand feet deep ran Alph, the Sacred River, flowing through caverns not altogether measureless to man, since I could unromantically check their depths with the aneroid, but undeniably down to a sunless world wherein deluded humans fought in darkness for ideals as brightly coloured as these very clouds … In the front seat Dante shifted awkwardly and dried the Lewis gun with a pocket handkerchief.

Climbing gradually to eleven thousand feet we patrolled up and down for the better part of an hour. Not a single aeroplane, hostile or friendly, was to be seen, and, considering the state of the weather at lower levels, I became convinced that by now all good German pilots must be comfortably at rest in their quarters exchanging *Prosits* and playing *skat*. No use waiting for them. I must go home. Diving through Alph's impressive gorge, I left the bright world of one poet's dreams to return to the dim Inferno of another's. It rained all the way down; Dante was drenched to the skin.

When at one thousand feet I obtained a clear sight of the ground what I saw was not reassuring. We were over woods, but I could not recognise them, neither could Dante. Beneath the clouds and in pouring rain we came lower, to within two hundred feet of the earth. I saw a farmhouse, a small stream, a ploughed field bordered by trees; all were unfamiliar. A horrible doubt crossed my mind – that we might have been blown across the lines whilst flying in that world of illusion above the mists. Could this be German territory? For nearly two hours we had been out of sight of the earth; although I had tried to allow for a possible west wind, it would require very little error to take us ten fatal miles to the east. With growing anxiety I scanned the few landmarks, still without recognising any of them. Visibility was bad. Before risking a further increase in our possible error we must be bold enough to land and ask the way. French peasants would help us wherever we might be. Turning into wind, I came down in the ploughed field and taxied up to the farmhouse.

In spite of the rain, one or two bedraggled people came from the building, plodding slowly towards us through the mud. I beckoned furiously to hasten their lagging feet, shouting to know where we were. They looked at us with gaping mouths as if we were monsters from another planet. They did not seem to know of any of the places for which we asked. At length I mentioned Merville; and at that a young farmer smiled broadly and pointed through the driving rain. In the direction of his outstretched hand I made out a church spire and the black hump of many houses, half-obscured by fog. It was my turn to gape. Merville – not a quarter of a mile away! We were under two miles from the aerodrome.

We waved our thanks, taxied stickily through the muddy field and took off ...

The other patrol flights, including M.C., had landed long before us. We had tea alone and in comfort. My observer, ex-Dante, sighed as he relaxed into an armchair.

'I made sure you were going to land us in Germany,' he said cheerfully.

In the evening we heard the news. The King had been seriously hurt by his horse rearing and falling upon him.

XXVIII

In the barge one day, I found Wilhelm examining a large-scale map of north-eastern France. At his side was another pilot from the same flight, a serious lad whose hobby it was to collect what he termed 'rare earths'. I am ignorant enough not to know what sort of 'ologist this made him, but he claimed that it was a very exciting study. Once, when he made a forced landing upon a heap of manure, it was generally supposed that not engine trouble but the needs of his peculiar vocation had brought him down. He was a very good pilot, but inclined to lord it over me because he had one hundred and fifty hours' flying to his credit, whereas at that time I had no more than seventy.

'What would you do,' he asked as I came in, 'if you had to come down on the far side of Valenciennes?'

I replied, I think, that I had not yet considered the problem, no one having invited me to go so far.

'There's nothing to laugh at,' I was told. 'You ought to start thinking about it right away. This squadron does the Long Reconnaissance next week and it's the turn of our flight to go.'

'But I thought it was Foxy's turn?'

'No, his Flight did it last time. And besides, Foxy is leaving the squadron. He has had some sort of row with the major. So *we* do the Long Reco. – and *you'll* probably have plenty of chances to indulge in your favourite pastime of air-fighting!'

I asked to be enlightened for this particular reconnaissance was known to me by name only. I wanted details, and I knew that Rare Earths would take a spiteful pleasure in announcing them. He was going on leave in a few days' time.

'You fly south from here,' he explained, 'cross the lines between Lens and Arras at the greatest height your machine can get to, pass over Douai, Orchies, Denain, Anzin and Valenciennes, circling each place – slowly, mind you – so that your observer can take notes and count the rolling-stock in the railway stations. Then you turn round and come back, well to the south so as to avoid Douai like the plague, recross the lines if you're lucky and come home.'

'Sounds rather tiresome,' said Wilhelm. 'But what's the matter with Douai?'

Rare Earths chuckled.

'Well, it so happens that the Germans have put a full-size aerodrome there. When they see you go over on the way out, they stand by to wait for you on the return. And it's not very nice to find half a dozen Fokkers sitting on your tail when you're heading back against a strong westerly wind and running short of petrol!'

'Short of petrol? Why, how long does this show last?'

'About four hours from start to finish. More if there's anything worth seeing at Valenciennes. But you don't want to waste time there – the Archie can be pretty nasty and there's yet another aerodrome nearby.'

'Altogether an unattractive business,' concluded Wilhelm, as we bent over the map. Rare Earths chuckled again. Valenciennes, I could see, lay some forty miles on the wrong side of the lines. I looked up at my tormentor.

'What's the answer to your question? What *does* one do if there's trouble at the far end of the reconnaissance?'

Rare Earths rubbed his hands together with fiendish glee.

'God knows, my dear fellow! But you'll probably find out in a week's time when you go there yourself. I should say the best thing to do would be to turn east, due east and land in that big forest there' – indicating a green patch on the map – 'then you might escape from the angry Germans looking for you. What are you laughing at? You don't think I'm serious? Let me tell you: the first fellow who went on this show was shot down; next time they sent two, one came back; then they sent three, and none of them returned!'

I stood silent.

'What you might call the Law of Diminishing Returns,' murmured Wilhelm.

Rare Earths laughed diabolically and went off to bottle some samples of Flanders mud which he was taking home for his collection.

XXIX

Foxy kept very quiet at dinner that night and I noticed that the major scarcely spoke a word to him. The rumoured trouble seemed to have some foundation in fact. Afterwards, while the other members of the Mess gradually dispersed, some to their cabins, some to take a stroll along the river-bank, others to disappear into holes in the ground (I must suppose that, for I could never make out where they all went to), Wilhelm and I lingered over a glass of port, to chat and also to listen to Foxy. As soon as the major was gone, he opened up and became his normal self again.

'Yes, I'm leaving,' we heard him tell his friend M.C. 'What happened? Oh, the silliest thing imaginable. No one but this old Starched Shirt would have made such a fuss about it. You see, the wing-commander turned up here before nine o'clock yesterday and saw me going round the flight with pyjamas on under my coat. Nothing wrong with that. We shan't lose the war because of it. It was my morning in bed, no dawn patrol. But of course the major has to kick up an awful lot of dust. He has thought up everything he can against me and written to the wing about it. Net result, I'm to be sent away from the squadron. All the major's worrying about is himself. He's scared to death of missing a chance of promotion ...'

'Well, what's going to happen to you now?' we heard M.C. enquire solicitously.

'Oh, I'm all right,' Foxy answered confidently. 'Right as rain. I'm being sent straight back to England. And I know plenty of people who will see me through, senior officers. Probably get my squadron shortly. After all, I'm a regular officer, and I learnt to fly long before the war; I'm about due for promotion. But I must say it will be funny going aboard the boat at Boulogne – remember that fellow who stands at the head of the gangway? Everyone who passes he asks: "Leave or duty, sir?" Remember him? Well, I can't answer that I'm on leave, nor that I'm on duty. I shall have to say that I'm in disgrace. *Tee-hee.* "Leave or duty, sir?" – "Neither. Disgrace!" *Tee-hee-hee!*'

Noticing that Wilhelm and I were tittering with amusement he turned to smile at us benignly.

'Ah, I feel sorry for you young chaps,' he exclaimed with mock compassion. 'Awfully sorry. I'm afraid you'll end by going west. A dud engine or a Fokker on your tail will see the last of you. That Long Reconnaissance – makes me go all goosey to think of it! I hope you'll remember me when I'm gone. There I shall be, with a foot on the rail of the Aero Club bar, drinking something long and strong, and you poor blokes will be freezing stiff over Douai. Then, when I'm sitting in the Piccadilly Restaurant with a steak cooking over the silver grill, I shall pick up a paper and read that you've been brought down and are feeding *behind* the grill in Potsdam! Brr – poor fellows! "Leave or duty, sir?" – "Neither. Disgrace!" *Tee-hee-hee …*'

And so he passed on; and such was his self-assurance that I dare say the trumpets sounded for him on the other side of the Channel.

XXX

The leaves had fallen from the poplars by the river. Gaunt branches pointed to the bleak heavens like a row of upturned brooms. No more did lovers stroll along the tow-path at nightfall; they stayed at home in Merville or Estaire, for the nights were cold. The reeds had withered on the bank near the barge whose decks were slippery in the mornings with frost, and the mud in front of the sheds crackled underfoot. Each day seemed scarcely to have dawned before it was already afternoon when pale mists arose to narrow the horizon. Over the quiet landscape the smoke of burning brushwood drifted to mingle its scent with the perfume of damp soil.

And with the dying of the year which had seen the death of so many hopes, there came to this corner of France a mournful yet disquieting hush. All day long the boom of guns shook the air: but now at widely spaced intervals, they were like the minute-guns of an interminable military funeral, sounding the knell for an ever-lengthening list of slain. Even the moan of shells was diminished as though they moved more slowly through the air; if occasionally an explosion was louder it was because of the hardness of partly frozen ground. At night, when the guns were almost silent, star-shells popped into the sky, hung drowsily swinging, descended glaring evilly at the tired earth. But their light was now no brighter than the white sparkle reflected from frosted ridges in furrowed fields or from tufts of grass beside the Lys. And the rifle fire coming out of the darkness was scattered and faltering as though the wakeful men in the trenches, accustomed to nightly alarms, could not be bothered to reply more warmly. On the ground the air struck chill, above the treetops it pierced through leather clothing.

An early winter. The first flakes fell. Then came the first blizzard. On the morning of our Long Reconnaissance the ground was white with an inch of snow.

'This *is* a ghastly life,' Wilhelm had said the night before. But in the morning he added: 'I'm glad we're going on this rotten show. We've been too much like spectators lately.'

XXXI

We started off in fine style. Wilhelm was the first away, for his was the machine that was to do the reconnaissance, mine was to provide escort defending him against attack. Vying with one another to see whose machine could climb fastest, we made a wide sweep to the west and south whilst gaining height for the serious work of the day.

I was rather proud of my machine. It was slightly newer than Wilhelm's and could put up a remarkably good performance. We so rarely flew in company, formation flying being unknown, that I relished the opportunity of showing off its powers. After one or two bursts of speed during which I managed to make up for my later start, I opened the throttle fully, pushed the nose down to obtain a few more miles an hour, and then 'zoomed' high over Wilhelm's head, maintaining the steep climb until my B.E. was on the verge of stalling. Then I levelled off and looked back. I had succeeded even better than I had calculated; the other machine was outdistanced, outclimbed. Wilhelm had vanished.

I must have been singularly blind that day, because at the time he cannot have been so very far away, but search as I might I simply could not find him. Turning the machine, throttling the engine to return to his level, banking hastily from one side to the other, I searched for him everywhere – save, it seems, in the right direction. It was as though his machine had exploded, been dissipated in fragments as impalpable as the thin mist rising from the ground. It was, of course, possible that during my foolish stunting he had made a vertical turn and dived for home – owing to engine trouble, or for some other cause – but I did not think it likely; I felt instinctively sure that he had gone on.

It was a bright sunny morning, although a few wisps of windblown cloud, mist from the melting snow on the hills and the glare of the sun in the east made it hard to see. Yet in the distance, beyond the lines, I fancied at length that I could discern a speck of an aeroplane. If that were Wilhelm I must hurry after him, for on the return journey when the Fokkers came up from Douai he might need my help. At all events I could not risk letting him down by turning back; it was my fault that we had become separated. Moreover, we had orders that if the first machine were forced to abandon the flight the escort was, if possible, to carry on with the work. At nine thousand feet (and still climbing) I turned east and headed for Douai.

Nothing much happened. I don't quite know what I had been expecting, but whatever it was it did not occur. The flight was as dull as any I had been on, made no pleasanter by the fact that I was insufficiently clothed and that it was freezing hard. Even the country over which we passed offered few features of interest, although it was a little mysterious-looking beneath that thin white drapery of snow through which points of earth appeared jet black like rocks washed by the foam of a receding tide. The towns, with firmly pencilled outlines and close-packed roofs gleaming with moisture, were lustrous. Staring down at them, it was as though we were gazing into the enemy's soul – a soul however with remarkably few secrets to tell. There was hardly any movement in the towns, on the roads outside or on the railways. There was not even much Archie.

Rapidly, with an occasional turn or two to give the observer a clear view, we flew over the three main points: Douai, Denain, Valenciennes. At the last place we circled for a few minutes whilst I searched around for the invisible Wilhelm, and the observer hung out over the side of the fuselage to peer down at the network of railway lines, count the rolling-stock and make awkward notes on crumpled, fluttering sheets of paper. My hands and feet were numb and I was shivering uncontrollably when at length we turned homewards.

As there were still no signs of Wilhelm (I learned afterwards that, finding the wind too strong, he had turned back on a northerly course after passing Denain) I decided to take the shortest way home. From a little to the south of Valenciennes we made for Arras, avoiding the perils of Douai. Rubbing hands and knees violently for warmth, I watched the course we followed above the ground, noticing to my annoyance that the top of the compass had frosted over and that however much I tried I could not clear the glass. Luckily there were no clouds or steering might have become difficult. But now we encountered an oft-experienced trouble of these distant flights; the prevailing westerly wind had risen considerably since our departure from the squadron and at ten thousand feet was blowing with great strength. From observation of the ground I estimated that we could be making no more than twenty-five miles an hour against it. At so low a ground-speed we were becoming an easy target for Archie, and we also risked running short of petrol before we could get home. We had to gain speed by losing height. At something not far from eighty miles an hour air-speed we hustled on, descending gradually, engine – of course – full out.

That last was another of the troubles of the Long Reconnaissance. The engine had to be used at full throttle almost all the time if one was to attain the necessary height, carry out the full programme of work and maintain sufficient speed to dodge Archie and enemy aircraft back to the lines, and this left a very small margin of either fuel or engine power if it came to a scrap at the latter end of the journey. Not only the overwhelming Fokkers had forced pilots to come down in enemy territory.

On that day, by way of a change, Archie was extremely inaccurate. But it was not for want of trying. The poor gunners must have given themselves stiff necks staring up at us to watch their bursting shells. And since we were moving so slowly I felt uncomfortably certain that their aim must soon improve. Only a few scattered and spent fragments, however, came near enough to tear small holes in the wings, and but slight deviation was necessary to disturb the poor marksmanship. It was for me the least alarming day of anti-aircraft fire, although I had never seen such heavy or prolonged shooting. When we were close enough to the lines so that if necessary we could glide to safety without engine power, I turned to look at the shell-bursts behind us. All the way from Valenciennes, hidden now by the haze of distance, to Arras, nearly beneath, the face of the sky was disfigured by a rash of black spots. I made an effort to count them; it was as usual quite hopeless, but in one cluster alone there were ten puffs of smoke. At least a dozen similar clusters could be seen distinctly while many other bursts had already faded: in addition those shells fired at us upon the outward journey had to be reckoned. At a rough guess therefore upwards of two hundred shells must have been fired in the course of a single morning – and not so much as a decent splinter by way of souvenir!

XXXII

But the morning was not over yet. As we reached the trenchlines where they curved about the eastern side of the town of Arras, I saw Archie bursts to the north-west. Our own fellows were hard at their equally unprofitable task. German aircraft were across the lines.

We spotted them almost at once – a couple of grey-blue two-seaters of a type I couldn't recognise – a mile or two away from the nearest Archie. With the engine at full throttle once more, we climbed towards them and almost immediately one of them turned back to the lines at speed, easily outdistancing us and firing a few rounds as he went. The second machine, although a little higher, could not get away so simply. By holding to our course we were bound to intercept him. At last, I thought, we would fight above our own territory.

For an instant, as our two machines drew near, the enemy disappeared behind my own top plane, and the first indication we received that he had turned straight towards us was when a sharp burst of machine-gun fire came spattering past our heads. Then he reappeared above us, still turning, trying to pass over us to reach the lines. My observer opened fire at once from the rear mounting, but an instant later the gun had to be changed. In response to my frantic waving he juggled it into the central 'candlestick' mounting. I had decided that since the enemy was above us I would try to remain underneath and just astern, so that the observer could aim over the top of the propeller. It was a difficult shot, but a good one if I could maintain the position.

Meanwhile the enemy continued to turn; from his observer's comfortable back seat I saw the gun spitting fire that fortunately did no more than hole the wings. But although I conformed to his circling it was some time before we could get in a decent shot in reply. Then with the nose down we had, for a few seconds, a clear field of fire and the observer let off about twenty rounds. At once the enemy turned away and began to dive.

Convinced that we had hit him, I looked hopefully over the side. And again I was disappointed. The enemy's latest turn was aided by the strong westerly wind, carrying us both swiftly across the lines. However badly damaged – and from a faint trail of oily blue smoke I fancied his engine was hit – he was going to get safely home. Taking the risk of running the engine to pieces by giving her full throttle, we dived after him. Archie opened up, trying to intercept us; we ignored him. Over the top of the propeller the observer kept up short steady bursts of fire. The enemy replied intermittently ...

We had to give up in the end. By the time my observer had finished his drum of cartridges the enemy had ceased fire. But now with growing anxiety I began to discern the outline of Douai aerodrome, less than two miles ahead. I could see the sheds on the aerodrome, machines waiting in the open.

The necessity for caution came to me suddenly. Fuel was running short, back at the squadron we were already overdue. Abruptly I swung the machine round, headed for home. No use climbing to safety; with the engine at half throttle to save petrol, we flew back nose down, trying to forget the uncomfortable proximity of ever-faithful Archie.

XXXIII

Even now I feel the need to excuse the ending of that flight. By the time we reached the aerodrome beside the Lys we had been in the air for well over four hours during the greater part of which my hands and feet had been more or less frozen. Much staring over the side at the moist shining earth or up at the glare of white clouds had tired my eyes; perhaps, too, the excitement of the fight had been something of a strain. Near Lens, we had run into a snowstorm, adding to our other worries the difficulty of finding the way. And when at length we sighted the aerodrome I dared not circle it lest what I supposed to be the last remaining drops of petrol should give out. Turning into wind I came in to land at once.

The wind blowing in violent gusts made it bumpy in the extreme. The machine rose, fell and swerved beneath me like a small boat in a tide-rip. Were I to let her approach stalling point she would pancake down with the weight of many tons, so that it seemed essential to land fairly fast for I could scarcely feel the controls. Never had that curving little strip of an aerodrome looked so uninviting for a difficult landing; never had the wind blown so erratically, it seemed to come from all directions at once. I landed as best I could, bounced rather badly, and then just as everything was beginning to come right a puff of wind caught the tail, swinging us around. For a few yards we jolted heavily over uneven ground whilst I kicked vainly at the rudder bar; then, slowing down just too late, we rolled into a mound of earth by the riverside. The machine tilted sharply forward – and came to a stop, nose down, propeller smashed ... In the distance a shell exploded, but the sound was much less emphatic than my curse.

XXXIV

As hot with shame I struggled out of the cockpit, elevated by the crash to the height of the driver's seat in a hansom cab, I saw to my horror that from the sheds the major was observing me. A group of officers stood about him. I could imagine what they were all saying; and I could imagine that some of them were delighted. Hitherto I had been rather pleased with myself as a pilot, dangerously pleased; they were justly gratified at my humiliation.

I jumped down quickly enough, but my feet were so numb that I had to sit on the mound which had caused my downfall and pull off my flying-boots before I could walk. Meanwhile the observer, who had been free to stamp back circulation during the flight, came valiantly to my rescue. Catching sight of Growl approaching ahead of the others, he marched up to him and presently I heard fragments of his rapid explanation: 'Four hours in the air ... freezing cold ... a fight ... two enemy machines ... bumpy ... snowstorm ...' By the time Growl reached me the venom had gone out of his glance, and after a sarcastic comment on the state of the B.E. he listened calmly to my account of the accident. At the end he became quite friendly.

'Well, young fellow, I suppose you couldn't help it. We all of us crash sometimes, and it might have been worse. Trouble is the wing-commander's here.'

Swinging round to face this new terror I saw the major coming up like an angry ostrich, stepping high and pecking his head at each long stride. At his side was a round little man with a monocle. The wing-commander! Others followed like mutes at a well-attended funeral. I saluted bravely, but no one took any notice of me; all eyes were upon the wrecked machine and the silence was grim with displeasure. In my ears there tingled suddenly a sinister echo: 'Leave or duty? Neither – Disgrace!'

Growl, who was a fearless sort of fellow, forced his way without hesitation into the august presence and began to give, as if it were his own, my explanation of how everything had happened. The major listened with apparent interest, even going so far as to ask a few questions in a hushed voice, but the wing-commander had already wandered off and was bending down to gaze under and into the aeroplane as though he had never seen one before. When Growl had stopped speaking, the major went to join him. The wing-commander's words were borne to me upon the wind: he had a thin, nasal voice.

'Tell me, what did the pilot – er – want to crash for?'

I thought that never in my life had I heard such a stupid question. But I blessed the major for his answer.

'Oh, he was in the air for a very long time, Valenciennes and back. And he had the very devil of a scrap – chased a German all the way to Douai, made him land!'

At that moment I felt genuine affection for my commanding-officer. It was the first time in my experience that he had seemed really human. And his words had their effect. The wing-commander opened his eyes. The monocle fell out. It had not been known to do so within the memory of living man.

* * *

'What did the Starched Shirt say to you?' one of the pilots asked me when the crowd about my machine had dispersed a little. I told him that at present I considered the major one of the best and kindest of men. Had he not spoken up for me to the wing-commander?

'And so he jolly well ought to,' was the reply. 'After all, he takes what credit he can for work done by the squadron, and you get the blame for crashing ...'

But on this occasion I argued the Starched Shirt's case with heat.

Near the sheds later on, M.C. accosted me.

'Damn' bad luck, that landing of yours. This aerodrome is simply impossible when the wind blows across ... Hear you had a fight. With two of them? How did it go?'

I was amazed. He was interested. His tone was warm, friendly. I wondered if I had misjudged him.

On the way to make out a report of the morning's doings, I found Wilhelm completing his. We compared notes as to where we had been and how I had managed to miss him at the start of the reconnaissance. He wanted to know all about the fight.

'By the way,' he exclaimed at length, 'that's four fights you've had now – you're level with me and ahead of anyone else in the squadron. Better stop for a while or I'll be getting jealous! But, I say, I am sorry to hear you crashed. Rotten luck!'

Four hours in the air may not seem very long nowadays, although in a draughty B.E. in winter, it could be tiring enough. But it occurred to me that I should not have attracted so much friendly attention had I made a perfect landing at the end of it.

XXXV

I was not, I soon discovered, in disgrace, and yet I could not help feeling that it was on my account the wing-commander did not stop to lunch. But then visitors very rarely did stay to lunch, in fact they seldom came into the Mess at all. Perhaps they sensed from afar the gloom, the chilly silences, the petty ill-feeling that disunited us. One could not blame visitors for looking at their wrist-watches and murmuring must-get-back, lot-of-work-to-do excuses. I sometimes felt I would like to go with them; the trenches must be warm and cheery compared to our dank inhospitable barge.

One day a general did come to lunch with us. His name was 'Boom'[5] because of his voice, but we were not privileged to hear more than a word or two of it. Save to put food in, he scarcely opened his mouth during the whole uncomfortable meal. The major kept up a droning monologue, like a country parson incanting the Litany, in a voice barely audible above the guarded clatter of knives and forks. Otherwise no one spoke except to ask for the bread, the butter or the salt, please. We all drank water.

Immediately after lunch Boom disappeared and we saw him no more. In the morning we had felt very nervous at the thought of his coming, of what his keen eyes would see, of whether he would quietly approve or thunder forth his stern condemnation. When he had gone we were disappointed

---

5. Trenchard.

that he had not inspected, that he had not spoken to us personally, individually. A word from him would have been encouraging. A pity he, too, was so aloof. It made his visit seem rather uninspiring. And somehow it confirmed my suspicion that we were neither popular nor interesting. In fact, we were not a good squadron; not a bad lot, only young, dull and very ill-assorted.

XXXVI

I was beginning to like Growl, possibly because he was beginning to like me. With his neat canvas leggings, hands thrust into the front pockets of his riding-breeches, coat flaps pushed back behind his wrists, feet firmly planted well apart, he had the appearance – enhanced by his clean-shaven, weather-beaten face, by a straw between his teeth, and by that gruff voice which could change so rapidly from wrath to good-humour – of something between a horse-dealer and a buccaneer. At times I would catch him looking at me with an expression, half frown, half smile, such as a pirate skipper might bestow upon a likely lad. It was a pity that he was never able to give me any hints as to how to fight the enemy in the air, but in those days each man had to learn and progress from his own experience and, as luck would have it, I was gaining mine quicker than most – too quickly perhaps.

'Do you know anything about bomb-sights?' he asked me one day.

'Not a thing,' I admitted. 'I've never even seen one.'

'Then, young fellow, you had better hurry and find out all you can. The mechanics are fitting bomb-racks to your machine … Hey! Where are you going?'

'To stop them before it's too late.'

'No use!' he exclaimed with a malicious chuckle. 'The job's more than half-done. Tomorrow you're to practise with the sight over the aerodrome near Béthune. And the day after that you and a lot of enthusiastic young pilots will go a-bombing.'

I protested that one day's practice would not be sufficient to teach me to hit any target with certainty.

'Never mind, young fellow, you do what your elders and betters think is good for you. You'll have plenty of company on the raid. Rare Earths is going with you; and M.C. will be among the escort. Several other squadrons are competing – something like twenty-five machines in all, each carrying two 112-pound bombs. That makes two and a half tons, on one railway junction – you ought to do *some* damage even if you miss the target altogether!'

Put like that, the raid seemed to offer immense possibilities. Excitedly I asked if the war were starting again. But at that Growl only laughed and told me not to be silly. He went on leave that same afternoon.

XXXVII

No sooner had I tried the bomb-sight in the air than I realised that it would be utterly impossible for me to learn to use it in under two days' time. A rather complicated apparatus, it required some skill and experience in the using. Above all it required two flights over the target; the first one to get the wind's speed and direction and to make sundry calculations with a stop-watch and notebook, the second flight to drop the bombs. Since observers had to be dispensed with owing to the added weight of bombs, all the calculations had to be done by the pilot. I did not fancy myself sitting above an angry Archie battery and scratching my head over a complicated sum in arithmetic, especially if the final result was to be the totally inaccurate placing of my bombs. The more I thought of it the less the prospect pleased me.

On the day of the raid I came to a decision. I said nothing to anyone, for Growl and Wilhelm were both on leave, but I made up my mind that if, after an attempt to aim my first bomb by means of the sight, I missed the target I would descend to a much lower level than was prescribed and deposit the second bomb exactly where I wanted it. When, at the last moment, I learned that we were to make two trips each, dropping four bombs apiece, I felt certain of achieving something by my own methods. It meant disobeying orders and taking extra risk, but I had some small confidence in myself and none in the sight.

The meet, at which our B.E.s supplied both the pack and the field, was timed for 11 a.m., and we were due to move off a quarter of an hour later from the neighbourhood of Béthune. Arriving punctually, I found three or four machines circling around; two more turned up from my own squadron, and between Béthune and the lines there were a few others. But there was nothing like the important gathering I had been told to expect. People coming from squadrons from far to the north had apparently decided to cut the meet altogether; I could see isolated machines in the distance already being Archied. Waiting no longer, I gave my machine her head and jogged off to the railway junction at Dron, from which if we could not actually draw a fox, we might at least hope to tempt a Fokker.

There was, of course, no question of formation – that additional peril to flying had not yet been invented. Machine arrived when they liked, dropped their bombs and dashed home to lunch. But the sight if not spectacular but was at all events rather impressive, with a score of aeroplanes scattered over the sky and many dozens of Archie bursts even more scattered. One advantage of do-as-you-please and no-formation was that Archie never quite knew at which machine he was aiming. Every one of us was at a different altitude, dodging in his own peculiar way and in his own good time. All the puzzled anti-aircraft gunners could do was to fire into the brown, hoping that the odd fragment might score a hit. And by the laws of chance it sometimes did; but not very often.

The wind was from the north, and on the south side of the junction a collection of machines assembled, each waiting its turn to fly into wind over the target. The crowd did not look any too safe to me; as if the field were hung up, bunched in front of the only gap over a dangerous jump. Machines were jostling each other in their anxiety to get ahead and have done with the job, and to add to the confusion, Archie, without doing any real harm, was beginning to find the range. At from nine to ten thousand feet – the height at which the raid took place – Archie was considered to be fairly innocuous, but I noticed that, despite the conscientious way in which some machines were circling twice over the target to adjust sights before dropping their bombs, he was putting them off their aim: a good many misses were being registered in the fields at the side of the railway track. I should do no better if I joined the crowd; I should only get in their way and in the way of Archie. I must strike out on my own, lower down, much lower.

To dive towards the railway with the engine at half-throttle was easy enough, but on the way the thought occurred to me that I might now get hit by one of the bombs from the machines above. The chance of this happening was no greater than of being hit by an unexploded Archie shell, yet the idea so alarmed me that I decided at once not to go round twice adjusting the sights, but to drop the bombs quickly by luck and judgement. For this it did not seem worth while going below two thousand feet, where ground machine-gunners were adding to the racket. Approaching the junction with the engine still throttled down I could also hear the uneven popping and crackling of rifle fire – heavier than usual, it seemed. Peering over the side, I could at first see nothing to warrant so much noise. The railway station was a bit knocked about and appeared to be deserted, but a short distance out of it, on a curve well way from the junction a train was standing motionless, the engine blowing off steam. Beside it there were many agitated black dots ... A troop train! The men had disembarked and it was from them that the rifle fire was coming. To use the sight now was out of the question; my one idea was to get rid of the two bombs without delay. No time to waste; I pulled both release handles. The bombs dropped off.

Watching closely, I followed them down to the ground ... Both missed the station – of course! The first one fell in a roadway not far from a level-crossing, but far enough to be quite harmless. A flash and a big puff of smoke from the second bomb appeared in the courtyard of a house twenty yards from the railway line and about two hundred yards from the station. My aim – from which I had expected such wonderful results – had proved to be hopeless. And yet in that courtyard where the second bomb exploded I saw motor-transport, and the smoke which hung over the place afterwards seemed to indicate that something had been set on fire. Better than nothing. But I wished that I had been given a few more bombs to practise with; half a dozen more and I *might* have hit the station itself.

Now that it was all over I felt very disappointed. It was a pity I had come down so low to achieve so meagre a result, whilst high above in the sky I could see a couple of Fokkers and a German two-seater with whom I might have had a more profitable engagement. M.C., I imagined, must be having a grand time.

On the way home, no sooner had I got clear of the worst of Archie than I flew into a snowstorm which, while it lasted, was so much more terrifying than anything the enemy had done that when at length I landed at the squadron, with the machine coated with ice, my account of the morning's work was incoherent.

XXXVIII

For once everybody in the Mess was talking at the same time. The three or four pilots who had been bombing had returned before me and were eagerly discussing the results, and I noted with embarrassment that they all claimed to have obtained direct hits on the station. The others, like M.C., who had acted as escort were commenting on the fights they had had and on whatever they had been able to see of the bombing. The major went from one to the other like an interested spectator after a football match, asking questions, faintly smiling, showing keenness, almost excitement, but unable to get a word in above the unwonted tumult. A few more shows like this, I thought, and he would become an enthusiast in spite of himself. It had made us all keener. If the raid had not been an unqualified success, at least it had given us something to do, something of an offensive sort against the enemy to lighten the gloom of winter. I was relieved, however, that my own answers to questions vaguely and hurriedly put were hardly listened to.

'Did you see that barge sink in the canal alongside the station?' someone asked, addressing the crowd in general. 'A bomb fell right inside it, direct hit – it sank like a stone!'

'Yes, I saw that,' someone else replied. 'But it seemed to me that it blew up before it sank – must have had ammunition on board. Personally I aimed at that train standing on the curve. Think I got a direct hit – knocked out some of the troops.'

The major was murmuring, 'Well done, well done,' whilst at my side M.C. was speaking.

'Archie *was* busy, wasn't he? Sending up a lot of those "Flaming Onions", too – nasty things, but they didn't do any good. I suppose the gunners were afraid of hitting their own side – quite a few enemy aircraft about. Did anyone see those two Fokkers?'

We answered in chorus. Everyone had seen them, some had tried to fight them.

'I thought one of them was going to dive on me,' someone said. 'But I fancy there were too many of us to make it attractive.'

'I chased one for a mile or two,' M.C. went on. 'I couldn't get near enough to shoot, so I came back to watch the bombing. It looked as though the station had been pretty badly hit.'

Suddenly he stuck out his jaw, glaring around in emulation of Growl's best pirate-captain manner.

'Who the devil was that silly ass flying at about two thousand feet, collecting all the machine-gun fire? Who was it?'

XXXIX

At noon I was weak with hunger, for which I ate a hearty lunch. Afterwards I was weak with indigestion, for which I took a large glass of brandy. After the brandy I felt mildly intoxicated, for which the only remedy appeared to be to leave the ground as quickly as possible. Scrambling into the B.E. I steamed hilariously away with two nice new bombs hooked up underneath.

Over Don other aeroplanes were returning one by one from the luncheon interval, but there was not the same dangerous crush as in the morning. Not that it would have worried me in the least had the crowd been twice as thick. I was in no mood for dallying. Now that the ice was broken – in a manner of speaking, for it was still freezing hard in the air – I intended to pursue the same tactics as earlier in the day, but more boldly. An easterly breeze had blown the snowstorm out of the sky, the air was crisp, the weather wintry but fine. I wished that I had with me that cavalry observer; I felt like making huntin' noises. Everything seemed favourable to the attack; even Archie kept a friendly distance, encouraging me with an occasional cough well above my head as I dived Don-wards.

There could be no doubt about my judgment this time. If *in vino Veritas* has any meaning, it meant just then that I was an extremely fine dropper of bombs. I don't want to exaggerate to my own detriment the effect of the spirit I had drunk, but it must have been Napoleon brandy – I had the eye of an eagle; damn it, I felt like an eagle! An eagle laying high-explosive eggs … Long before reaching the site I saw black dots moving. German dots: '*Entschuldigen sie bitte, meine Herren,*' I murmured and pulled the first release handle.

I was sure of having pulled it too soon; the bomb would fall so far from its mark that the very sound of the explosion would be inaudible in Don. And then I saw a flash in a big building between the station and the canal, debris flew high and wide, a column of smoke shot upwards. It was rather satisfying. I circled round quickly for the second shot. Near the station more black dots were moving. '*Bitte, meine Herren, ruhig bleiben. Es kommt noch eine* ...' I watched the bomb go down, diminishing rapidly to a pinpoint, then suddenly expanding again as it struck a building in the goods yard. A flash, bricks and dust, and lots of slow-spreading smoke ... I flew home, humming a tune.

Twenty aeroplanes – two bombs each, two trips each – four tons of bombs upon one small railway junction. The biggest raid the Flying Corps had yet carried out ... At the squadron office we wrote our reports feverishly, anxious to know what would happen next.

Next? Well, the excitement died down. The reports went in and were filed. Aerial photographs were taken of the damage done. Press *communiques* mentioned the raid cautiously, observing that similar bombardments had preceded the battles of Neuve-Chappelle and Loos. But the opposing armies made no move. The incident seemed to have no meaning or value in the main trend of the war. It was soon forgotten. An extra number of star-shells lit up the countryside for a night or two; there was a little more rifle fire than usual; the enemy was nervous. Nothing else.

Nowadays when I recall Don Junction, which is not often, it is to wonder how many luckless French civilians were in or about the station whilst we flew carelessly overhead thinking it all rather good fun.

XL

The bombing of Don took place upon the 27th of November, and early on the next day an urgent message came through from the watchful anti-aircraft batteries in our neighbourhood announcing that the lines had been crossed by a number of enemy aeroplanes. The squadron came to life. M.C. and Rare Earths made ready their respective machines. My observer came running breathlessly from the barge to the hangar where I was already waiting, with orders for us to leave at once. Quick to obey such a joyful command, we were off the ground before the others.

And almost immediately we sighted an enemy, a big white-winged two-seater Albatross, far above us and flying parallel to the lines, reconnoitring our positions. So far above was he that I doubted if we could ever climb up to his height to catch him before he went home; like most German machines, he had a greater turn of speed than we had.

The chase started over Neuve-Chapelle when we were at two thousand feet and he at about eight thousand. It continued in a straight line as far as Armentières, by which time – the enemy having descended a little – we had drawn nearly level at six or seven thousand. Then to our chagrin he turned eastwards and before we could fire had crossed the lines. Forestalling this turn, expected since the beginning of the pursuit, by keeping well to eastward of him I managed to get ahead, only losing a little in height in gaining the necessary speed. Five miles across the lines, with the machine-gun on the rear mounting, we engaged him.

Strangely enough I do not think that until the instant when we opened fire he had been aware of our presence. Probably he had been intent on gazing to the west, giving only an occasional glance to the east where, with the sun in his eyes, the B.E. had remained almost invisible. Thinking himself safe, he throttled down to glide towards Lille; and passed within twenty yards of our starboard wing-tips ...

Twenty or thirty rounds my observer fired, not more, then, as the enemy turned across our bows, ceased fire to change the gun to the forward mounting.

I had expected to hear heavy fire from the enemy's back seat, for, while the gun was being changed and as we started to dive after him, he had an easy chance to get us. But to my astonishment not a shot came in answer. When the gun was ready the observer gave him another burst, a very short one because the Albatross was turning faster, gliding more steeply. His glide was becoming a dive; a dive at so steep an angle that I could no longer make the B.E. follow. And the turn he was making now had something unnatural about it – he was going down out of control! For a moment we both watched, fascinated.

A sudden crack of bullets made us swing our heads round; made the observer jump for the Lewis gun with a movement that shook the machine. Over our heads sailed another Albatross. And even as I banked the B.E. swiftly away from this new danger I saw, returning from the west, two more enemy craft.

Bullets cracked by. Our gun replied with several long bursts, its barrel getting as hot as the observer changing it hastily from one mounting to another. The B.E., jarring from frequent impacts, banked, dodged, dived and zoomed as though she knew what was wanted, accepting all that I could give her from the immense store of my eighty-three hour's flying experience. And while we were firing and wheeling, from out of the skies came a fourth enemy. It seemed as if the curse laid on those who shoot an Albatross had descended upon us.

Four German aeroplanes, one curveting B.E. Even Archie stopped to watch.

XLI

When an hour or so later we returned to the squadron it seemed that at least a week had passed. I felt as though I had not slept for days, although I might have dreamed. The morning was sunny, the air calm. I brought the B.E. down carefully; the wind was in just the right direction, I made a good landing. As the machine came to rest in front of the hangars I remember calling out to the observer, in the sudden silence after the stopping of the engine, 'Well done – good show!' And so it had been; swinging that gun around from mounting to mounting, hanging on whilst I did the wildest of turns, keeping a cool head in an emergency, demanded from the observer the qualities of an acrobat, a strong man, and a juggler. And whereas his many bursts of fire had eventually driven off the whole pack of enemies, his first few rounds had been accurate, deadly. No doubt of that; the enemy had gone down and crashed. Ten miles inside his own lines, but crashed nevertheless. A satisfactory, almost an unhoped for, result; previous to this fight I had begun to doubt the possibility of ever bringing down an enemy until we were better equipped. I had been reminded of that Cautionary Tale in which Algernon, playing with a loaded gun:

'... pointed it towards his sister,
Aimed very carefully, but missed her.'

It had seemed that we were destined always to aim very carefully, but miss the enemy. At last we had aimed and hit. 'Well done!' I repeated.

The observer turned to look at me with open mouth and raised eyebrows as though he did not quite understand.

'Good shooting on your part,' I said. 'Just one big burst and down he went.'

His brows were still raised in surprise. 'Did he *really* go down?' he asked at length. 'I *thought* I saw him dive out of control, but I wasn't sure – it all seemed so unreal. Good thing you kept dodging – I couldn't move that gun any quicker, my hands are still numb from hauling it around. I suppose it *must* have been real!'

I laughed at his doubts, though I was not far from sharing them. Aerial fighting, more than any other, seems so immensely far away when one stands once more on the earth, with the machine-guns silent, the engine still, the sky empty.

'Come and look at the damage,' I said. 'That's real enough.'

It was not so much the quantity of hits as the quality of the damage done. One of the interplane struts was shot through, a rudder control cable cut away, the air-speed indicator smashed, the propeller chipped, a longeron in the fuselage pierced and splintered (that last bullet had grazed the back of my seat) – twenty hits altogether. But we had won something of a victory. Later on *The Times*, meaning to be kind, described it as a 'gallant fight against odds', as if the odds had been of our choosing! As for 'gallant' – well, one of its meanings is courteous, and that the fight was – at least for a moment or two. A sharp turn to avoid one enemy had brought us close alongside another, dangerously close, within pistol shot. Our own gun was momentarily out of action, between mountings, and we could see the enemy observer working over his as though reloading or clearing a jam. We were actually close enough to see the expression upon each other's faces, but powerless to do harm. I don't know yet what came over me, whether nervousness, excitement, or just a fellow-feeling for the man opposite in the same position as myself; but it was at any rate a joyful impulse that made me raise my arm to wave across the narrow air space. And from the gunner's cockpit of that enemy biplane, the German waved back to me. Just a single wave of the arm above his head, a salute as it might have been in the days of tilting, of knights in armour and of wooden lances. Then, his gun being ready, he opened fire. My observer was still loading, I was forced to turn away in self-protection. I had only an automatic pistol, but I discharged it defiantly …

* * *

In those days a machine was repaired sooner than scrapped or replaced. It took two days for mechanics working morning, noon, and night to repair my B.E. The day after they had finished I had reason to wish that they had taken longer.

XLII

In the Koran it is written: 'The fate of every man have we bound about his neck.' The words might well have been painted over the companion of our drab and unromantic barge. For, if I cannot profess to speak for the respective fates of the other officers in the squadron, of the inevitable nature of my own small destiny I have no remaining doubt.

The bombing of Don had roused the German airmen to activity over our territory. Whether they came to see what we were up to or to take reprisals for our raid mattered not, they had to be chased away. In the course of such a chase I had had that fifth and biggest fight in which an enemy machine had been brought down near Lille. In an attempt to confirm the wrecking of this enemy craft, Wilhelm, just back from leave, was sent into the air to locate and photograph it. The enemy, possibly expecting further trouble in the vicinity of Lille, had their Fokkers ready. One of them surprised Wilhelm at his work, outfought him and shot him down – a prisoner and wounded.

The Long Reconnaissance was coming round again. The third flight (the one which did not live on the barge and which enjoyed a measure of independence in a farmhouse) was now wholly occupied in artillery observation; they did no Long Reconnaissance work. The flight which Foxy had commanded had been the last to attempt the job (they had abandoned it owing to bad weather); it was therefore the turn of the flight to which I belonged. But with Wilhelm captured, Growl away on leave and Rare Earths' machine laid up for overhaul, I was the only pilot available: the other flight would have to do the reconnaissance after all. But now they, too, claimed that they were short of machines and pilots, or would be for a few days. Moreover the weather looked as though it might remain unsuitable for a week and at the end of that time the Long Reconnaissance duty would lapse, passing to another squadron. The flight that had been Foxy's was quite willing for this to happen because only M.C.'s machine was ready to take the air.

Growl was returning from leave in a day's time. During his absence we had done a lot of good work. Patrols, reconnaissances, the bombing raid; we had had the big fight; but we had lost Wilhelm. It would be a great thing, I thought, if we could produce the achievement of a successful Long Reconnaissance with which to greet him on his arrival. The result of the big fight had brought me some small *kudos*, but it was clear that to please the major I should have to keep up the good work and not rest upon whatever swiftly fading laurels I might have earned. The day before the reconnaissance was due I made up my mind.

With all the insane enthusiasm of improvident youth I volunteered to go, with M.C. as escort. Till then only a slender concatenation of circumstances had led me forward, but from the moment when I made my choice the chain was finally welded. I had tempted fortune too far.

XLIII

Still rather dejected by the loss of Wilhelm and his observer, we were nevertheless an unusually jolly party in the Mess on the night before I went on my second Long Reconnaissance. And the reason was not far to seek. The major was dining and sleeping at headquarters, Growl was in England, Foxy was in 'disgrace'; with the possible exception of M.C, the entire range of cats was away and the mice therefore put up a bold squeaking. Even so there were too few in the mess to make a really cheerful din.

'This squadron *is* getting small,' a young pilot remarked, looking round the table. 'Hardly enough of us to do the work! Wish they'd send some more out from England.'

One of the observers gave a chuckle.

'"Nay, wish not one man more …"' he quoted.

The young pilot was scornful.

'You imagine the fewer of us the greater the share of honour?' he retorted. 'Balderdash! There's only one man in the squadron liable to come in for any honour – and I don't suppose you'll claim that our old Starched Shirt has the personality of Harry the King. Wonder what he would be like in a real emergency, a tight corner – if the Germans came here, for instance?'

'Not much likelihood of that,' M.C. declared. 'It's much more probable that we shall go and join the Germans. Personally I think Foxy is well out of it – sent back to England with nothing against him except a vague complaint about his pyjamas. Think of him now, sitting in his club or in some swell restaurant in London, cocktails, dress clothes, carnation in buttonhole, beautiful lady dining with him …' He broke off to make a pretence of shuddering. 'Brrr – makes me go all goosey to think of him!'

The observer who was to accompany me on the morrow grinned.

'Yes, Foxy *will* laugh if we go and dine in Potsdam after the reco, won't he? What do you think,' he asked me, 'do you suppose we are scheduled to "go west" tomorrow?'

I shook my head emphatically. Not on my life, I maintained stoutly, would anything so disastrous occur. If we went at all, and the weather made it uncertain, we would return just as we had done from a score of previous flights across the lines. My leave was due at Christmas and on that day I had every intention of dining at home. I laughed at his fears.

But I must have forgotten to touch wood.

XLIV

We stood upon the canal bank near the hangars. It was after breakfast on the following morning.

'Do you think it's good enough?' M.C. asked, looking doubtfully at the sky.

My observer answered him firmly, resentful of the suggestion behind his words that we should not go at all.

'Certainly it's good enough – to make a start at any rate. There's not too much wind and there are gaps in the clouds – look, the sun's coming through!'

They both turned to me. As the actual reconnaissance pilot my judgment must be final. Avoiding their gaze, I stared at the clouds and listened to the wind in the poplars. The waters of the Lys were ruffled; dead leaves whisked along the towpath, tumbled into the river and sailed upstream in crescent formation like a miniature armada. Small waves broke against the bows of the barge, brushed past leaving a track of frothy bubbles. The canvas walls of the hangars billowed steadily for a while with the pressure of air within, then collapsed suddenly against the poles with a dull boom like the sails of a ship taken aback. In front of the sheds stood the two duty aeroplanes, rocking slightly as the breeze caught their wings. From their wires, as from the bare branches of the poplars, came a mournful soughing.

I shivered; the air was cold and damp … How far away the summer of Shoreham and Gosport seemed! Then there would have been no doubt about a day like this; 'unfit for flying' or perhaps 'no lift in the air' would have been the decision. But it was for such weather and such work as this that I had been trained. Orders had been left at the squadron office that the reconnaissance must be made if the weather were at all possible. Could it honestly be termed 'impossible'? I thought not, although I longed now for a definite order to cancel the flight. But Growl was away, the major had not yet returned from headquarters; it was for me to decide. I glanced about, taking in all the signs of the weather.

Mechanics stood by the machines, holding on to the wings. They looked cold, only half awake. Poor fellows, they had a dull life of it; no flights on fine sunny days, no adventure, no aerial combats. But their quarters were hardly less comfortable than ours – better than the trenches! – and they were not called upon to make fateful decisions, to risk 'going west' … A flight-sergeant hovered nearby, keeping an eye on the mechanics, ready to spring to attention when called. M.C. frowned gloomily as if to emphasise his own unfavourable opinion, and the two observers having had their say waited in silence, holding maps and notebooks.

And all these men were watching, I could feel their eyes upon me. They were watching as I blinked up at the sky, watching when I stared at the horizon, watching and waiting for that final verdict which it was mine to give and so direct their immediate actions. I could have stood there all day irresolute – but my observer was right, we must make an attempt.

'Let's go,' I said to M.C. at length. 'I believe we shall find clear weather beyond the lines. We can always turn back if it gets too bad.'

But I was inwardly convinced that, once we got under way, there would be no returning until we had circled Valenciennes.

My observer led the way to the machine.

'Start up!' the flight-sergeant shouted to the waiting mechanics. 'Get those engines going. Smartly now!'

The die was cast.

XLV

Down the curving stretch of the aerodrome the wind blew lustily, lifting us vertically over the trees at the far end. Holding straight on, I prudently gained height before turning; it was not a day to risk a landing down wind. At fifteen hundred feet we passed back over the squadron.

The escorting machine with M.C. as pilot was well below and behind; apparently he had wanted to see me safely away before taxi-ing out to take off, but I was momentarily puzzled for there were two B.E.s in the air below me. As I watched, one of them went down to land, taxied along the riverside, stopped by our flight sheds. Now that it was on the ground I could see it was not M.C.'s machine; there was a newness about the colour of its wings – Growl had returned, that was it, bringing a machine to replace the one lost with Wilhelm. He would be pleased, I thought, to see us going off punctually despite the poor weather. I watched the brown dot of him striding towards the barge.

The narrow world in which I had dwelt for nearly three months moved swiftly by. In spite of its restrictions, in spite of its atmosphere of ill-feeling, of distrust, of envy and of hidden malice it had taken a friendly, almost a home-like grip upon me. It was not the fault of one more than another among us that we were so cheerless and so stiff; it was the closeness of our confinement in the barge, the small circle of our daily horizon, the dismal winter futility of the war. With a little generosity one could afford to absolve the major from blame, because there can be no doubt that he suffered from a constitutional disability to inspire comradeship. That he was willing to meet changing conditions seemed evident from his having left the gunners for the Flying Corps; and despite my early prejudice I had found myself liking him at times, but they certainly did not think much of him in the squadron. He must have sighed with relief when at length he left it. Some time after the war I saw him, dressed in the new blue uniform of the Royal Air Force. He still walked like a melancholy bird. And appropriately enough, considering the circumstances in which I best remembered him, he was judging a competition for landing aeroplanes within a small space ...

Although he had been expected back early at the squadron he was not there to see me off when I left on that Long Reconnaissance, and once I had started it made no difference where he was. Even had he and Growl met in anxious conference near the farmhouse where the squadron office was situated, there would have been no means of recalling me. But, Growl gone, the aerodrome remained deserted. The pilots were at breakfast or, profiting from the bad weather and general inactivity, still in bed. The farm buildings and transport lines passed beneath; a hedge, the corner of a ploughed field; then the barge, dirty grey with an untidy deck – I could make out the skylight of the Mess, the porthole of my cabin next to it. The Lys, its surface the hue of steel, was curved like a sabre, the edge to the east. The poplars straight as guardsmen on parade became foreshortened, became dots, then rapidly lengthened again. Merville passed under my right wing. The squadron lay astern.

I faced forward to pick out the landmarks on the southerly course to Arras. The machine was climbing rapidly, we were already through the first thin bank of scattered clouds and the trenchlines to the east and south were visible. No one could have called it a fine day, yet it seemed good enough for our purpose. There were heavy clouds above us, but the sun was shining through the upper layers and over German territory the air was clear. If only the westerly wind, against which we should have to struggle on the return journey, did not strengthen ... Contrary winds, however, were only to be expected as a part of the day's work; the reconnaissance had to be done.

I looked back once more to check my course and the drift of the wind; but Merville and the aerodrome were obscured by a rain–cloud.

Chapter 3

The Wings are Clipped

I

We were nearing ten thousand feet when we approached Arras from the west, for this time I did not intend to commence work at anything less than that height; I wanted to be sure of seeing my way clearly above the clouds. Arras itself was partly hidden, but there were plenty of gaps to show me the lines, and to the east there was a vast area of clear sky. That hornets' nest of Douai showed up distinctly, bright in the wintry sunlight. Hazy in the distance lay the towns we had to visit. An easy course to steer, only the wind to worry about.

As we reached the lines I looked back to seek M.C. in the escorting aeroplane, but he was nowhere in sight. That he had been with us as far as Lens I knew, I had seen him several times. Of course it was possible that I had outdistanced him since my machine, I had reason to believe, could climb faster than his; he might even be hidden from us by one of the many big cumulus clouds. At all events it seemed unlikely that he, our escort, should already have turned back. I waited, making figures of eight above Arras.

Bad weather was coming up from the west, no doubt of it. If this job were to be done at all, 'twere best done quickly … Again I searched the sky. No, not a sign of M.C. We were above ten thousand feet, time was precious, I dared not wait longer. Heading east we crossed the lines. My observer made ready his map and notebook; the Long Reconnaissance had started.

II

Almost at once we sighted a German two-seater. One thousand feet below us, heading north-east to cross the lines. I increased to full speed, losing height so as to get to the eastward of him and drive him towards our own territory: then, signalling to the observer to place the gun on the forward mounting, turned to attack.

There was a flash from the enemy's back-seat gun as he opened fire, but I could not hear the bullets pass; his aim was poor and the range none too close. I pushed the nose down for a further increase of speed, but before my observer could get in a shot the enemy wheeled and went into a dive. A big mountain of a cloud rose up in front of him. He plunged into it, effectively checking our pursuit.

As I glued my eyes to that cloud, watching like a terrier in front of a rat-hole for his reappearance, my gaze fell once more upon the war-scarred town of Arras with the chalk-white line of trenches running through its eastern suburbs. We were recrossing the battle front, back to our own lines … I hesitated. Somewhere in the big cloud was the enemy, trying to elude us. Were we to wait for him and then follow, there would be a long, probably a disappointing chase. We could not hope to surprise him; it was quite on the cards that we should fail to overhaul him. M.C. with his escorting aeroplane might have helped, but he was not in sight. I looked to the east. The open country, clear of clouds, seemed to be inviting our inspection. The Long Reconnaissance was more important than any aerial combat; we had orders not to force an engagement on the way out. On the way back – well, there might yet be plenty of excitement if the Fokkers rose from Douai.

On the far side of the cloud the German two-seater came out of concealment, heading due north. He was travelling fast, the range had already opened a great deal. My observer caught sight of him, pointed enthusiastically. But I shook my head and steered east. The observer replaced the gun upon the rear mounting, brought out his map, rearranged his notebook.

III

Aided by the west wind we made rapid progress. Douai we left a mile or two to the north, time enough to visit it on the return journey if all went well. The principal objective was Valenciennes. I made haste to reach it before the unsettled weather changed for the worse.

In a comparatively short time we were above Denain, where the observer – he was that same Dante of the patrol during the King's visit – Dante, began a feverish taking of notes. Every now and then he would wave one arm or the other to indicate the way I should turn to give him a better view of road or rail, transport or trains, of anything new or unusual to interest the Intelligence people. It was hard for him to see what was happening in the stations for we were now at twelve thousand feet in brilliant sunshine and below us the light was poor, misty. For some ten minutes we cruised around over the town. It was very quiet. Archie sent up three shells.

On to Valenciennes. The wind must be increasing in strength, I thought; the earth passed very swiftly. On the roads and in the country generally, nothing much worth observing other than a train or two in the sidings. And not a machine in the sky, not a speck anywhere, not so much as a shell-burst. Only a threatening bank of clouds to the west.

Valenciennes at last. Still in France, and yet to us it seemed the very heart of the enemy's territory. What unpleasantness were they preparing down there? We went beyond the town for a couple of miles, staring curiously at the mysterious land. A road and a railway led to the east – to Mons! No use in going farther that way; there was nothing doing in that direction now. I turned back to circle the town. The glare had gone from the surface of the ground, the haze had been blown away, the air was clear. We had reached thirteen thousand feet, but above us the sky was clouding over even as Dante hung over the side to count rolling-stock. Not much movement in the big railway station, nothing out of the ordinary; but to the south a long train was winding down the track towards Cambrai, another moved in the direction of Avesnes. I could see that Dante had noticed them and intended to deal with them later; meanwhile he wanted to have another look at Valenciennes. He waved for me to circle again.

This time as we turned I observed how almost stationary we appeared to be when facing west; the wind had risen. It would be a slow and tiresome business flying back against it, there were rain or snow clouds on our course; already it was bitterly cold, my hands were numb. And the top of the compass was frosted over as on previous chilly occasions when, in obedience to Dante's waving arm, I turned south, glad to be off from the neighbourhood. Its silence was uncanny. An old French fort stared up at us like the eye of a Cyclops. Why didn't Archie fire? Had the gunners not seen us, or did they think the weather so bad that they need not add to our difficulties?

Perhaps they were right; it was a stormy day and ours was the only machine in the sky. Thank goodness the reconnaissance itself was nearly completed. We were well to the south of the town now. In a few more minutes we could turn west.

IV

How they dragged by, those minutes, interminably slow! *Tick-tick-tick* – I could hear the seconds hammering by in my head, like an uneven pulse. A flicker of sunlight spread over our wings, gilding them, making them shine, but the world below had darkened. It was raining in the country through which the long train was leisurely steaming. Was it carrying troops or freight? Any train in occupied territory was worth while examining. I banked slightly for Dante to see more clearly. He leaned over the side of his cockpit, carefully counting the trucks. *Tick-tick-tick* – the engine revolutions seemed to be checking his tally. I wished he would make haste. Apparently he found this train of great interest, he was taking copious notes. *Tick-tick-tick* – sounded like the scratching of his pencil – or was he tapping it against the edge of the fuselage? Absurd thought! But there did seem to be some unusual rattle mixed up with the more ordinary noises of a B.E. Or were my ears playing me tricks because of the altitude?

Dante was waving me to change course. From south to west. It was the beginning of the journey home. And about time, too, I thought.

On completing the turn I glanced northward to get my bearings from Valenciennes. The town was much farther off than I had expected; then the wind was not due west, it was blowing us to the south. I must watch that drift on the way back; it would not do to go too far south of Arras. Forty miles to the lines, against this wind it would take us an hour at full speed losing height. I looked at my watch. We had been in the air for well over three hours. There was fuel for only one more hour with certainty. Yes, I must lose height, hurry back. *Tick-tick-tick* – something seemed to be shaking in front, near the engine. On the instrument board the revolution-counter stood fairly steady, but now I had no doubt that there was some slight, growing vibration. *Tick-tick-tick!* A menacing, horrible sound such as one might dream of in nightmare. Engine failure? The thought crossed my mind; I rejected it furiously. Those three miserable Archie shells from Denain – I had heard something strike the machine – had they done some fatal damage? Cracked a cylinder, caused an oil leak? I peered forward, afraid of my thoughts.

Dante was still busily taking notes, calmly, cold-bloodedly, unconscious of danger. He had heard nothing. Was it just my foolish imagination, after all? No, the damnable *tick-tick-tick* had become a hard knocking, louder than ever. It was sounding the knell of our hopes …

Over the side I gazed downward, trying to estimate from the far distant earth the amount of our drift. It was hard to judge, the wind appeared to be north of west, but only a little. Drawing my head in, I crouched low in the cockpit to scrub with my glove at the glass top of the compass. No use; the frost was inside the glass. I could not see the compass card. A cloud passed over the sun, and at the same time the earth below began to grow dim from oncoming rain, the principal landmarks were obliterated. Dante turned to look at me anxiously, pointing ahead once or twice as if to ask the way. I shook my head in doubt. I had to guess the way home.

V

The knocking developed into a loud clanging which, I feared, was bound to terminate disastrously. It did. Suddenly. There was an explosion as loud as the bursting of a well-aimed Archie shell, pieces of metal flew past Dante's head, a big puff of blue-black smoke momentarily enveloped the engine; a flash, and the whole machine vibrated with the shock. Fire! – the thought came irresistibly into my head. Off went the switch, petrol cock closed, stick forward, throttle wide open – an engine fire might be extinguished by quick action. I dived a thousand feet off our height.

At the time my mental anguish was so great that I retain little more than a blurred impression of the whole occurrence. I had no time to think it over. After these many years, however, I feel more than ever convinced that I did the right thing, that the engine was for a few moments actually on fire quickly extinguished by the dive. We lost some valuable height, but at all events the worst catastrophe was averted, even if the inevitable end of the flight was but postponed. Slowly I flattened out, switched on again, turned the petrol cock. The engine started.

But, ye gods of machinery, how she ran! The vibration was such that the control stick jumped from my hands. This could not last, the whole machine would fall to pieces! I dared not run the engine at more than half throttle and yet I had to use it as much as possible in the hope that it would still drag us back. Where the devil were we now? Dante did not seem to know. I admired his fortitude; he sat calmly, almost rigidly in front of me, occasionally staring over the side at the gathering clouds. He must have felt horribly frightened. It is no joke to have to sit still and in silence, twelve thousand feet up in the air, behind an engine that is breaking itself into small pieces and in front of a pilot of whose thoughts you are entirely ignorant. He could not even help me steer, save by guesswork, and at that he was no better than I.

We came to a break in the clouds and, while the sun shone again for a few minutes, we looked earthwards. But it was in vain that we searched the small visible patch for familiar landmarks. Two white roads, straight as the legs of an isosceles triangle, converged; at the apex must lie a town, though we could not see it. Probably Cambrai. All right so far. A little south of our true course, but that was the fault of the north-west wind. No use heading into it more directly, it was too strong for us to fight with our failing engine-power. Better to accept the small amount of southerly drift, it might drift us over the lines. Even so we could not avoid having the main force of the wind against us.

Ahead, right across our path, rose a great mountain of cumulus. There was no going round it, we should have to fly straight through, even though the engine was running worse, the vibration tending all the time to increase, so that every now and then I had to throttle down a little more. And the compass was entirely useless; the mist had cleared to some extent from its glass, I could just make out the card, it was swinging in meaningless circles …

The towering cumulus mountain stood before us like an iceberg at eight thousand feet. One last look at the ground: open rolling fields, a hedge, a track. Not a landmark. The earth faded from our sight. The machine lurched suddenly and damp, grey vapour whirled past.

VI

It was dark in the clouds and bumpy enough to make me appreciate my safety-belt. Snowflakes that smacked my face as though they had been fired from a gun rushed by, changed presently to rain-drops like whiplashes. The air became warmer; we were descending by swift stages. Every bump seemed to lower us by a hundred feet or more, and still there was nothing to steer by. I kept as straight and as even a course as my bewildered senses could suggest, but the trembling engine blurred my sight, its rattle drowned the whistling of the wind in the wires.

Where was this journey going to end? Would we cross the battle-front without knowing it, in the dark? Would the wind, less strong at lower altitudes, allow us to reach safety by a narrow margin – or were we to 'dine in Potsdam'? The suspense whilst these hopes and fears passed through my head was intolerable. Foxy was not far wrong; even at this distance of time I 'go all goosey' at the unhappy thought of it. And yet I clung to hope long enough, until in fact there was none left to cling to. I refused to believe that we might not get home, that we might fail – that we might be *captured*. I would not think of it, but even as I declared my faith in ultimate success, I found myself longing to be anywhere but in the pilot's seat of this doomed craft.

They were endless, those clouds, and the bumps they gave the machine so fierce that I had perforce to throttle the engine still more, fearful that something vital might snap under the increasing strain. Not a sight of the earth, nor of the heavens, barely enough light in the gloom to be sure of a moderately straight course. West – approximately west. In the disturbed air the speed indicator rose and fell alarmingly; it helped me to maintain an average, but that was of little use by itself. It was the wind's strength I feared, and that strength I could not measure.

Alone the altimeter held my attention. Its information was positive. Like a clock ticking away the last seconds of a condemned man's life, the needle moved ineluctably downwards, ticking off the feet: three thousand, two thousand, one thousand. Five hundred.

VII

And then, as though through a misted glass, the earth reappeared. An empty field, a deserted road with many puddles, the clustered houses of a small village, a man walking, his head bowed against the driving rain; then more fields, a clump of trees. We both stared down in dismay. There was nothing one could recognise in those few acres. I felt horribly uneasy. The sight of trenches, wire, shell-holes, the wreckage of war would have been reassuring; but this land was as peaceful as though we had left the quarrelling world behind and come from the clouds to another planet.

The ground rose sharply. A big wood lay ahead above which I should never be able to rise with the failing engine. Should I turn towards it, switch off and crash into the branches? The wreckage would be useless to the enemy, if indeed we were in their midst – and on foot we might yet escape. But there came to my mind the story of a pilot lost in the clouds as we had been and carried by a sudden change in the wind far back into friendly territory. He had jumped out of his machine and hidden in a bush – until 'captured' by the men of his own side. After all our trouble and anxiety we must not become the laughing-stock of the Flying Corps. Yet another pilot had been wafted across the Channel in a fog, and coming to ground in an unrecognised land had startled the inhabitants of Kent by asking in voluble French for the whereabouts of the Germans. And also there came to my memory the landing I had made at the end of the King's patrol to ask the way, and how I had found to my joy that we were but two miles from the squadron. The same thing might happen here; a French peasant might with a word banish all our fears. I had to land, no doubt about that – the engine was finished, the ground very close – but I must land with care.

On the summit of a low hill, in a ploughed field whose soft soil in the heavy rain was fast becoming mud, I completed as good a landing as any I had ever made. The machine was safe if *we* were. Switching off I silenced the last splutters of the engine. We had been in the air over four hours.

The unusual sound of my own voice after the uproar in the machine was startling; even to me it sounded high-pitched and nervous.

'Do you think we can have crossed the lines while we were in the clouds?' I called with as much hope as I could force into my tone.

Dante climbed out of his seat, jumped down beside me.

'No,' he said, 'I'm afraid *not*.'

VIII

With Dante's reply I could but agree. He had merely put into words something I had not yet dared to say even to myself. His opinion that we had landed in German territory coincided with my own secret belief, and with the stating of that opinion my hopes were virtually extinguished. A last spark remained among the embers: I asked him to go back on foot in the direction whence we had flown, as far as the brow of the hill. From behind a hedge he would be able to see the village, spy out the land, watch who came. If French peasants all was well; if no one, we would have time to deliberate; if the enemy ... He nodded assent and jogged off in his heavy flying-kit through the squelching mud. In days gone by he had done good work as an aerial gunner, as observer he had been painstaking, indefatigable; in several combats he had acted as calmly as during the recent trying moments of our descent. Now he made his last reconnaissance whilst I stood by the machine preparing for my own final duty.

Not twenty seconds passed before I heard his shout. The words shocked, yet did not surprise me; they but brought to a climax a morning of anguish such as one is not often asked to endure.

'Look out,' he cried. 'Germans! Hundreds of them – they're coming! Quick – can you light her up?'

Yes, I could do that. I had never thought of it before, and there was not much time left now. But I knew that I could do it.

In a cubby-hole behind the pilot's seat was stored a flare. I had seen it there many a time; but to this day I do not know whether it was intended solely for setting machines on fire or whether it had originally been meant to serve as a signal of distress for machines coming down in the Channel. Perhaps both emergencies had been envisaged. At all events it served my purpose well enough, although in this as in so many other matters no instructions had ever been given. But I knew my way about that aeroplane, and I knew the easiest of the petrol connections to get at. My one fear was that after our long flight there would not be enough petrol left for a big flare-up.

For the last of my anxieties, however, there was fortunately no ground. A good three or four gallons of petrol remained, and as I wrenched away the rubber connection a steady, clear stream gushed forth. I struck the flare. Thrust it forward. And the sudden blast of the flames as they shot up and spread was like a gasp of astonishment sent up to the weeping skies. I sprang back, my face scorched by the blaze.

For an instant we both stood watching, gaining some small satisfaction from the success of our final endeavour; then Dante ran forward to throw maps and reconnaissance notes into the flames. Nothing should be left for the enemy, nothing save only our wretched selves. That we could not remedy; we were burdened by flying-kit, mud held back our heavy boots; the Germans were coming up on two sides, at a run. We pushed more things into the fire, making sure that all were destroyed. On the rear mounting the Lewis gun pointed defiantly at the heavens. The flames licked about it, rising from the fiercely burning fire, roaring in that same west wind which had completed our downfall.

I thought of Shoreham. I had seen many crashes since then, but no fire. It had been my first experience in the Flying Corps and now – for a time – it must be my last. But at least there was no tortured victim in the crumbling front seat. No human being had suffered from my piloting, except a few of the enemy. And yet both machines – here as at Shoreham – were B.E.2cs. There must be some significance in the flames, something of my own self ascending in smoke and fire from the aeroplane in which I had dreamed and hoped, fought, striven and feared ...

'You speak German, don't you?' Dante said. 'Better say something to them.'

I turned away from the machine. Large numbers of German soldiers were beginning to appear from over the brow of the hill. They were out of breath from hard running and as they came near they slowed down to a walk. Through the centre of their long, ragged line a man on horseback approached at a gallop, drew rein within ten yards of us. He wore a spiked helmet, a sheathed sword hung by his side and upon the shoulders of his long coat were the insignia of some rank or other. I judged him to be a senior N.C.O., but it seemed wise to give him the benefit of the doubt.

'*Herr Leutnant*,' I called, 'we are English officers. We have had trouble with our engine and have been forced to come down. We wish to surrender.'

Something had to be said by way of introduction, but I felt rather an ass making such an obvious speech. Especially as I had not used so much German since before the war; I fancy my words must have smacked too much of the courtly surrenders of another age, they did not fit in with the angry rudeness so necessary to twentieth-century warfare. They certainly puzzled the man on the horse. '*Ja*,' was all that he could find to say.

And then the Lewis gun spoke its last words to the enemy, barking like a watchdog at the approach of danger. The ammunition had become red-hot; it burst with a series of loud crackling explosions. At that the horse took charge of the man; together they galloped off the field.

IX

The men who presently advanced towards us were from a German air-squadron stationed less than a mile away. In a short time we were surrounded by a dozen or more young flying-officers.

I have today no warmer a feeling of friendship, no deeper an understanding of the men of the German Flying Corps than I had on the day of my capture. And this for the very good reason that in the course of one winter's afternoon in 1915 I learnt so to appreciate their qualities that no mode or trend of opinion can ever change my sentiments. They did much more than spare our lives; they spared our pride. With fellow-feeling for airmen in distress they solaced our despair. Towards us, captives from an alien and hated race, they made no gesture of anger or of reproach. Their hands were raised; but to salute us. They spoke to us not with words of triumph, of wrath or of scorn, but with a ready sympathy for our plight, a knowledge of all that our misfortune must mean to us. We were their enemies, British, and at their mercy; but they did not show by word or deed that they were aware of the fact. It may have been wholly that much-exaggerated 'comradeship of the air' which linked us, but I prefer to believe that our mutual understanding ran deeper. We wore the uniforms of our respective countries, we stood for different causes, but, beneath all the superficialities, we knew that we were actuated by the same motives. Youth, adventure, high spirits – those things wound up for us the mainspring of life. We would have fought just as well without propaganda; we had no need for bitter hatred. So may it have been in the days of chivalry.

After the first stiffness and formality were over, one of them asked me: 'But why were you flying on this of all days – in weather too bad for any of us to go up?'

'Just paying a little round of visits to certain places such as Valenciennes,' I answered, anxious not to give anything away.

'Valenciennes?' he exclaimed. He seemed amazed. 'But have you been there often?'

'Once too often!' I replied ruefully. Whereat he and the others were good enough to laugh.

'And what made you come down?' they wanted to know.

For answer I led the way to the front of the machine and pointed at the broken cylinder. I was never able to find out what had been the first cause of the trouble, although at the time I naturally suspected faulty lubrication. It may have been Archie, but I doubt it. A flaw in the metal, a worn bearing – without taking the engine down there was no possibility of making sure. And, after all, engine failure was not uncommon; only unpleasant. But it was plain enough to even the most unaccustomed eye that no machine could hold the air long with one out of eight cylinders almost entirely absent. The German officers clicked their tongues and shook their heads at the evil sight. They smiled at us understandingly and murmured their sympathy in a way that implied a share in our sorrow, a compassion for such ill-luck.

I am not sure it was through no fault of theirs that later on, while we were in the Mess, certain men of the squadron went through the pockets of the coats we had left hanging outside. It was not an 'official' purloining that deprived us of money and cigarettes.

Long afterwards I found that our point of landing was within six miles of the front lines. Five more minutes' flying time would have seen us safely over.

X

It was a phrase used during luncheon – at which we were the honoured guests – that brought home to me the full meaning of our calamity. We had been talking shop with so much animation that I had nearly forgotten the circumstances of capture and the misery of being a prisoner of war, when one of the pilots happened to ask me if I enjoyed reading German books. Reading, he remarked, would lighten *'die furchtbare Langeweile'*. And all at once I perceived that in those words the future was summed up for me: the frightful boredom – of being held captive, of sitting idly waiting for the time to pass, for the war to be over; while all the time these men would be able to go on flying, fighting, achieving something however small, at any rate living, adventuring. The sudden realisation of coming inaction was less merciful than a blow on the head, it was sentence of living death; and it was on the tip of my tongue to retort that I had no intention of sitting still to endure it, that there was such a thing as escape and that I should take the first opportunity to try it. But where they had been courteous, I must be tactful. Already I was learning that of a prisoner's valour by far the better part is dissimulation.

But that night, after we had been transferred to less hospitable surroundings in the town of St Quentin, the thought returned to me with renewed vigour. I could never resign myself to spending the remainder of the war in prison; the hope of flying again – all that was left to me – *that* I refused to surrender. It simply could not be that I had flown for the last time. I must get away from this intolerable captivity; I must get back to the squadron, to the barge on the River Lys, to the tall line of poplars and to the slippery mud of that narrow L-shaped aerodrome. I saw now how much all those things had meant to me … Boredom? Yes, I had been bored there sometimes, but not as I was going to be bored if I did not at once strive for freedom. Life in the barge was dull no doubt, yet outside it there had been action, flying, fights in the air, work to do; prospects, distant perhaps, of something startling happening to the war. It was hard to lose so much, impossible not to wish to regain everything by a bold yet cunning stroke.

If only I could get away from my captors – sometime, somehow – elude them, run, hide, cross the frontiers of Belgium and Holland; or else sneak cautiously through the trenches on some dark night. I didn't care how it was done so long as I could return to the squadron I had left that morning. It would not be easy, on the face of it I could see that much; I must think it out calmly, with determination. And then some day I should see again the Lys curved like a scimitar, the poplars straight as well-drilled soldiers, the grey barge – with men waiting open-mouthed in the Mess, to whom I would tell my story, to whom I would explain the events of this day, explain why I had been forced to land. And the major would smile rather more broadly than usual and put just a little warmth into his 'Well done!' And Growl would clap me on the back and say, 'By jove, young fellow-me-lad, come and have a drink! ...'

Victory when at length it came was not like that. It never is. Success, hard won, can never be as sweet as the sanguine dreams of youth would make it. For it is in the nature of things that every real achievement must come a little too late. When next I flew over Merville, the quiet fields near the river were pitted with shell-holes, the stems of the poplars were broken and the barge had gone from the Lys.

The friendly reception of the German flying-officers had ill-prepared me for the night spent in a cell in St Quentin gaol. Lonely, dejected, I was overwhelmed by the day's disaster. Memories of the past months came to taunt me. Foxy's titter: so this was 'Potsdam', this moist foul-smelling cell? Rare Earths would have been able to collect some fine samples from the walls, let alone the floors. Where was Wilhelm in all this? At the German squadron they had not been able to tell me anything about him. At any rate he must be in hospital, better than being here unwounded. 'What would you do if your engine were to fail over Valenciennes?' That damned question! And how had I answered it? I supposed that I ought to have landed unseen in a forest somewhere to the east, waited till dark, made a bolt for the frontier and freedom ... And my leave had been due at Christmas!

Outside, somewhere in the town, a clock boomed the hours. The long vibrating strokes rang in my ears, echoed in my heart: 'Escape-Escape-Escape!' I prayed that when Opportunity came my way she would not be 'veiled like an Eastern bride', and that I should be prompt to recognise her.

But I am glad that I did not know how long it would take.

Part II

Chapter 4

The Wings Grow Again

I

His Majesty[6] lit a cigarette, inhaled, blew out the match.

'And what are you going to do now?' he asked.

He had moved to one side whilst lighting that cigarette, so that my eyes were no longer upon his face. I looked out of an open window upon the Green Park. The trees were in leaf, the sun shone. A faint breeze ruffled the loose-hanging curtains and bore in from Piccadilly and Hyde Park Corner the subdued roar of London, a roar that to my unaccustomed ears was like a distant roll of drums, an eternal call to arms. It was May, 1918.

'What are you going to do now?'

The King had come forward again, between me and the light, and now his head was framed by the tall window and the green grass beyond. London was behind him. The call to arms came from over his shoulder.

'I'm going back to France, sir.'

I had no hesitation; France it must be. I had given the matter a great deal of thought, and my answer to that particular question was decided upon long before I reached Buckingham Palace. But I have no doubt that, had I been in any uncertainty, those twenty minutes of the King's audience would have compelled me to make up my mind without possibility of change. For the telling of my story had reawakened old voices heard upon the banks of the Lys, in the keen air above Artois, and in the less wholesome air of St Quentin gaol. And, as I see it, the reasons for such a reawakening are easy to understand, since after long years of endeavour, of frequent failure and occasional despair, the great, the longed-for, the romantic climax had come. Fortune had smiled – if rather late in the day – and the adventure seemed to be concluded.

----

6. King George V.

Seemed – for I saw clearly that it was not yet ended. Real success could only be claimed when I had completed the circle, returned to the point from which I had started ...

'I'm going back to France!'

I had caught myself wondering, before the interview, how the King would receive this declaration of mine. Would he, like certain kindly people at the Air Ministry and elsewhere, say: 'No, no, my boy, you've done enough'? I hoped not. The remark made me shudder, for they were dead who had 'done enough'.

The question that came by way of reply was more to the point. It showed understanding, not only of the attitude of those in authority, but also, I think, of my personal desires and their probable frustration. Just four words:

'Will they let you?'

I said rather meekly: 'I think so, sir.'

It was not quite true. I was beginning to be afraid 'they' would *not* let me go. The fear had become more real during the past week or two, but I think it had been growing ever since the day when the train carried me from St Quentin to the Rhine.

II

That was an afternoon of unalleviated melancholy, of sadness growing more intense at each rhythmical click of the wheels upon the rails. For as long as we were in France some faint hope still beat within me that something would happen – that the train might be derailed, that a bomb might fall from the empty sky to kill my captors, even that a sudden and wholly unexpected offensive by the Allies might sweep through the trench lines into the back areas, so that presently I should see cavalry or armoured cars dash across the rolling countryside to stop the train. Hope clung to me through Bohain and Busigny on to Le Cateau – had not British troops fought there? There might yet be survivors, stragglers cut off from the retreat, hidden among the friendly woods and villages of this last corner of France ... The express train rushed on. The sort of 'something' which I so wanted to happen did not occur. It seldom does.

At dusk we crossed the Belgian frontier.

'Do we pass through Mons?' I asked.

'Mons?'

'Yes, where a battle was fought in the early days – the first battle in which the English were engaged?'

'Never heard of it,' was the answer. And at that the war, active operations at all events, became suddenly immeasurably distant …

Between Liège and the German frontier the train chanced to run at reduced speed. A dark night; from the compartment windows I could see nothing of the countryside; but, aware that only a few miles to the north lay Holland and freedom, a wild hope seized me. I tried the lavatory. The German guard who escorted me kept his foot in the door, the window was fixed shut, and it was plain that there would be no time to break through it before the guard took action. Nothing doing. A few minutes later the train ran into Herbesthal, first station inside Germany. It was a long time before I came so near to the Dutch frontier again.

A change of trains and of guards at Cologne, a long wait and a longer journey up the Rhine valley; at four in the morning, leaving the train at Mainz, we marched uphill into the Citadel barracks. There, in the company of some four hundred other prisoners – Russian, French, British and Belgian – I settled in to spend my first Christmas in captivity and, presently, to make my first feeble scratchings in a tunnel.

A futile affair, the Germans must have thought it; for of course they knew. The entrance was in the basement next to the bath-house and the fact that we, the diggers, made use of the bath-house every afternoon yet came out of it dirtier than when we went in was rather too obvious to be tolerated. In January (1916) half a dozen of us were transferred at a moment's notice to Weilburg, a pleasant little place – or so it would have seemed to eyes less jaundiced than those of war-prisoners – where we were lodged in a large two-storey house, formerly a school for N.C.O.'s in the picturesque valley of the Lahn.

Down the steep and wooded sides of that encompassing valley, by some freak effect of acoustics there rolled before the end of winter a distant thunder of gunfire. Barely audible yet unmistakable, from a hundred and fifty miles away: the remote thunder of massed artillery at Verdun. An inspiring sound, that raised our eyes to the echoing clouds and sent us, paradoxically, underground, to tunnel hopefully from a disused cellar. Russian officers had already started the dig before our coming; we joined them enthusiastically in an atmosphere of night-time conspiracy, driving the shaft forward with a will, thrusting it out beneath the camp boundary; only to fail within a few yards of success. Driven too near the surface, the roof began to cave beneath the unexpected weight of an exceptional snowfall; shored up, it withstood the pressure until the first thaw; then gave way to the heavy stamp of German guards marching overhead.

A fragment of wood from a crate, used in shoring up the roof, bore the barely decipherable name of one of our own accomplices. Whereat the German commandant summoned the dozen or so British prisoners before him and, pink-faced with agitation, denounced our crime: this was a *Schweinerei*! It was forbidden to escape! If we made any further attempt we would be immediately shot dead: *sofort todtgeschossen*! … Without delay we started to evolve new plans, learning the tricks of the trade as we went: the making of false keys to open the doors of German offices, the typing – on a 'borrowed' typewriter – of forged passes to facilitate travel by rail, the copying of such rare fragments of maps as the French were able to purchase from sympathetic Alsatians among the guards. In the end we were not too badly equipped; but in the execution of our plans nothing went right for us. A new tunnel ran into solid rock; a well-planned exit in laundry baskets was foiled by a last-minute change in camp routine that put the baskets out of our reach. One night in April, helping to fuse the camp lights to aid an escape attempt, I was caught in the act. Enjoyed the experience of a court martial in Frankfurt, less the ensuing month of solitary confinement in the Weilburg prison; so that it came as a relief to be transferred, at the end of May, to a new and supposedly superior establishment at Friedberg-in-Hessen.

But however clean and well regulated as a prisoner-of-war camp, from an escaper's point of view it was an unpromising place. Its two modern barrack buildings, surrounded by a palisade and two rows of sentry-guarded wire, stood in flat, open country that discouraged all thought of a direct attempt upon the defences. A tunnel? Impossible indoors; the barrack basements, daily inspected by the enemy, had cement floors above concrete foundations. We began to dig in the open; sinking a shaft in the half-acre of wasteland allotted to prisoners for the planting of small 'gardens'; concealing its mouth ingeniously enough within a summer-house tent, distributing the spoil evenly over our patch of land embellished with potted plants, obtained through the camp's canteen. Throughout the summer we worked at it, carved our way through firm clay soil, hid the entrance beneath some three feet of earth at the end of each day's stint, effaced all trace of work upon the tent's floor with a liberal sprinkling of granite chips. By mid-August, with more than thirty yards dug, we had passed, according to our careful measurements, beneath the wire and the palisade, beyond the outer line of sentries, to reach a fold in the land bordering an orchard. The time had come to break surface.

At that same moment luck deserted us. An unrelated escape attempt from the nearby *Kommandantur* roused to violent activity the hitherto unsuspecting Germans; a camp-wide search was followed by a general digging up of the 'gardens' that revealed, in the end, our tunnel's entrance … The Germans were even more surprised than angry. 'Why,' one of them remonstrated with me, 'why do you want to escape? It's not unpleasant here, and even if you succeeded in getting out you'd never get across the frontier.' I was to hear it many times again later on: *'Ueber die Grenze kommen Sie nie.'* It was, just then, the least of our worries.

Other plans were considered, some wild, some desperate. Late in September we tried one of the most fanciful. As many a would-be escaper had noticed there was a close similarity, in texture as in colour, between the overcoats worn by German and Russian officers. By friendly exchange and barter two Russian coats had been obtained and, the cut being different, suitable alterations made by the camp tailor, a gallant Frenchman who cheerfully risked imprisonment to score off the *sales Boches.* Accessories, caps, bits and pieces of equipment were collected from two other prisoners who had long considered the scheme and worked upon it but no longer believed it to be feasible. At length ready, the camp routine meticulously observed, we put it to the test. At nine o'clock on a morning of hazy sunshine, three of us – two as German officers, the third a sort of secretary-assistant in civilian clothes – marched out of the *Kommandantur* to which we had gone one by one, ostensibly to collect food-parcels, in reality to make a quick change from khaki to field-grey in a cubby hole beneath the stairs. Marched some thirty yards towards the gate most generally used by the authorities; taking pains to advance only at a slow and dignified pace whilst I, the one German-speaker, almost paralysed with stage-fright, talked incessantly to cover the silence of the other two and anxiously watched the behaviour of the sentries. Within ten yards of the gate I dared to raise my voice; barked out the magic word: '*Aufmachen!*' It did the trick. The sentries sprang to attention, clicked heels; one of them rattled keys, turned the lock, flung open the gate, stood back. And then, as for the immortal *Mr Toad,* the soldiers all saluted as we marched along the road ...

Marched on in agony of discomfort both mental and physical; across country, over open fields, past staring peasants; marched half-strangled by the closely packed provisions tightly strapped beneath our German overcoats. Marched for two hours towards the wooded slopes of the Taunus; reached them at last, climbed high up the hillside and, discarding our German uniforms to reappear as nondescript civilians, rested in security waiting for nightfall ... A still day of late summer whose deep silence was broken intermittently by that immensely distant yet immediately recognisable rumbling: the thunder of guns massed upon the Western Front. 'March to the sound of the guns' – no, we couldn't do that. Coming down from the hillside at dusk, we marched east. Passed to the north of Homburg and then, on successive nights, to the north of Frankfurt, to the east of Hanau, south to Aschaffenburg, narrowly avoiding unexpected perils on the long road to Switzerland. Before dawn on the fifth day an error in navigation led us to camp at the foot of a low embankment; revealed for what it was when, at first light, a train rolled surprisingly overhead. The sharp-eyed driver spotted us, raised the alarm at the next station; the railway staff came out in force, surrounded us in the woods, marched us off to gaol.

A month's solitary confinement in the town prison at Friedberg; then, for me, a journey via Berlin to Fort Zorndorf, a few miles to the north-east of Cüstrin and notorious as a special camp for persistent escapers. No one could break out of it, they said. No one. On a bleak January afternoon, unkindly tricking the commandant who had invited us to his house amid the trees outside the fort to discuss camp routine, three of us eluded our escorts and, vaulting a fence, made a bolt for it and got away. Almost at once the alerted guards were in hot pursuit; we had to sprint through the woods at top speed for the better part of a mile and we were none too fit. One lagged behind, was overtaken by the guards and hauled back to the fort. The surviving pair of us kept on, shedding khaki overcoats as we went, heading north into the darkening pine-forest.

Our aim was to outwit the enemy by reaching, at dawn, a branch-line railway station beyond any point he could reasonably expect us to make. A night of considerable discomfort followed, memorable chiefly for the distance covered: forty-five miles across country in under fifteen hours, for the most part against driving rain turning to sleet. Thinly clad in makeshift civilian clothes, with scarcely any food, it was far from pleasant. But we made the objective in good time; took train for Berlin and, absorbed into the crowd of fourth-class passengers, thought ourselves safe. Two stations later a guard, sent specially from the fort to head us off, came on board and held us up at pistol-point. The third man of our team had been unable, on recapture, to destroy his map; it had given away our intended route …

Ten days in Cüstrin gaol. Back to the fort. Out again for a night attempt in February. This time to exploit a scheme patiently evolved by some French officers who, prematurely transferred to another camp, had bequeathed it to three of us, together with all its equipment. Deep snow lay on the ramparts when, on the appointed night, we sallied from a casemate on top of the fort and concealed by white overalls, crawled unseen past a line of patrolling sentries, bearing with us as well as our kit the three parts of a ladder to be assembled in the ditch for the scaling of the fort's outer wall, an obstacle rising up a sheer thirty feet to the level of the surrounding country. The ladder, brilliantly contrived by the French out of chair legs reinforced with angle-irons taken from camp bedsteads, was just over twenty-nine feet long. Enough; but no allowance had been made for the unforeseen foot of packed ice and snow now overhanging the wall's crown. With the ladder in position before dawn, when the night guard in the ditch had been withdrawn and the daytime guard on the fort's summit had not yet come on – an observed interval of ten minutes – we found to our dismay that we were unable to surmount the slippery ice-cap. No remedy was available in the time; we had no pick and fingers alone could not break the ice, nor could the ladder support more than one man at a time … When the German garrison gathered in the ditch for the morning parade they stared in consternation, barked their displeasure, and took us back into the fort.

Three months solitary in Cüstrin gaol on a charge of stealing angle-irons from the Kaiser's bedsteads, then back to the fort to plan anew. To scheme, to discuss, to argue, sometimes to quarrel, but always with the one end in view: to get out of Germany and back into the war. Of course we knew well enough that not one man in a hundred of us would ever succeed – and, knowing it, some gave up, settled down to learn Russian. They were wise. But the obstinate few whose youthful unwisdom transcended the mere need for adventure to alleviate the tedium of captivity clung with an almost religious fervour to the belief that Chance would some day reward their restless perseverance. *'Ueber die Grenze kommen Sie nie'* – we knew *that* was nonsense; others had crossed over before us. Nor did we forget that the German stood in Belgium where he had no right to be; he must be thrown out before the war could end; and in that ousting we intended to play our part. But for me as, I suppose, for any young pilot there was something more: the unflagging desire to fly again, to climb above the clouds, to hear anew the steady hum of a smooth-running engine and the comforting music of the wind in the wires.

With the German authorities now striving to efface the sinister reputation of Fort Zorndorf as a 'special' camp, new British prisoners were brought in, some straight from capture. From one of them, a Scot and a pilot, I learned of great changes in aviation, of new machines and new methods, of whole squadrons of single-seat fighters flying in formation, engaged in daily combat. Heard too of those achieving fame in the crowded skies of north-eastern France. The Germans sang loud the praises of Immelmann and Boelcke; the French glorified Guynemer. The British, for sound reasons, did not advertise their successful pilots; but from my Scottish friend I learned of many names new to me. One in particular, that of Captain Albert Ball, stuck fast in my memory ...

In August (1917) a few of us were unexpectedly transferred to the camp of Ströhen Moor in Hanover. An unhealthy spot and ill-equipped, with dysentery afflicting its three or four hundred all-British inmates; worse than that, already before our arrival there had been so many escape attempts that, with the Germans thoroughly alerted, there were few sound opportunities left. Eventually, after a succession of minor failures, six of us evolved a bold scheme in which, once again, I was to wear German uniform. This time, disguised as a *Landsturm* guard – complete with home-made gear and dummy rifle – I was to lead out of one of the side-gates the other five dressed as British orderlies and wheeling a baggage cart 'to the railway station', a more or less daily occurrence. Weeks were spent building up the rifle, contrived with odds and ends of iron and wood, with a bolt mechanism made from pieces of tin-can shaped and sandpapered to look like steel. At long last ready, we paraded early one morning. Barking out German commands at my apparently reluctant and appropriately slouching crew, I led the way to the gate; and showing a forged pass, demanded its opening.

A scheme of such effrontery deserved to succeed. And succeed it did: until, outside the camp, a sharp-eyed sentry – who from long service at Ströhen knew many of the prisoners by sight – chanced to recognise as officers first one then another of the 'orderlies'. I suppose we were lucky not to be *'todtgeschossen'* ... Gaol was followed by a court martial at Hanover – I forget on what charges – and a three-month sentence, served partly at Ströhen, partly at Neunkirchen to which about eighty of us were moved in November.

Neunkirchen was one of several camps the Germans established in the Saar in the hope that the presence of officer prisoners of war would ward off allied bombing of the area. The hope proved vain; to the remote thunder of guns on the Western Front there was added presently the sharper thudding of local anti-aircraft guns, to us a welcome sound. But the very nature of the camp – a single building in the centre of the town, its small courtyard overlooked by neighbouring houses and heavily guarded – made escape more than usually difficult. A tunnel was the best bet; and throughout long snowy weeks of winter we worked at it. Organised and equipped, it expertly made ready to evacuate a good half of the camp's inmates, providing many with sketch-maps and home-made compasses; thrust out, once again, to within feet of the proposed exit. And then the snows melted and the rains came, and the camp's drainage system was choked. Drainage engineers, brought in to inspect and repair the damage, laid bare the tunnel's well-concealed entrance.

A fortnight in the local gaol brought my total time in solitary confinement to eight months, with success as far away as ever. But with the spring came new hope. Neunkirchen camp was to be closed, the prisoners transferred to camps deeper in Germany; at the same time an Anglo-German exchange scheme came into operation whereby long-term prisoners were released to enjoy the relative freedom of internment in Holland. Still believing in ultimate success, I refused the exchange; but the authorities insisted: I must go to the transit-camp to certify my refusal lest Germany be accused of holding prisoners back. In mid-April half a dozen of us were moved to Aachen. Close enough to the Dutch frontier certainly, but, we learned, for a stay of no more than thirty-six hours.

A daunting prospect. A challenge to all the knowledge and experience gained from the years of effort. A new camp, only the daylight hours in which to survey its defences, to note its routine, to devise a plan. Only one evening in which to make good an escape, one night in which to march a roundabout twenty miles so as to reach the frontier – and cross it! – before daybreak. The escape must go unnoticed by the camp guards, since with the frontier so close it would be easy to alert the area once the alarm had been raised. For much the same reason it would be impossible to lie up near the frontier, study the landscape and cross over on a second night: as soon as we were missed from the camp during the day the border guards would be reinforced. Nor was the country easy to cross; hilly, wooded, intersected by small streams, in the open it was studded as well by farm buildings as by mining villages. Quite a problem! But this time the luck was on our side. My chosen companion – Beverley Robinson, a Canadian pilot who had served his time at Zorndorf – was a tower of strength, moreover he possessed an excellent map. By a narrow margin we made it … Nearly two and a half years had gone by since a train's lavatory window had barred my way to this same frontier. Now, humbling circumstance, it was through a lavatory ventilator that we climbed from our camp into a lavatory of the adjoining German transit camp; thence down an open drain, under the wire, away into the night, unseen.

It was still night when we reached the frontier. Before dawn we crossed it unawares; strode on anxiously, checking our position by map and compass at first light. Verified it again from the cover of a bramble patch as day broadened, until no possible doubt remained. '*Ueber die Grenze kommen Sie nie*'? Rubbish! We stood in Holland. Success had come at last. Sweet success!

* * *

III

I cannot for a moment pretend that these memories of escape 'flashed' through my head while I answered the King's questions. But all of them and many more were lodged in that mysterious locality known as the back of one's mind. And in the effort to extract events necessary to make a brief and coherent story, I found that the whole lot had come floating to the surface.

With the result that when, at the end of the interview, I left the Palace it was to seek forthwith that sanction which alone could crown the long adventure. A taxi took me to the newly created Air Ministry, then in the Strand at the Hotel Cecil. There from a senior but sympathetic friend I begged a straight answer to the essential question: Would 'they' let me return to the front in France?

To my relief I heard him say that he thought it could be arranged. The trouble was that hitherto no one captured flying in France had been allowed to return to fly in France, because – and I had to admit the truth of this – capture was one of the things most likely to happen to an air-pilot. And apart from the vague possibility of an officer, captured for the second time, being an enemy agent, there was the more serious probability of his being harshly treated by the Germans. Personally I thought that the likelihood of being recognised on capture would be exceedingly remote, and afterwards – but, touching wood, I had no intention of being captured.

'It may happen, however,' my friend insisted, 'and therefore it will be best if you adopt another name when you get to the front.'

'When I get to the front! But how *am* I to get there?'

'Well – I think if you go back to your training squadron, pass through and *say nothing*, the Air Ministry will forget about you in time. Then, when a batch of pilots is sent out to France, your name won't be noticed amongst the others. And I promise you my department will make no objections.'

I took him at his word and returned to London Colney where I had been posted shortly after landing in England. I had taken no leave, for I knew that I could always get occasional days and week-ends off while learning to fly. There was plenty of time. The great German attack was held up; there would be a return push in the summer, driving on through the winter; and the next spring, with the Americans properly in the field at last, the final battles would be fought. I curbed my impatience and took up the 'new' flying with enthusiasm.

It was a long job. Longer than I had expected. Slowly I passed through the usual business of engine-fitting, rigging, machine-gunnery, and graduation from the Avro to the Sopwith Pup, to the Spad, finally to the S.E.5a. I was shown all the mysteries of aerobatics and taught – very badly – how to fly in formation. At length, in August, I was ready. The Air Ministry said nothing: 'they' seemed indeed to have forgotten all about me. Young pilots who had started their training just before me began to move off overseas. Only the shortage of S.E.5 practice machines held me up until the middle of the month.

And then one morning orders came for me to join a School of Aerial Fighting in Yorkshire.

IV

There was something very puzzling about this posting to Yorkshire. It was not absolutely essential for a pilot, especially for one who had been to France before, to pass through an Aerial Fighting School; to my own knowledge several fledgelings had gone direct from the training squadron to France. I had now all the necessary qualifications and my friend at the Air Ministry had kept his word about letting my name through in the ordinary way, without mention of capture or escape. Why, therefore, had I of all others been selected to go so far north as Yorkshire? A Fighting School was, of course, another step on the way to the front, but it was also another delay. I began to see in this move the action of some well-meaning but misguided individual, someone who saw that by sending me to Yorkshire a little more time would be gained, another chance that I might change my mind. After the course of fighting instruction there were other stations to which 'they' might send me; Home Defence loomed menacingly near.

With these uneasy suspicions in mind I kept my eyes open as soon as I stepped into the headquarters office of the Fighting School. Presently my name amongst others was called out by one of the staff, and on hearing it a clerk rose from a corner of the room, crossed over and handed me a small bundle of papers.

I glanced through them. There were a couple of letters forwarded to me by the Air Ministry, a claim for some allowance or other, and an open envelope with my name in one corner and the commanding-officer's in the other. An envelope which at once increased my suspicions and my fears of interference. I turned it over in my hands: what was it? – a sort of letter of introduction? In that case the open flap and my name in the corner gave me a right to read it … Dodging behind the line of waiting pilots, I opened it and read.

When I came to the end I fancy I must have smiled at the luck which had allowed this letter to fall into my hands before it reached the CO. It was from a fairly high-placed and influential friend at the Air Ministry. It contained a flattering account of my captivity and escape; but it ended with the statement that, whereas I was anxious to proceed overseas, it was considered undesirable that I should return to France. Italy was suggested …

In the days of my captivity I had learnt that on recapture, after an attempted escape, the first thing to do was to destroy efficiently the maps and other incriminating documents one was carrying. Months of concentration upon the one subject of escape had brought such lessons in habit up to the level of instinct. In this office of the school on the distant Yorkshire coast, seeing that I was in danger of recapture, the instinct asserted itself. I tore the envelope and the letter to small pieces. And no one in that gathering of newly fledged pilots realised that I was escaping again.

Two days later, the school being greatly overcrowded, it was decided to send away a batch of those pilots who had some previous tuition in aerial fighting and sufficient flying-hours to their credit. The majority of these pilots were young Canadians and Americans serving in the British forces, light-hearted, keen for adventure in the air, elated that their stay in Yorkshire had been cut short. They left the school singing and cheering happily, for their orders were to report at the Air Ministry on their way to France. And I can testify that they sang and cheered and were happy, because it happened that I was one of them.

V

I had no idea of the intricate organisation which had grown up for the disposal of pilots in France. I had imagined that, as on a previous occasion, I would have to wander about looking for a headquarters or an office of sorts, that I might have difficulty in finding anyone who cared a damn where I went to or when, but that by the end of twenty-four hours I should somehow have drifted off to a squadron and that there the fun would begin at once.

It wasn't at all like that. The number of officials at Boulogne surprised me; it seemed dismally certain that the army in France had been overtaken by efficiency. They were like ushers in a cinema, inspecting your tickets before letting you through to the performance. And as in a theatre, so here there were clear distinctions between tickets of different value. Staff ticket-holders were bowed into cars and driven to the stalls and boxes; subalterns and other ranks crammed into the same old tumbledown trains which would eventually deposit them within walking distance of the pit. As for air-pilots, we were the cheap seats. But instead of allowing us to go straight up to the gallery, they pushed us into a train that steamed off in the wrong direction – away from the front!

It was not until we had passed Etaples and were almost at Berck that I understood we were going to a sort of livestock depot known as a 'Pilots' Pool'. We arrived late at night and I could neither see nor discover anything of the place until the following morning. Then to my horror I found that I was back in prison … The offices were set apart and labelled 'No Admittance' and 'Keep Out'. Here and there guards were mounted on sentry-go. Why, there was even a stretch of barbed-wire about the place and over the sand dunes!

And the reports which other pilots gave me were not encouraging. The place was full to overflowing, there had not been many demands from squadrons recently, there was a waiting list a mile long. Many of the pilots did not care; they had been out to France several times before and were content to wait their turn. Some of them had been waiting two or three weeks, and were expecting to stay for as many more … 'They also serve who only stand and wait …' I was bored and discouraged.

During my first day more than twenty pilots arrived; not half a dozen left. There was nothing to do all day and nothing but a bar to sit in at night.

On the second day the same thing happened: many officers coming in, few going out. Someone who had been to the office told me that the list of pilots was in a terrible muddle; the single-seater people were mixed up with the heavy bombers, and it might be weeks before things were straightened out. There was no flying, and on the coast we could not hear the guns. The wind hummed, but in wires that were barbed, not streamlined.

Early on the morning of the third day I went to the office to have a look round. There were many pilots hanging about, some old, some new; they were giving particulars about themselves to be entered on the new lists which were being compiled by a couple of clerks. Some of us strolled into the orderly-room – the C.O. being absent at breakfast – to look at the lists, at the numbers of those units requiring pilots, and so on. I was reading through some routine orders when all at once I caught sight of the new list of single-seater pilots. It was lying beside the typewriter upon which it had just been made out by one of the clerks, ready for submitting to the C.O. as soon as he came in.

I glanced down the list. It was very long, covering two pages of foolscap gummed together. Pilot's names were thick on the paper as autumn leaves. It took me some time to reach my own – near the foot of the page! Just as I found it one of the clerks came by.

'I say, Corporal, surely my name ought to be higher than that,' I exclaimed, bitter with disappointment. 'I've been here three days already. I can't wait for ever!'

He laughed as he came up to me. He was a friendly sort of fellow.

'Some of them have been here for three weeks, sir. But perhaps there's been a mistake. Let me see – which is your name?'

I reached forward to point it out. As I did so my sleeve caught against some light object upon the table.

'Look out!' cried the Corporal.

But he was just too late. A river of ink streamed over the page and cascaded to the floor. The bottle rolled slowly through the black stream, splashing over the names.

'O-o-h ...' said the corporal. 'You ...' He paused, only the regulation respect for rank preventing a comment upon my parentage. 'You – you've spilt the ink!'

'Couldn't help it,' I told him. 'Bottle on table – uncorked – caught in my sleeve – an accident. I can't tell you how sorry I am!'

He was kind enough to be pacified at once.

'That's all right, sir; can't be helped. Trouble is it's the only completed list we've got. And the C.O. will want to see it – he'll be here in a minute.'

I bustled about as anxious as he.

'Then let's get it re-typed at once. Come on! I'll help you. Sit down. Got some foolscap? Right. I'll read the list out – I can manage to see through the ink. Ready? First, the heading ...'

'Oh, I know the heading, sir,' he answered, settling down before the typewriter. 'It reads: "List of Pilots".' He began to tap the keys. 'Pilots for Single-seat Fighters ...' *Tap – tap – tap. Tap-a-tap. Tap.* 'S.E.5, Sopwith Camels and Dolphins.' *Tap – tap – tap.* '"Name and Rank".' *Tap-tap-a-tap.* 'Now, sir, if you please?'

'Yes, what is it?'

'The first name, please, sir.'

'The first name?'

'Yes, sir, the first.'

Mine is a difficult name to catch. I spelled it out carefully.

Tap-tap. Tap-a-tap. Tap-tap ...

After an early lunch a Crossley tender bore me off in the direction of the front. I was sorry for those who had been waiting for nearly three weeks, but then I had been waiting for nearly three years.

Chapter 5

Wings of Victory

I

Those drivers of Crossley tenders who ferried air-pilots across northern France always seemed to me a most mysterious lot of men. Their knowledge of the country, of the roads and byroads – some of which I was never able to find again – smacked of the supernatural. The way in which they drove, unerringly and in silence, direct to squadrons of whose location, of whose very numbers the passengers were ignorant attained to the miraculous. They were a race of men apart, inscrutable, possessed of a knowledge beyond our divination; for while they carried us behind them they were the sole arbiters of our chosen destiny. There was an uncanny family likeness about all of them, particularly in the set of the jaw.

A curious similarity, too, linked my first journey to this my second. True, the first commencing in St Omer had ended after a halt at Aire, upon the banks of the Lys, whereas the second took me from Berck to south of Doullens. (And there is a world of difference between Flanders and Picardy.) But there were other close resemblances, close enough to bring back memories of what seemed a long-forgotten war in a bygone century. It was, in fact, within a month of three years since I had last approached the front in a Crossley tender. The season, the weather were almost the same. The roads, winding over undulating fields or rushing straight down long tree-lined avenues, were white and dusty. Lorries were more plentiful, and ambulances and staff cars, but horse transport was still in evidence. There were still farm-carts on the roads, and wagons laden with hay. There were still peasants in blue smocks and wooden shoes in the fields, cattle in the farmyards, women at the doors, and smoke from old chimneys. France in the back areas had not, I fancied, changed much in a hundred years – although no doubt Corot would have been surprised to find his dancing nymphs replaced among the poplars in the meadows by Chinese coolies.

But the lack of change behind the lines made me wonder again whether I had not imagined the period of captivity. It was hard to realise that I had been absent during the immensity of those years between. So many men – millions of them! – had marched down these same roads since I had passed by. Day and night for a thousand days the guns had muttered behind the horizon to the east, rising to thunder during those incredible battles – the Somme, Arras, Messines, Ypres, Cambrai and the great German attack. Had I really missed so much? I could scarcely believe it, could scarcely credit that battalions, divisions, armies of men had vanished, that a score of young men whom I had known intimately – at school, in the infantry, in the Flying Corps – had no longer a voice in that everlasting clamour of war a few miles away. I was not 'coming back'; it was into another war that I was being drawn, as though I myself had been killed during the Long Reconnaissance on that blustering December day in 1915, to be reincarnated, after an uneasy stretch in purgatory, amid surroundings familiar enough but amongst men unknown to me. Not one of the half-dozen pilots in the tender knew anyone I knew, and they spoke of squadrons and their histories with an ease that left me silent and alone with my memories.

They left the tender, those six pilots, at various points along the road where squadrons had their headquarters, until at length I was the only one remaining behind the taciturn driver. That, too, was just as three years before. I found myself wondering to what sort of a temporary home I was being driven. Would I meet with the same chilling reception as in the barge? Would I find a Starched Shirt in command, a Growl to insist upon salutes and standings to attention, a Foxy to make me feel 'all goosey'? I was very much afraid that my history might repeat itself far too accurately.

We came to a farm, turned off the main road, bumped over the ruts of a winding track. My head began to nod, for the drive had been long and the evening was warm. When, after one exceptionally long doze, I opened my eyes, I saw a line of poplars and thought myself back upon the Lys ... But there was no river here; a wide expanse of open field was spread before the poplars, themselves bordering a wood upon the brow of a low hill. There were canvas sheds at the side of the field, two groups of them with the usual adjuncts of transport lorries, workshops, store tents. We passed the first group – I had already begun to collect my belongings, but the driver shook his head – and driving round the aerodrome went slowly down a lane between the second group of sheds and the small, dense wood. At a gate leading into an orchard we came to a halt.

'Here you are, sir,' the driver announced, speaking to me for the first time while, with a stub of pencil, he ticked my name off the list. 'This is your squadron. Name of the place? Valheureux.'

I got down. The driver hailed a couple of men near one of the sheds to help unload my kit, and I turned away to advance reluctantly through the gate into the orchard, wishing I had one of my prison friends with me. Now that I had arrived I positively dreaded the first moments in a strange Mess with strange pilots.

My feet lagged in spite of the necessity to go forward – under the eyes of the tender-driver I could not turn back – and I had time to look about me at scattered tents and small huts, the grass was growing long between them. Ahead of me, half-hidden by apple trees, was a large Mess-tent connected by a short canvas passageway to a wooden building rather like a cricket pavilion. It was painted green and had small lattice windows, a sloping roof and a wooden porch along the front. Evidently the Mess. A comfortable looking place, snug and homelike, tucked away amid the trees and lush grass. I hoped devoutly that the inmates would not turn out to be unbearable ...

A voice called to me from the porch; a young pilot, whom I recognised as one I had known in England, rose from a camp-chair and hurried towards me as I looked hesitatingly around.

'I'm awfully glad to see you – what luck your coming here! I didn't think you would get out to France for months yet.

How did you do it? Come on into the Mess. I'll show you round the squadron presently ...'

As a first step I could not have wished for better. To be greeted as an old friend by someone, to be told that he was 'awfully glad' to see me was just the tonic I needed. Confidence began to return with the first sip.

On the porch I met and shook hands with two pilots, both friendly and both Americans: Larry Bowen and Johnny Speaks, and then my friend led me into the main room of the pavilion. It was empty just then, so that I was able to get my bearings before meeting the rest of the squadron.

'I say, do you realise what squadron this is?' my friend went on – the corruption of his name most generally used in the squadron was Shutters.[7] 'You're in luck to be sent here. This is the most famous scout squadron in France – Ball was in it, and McCudden, and Rhys Davies, Gerald Maxwell and a flock of others ...'

I thought of a dark, stone-vaulted room in a German prison and of a Scottish pilot, recently captured, telling me of the squadrons and the airmen in France: 'the best of the bunch – Captain Ball ...' That pilot had been taken at the close of the winter's fighting on the Somme. Now, of a sudden, it seemed that no time at all had passed since I had heard him speak. Prison – the Somme and Cambrai – the concentrated efforts to escape – the Dutch frontier – and so to France, to Ball's squadron: it was the only logical sequence. Once more the Army was attacking, past the ruins of the Somme, on towards Cambrai and St Quentin and the Hindenburg Line. The enemy had been held, repulsed, was at length being forced back. I was ready to play my own small part in the air again. But Captain Ball was dead ...

Shutters went on.

'And do you know that this squadron has brought down more German machines than any other in France! Look at that list of honours!'

He pointed to the far wall. Beneath a wooden propeller of German make and between two black canvas crosses cut from an enemy aircraft, a three-ply board was fixed in a carved wooden frame. The number of the squadron was at the head: below were the names of men who had won decorations.

Bravery, I suppose, is relative like everything else and the displaying of it in such a manner as to earn a decoration must generally be a matter of chance; yet in this squadron the number of awards and the period over which they were spread under successive commanders seemed to prove beyond doubt that the work of its pilots had been consistently courageous. Ball headed the list. The date against his name was June 6th, 1917. From that date until my

---

7. Derived from an absent-minded habit of keeping radiator-shutters closed during the climb, causing his engine to overheat, with unhappy results.

arrival a year and three months had passed, and in that time the members of the squadron had collected two V.C.s, six D.S.O.s, fourteen M.C.s, eight bars to M.C.s, and six D.F.C.s … I remember laughing out loud as I looked at that long list – much to Shutters' surprise.

'What's the matter?' he demanded rather crossly. 'Aren't there enough names there?'

'Oh, yes – almost too many. I was thinking of the squadron I belonged to in 1915. There we had one M.C. between the whole lot of us. It would have been funny to have seen that lonely name on a board in the barge!'

'Perhaps you didn't have the same opportunities in those days,' Shutters was kind enough to remark. 'Who was your C.O.?'

'The Starched Shirt,' I told him, giving the name.

'Never heard of him,' murmured Shutters. And somehow I found his answer full of meaning; the Starched Shirt was a general now, in charge of training or something, a successful senior officer, not a bad fellow at heart, and fond of Surtees I recalled. Yet the younger generation of war pilots had 'never heard of him'. But these men – these names headed by that of 'Captain Ball, V.C., D.S.O., M.C., Légion d'Honneur' – they would not soon be forgotten by those who fought. Indeed the final and greatest Decoration to which so many had already attained would ensure that their names lived on for evermore. So that on joining such a squadron and seeing such a list for the first time one might well believe oneself to be standing at a parting of the ways; the way of the excellent Starched Shirts of this world, or the way of Ball, Rhys Davies, McCudden and others.

A Gilbertian verse tugged my memory:

'Is life a boon?
If so, it must befall
That death, whene'er he call,
Must call too soon!'

Too soon? I forgot about the squadron on the banks of the Lys, and read slowly through the names on my new squadron's roll of honour …

'Let's go down to the sheds,' said Shutters impatiently.

II

On my way back from the aerodrome I met the C.O. for the first time. I was following Shutters along a narrow path through the orchard, when he came out from a trim wooden hut amid the trees. Shutters stopped and saluted. I did likewise.

'Hullo – what's the game?' said the major. He was tall, lean, young; his small moustache seemed almost black by contrast with his exceedingly pale face. He wore the uniform of the 9th Lancers, Wings, and a Military Cross ribbon.

'New pilot, sir, just arrived,' Shutters announced. And then like an ass he added, after mentioning my name: 'He's an escaped prisoner.'

The major smiled, but I could see at once that he was scared. He evidently remembered something about the authorities' attitude to prisoners. His questions were asked in a mild manner, but quickly and to the point. Where had I served before – when had I been captured – when escaped?

'Good Lord – I suppose it's all right?' he exclaimed at the end.

'Oh, perfectly all right, sir,' I answered airily. 'I've fixed it all up with the Air Ministry.'

He was silent, and for a moment I was horrified by the thought that he was going to announce his intention of making inquiries. Then his smile broadened. He did not speak, but I seem to read the word 'Liar!' in his eyes. And I smiled back at him, for I felt sure it was a friendly reproach.

'Well, I suppose you're anxious to get some of your own back,' he said at length. 'I expect you've got a score or two to pay off?'

I told him that that was my main idea in returning and that I should like to start as soon as possible.

'Oh, there's plenty of time,' he replied. 'Besides, it's a rule that new pilots don't go over the lines until they've been three weeks with the squadron.'

Three weeks! I protested in alarm. In three weeks anything might happen. I wanted to get going at once. I had been over the lines before – that must be obvious or I would not have been captured – I had plenty of flying-hours to my credit, experience with S.E.5s and so on. The major went on smiling.

'I dare say I might make an exception in your case,' he conceded as he turned away towards the sheds. 'You'll have to do some formation and firing practice first though. You don't want to be shot down the first time you go on patrol over the lines!'

III

It was getting late. Shutters and I strolled back to the Mess where already most of the pilots had gathered for cocktails. The majority were very young – that is, few of them were any older than myself and few wore decorations, for the squadron had had heavy losses in the past month or two. I will not claim that I was welcomed like a long lost friend, because I did not know any of them by sight or by name, but there was a hint of geniality about their greeting that put me at ease. At first I was more diffident than they were, since, with memories of my first night in the barge, I rather expected to be given the cold shoulder, but with the arrival of a round of drinks what little ice there was melted rapidly.

Everyone was in good spirits. Two German machines had been shot down that morning. The squadron's total bag since coming to France was nearing the four hundred mark – an average of almost one a day over a period of more than a year! Of course, things were slowing up because the older German aircraft over which the S.E.5s of the squadron had had an undoubted superiority were being replaced by more efficient machines. The Fokker D VII biplane was the principal enemy to be fought now, and against that good little machine the S.E. had to be careful. 'Dive and zoom,' I was told, 'dive and zoom – don't try a dog-fight with them until you've had plenty of experience. They can generally outmanoeuvre you.'

'But we're faster on the level and in a dive,' said the American Larry Bowen. 'Keep the old S.E. going fast and you can beat anything in the sky.'

'Yes, but those darned Fokkers can outclimb us,' put in a Canadian flight-commander. 'The best thing to do is to get height at the beginning of the patrol, between eighteen and twenty thousand feet, manoeuvre for the sun – then, when you see your Huns, half-roll and dive on to their tails.'

'And keep going,' Larry repeated. 'Don't stop to argue unless you're mighty sure of yourself – just dive straight through them and zoom up later to see what's left. Then you can half-roll and dive again …'

I was back in France! In a famous and efficient fighting squadron whose pilots were still eager and ready to add to their laurels. Their feelings, their desires, their ideals were also mine. There was no cold water to quench enthusiasm here. To the younger pilots I might appear as something of a curiosity, a sort of Rip van Winkle of the air who compared all that they told of modern fighting with conditions existing in 1915; but they soon realised I was keener on flying than on talking about the past, which was all that really mattered to them. And to me their old-new jargon spoken within sound of the guns was very thrilling.

Presently 'Gilly' came into the Mess. Gilly was the name of the C.O., though not, of course, used to his face. I had not noticed any particular stiffness about him at the first meeting, but now, the day's work over, he seemed to have unbent completely.

'Well, chaps, how about it? A slight celebration tonight I think,' were his first exclamations. 'Now then, where's the Newt?' The 'Newt', I discovered later, was the diminutive adjutant. 'Newt, go and tell the band to fall in here at once. And – where's that Mess-corporal? – Corporal, ask the officers what they want to drink …'

A band? I watched the six members of the orchestra file in by a side door past the small bar and pantry. A piano stood in a corner of the room; drums, fiddles, a double-bass gathered round it – men of the squadron, led by a broad-shouldered moustachioed sergeant with a violin.

'Strike up!' ordered Gilly. 'And start off with the squadron tune.'

To some it might make pleasant reading were I able to record that, with the squadron-commander and his gallant officers standing stiffly to attention, the orchestra played a selection from 'Pomp and Circumstance', beginning with a noble and full-throated chorus of 'Land of Hope and Glory'. Or perhaps, with Americans present, 'The Star-Spangled Banner' would have been appropriate … The melody chosen by the squadron to which I now had the honour to belong could only, I am afraid, be regarded as frivolous. It was called 'The Darktown Strutters' Ball', and the first line of its refrain informed some unnamed lady that: 'I'll be there to get you in a taxi, honey.' But nobody worried about the words and the rhythm was invigorating. It was – it is – a damn' good tune! And the orchestra played wonderfully well, superbly I thought. It may have been the cocktails, but I began to bless the good fortune which had brought me to this happy squadron.

After dinner Gilly, solemn for the moment, read out the names of those going on the Dawn Patrol. I was foolishly disappointed to find that my own name was not amongst them.

IV

On the way to my tent that night I made a detour through the orchard so as to come out into the open on the eastern side of the aerodrome. I was impelled by some strange excitement – not alcoholic! – to see what was happening in the direction of the front lines.

It was a dark night, but the horizon was aglow with intermittent gun flashes. We were too far from the retiring line of battle for me to see the flares sent up from the trenches, but their wavering light shone from behind the skyline with unearthly effect, as if playful giants were striking box after box of titanic matches. Owing to the recent German defeats the distance to the front was nearly fifteen miles, so that the sounds reaching me were softened and confused. A continual vague rumour kept the night alive, occasionally a long burst of machine-gun fire would rise and fall as though borne upon an impalpable breeze, but in the main it was the thudding of the guns which alone was plainly audible, the flashes which gave the scene reality.

Gun-fire held, for me that night, the utmost significance. The last time the sound had come to my ears from the front in France I had stood peering *westwards* from the window of a prison camp in the Saar. Now I faced over open ground – to the east!

From between the orchard trees at my back came the strains of the orchestra playing the final piece of the evening: the squadron's tune, 'Tomorrow night at the Darktown Strutters' Ball.' Tomorrow – I would fly again in France. Only a practice flight, but with what meaning for me! The squadron lay not far from the Somme battlefields. I would fly to the neighbourhood of Bapaume, fly over the very place where I had landed to become a prisoner.

V

It was actually something like ten days before I was allowed to cross the lines officially. I say 'officially' because of course I could not resist the temptation to sneak across during various practice flights; but not too far over, for I was mortally afraid of displeasing my new squadron-commander before I had had time to achieve anything. Gilly was willing to let me take my full share of the squadron's work as soon as possible, but he was right in holding me back. It would have been very awkward, when some of the Air Ministry officials concerned were not even aware of my presence in France, had I disappeared or been recaptured on my first flight.

Every day I was allowed to take up an S.E., either for formation flying or for firing practice at a ground target, so that gradually I became more confident of doing my share alongside those pilots whose experience seemed, at first, so much greater than any I could hope to acquire. Firing at a ground target was good practice for attacks on trenches and troops as well as for aerial combats, and with hints and tips from Gilly himself I began to learn something of both forms of fighting. The squadron was now frequently employed on operations such as aerodrome raids, bombing of troops and transport and harassing tactics generally, in addition to its normal occupation of high altitude fighting; for the ebb and flow which, since the German offensive in March, had come into the hitherto stagnant position-war had greatly increased the importance of guerilla attacks by fast single-seaters. 'Risky work,' I was told, 'but well worth it.' Later on indeed these operations became of such value as to outweigh by far the bringing down of a few more enemy aeroplanes.

Meanwhile it was our business to be ready for both jobs and I took the firing practice seriously, believing that, as Gilly had said, there would be plenty of time to pay off old scores. I had waited for so long, a little more patience was easy to command. The war would slow down during the winter months whilst I gained experience; in the spring and early summer I would be ready for the final victories.

Casualties, however, brought suddenly nearer the day when I was to be sent off to measure my skill and my luck. A flight-commander was wounded not many days after my arrival; then a young pilot was reported missing, a third fell ill and was taken to hospital. Not heavy losses, but persistent enough to make replacement necessary even by such novices as myself. An aerodrome raid – upon Estourmel, at which I was a mere spectator, high up in the sky with the protective flight – was hailed as a success, but it cost the life of the young American Larry Bowen. And then another pilot was reported missing …

And thus stepping into dead men's shoes – or more accurately into the cockpit of a vanished pilot – I found my name one evening at the tail end of the list for the Dawn Patrol.

VI

That Chance which, alternately good and evil, had steered my course throughout the war now showed itself clearly. For with that very first Dawn Patrol my carefully laid plans were blown to pieces as though they had been struck by a direct hit from an Archie shell, and I became involved in a whirlwind of events which did not cease blowing until the war itself ended.

And yet the day began in a normal manner. We left the aerodrome in the grey light, taking off in formation and flying east into the brilliant sky of a perfect morning, climbing steadily to cross the lines south-west of Cambrai and head for the rising sun, testing our guns as we went. Below us lay the ruined country of which not even Sir Thomas Browne could have said that it had survived the drums and tramplings of three conquests. On both sides the artillery was busy, presaging a heavy day in the air. Presently Archie opened up on us, keeping his usual fairly safe distance so that I rejoiced to hear the old familiar sound of his chronic cough. At eighteen thousand feet we turned north-east, and a few moments later, somewhere above the line Valenciennes-Cambrai, we sighted a large enemy formation.

I say 'we' because I suppose everyone saw the enemy machines at more or less the same time, but actually it didn't much matter whether I sighted them or not. I was the last man on the right of the top, protective flight; it was for the leader of the lower flight to find and attack the enemy – which is what he did. Hardly had I recognised the distinctive silhouette of Fokker biplanes than I saw a red light shoot up from our own leader and down he went in a steep dive to support the lower flight. For a moment it seemed as if the enemy were going to dive too, then his formation broke up, scattered and engaged our machines. This caused our own flights also to break up, each man going after the enemy nearest to him, and in a few seconds, instead of neat 'V's' manoeuvring for position, the air was full of machines hurtling in all directions like traffic at a badly regulated street intersection. The, for me, ticklish operation of a dog-fight was in full swing.

'Dive and zoom,' they had told me, so I dived and zoomed. For an instant a Fokker flashed full into my sights; I dived hard, pressed the trigger-release and prayed for victory. But with what seemed no more than a flick of the pilot's wrist he swerved off at right-angles, and a second later shots from another enemy crackled past my head. 'Dive and zoom!' I made haste to obey. 'If the enemy fire is too hot – hard rudder and no bank – side slip!' I tried that too ...

All at once I found myself outside the dog-fight. I looked round hastily. Two of the enemy had gone down as the result of our first attack, but already the fight was practically over, with the enemy chasing our people away. 'Attack – dive and zoom ...' it had been, now it was 'dive for home'. Until we could get clear and re-form the V, it was each man for himself. Fortunately my last zoom had taken me above and away from the main group of the enemy, for having started at the tail-end of the flight, I had been left a considerable distance behind. Opening my engine to full throttle, I pushed the nose down along the shortest course for our lines.

And then, looking about to see that no enemy was sneaking up to get a shot in from astern, I noticed something very odd. The clear blue sky was streaked with condensation, criss-crossed with the smoke of tracer bullets, the thin lines of greyish vapour shining in the bright sunlight. Archie puffs were dotted here and there, and a dark trail showed where a machine had gone down in flames. But there was something else. A thick blue-grey streamer of smoke was festooned over the scene of the recent fight – circling, diving; zooming – following the course of one of the machines engaged. I could see no craft, friendly or hostile, from which this streamer could be coming, but glancing over my shoulder I saw that it became thicker and darker the nearer it came to me ... I jerked my head round anxiously. It came from my own machine.

I was not on fire, that was my first joyful thought. The thick oily smoke came from the starboard exhaust pipe, and watching the end of the pipe I saw small pieces of metal come trickling out. Something was very much the matter. I had heard the click and rattle of a couple of shots getting home on the machine at the beginning of the fight, and now that I came to notice it the engine was vibrating a lot, the revolution-counter wavering slowly downwards. I must hurry to recross the lines. I looked over the side to make sure that I was following the best course.

We had gone a long distance east to find the enemy and the usual west wind had carried us still farther during the fight. I had made good headway so far, but as near as I could judge the lines were twelve to fifteen miles away. Cambrai lay beyond my starboard wing tips, below were open fields – a queerly reminiscent stretch of country. I glanced back. Valenciennes showed up unpleasantly close, almost directly under my tail-plane. The altimeter pointed to less than fourteen thousand feet. Fifteen miles to go, against the wind, with a failing engine … I had done all this before! Exactly the same thing over this identical course. Valenciennes, the west wind, engine trouble – it was happening all over again. A bit of history, unimportant to anyone save myself, was bent on repeating itself.

Archie crept close and a cloud passed over the sun. It was so bumpy at low altitudes that I lost height more rapidly. There was heavy fighting going on below, clouds of smoke, and a terrific bombardment; I could hear it plainly above the tired rumble of the engine and the dreary humming of the wires. I was getting close – but I was hearing the guns from the wrong side of the lines. If only the wind would drop …

At three thousand feet the failing engine subsided altogether. I switched off. The bombardment became menacingly loud.

VII

I must suppose that Chance wished to show me the other side of the picture – what might have happened with a bit of luck nearly three years before. Because I landed amid the shell-holes near the village of Queant, about a mile and a half behind the British front. Somehow or other the machine had managed to drift over the trenches in spite of Archie and I landed her, much to my surprise, without breaking any thing. But I was still very worried when I got out of the cockpit; the sensation of being doomed to recapture had been so strong I could not easily shake it off. Anxiously I looked into the cubby-hole behind the pilot's seat to see if the flare for setting her alight was safely stowed. The guns were loud, but even now they seemed to be firing in the wrong direction. I had lost my bearings in the last moments of that uncomfortable glide …

A voice hailed me. I jumped round in alarm. But it was a friendly head which poked itself out of a dugout doorway.

'Come on in,' said the owner of the head. 'Must have been cold up there this morning. Have some whisky!'

I did.

And later I got on the 'phone to the squadron, spoke to the Newt.

'I'll send a tender for you,' he said. 'Glad you're safe, we thought you were missing. Don't forget to bring back the watch!'

The eight-day luminous watch was the one item on the instrument board which appealed to all men. It was easily detachable, so easily that any machine left untended for more than a few minutes was invariably looted of its valuable timepiece. The first thing a pilot had to remember, no matter how serious the crash, was to unscrew the watch. But the morning's events must have unsettled me for I left it in the machine.

The tender arrived at noon and that same evening I dined again in the Mess instead of, as I had for a while feared, in St Quentin gaol. The Newt was a little upset at my having forgotten the watch, but Gilly was good enough to say that he was pleased to see me back; he too, it seemed, had had a nasty feeling that I might have been retaken, and I think he knew what the thought of recapture meant to me. That, however, was something more than one of the junior pilots understood. At dinner I happened to sit next to him. He came from somewhere near Glasgow and so was called, I suppose inevitably, Jock.

'What was the major talking about?' he asked. 'Something about your having been a prisoner – surely you were never such a fool as to get captured?'

I admitted that it was so, that I had been just such a fool.

'But, good God, man – how did you manage it? And you were there *two and a half years*? Unwounded at that? I can't believe it!'

'I'm afraid it's true,' I told him sadly. 'And it really couldn't be helped.'

'Nonsense! No pilot ever needs to be taken prisoner.'

'Supposing it happens to you some day, what then?'

'I'll get back before I'm caught.'

I began to feel uncomfortable – worried for him.

'But if your engine fails when you're, say, fifteen or twenty miles on the wrong side of the lines?'

'I'll glide home.'

'And if the wind is against you and you haven't enough height to glide over the front?'

'Those are absurd suppositions, but if it did happen that I was forced to land in enemy territory I would know what to do.'

'What's that?'

'Run away – hide in a wood – take cover somewhere. And crawl back after dark through the trenches. I'd know how to do it – I've served in the infantry.'

So might I have spoken in the days of the barge on the Lys.

'Well, if you didn't have the luck to do any of those things, you might still be taken prisoner.'

'And be put in a German gaol? Pouf – I'd be out of that before they'd had time to lock the doors!'

Ten days later the Dawn Patrol returned after a sharp engagement with a large number of Fokkers. It was my morning off and I stood on the aerodrome counting the S.E.s as they came in to land. Two were missing. One of them contained Jock.

My sorrow was genuine, for the loss was the squadron's and it seemed probable by all accounts that Jock had been killed. But before the end of the week we heard that he was safe – a prisoner and unwounded. Then, I must confess, I laughed. And I think we all wondered if we should not soon see him back, a free man after breaking gaol and crawling through the lines. Presently we forgot all about him – as they must have forgotten about me on the Lys.

VIII

At some time during the war Rudyard Kipling wrote a number of verses dedicated to various categories of people engaged in the struggle. In a moment of poetic aberration he wrote of a young pilot diving through clouds, 'his milk-teeth yet unshed …' Merciful heavens! we were young, but not that childish and by St Apollina, patron saint of dentists, there were no loose teeth in Gilly's squadron. Think of stopping in the middle of a dog-fight to spit out a couple of pre-molars!

However, even supposing Kipling's picture to have been accurately painted, I would assuredly have lost the whole galaxy on the afternoon of September 28th. I came near to more than that.

'Now then, chaps, a big show today,' Gilly had told us in the morning. 'There's a full-size war in progress – attack on the Hindenburg Line. We do high patrols first, and this afternoon *trench-strafing.* The Boche is taking it in the neck – got to stop his reinforcements coming up and harass his retreat, if any. Now off you go – dive and zoom – and if their fire gets too heavy remember the safest thing is to *keep low down!*'

We left at intervals in flights of three, loaded up with ammunition and four 25-pound bombs apiece. My own party, led by a senior pilot, made for Cambrai, crossed the lines at two thousand feet and began circling the country to the south of the town looking for targets.

There was a great battle going on underneath, to the west of the Scheldt Canal; the air was bumpy with explosions and with the flight of high trajectory shells. Comparatively undamaged country was rapidly being battered to pieces, villages were collapsing like sand castles overwhelmed by the tide, churches went down in clouds of dust, farms and isolated houses blazed furiously. Of course, the main clamour of warfare was inaudible to us above the roaring of our engines and the persistent singing of the wires, so that flying low it was ever surprising to see, without warning sound, a mass of broken earth fly into the air as a heavy shell burst nearby, or to observe a stout wall suddenly collapse in smoke and debris without so much as a murmur having reached one's ears. Rather like a silent film … Few troops were to be seen on the German side and little movement. At first it was hard to find suitable targets, especially since we were flying in formation.

Keeping formation even at high altitudes always bothered me when a scrap was imminent, I suppose because my early training had formed an instinctive desire to be alone and unhampered. Certainly I never learnt to feel comfortable fighting in V-formation and near the ground the proximity of other pilots was to me intolerable. On this occasion our first few dives at small parties of enemy infantry seemed positively feeble, for we were worrying far too much about keeping the right distance from one another, and about pulling out of each dive as soon as the leader did, to aim properly or to fire with any enthusiasm. Moreover, cruising about at some fifteen hundred feet from the ground we were offering an easy target for machine-gunners as well as for Archie. At the first objective worthy of my bombs I decided to break away from the others and work on my own.

Presently my interest was aroused by a small railway station south-east of Cambrai. It seemed at first glance to be deserted, but we had come gradually lower and I happened to notice some half a dozen German soldiers standing motionless beside what must have been the waiting-room. In their field-grey uniforms they were practically invisible and I should never have seen them but for the white circles of their upturned faces. It was funny seeing German faces so close to me again. Like being half-way back to prison. Funny? Well, I didn't exactly hate them, but I disliked them a good deal and this was war; I broke off from the formation, circled round and dropped two bombs.

Since I was not more than a hundred feet up the bombs made a nasty sort of *Clang – Clang*! under my S.E.'s tail, but there was no other response from the ground. When I looked back the signal box was hidden by a cloud of black smoke and there was a big dent in the roof of the waiting-room … So far so good. I searched around for other targets.

This was rather fun, I thought, and not too dangerous if one kept as low down as Gilly advised. The trouble was that to put in a reasonably long burst of fire one had to zoom up to about five hundred feet where concentrated rifle and machine-gun fire was apt to become much too hot. However, with a bit of turning, twisting and side-slipping I hoped to counter that.

By this time the other two machines of the flight had vanished, had found other targets I supposed. I was alone again; if I got shot down no one would know where I had gone to. Time enough to think of that later … I found some Germans in trenches – half-rolled, dived and zoomed. Then a party strolling through a cutting between two hills – dived and zoomed again. I heard them return my fire, but they did no damage, and a few moments later I saw a cart drawn by two horses moving briskly down a road. There were a number of men in the cart – I saw the details clearly as I passed within a hundred feet of them. I don't know what they were doing, whether retiring or going up the front, for the winding road ran approximately parallel to the firing line. But it was a tempting target, and again the sight of those

German uniforms gave me an odd sensation of annoyance. I dived from eight hundred feet.

When he heard me coming the man on the box whipped up his horses. Why he did that I cannot say, for there was nowhere for him to go, and it made little difference to me whether his cart travelled fast or slow. I suppose the men in the cart got excited when my first shots fell amongst them, perhaps they yelled. At all events the horses bolted, left the road, the cart tipped over and rolled down a grass bank into a stream. My last glimpse of the man who had been on the box showed me a face strangely reminiscent, at that distance and in that second, of an extremely disagreeable *Feldwebel* at Fort Zorndorf. I felt that I had paid off a score … And when I pulled out of the dive the wires were screaming triumphantly like the blare of brass in the ride of the Valkyries.

I stared ahead. Beyond a line of trees three or four flashes of yellow light winked at me. Guns! Not very well concealed, they had evidently moved up hurriedly. I had two bombs left – just the thing. Approaching from behind the trees, I zoomed up a couple of hundred feet to see what I was doing, and pulled the bomb-release handle …

And then I don't know what happened. Rising instantly above the *clang* of my bomb there came a roar like the ending of the world. Something kicked at the tail of my S.E. lifting it up as if it were paper, throwing the nose down into an almost vertical dive, out of control …

I know that what I am describing sounds incredible, but I also know that it happened, and that men in the squadron, Gilly amongst others, saw the machine afterwards and testified to its condition.

To estimate how long that dive lasted is beyond my powers. Perhaps it was two seconds, probably less. Reckoning that I was travelling at well over a hundred miles an hour and that when the dive started I was three hundred feet up, it must certainly have been less. And yet I had time for coherent thought. No past life flashed before me; my eyes remained open and it was the immediate future I looked into. I saw the ground appallingly close coming up at speed. I felt the control stick rigid in my hand, as hard back as I could get it – but jammed. I thought that I was 'for it'. In those infinite fractions of time I passed through fear, beyond despair, into a bleak region where without hope I *knew* that I was going to dive into the ground.

And so I did.

How it came about that I survived I can only explain in this manner. The machine had come slowly and almost of her own accord out of the vertical, but she was still descending steeply and at great speed when she smashed into the earth. There was a ghastly noise of breaking and splintering, I was flung forward against the safety-belt, my head hit the windscreen; but the machine quivered, bounced, and went on – minus her undercarriage. There must have been a slight fall in the ground just at that point, for had it been level or sloping up I would have crashed irremediably and fatally. As it was the machine seemed to stagger forward, her speed reduced almost to stalling-point; gradually her nose came up until she hovered along a few feet from the ground. She could still fly; by some tiny fraction of time and distance she had missed stopping altogether.

And now fear returned like pain after an operation. Dead certainty of the end had acted as an anaesthetic, returning hope brought new terror. What would happen next? The control stick was impossibly heavy, stiff, something had gone wrong with the tail. I glanced over my shoulder, and sat aghast at what I saw. On one side the fuselage had been stripped bare of its tail-plane and elevator, which now trailed, broken and tattered, at the end of a bracing-wire. The rudder was partially jammed by the wreckage; I could scarcely steer, dared not use too much force on the rudder-bar. The undercarriage, I knew, was gone, but worse than that the tip of a propeller-blade had been carried away. The engine vibration alone was nerve-shattering, and I could only guess what other damage must have been done to the frame-work of the machine. The extraordinary thing was that she flew at all; for the moment that was all I cared about.

By careful manipulation of the engine throttle and of the half-jammed control stick I succeeded in obtaining more or less level flight at an altitude of about one hundred feet. Lateral control was not too bad, but with only half a tail the machine had a horrible tendency to pitch uncontrollably. The best speed, I found, was about eighty miles an hour, and to obtain this I had to run the engine at three-quarters of full throttle, thereby bringing on such a vibration as made me fear the engine would break loose if I did not land soon. But to land in German territory was something that did not occur to me.

The likelihood of a crash was brought home by the attitude of the enemy. I passed over a nest of German machine-gunners. I saw the gun pointed, the men in field-grey crouching behind it. But the gun did not fire. Looking down at them I watched their heads rise, looked into their upturned faces, almost caught the expression of blank surprise in their open-mouthed immobility. They were too startled by my wheel-less, tail-less, rattling machine to think of firing ... I overtook a solitary steel-helmeted German walking towards the front. He spun round in alarm when he heard me coming, bent down to take cover; then slowly straightened up and stood regarding me, legs apart, as I passed unsteadily on my way. It was the same with the rest of them. The enemy did not think it worth their while to waste ammunition on a doomed and harmless craft.

I had been heading almost due north at the moment of impact and, although I could not see much of the country when I came out of the dive, I knew enough to realise that I was making for Cambrai and not for the lines. With infinite care I pressed the rudder-bar to bring the nose round from north-east, through north, to north-west. More than this I dared not attempt, for the remains of the tail were now vibrating as much as the engine; greater pressure on the rudder might bring about a final collapse. But in a little while, clearing some treetops by a few feet, I saw the Scheldt Canal go by beneath me. It was the first reassuring sign since the crash and it gave me confidence to continue, though by now I was as frightened of coming down as of staying up, knowing that I would have practically no control of the machine on landing.

Then I began to see the *backs* of Germans in trenches, in shell-holes, behind mounds and in the ruins of houses. The earth started to spout broken fountains of mud, earth, stones. Clouds of smoke rolled by, whilst above the banging of my engine I could hear the deep shuddering boom of guns. It took an age to cross the battle-zone, and all at once I noticed that I was getting much lower. Less than fifty feet from the ground. More like twenty. I tried to climb a little. Impossible. The machine lost speed at once ... There was a hill ahead of me – a well-known hill, wood, village: Bourlon! Our people had attacked it that same morning. Question was, had they taken it? If so I might be safe yet ... The ground came closer.

I began to see faces, not backs, in the trenches and shell-holes. Dimly through the smoke, I distinguished khaki uniforms. The shell-fire was less heavy. Ahead a gun flashed in my face, firing in the direction whence I had come. The ground drew still nearer, so near that had I possessed an undercarriage the wheels must already have been rolling upon the pitted earth where dead men lay as well in khaki as in field-grey. I tried to pull the nose up, got the speed to just below eighty, switched off; slithered along the ground, hit the rim of a small crater. There was a final crashing and splintering, from the wings this time, and the machine burying her engine in the ground thumped over on to her back.

IX

When I came to, a few seconds later, I was being hauled out of the wreckage by a couple of burly private soldiers. An officer with a very red face stood by, directing operations as though he were assisting at a rather uninteresting bit of salvage work.

'Blimey, sir,' said one of the men, 'look at all the berlood!'

That remark brought me round. I struggled to my feet, anxious to find out where I had been hit. The officer hurried forward solicitously.

'Are you wounded?'

Then if ever I should have quoted Browning: 'Smiling, the youth fell dead ...' I was too slow. It was the private soldier who answered for me.

'Garn, sir, it's only 'is nose what's bleedin'!'

The place where I had landed (in a manner of speaking) had been captured an hour previously, so that I had timed my descent rather well. The hill-side was no longer under rifle fire, and the fact that it was being shelled at odd intervals was not sufficient to deter the rank and file; a crowd of idlers soon collected such as, in peace time, assemble to watch a city street being taken up. Through the midst of them there hurried presently a dapper gunner subaltern. He clicked his heels and flung me a salute that would have shamed the guards at Buckingham Palace.

'Battery-commander's compliments, sir, and if you wish for assistance we shall be happy to do anything in our power.' He saluted again.

'Thanks,' I said, holding my nose and feeling very giddy. 'But why the "sir" business and all this saluting?'

It had been a warm day and I was not wearing flying-kit over my uniform. I saw him glance down in a puzzled manner at the badges on my sleeve, and when he spoke again it was in a much less humble tone.

'Oh – I thought you were at least a wing-commander. You had such a very big streamer on your machine.'

'Streamer be blowed!' said I. 'That was my tail-plane.'

I went on to tell him of some of the peculiar things which had befallen me, thinking that being a gunner he might be able to find an explanation for my having been blown up. But he was listless from the start and at the end plainly disappointed.

'The battery-commander thought you were flying a new type of machine – very fast, without the wheels, don't you know ...'

I left him gazing at my wrecked aeroplane, and walked back to the balloon line where they gave me a much-needed whisky-and-soda. Then, finding a tender returning empty to the depot, I hopped on board and was driven back to the squadron by easy stages.

X

'We were afraid you had "gone west", sir,' said the clerk in the squadron office when I arrived after dark. 'The returns are all ready to go off to the wing. Another half-hour and you'd have been reported missing.'

He seemed rather disappointed at having to make out a new return.

I made my way to the Mess, where Gilly and his officers were at dinner in the big tent. It was a calm night, and I remember noticing how few sounds issued from the open flap through which a broad shaft of light came to colour the stems of the apple trees and chase the shadows through the long grass. The pilots seemed unusually silent. Considering who was believed to be missing, I was surprised and rather gratified that free champagne had not been served out nor the orchestra called in. But on approaching the entrance I was overwhelmed by a stupid self-consciousness. I was beginning to feel tired and incapable of giving lengthy explanations of the day's happenings. I would far sooner have met just one pilot on my way to bed: 'Hullo, so you're back?' – 'Yes, I'm back.' He would have spread the news and I could have told them all about it in the morning. However, I was hungry as well as tired. There was nothing for it but to go on.

As I came into the tent I could hear one of the pilots talking to Gilly about the results of the afternoon raid. Suddenly Shutters, who was nearest the entrance, called out: 'Good God – here he is!'

There fell immediately the sort of silence which makes superstitious people observe that it must be twenty-minutes-past or twenty-minutes-to, while all heads were turned anxiously as though to look at an unwelcome ghost. Not knowing exactly what was expected of me, I advanced to the head of the table where Gilly sat. The usual formula employed on entering a Mess after dinner has started came to my mind.

'I'm sorry I'm late, sir,' I said and was astonished to hear them all laugh.

'What happened?' Gilly asked.

I began to make as good a story as I might out of the adventure, and, fortified with a drink, I was just warming up to the nerve-racking climax when an abrupt question fell like ice upon my conscience.

'Did you remember to bring back the watch?' asked the Newt.

Amid further laughter I turned away, sat down in a quiet corner. I had forgotten the thing again!

XI

Perhaps it was a stubborn desire to bring back at least a watch from future engagements which made me so anxious to start again at once. Certainly Gilly was not keen that I should indulge in any more low raids until I had recovered from the shock of the first. But I did not then understand why he should insist so firmly upon my having a rest; I felt none the worse for my adventure, and I would not admit even to myself that I had had more than a bad scare. It was not until afterwards that I understood the wisdom of Gilly's decision. He knew well the sort of thing likely to affect a pilot's nerves, and how a strain upon those nerves, unless cared for in the right way and in time, may become so serious as to break even the best of health. Gilly knew, because his own health was strained to breaking-point.

He had started the war in German South-West Africa, and had followed it up with a long record of service in France. As a result of one of his aerial combats, he had suffered a serious crash, but on recovering he had insisted on flying at once and, as it turned out, much too soon. He was never really strong again, and hard work as a squadron-commander had worn down his resistance. Nevertheless, on any important raid or at any time when the squadron required experienced leadership he was the keenest man in the air. And I must emphasise that by saying that it was no part of a squadron-commander's duties to fly; on the contrary, organisation generally required his presence on the ground. To a pilot with bad nerves and in poor health the excitement and strain of aerial fighting generally and of ground attacks in particular were very great. On returning from the aerodrome raid in which Larry Bowen was killed, Gilly, who had been the enthusiastic promoter and leader of the whole show, landed successfully, taxied up to the sheds, and remained sitting motionless. Mechanics ran up to find him white as a sheet ... Upon another occasion he had to be helped out of the cockpit after a fight, and much later he confided to me that once he had nearly blacked out during a ground attack.

But he refused to give up. His was the sort of courage that, however hackneyed the word, can only be termed indomitable. For the sake of the squadron, for the sake of us, his pilots, he was determined to stick it out – at any rate until the winter, when, he had been told, the squadron would return to England to be equipped with a newer and faster type of machine. Then rested, practised, reorganised, we would return in greater strength than ever to take part in the final victory ... In his lighthearted way he kept us all in order; warm in his praise of anything that, in our daily flying and fighting, accorded with the spirit and traditions of the squadron. On the evening of some day's achievement in the air he would order in the orchestra to celebrate or else bundle us into tenders and carry us off to the nearest town for dinner. Once we went as far as Dieppe, orchestra and all, in search of entertainment, returning in the small hours to wobble into the air in erratic formation. Any adventurous scheme for annoying the enemy won his approbation, and he himself was continuously seeking fresh methods of prodding the Germans.

I had the good fortune to see one example of Gilly's work at very close quarters. In fact, I couldn't well have been closer. It happened – as far as I can make out from the tattered leaves of my Combat Reports – on October

8th, on which day Gilly honoured me with an invitation to go and shoot down a balloon with him.

But before that a number of incidents had occurred combining to give me a certain footing in the squadron as one likely to survive more by luck than by judgment.

For the first few days after my 'tail-less' crash I was sent off quietly on patrol in formation with the rest of the squadron.

We had one or two fights, but nothing memorable in the way of victories, enemy aircraft just then being rather scarce on our sector of the front. On October 3rd trench-*strafing* began again, and for a while all went well. We found plenty of good targets for bombs as well as for machine-guns, so that the war seemed, from our point of view, to be going on at a rattling good pace ... On the 5th I shot down a balloon in flames, and scored a direct hit on a train in Busigny station – Busigny, through which I had steamed miserably in December, 1915, on my way to Germany. Later in the same day I dropped other small bombs, this time on some infantry who were showing their resentment at my presence, and finished up with five hundred rounds of rapid fire into an old archway in Cambrai where a company of Germans were misguidedly sheltering. A good day – but the next was nearly disastrous.

It was my fault this time. I tried too many conclusions with ground machine-guns, which I had foolishly thought could be mastered with a few steep, hard-firing dives. The success of the last days led me to take risks such as I would normally have had the sense to avoid; instead of diving swiftly once or twice and making that quick escape – flat along the ground, round corners of houses, behind trees, following the contours – I allowed myself to get annoyed with the tenacity of some German soldiers. Forgetting all my valuable lessons, I went on diving as though at practice upon an aerodrome target, until one of the nests which I had not been able to silence registered mortal wounds upon my poor S.E.

There had been the usual *crack-crack* of machine-gun bullets all through the engagement, but as I was zooming away from my last dive, ready to half-roll and attack again, the angry little sounds became much louder. Within three seconds I saw a group of holes appear on the left lower wing, a splinter flew off an interplane strut, a flying-wire broke with a twang like that of a bass fiddle. I tried side-slipping, but they held their aim. The fuselage began to rattle like a can of dry peas, something kicked the rudder almost away from my feet – and an instant later a hard *smack!* and a stream of petrol in my face told me that the main tank had been hit.

Frightened of fire more than of anything else, but also of the next shot which I felt would get me personally, I made for home. The gravity tank was hit too, but there was enough in it to carry me, helped by the height I had gained on the zoom, to safety a mile or so beyond the lines.

They certainly knew how to hit back, those German machine-gunners. There was no scaring them away from their posts; you had to lay them out flat before they would give in. There had been three nests of them that morning, skilfully disposed about the outskirts of a village, covering the retreat of the infantry. I had knocked out the first two – seen the gunners fall, seen new men take their places, seen them fall too, seen one of the guns overturn – but the third, concealed in the ruins of a farmhouse, had given as much as he had received. My machine was more or less of a wreck when I landed.

XII

'I say, if you don't look out you'll get what's coming to you!' Shutters informed me upon the following day.

I was back at the squadron, tuning up the new machine allotted to me and painting her name – *Schweinhund* – upon the three-ply panel below the engine. I can't remember exactly why I chose this name, except that I had been called it more than once and that now most of my work was being done at an altitude where the Germans could read it plainly ... Shutters' remark was disturbing. I was beginning to think that if the enemy had not recaptured me so far they were not likely to succeed in the future. But such an observation was discouraging, and I told him so.

'Oh, I don't mean that you'll "go west",' he answered quickly. 'I mean you'll be getting your name on the squadron board – collect a D.F.C. or something.'

That brought me up with a jolt. My name on the board at the end of that long list? I had not seriously considered the possibility since coming to the squadron, having been far too busy for such delightful day-dreaming. Moreover I was too much impressed with the achievements of my predecessors to think that either decorations or promotion would ever come my way, certainly not until many hard months of flying and fighting had passed. Once long ago in the barge, I had dreamed of these things, and capture had been the only result. Later on, I think I had a sneaking feeling that there might be something to be had on my return from captivity, but as no one had ever suggested anything so pleasant I had soon forgotten all about it.

And now came Shutters to recall silly boyish hopes of honour and glory, childish longings for distinctions such as, I suppose, we all have. I wondered if he could have heard anything from Gilly, in a roundabout way. Was it possible that my name was being mentioned 'behind my back', in a pleasanter manner than that phrase usually implies? I hardly dared to hope so. I had been with the squadron for so short a time and, although enemy machines had been brought down when I had been on patrol, I could claim none of them for my own. As for my trench-*strafing* work, it did not really amount to much, and the fairly successful performances of the past few days had not been reliably witnessed. No 'confirmation' was obtainable.

That word 'confirmation' – which on first hearing I had mistaken for a religious ceremony – sounded the knell of many a young pilot's hopes of glory. Coming back from some furious fight a machine would land, the pilot jump out and report enthusiastically: 'By Jove – had the hell of a scrap! Got two Huns down in flames!' To which would come the chilling reply: 'Can you get confirmation of that?' It was just as well: optimistic hopes of victory have led us all a good deal farther than the facts at one time or another. Personally I had not hitherto been much interested in 'confirmation'; I had, to pursue the analogy, my own private communion with the enemy – or rather, my personal vendetta to satisfy. Given an aeroplane and ammunition I needed no endorsement on my Combat Reports to make me happy. But the authorities had to be considered, and, more important, the record of the squadron.

While Shutters was still trying to persuade me that a decoration was something more than an extremely remote possibility, Gilly came down from the squadron office and strolled up to my machine.

'Hullo – why the paintwork? And what does that name mean?'

I tried to explain that it was meant to be a bit of 'frightfulness' to annoy the Germans, and that in addition I hoped soon to have sketched out a portrait of the Kaiser on the radiator, painted so that when the shutters were opened and closed rapidly, the Imperial moustaches would wiggle and the eyes blink – the idea being that a picture of the All Highest might put the enemy machine-gunners off their aim. But Gilly did not seem altogether pleased.

'Don't you know there's an order against the painting of machines?' he said. 'And, by the way, the general wants to see you.'

'Good Lord! – shall I rub out the "*Schweinhund*" at once?' I asked nervously, for in those days when a senior officer wanted to see me it was usually to complain about something.

'No, you needn't worry,' Gilly reassured me. 'He doesn't want to see you about that. He wants to confirm you – '

'Is he a bishop?'

'Don't be silly! He wants to confirm your report of yesterday – your attacks on those machine-gun nests.'

'But how the deuce can he do that?'

'Well, it seems he was up visiting the balloon line. And for some odd reason he decided to go up in one of the balloons. While sitting up there admiring the view, he saw an S.E. diving at the village you mention in your report. When the machine came back he saw the squadron markings on it ...'

I scarcely listened to the rest of the tale. It sounded like a yarn from another war: Edward III in his windmill watching the Black Prince at Crecy – Napoleon 'upon a little hill' ... What luck! To have a real, live general watching the arena and the *morituri* and putting in a favourable report about it! Perhaps, after all, that Squadron Honours board ...

'And there's another thing,' said Gilly as we parted. 'I want you to take command of your flight from today ...'

XIII

Next day Gilly's balloon *strafe* took place.

Our objectives were two observation balloons operating to the south-east of Cambrai. The enemy, beaten all along the line, was still holding obstinately to that town and to the country south, protected by the remains of his trench system and by the Scheldt Canal – as yet, with all bridges broken, impassable for cavalry or tanks. In this salient fighting continued fiercely, the Germans in force, their machine-gunners valiant, with orders to hold up our advance at all costs. But reinforcements were reaching them with difficulty; artillery searched their back areas, aircraft of all types – heavy bombers or single-seaters, flying high or low, near to or far from the front – were busy destroying communications. Enemy supplies were running low, for they had lost a tremendous amount of material during the past two months' fighting. Even observation balloons were becoming scarce. And that was where Gilly's scheme came in.

It had been observed that the balloon which I had shot down had not been replaced, nor had one to the north of Cambrai which had been seen coming down in flames a few days previously; many others had been withdrawn from more distant parts of the line where the war of movement was getting under way. In the Cambrai salient only two remained in daily use, evidently doing important work observing the gathering mass of our attack and directing fire upon the Scheldt. The Germans took the greatest care of these two balloons, probably because they could get no spares, and at the first warning of danger hauled them down at a truly astonishing speed whilst every gun in the neighbourhood opened up – Archie, machine-guns, 'flaming onions', rifles, even anti-tank guns. Several of our people had tried to attack these balloons when returning from high patrols, but with no result other than to make the enemy more wary. The only chance of success lay in a direct attack, at a comparatively low altitude, from straight across the lines, so as to surprise them in the air before they had time to go down.

Gilly's plan was simple. In the early afternoon a strong flight of the squadron was to cross the lines carrying bombs. They were to look for targets and later descend to attack troops and transport – thus diverting attention from Gilly and me, flying together and some distance beneath them ...

A pilot landing at Valheureux at the end of the morning reported that, although one of the balloons was not to be seen, the other was sailing, bloated with pride, at an altitude of some four thousand feet, to the south of the small town of Caudry. After a very light lunch we set out.

I mentioned the lightness of the lunch because we had to make sure of being alert on reaching the objective. The Germans on the other hand would, we hoped, be somnolent after beer and *blutwurst*, and therefore unlikely to notice us until too late to save their balloon. Wide awake and full of nothing but zeal we rushed across the lines at five thousand feet, Gilly slightly ahead, with me in the *Schweinhund* at his elbow and the protective flight high up so as not to alarm the enemy prematurely. For a moment the whole show appeared to me in bright colours, an exciting but not too dangerous adventure. Gilly waved an encouraging hand – I fancied I could hear him shout, 'Come on, chaps!' while the engine harmonised with the wires in that cheerful refrain of 'The Darktown Strutters' Ball ...' But not for long. When we were no more than half a mile beyond the German front lines, Archie opened up with a roar.

Perhaps, after all, the enemy had had a light lunch that day, at any rate they were not at all sleepy. By the time we reached Caudry several batteries of Archie were making good practice on us and 'flaming onions' were coming up in long strings of green fire. No chance of surprise. And, worse than that, not a sign of the balloon anywhere in the sky!

On most days an observation balloon would be plainly visible for many miles, but its neutral colour – in autumn sunlight, with a faint mist in the air – sometimes camouflaged it so successfully that one might come within a thousand yards before remarking its ungainly shape. We hunted for it in all directions, high and low, into the sun, behind small clouds; until of a sudden I noticed Gilly banking his machine rapidly from side to side to attract my attention. I drew closer, saw him pointing down, and looked over the side of my cockpit. The balloon was on the ground – squatting ugly as a haggis, not a mile from Caudry. I glanced back at Gilly ... He was wagging his wings again. He was going down to attack.

Now given that you surprised the enemy there was no reason why you shouldn't attack his balloons on the ground as easily as in the air. More easily in fact, for his guns had no time to come into action. That was how I got my first balloon: came upon him suddenly from over a ridge of hills, dived quickly, set him on fire, and away before Archie had fired a shot. But this was a very different matter. The enemy was warned of our coming and had a splendid view of our manoeuvring; every machine-gunner must have been standing to, waiting to let fly.

That didn't stop Gilly. He had come out specially for that balloon and he wasn't going home without it. A moment after he had wagged his wings for the second time, he went over in a half-roll and shot downwards with a vertical dive like that of a stooping hawk. I remember the glimpse I had of his machine as it went down, and I remember, too, the thought which came to me: that in the face of the enemy's preparedness and of the barrage he was putting up, I would never have gone down alone. I was very thankful that he was the leader; it spared me any uncertainty as to what I had to do. Imitating his manoeuvre of a half-roll, I followed him, stick well forward, engine at full throttle.

For the first few seconds of that dive I experienced a feeling resembling relief. The tension of waiting was over, we were going into action. And whatever trouble might await us below we had at least fooled Archie, leaving his shells to explode harmlessly a couple of thousand feet above us ... Gilly's speed increased tremendously – soon we must each of us have been doing two hundred and fifty[8] – and I had a hard time keeping up with him. I saw him whisk his head round once to see if I was following: imagined him calling, 'Hurry up, chaps!' and through my own mind there ran the answering yell, 'I'll be there to meet you in a taxi, honey ...' At fifteen hundred feet he opened fire.

I could see the long white smoke-streamers of Buckingham incendiary bullets tearing down into the balloon – and I could also see a string of 'flaming onions' coming up from close alongside. At about a thousand feet from the ground I too opened fire. For a few moments four machine-guns were firing at one balloon; its upper surface was becoming hazy, obscure; it was getting hot.

By now the earth was coming up pretty quickly. Intent on keeping my two guns upon the target, I missed seeing Gilly come out of his dive and I was so close to the ground myself when I pulled out that it seemed the earth must have swallowed him. No time to ponder the mystery of his disappearance. No time to think, no time to do anything except stop firing and flatten out of that intoxicating dive. Only just time to see the big bulge of black smoke

---

8. The S.E.5's terminal velocity in a power dive was 275 m.p.h.

coming from the balloon. The job was done. She was burning. I skimmed over the roof of a house. Made for home.

As if they had been waiting for this particular moment – as perhaps they had – the wakeful Germans now opened as hot an anti-aircraft fire as personally I have ever known. Effective shooting had not been possible hitherto owing to the great speed of our dive, but now that we were flying level again they had their chance and they took it. The amount of stuff they threw up in the next few seconds appalled me. And for once I couldn't find cover. Scattered houses and a line of trees barred the way back in such a manner that I could not get really low down to that contour-chasing flight which is safest of all in wartime. Holes began to appear in unpleasantly large numbers upon my wings, things jolted and rattled; I could see shell-splinters fly past, together with small splinters from the *Schweinhund*. And all at once there was a sort of explosion right in front of me, a puff of blue smoke, and a wave of petrol splashed into my face, half blinding me.

To this day I don't know whether it was an incendiary bullet, a 'flaming onion', or merely a bit of Archie, but a great hole opened up in my main tank, and that puff of smoke was thick and hot ...

Fire-terror seized me. I knocked back the throttle, groped unseeing for the switch, side-slipped violently to avoid the flames I expected ... The wind was cold on my cheek. I forced my eyes open. Petrol still whipped by, smarting intolerably; but there was no fire. I switched on again; nothing happened. No pressure, of course, and therefore no petrol. The voice that breathed o'er Eden bawled in my ear, 'Switch on to Gravity, you fool!' I fumbled with the petrol cock, the engine was slow in picking up. I was only a few feet from the ground, coming down very fast in an open field beyond the line of trees. No doubt of it, I was going to land – in German territory. The engine coughed. I juggled frantically with the throttle-control.

And then the engine roared, jerked the machine forward, at length settled down to steady running. Air-speed rose quickly – eighty-five, ninety, a hundred. Heavy fire opened up ahead, machine-guns and rifles. I held the *Schweinhund* down, banked sharply round a clump of trees, dived over a low ridge, sped westward. The firing died away ...

The author in 1921.

Below: Maurice Farman Longhorn – the type of
aircraft on which the author learnt to fly in 1915.

Bottom: B.E.2c, the RFC's all-purpose aircraft of
1915.

Shorthorn assaulting a German balloon, October 1915. (*Painting by James Leech*)

Down on the Lys. (*Sketch by the author*)

Remains of 4086.
German photograph
of the author's B.E.2c,
identified from the
official records by the
serial number on the
fin.

St Quentin, December 1915.
Taken a few days after capture.
German guards (l to r – back
row) author, Two British Privates,
French Pilot, Strong (l to r – front
row) Hunter, French Staff Officer,
German Prison Govenor.

Medlicott, the author and Grantham (l to r),
Weilburg, February 1916.

Escape from Friedberg, 25 September 1916. (*Sketch by the author*)

A typical room in one of the best officers' prison camps in Germany, 1917.

Elementary form of forged pass,
made at Neunkirchen, 1918.

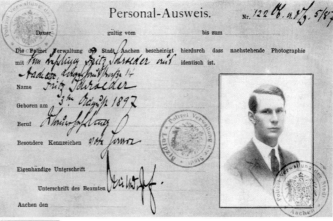

Finished specimen of forged
pass, 1918.

Captivity: end – Dutch frontier, 17 April 1918.
Beverley Robinson left, author right.

In flight: rivals of 1918.
(*Above*) S.E.5a; (*right*) Fokker D VII.

Larry: Lieutenant Laurence G. Bowen RFC
and RAF (American). Killed in action
15 September 1918.

Gilly: Major Euan Gilchrist MC, DFC, OC
56 Squadron RFC and RAF.

'… at least a wing-commander'. Return from ground-attack, 28 September, 1918. (*Sketch by the author*)

Johnny: Captain John Speaks DFC, RFC and RAF (American).

Bloody Bob: Lieutenant Robert A. Caldwell DFC, RFC and RAF (Canadian).

Schweinhund – the author in his S.E.5a. Photograph taken after the Armistice, with Lewis gun and mounting removed from top plane.

Fifty years on. Author with S.E.5a at the Royal Aircraft Establishment, Farnborough, 1968. (*Daily Telegraph*)

XIV

It was later than usual when a motor-cycle and sidecar deposited me at the squadron. The orderly-clerk looked quite startled when I appeared in the doorway. But he seemed better pleased than on previous occasions.

'Fact is, sir,' he said, 'the returns have gone off to the wing. You're down as "missing, believed killed". I'm very pleased you're safe, sir, but – well, I'm glad I shan't have to do the returns all over again tonight.'

Apparently one of the protective flight pilots had seen me going down under heavy fire, and mixing my machine up with the flames and smoke of the balloon had reported me to have been '*carboneezay*', as Foxy would have said. Hence consternation in the Mess, for the squadron, having had a good day, wanted to celebrate Gilly's destruction of the balloon, but felt a little doubtful about feasting until quite certain that I was good and dead. My sudden reappearance in the doorway of the pavilion, therefore, elicited a loud cheer, and after the usual shout of, 'Well, chaps, what happened to you?' the wine began to flow.

I was glad of that cheer because it showed that the squadron appreciated my luck. But later in the evening, just before the band began to play the squadron song, a second and louder cheer hailed the much more remarkable fact that I had remembered to bring back the watch.

XV

The war hurried on. And the time came for us to leave that quiet orchard at Valheureux where in the intervals of long and perilous hours in the air, we had lived happily enough. Henceforth we moved restlessly forward from one aerodrome to another. For the long agony of the infantry in the trenches of the devastated areas was over at last, and although there was still much fighting to be done it would be mainly in the open and with the help of cavalry and tanks. Cambrai was in our hands, the Hindenburg Line a thing of the past. The troops were advancing over country hardly touched by war, to Le Cateau and Valenciennes.

The first aerodrome we settled at gave me something of a shock. The ground itself and the surrounding country had been badly knocked about in the past three years, but the features were still recognisable, which was more than could be said for most of the land from the Somme to the Scheldt. A German squadron had been stationed in the neighbourhood. They had lived and messed in a château nearby. Walking over their old aerodrome, I looked into the house. And fancied I could hear keen young voices talking of aerial fighting, of flying and of the performances of new machines; sharp, high-pitched voices, yet not wholly displeasing, although one of them spoke of *furchtbare Langeweile* … Voices of the dead! It was the aerodrome close to which I had landed in my B.E.2c, and to which I had been taken a prisoner.

A few days later when I was driving with Gilly, helping to choose another more advanced aerodrome, we passed close to a squadron also about to move forward. A squadron engaged in artillery observation work. We drew up at the Mess to ask for information about landing-grounds in the vicinity. I went into the Mess-tent at the invitation of one of the officers, but that, it appeared, was as far as their hospitality went. Rather shamefacedly the officer accompanying me explained that the offering of drinks, meals, a packet of cigarettes, or indeed anything – except, I must suppose, first-aid to a wounded man – was against the rules of the Mess. The coldness of our reception caused me to ask the number of this squadron. I was not surprised at the answer. But the officer who told me had never heard that his unit had for long been stationed on the western bank of the Lys. Nor did he know that the Starched Shirt had once commanded it …

By the end of October we had advanced across the Scheldt to an aerodrome in the midst of that area, to the south-east of Cambrai, where but a little while previously German uniforms had daily drawn our fire, where desperate German machine-gunners had fought heroically. It seemed curious to be living and flying now from the district whence the enemy had faced so proudly and so long towards the Somme from the vaunted security of the Hindenburg Line. The French inhabitants, dazed by a liberation for which they had almost ceased to hope, stammered out tales of the years gone by, remembered the dates of our raids and fights, could tell us where pilots long dead had come down, where others had been captured. We discovered Larry Bowen's grave in a cemetery not far from the aerodrome he had raided; another, marked with a German cross, at the side of a quiet country road … And at finding myself in this land over which the flame of war had passed like a forest fire, I had a strange feeling of disillusionment, almost amounting to sorrow at the enemy's departure. There came to me a sensation of emptiness, an inkling of futility – as if in grasping at what had seemed the bright substance of victory we had but stumbled a little farther into shadows.

It was then, too, that I chanced to read a sentence of Shaw's writing: about the joy of life – about 'being thoroughly worn out before you are thrown on the scrap heap'. The scrap heap? A pilot's life in France – allowing for death, injury or capture – averaged under six weeks. My time was more than up. How much longer would the luck hold? Towards the end it seemed to be a question of which would be finished first: myself or the war ...

There was much to be done yet. Bombing of troops and transport, machine-gunning of the retiring enemy, destruction of his strong points. And renewed fighting at high altitudes for the German aviators were busy again on our sector, struggling gamely to avert the now inevitable end. We banished gloomy thoughts and carried on somehow, seeking fights wherever they were to be found, anxious to raise the numbers of our successes for the greater glory of the squadron. But the canker of disillusionment gnawed at my heart. In Germany I had striven for liberty so as to return to France and flying. Now in France I was striving hard enough, but I scarcely knew for what. Final victory in the war was certain – but beyond that? I was becoming introspective, conscious of a deep change within myself since the days of the barge on the Lys, a change not wholly for the better. Eagerness, enthusiasm were still there, but blended with something very like despair.

XVI

The whirlwind continued to blow, but now the vortex shifted to higher altitudes. Although ground attacks were still almost daily events, my personal adventures were more concerned with aerial combats. It was a welcome change, but one which made matters none the easier, since owing to my aversion to fighting in formation I frequently became involved in fights from which – one S.E. versus many Fokkers – I was lucky to escape with a whole skin and a no more than badly battered *Schweinhund*. In the S.E.'s superior speed on the dive sometimes lay the only road to salvation.

A small share of victories did, however, come my way, in spite of unorthodox methods and inexperience, although I knew that I could never hope to achieve the virtuosity of the squadron's great pilots. It is on record that McCudden once brought down a German aeroplane with a single shot – luck if you like, but a sign that his methods were sound, his aim accurate. It is also on record that in the destruction of a solitary Fokker an S.E. pilot once expended five hundred and fifty rounds. I see no reason why I should reveal the identity of *that* pilot.

But I was no longer making a practice of fighting entirely alone. The American Johnny Speaks, a lanky Canadian known as Bloody Bob Caldwell (whose field-boots, however grimy his hands and face, were always speckless mirrors) and I now did much of our hunting together, whether on high patrols or near the ground. We were now almost the senior pilots in the squadron, the maintenance of its traditions was in our hands, so that closer co-operation in air-fighting brought a depth of friendship that had in it something of the 'Musketeers'. And like those jolly warriors labelled Three for the sufficient reason that they were Four, so we had in Gilly a d'Artagnan who was both friend and leader.

I wish it were possible to give an ampler account of the doings of Johnny and Bob, but memory does not stretch that far. And though we compared notes of daily fighting and laid plans for future raids, when the four of us sat round the fire in the evenings it was not usually to talk of bloodshed. Moreover, it was an association which Chance did not permit to last very long.

XVII

One evening when I had just landed the *Schweinhund*, after she had had the good fortune to bring down a couple of Fokkers with no more damage than two holes through her radiator, I found Bob in the tent 'office', where I had gone to make out my report. His boots were immaculate as ever, but his face was long as a winter's night.

'Any luck?' he asked gloomily.

I told him the news, restraining my elation with difficulty.

'That's good!' he exclaimed grinning. 'Johnny got one too. The squadron record *is* going up.' His face grew sombre again. 'I'll have to hurry to catch up – it will soon be my last chance.'

'Why?' I asked in alarm. 'They aren't transferring you to another squadron, are they?'

'No, but it's all over now, bar the shouting.'

'What is? The squadron? They're sending us home to get the new machines?'

'No, not that either. We'll never get those new machines. It's the war – she's finished, done for. Fritz has thrown in the towel. Asking for peace …'

I couldn't believe it. Nor could anyone else, not for days. It seemed impossible that it should be so. That great, strong German who had held us back for years – on his knees? True, since August he had been beaten everywhere, on all fronts, beaten so that he could not hope to attack again; but although he was now in full retreat he had not yet been pushed back as far as he had advanced. He still stood on French soil. And already he was crying for mercy? Couldn't stand up for the last round? No, it couldn't be true! It was just the usual peace talk, a trick on the part of the enemy … Had we been in supreme command I think we should have refused him the armistice he begged for.

XVIII

My last fight with a Fokker took place on November 3rd, and my last aerial engagement – which is not to say that it was when I fired my final shots – on November 5th. I suppose that to celebrate the day I had hoped to arrange some specially attractive display of pyrotechnics, but in that I was disappointed. For although, leading my patrol, I tried to force a fight upon a formation of Fokkers they would have none of it, so that at length I was compelled to demand satisfaction from a humble, but by no means defenceless, kite-balloon sitting over the eastern edge of Mormal Forest. And with defective ammunition halting my attack it was the enemy who once again provided the fireworks.

It did not occur to me at the time that this last engagement was the counterpart of my very first. Just over three years since, greatly daring, I had sauntered along in the Shorthorn to vent my spite upon a German balloon near Loos. Then the wind had whistled through piano wires like a gale amid pine trees. Now I dived steeply in *Schweinhund III* and her streamlined rigging screamed Wagnerian music. The result was the same: the enemy hauled down his balloon.

Two days later something happened that was to mark my memory for life, though the incident itself was commonplace and small enough. It came about in this way. Leaving Johnny to take over leadership of the Dawn Patrol, for the heavily overcast skies were empty of enemy aircraft, I had gone down to seek targets on the ground. Hunting around just before sunrise I came presently to a more northerly sector of our now rapidly changing front, where a small force of British infantry, a battery of guns in support, could be seen moving forward up the pock-marked western side of a long slope. To the east, perhaps a hundred yards ahead of the most advanced troops, the ground fell away over a low chalky cliff. The German position, upon which our guns were dropping occasional shells, must be below the cliff; circling round at a distance I could tell almost exactly where it lay. I would have an easy target, diving over the cliff from the west, unseen by the enemy until I opened fire. There was to be an attack – I thought I would start it.

Skimming over the heads of our men I reached the edge of the cliff; and dived, engine roaring. With a thumb on the gun controls, I peered forward through the Aldis sight; and once more there came to me the sudden tightening of the nerves and of the heart that always returned whenever I was about to open fire, knowing that fire would be answered, that the next few seconds would be decisive one way or the other. I saw some half-dug trenches, a stunted tree, a patch of brushwood; a little way back from the foot of the cliff a number of gun positions, between them a road, a dead horse. And all at once I seemed to see, in a fleeting vision that compressed time into an instant, the whole melancholy prospect of our tardy victory.

And this is how I see it even now. A narrow country road, grey-white, stretches away to the east, cutting in two a monotonous brown plain. At broken intervals along the road, bordering untitled fields, rows of slender poplars stand straight and motionless. There is no wind; in the damp stillness of the autumn air I can see leaves falling vertically. Near at hand a ruined farmhouse stares through a pair of shattered windows like one whose eyes have not been closed in death: beside it a barn smothered in smoke burns steadily. From local flooding have come dark pools of stagnant water in the farmyard, at the side of the road, in the fields. Recent shell-holes grouped unevenly have a sickly yellowish look as though the land has been stricken by some repulsive disease. Through their midst the wet, faintly gleaming road leads on, growing ever narrower to vanish at last into the November fog as though into the heart of infinity – the long hard road back into Belgium where, for us, the war had started. In the distance beyond the farmhouse a handful of men in faded grey uniforms push, drag, hurry beside a hand-cart heavily laden. Of the might of a great nation, of its arrogance and military pomp, they are the sole remnants. At their thoughts as they return, perhaps not empty-handed but certainly defeated, to the fatherland whence they marched so proudly, I can but guess. Yet in their manner of striding on there seems to be a purpose, a common resolve urging them to follow the road to its mysterious end.

So much I saw in a matter of seconds as my aeroplane rushed towards this desolate land – perhaps the more desolate for not being utterly devastated. But before I had time to absorb it all, I received another and more disconcerting impression. As I dived over the edge of the cliff and looked down into the shallow trenches I saw that they were empty. Bits and pieces of equipment, barbed wire, a smashed limber, corrugated iron from a temporary shelter – the refuse of war – lay scattered; but not an armed man was to be seen. In uncompleted gun-pits three or four howitzers remained, rendered useless no doubt; but the attendant gunners had gone. The position was deserted. And then, through the narrow circle of the Aldis sight, I saw him – the only enemy soldier left in the vicinity of this hastily abandoned strong-point.

That one unexpected glimpse as I flattened out of the dive less than fifty feet from the ground will stay in my mind for ever. In the course of the war I had seen, like everyone else, dead men in every sickening phase of putrescence; had heard the wounded cry out; had watched, without power to help, men burning to death or falling from the sky; I was inured to horror. Yet this, seen at the very moment when in unthinking anger I was about to fire both guns at a supposedly numerous enemy, filled me with sudden dismay. I shall see that German soldier always. He is for me the Beginning and the End of war. He lies across the road by which his friends have marched in triumph or in sorrow first in one direction, now in the other, but always, I think, with the horizon obscured by mist. He is young, fair-haired – his steel helmet has fallen off; from the length of his limbs he must have been tall. He lies on his back mortally wounded. Something – perhaps a steel splinter, for the earth close by is newly shell-torn – has severed his right arm near the shoulder and laid bare his breast so that I can almost see the ribs through the dreadful red tatters of flesh. His mouth hangs open; he gasps for the breath that will but prolong his suffering. He is alone, forsaken. As I thunder over his head he draws up a leg convulsively, the boot scraping a little trench in the mud beneath which he will presently rest. He lies between the armies; just one dying youth, nothing in the war; uncared for, unnoticed. But not unnoticeable, for he bars the road. They will have to move him before they pass, whoever they are. Behind the slope above the cliff our own young men are advancing. To attack what? After all the years of hope, of failure, of stubborn courage, of lives thrown away like burnt match-sticks, leaving a million dead behind them they are to strike at – nothing. Their wrath, like mine, will spend itself in the air. And they will only march to victory across the body of dead Youth ...

As I flew on eastward above the muddy road, I overtook the half-dozen German soldiers struggling along with their hand-cart. Before I reached them I saw one unsling his rifle and throw it up to his shoulder. Standing firm, legs apart and aiming well ahead of my machine, he looked like a statue of exasperated humanity firing its small thunder at the mute, uncomprehending heavens. One of his shots cracked past, close to my head. I did not reply. It was no longer worth while.

That same evening I left for England. My turn for leave had come. It was about time. Over nine weeks had passed since my return to the front. The luck could not have held much longer, and this was the leave that had been due in December, 1915.

XIX

It would have been easy to have stayed on in England after my leave was up, but France drew me back irresistibly. Even now many of us were not sure that the war was over, it still seemed incredible that Germany should have collapsed so suddenly and completely. We thought it more than likely that back on his own soil, rested, reorganised, strengthened, the enemy would make a stand, defy us to come farther. The Armistice would be denounced; there would be a flare up of fighting from the embers of war; we should have to force our way into the Rhineland, and final victory would still await the coming of spring. After the noisy celebrations in London we trooped back.

Gilly had told me in London that he was to be invalided home; I was to be in command of the squadron, of *the* squadron – that alone was sufficient reason for rejoining. We had changed aerodromes once more, to quarters not far from Caudry – and near the very spot to which I had once followed Gilly in that wild dive upon a balloon. The place was silent now, too silent. All through the old war areas, from Albert to St Quentin, from Arras to Cambrai and on to Le Cateau, the land was desolate, deserted, for the armies had already moved on, the French civilians not yet returned. Sometimes at the end of a misty autumn afternoon the silence would become appalling – like the grave, like being buried alive. Amid the wreckage of a war that was over, with the litter of equipment, the shell-holes, the scattered crosses all about one, there seemed to be more than just silence in the air. It was as though from each day of the Four Years some ghostly event were rising to call to us, to remind us of the dead past; as though the dead themselves were calling us back … We made a great deal of noise in the Mess to drown such mournful sounds, and spent as much time as possible in the air.

Schweinhund III had survived the war, although the wind hummed through her wires more gently now. Without Archie's alarming cough or the sharp crackle of machine-gun bullets there was no need for them to sing too loud a song. But I made them scream again when the troops moved forward; dived at abandoned German aerodromes, hedge-hopped over liberated Belgium, overtook joyfully waving infantry advancing with the Army of the Rhine.

The Rhine! I flew down it, dived to the water's edge at Cologne, zoomed over the Cathedral and the railway station where, a prisoner, I had spent many cold and depressing hours; followed the railway to Aachen, circled the town, flew to the Dutch frontier, stared down … There I had crossed to freedom, along that white thread of a road beside that wood. Now I roared over the spot in an S.E.5, its nose painted bright red, with *Schweinhund* in large white letters to annoy the enemy. A triumphant return! But somehow, even as I looked down at that little corner of the earth which I had been at such pains to reach, an inexplicable fit of melancholy seized me. Disenchantment had made rapid strides. The Dutch frontier, the war, even flying seemed to have lost their meaning. Things which for years had mattered more than life itself were no longer of any great importance – to me or to anyone else.

Banking the *Schweinhund* steeply I turned away and, without looking back, laid a straight course for Brussels, wine and women ...

'Brussels by Christmas' – no difficulty about that any more! But we did not go there then; we preferred to spend Christmas in the squadron, having our own ideas of how to celebrate. And considering the miserable state of things – half peace, half war – we made quite a good show of it. Turkeys? No, they were not to be found. With their antiquated knowledge of aerodynamics they must have succumbed to Progress in northern France at about the same time as the Shorthorn. But geese there were, and we purchased them in quantity for the men as well as for the pilots.

I fancy the men had a reasonably good Christmas that year. In addition to the geese, valuable supplies were secretly obtained, a barrel of beer was set up in the Mess-room, an extra ration of rum issued. And the only incident worthy of the name was when an exasperated engine-fitter, armed with an axe, chased the disciplinary sergeant-major round the aerodrome in the cold dawn of Boxing Day ... But such high spirits were natural to the men of that squadron. Each man an expert in his own line, they had worked with a will. Upon their careful tuning of engines, their skilful adjustment of rigging wires, their accurate sighting of machine-guns, many lives had long depended. The squadron's successes are theirs to share with the boldest of those pilots whose names still head the Honours board. The magic brilliance of those letters, 'V.C.', twice repeated, shines on them as well; they helped to carve them.

XX

Johnny, Bob and I flew to Brussels to hail the New Year. It was our last celebration. Early in January we were informed officially that the squadron was not going up to the Rhine as we had hoped it would, and that demobilisation would commence at once.

For a few weeks more we carried on working, flying, practising formations and firing our guns at targets hoping against hope that something might yet occur to keep us together; and then slowly but with gathering speed the squadron began to dwindle like a community stricken by the plague. The men went first and the officers from overseas. Each morning in the office I would find a fresh list of those to whom release had come much as the Summons came for Mr Valiant-for-Truth, but in place of the Pitcher broken at the Fountain were the tokens of equipment, of tools, of flying-kit returned to store. The orchestra played 'The Dark-town Strutters' Ball' for the last time and were dispersed. Skilled mechanics vanished one by one, men who had been with the squadron from the start, ever since the day when, proud of its new S.E.s, it had come to France to put fear into a strong and determined enemy. Pilots flew for the last time and packed up their kits; the Mess grew smaller. Young Canadians, South Africans, Americans whom we had just had time to understand and to like disappeared from our lives forever. The senior N.C.O.s, without whom the squadron could not function, shook hands and entrained – rather regretfully, I thought – for demobilisation camps in England. The silence became so much the heavier that at length we were too few to lift it.

Then the final blow fell. In February our machines, our beloved S.E.s which we had come to regard as our personal property to endow with all the affection men give to ships, were taken away from us – flown down to a depot to be, in the official phrase, 'reduced to produce', destroyed.

Before she left I cut from the side of *Schweinhund III* the three-ply panel bearing her name. I took it home with me, a vain reminder of the days of her greatness ...

In the end Bob Caldwell went on leave to England and did not return. He wrote me from the ship in which he sailed to Canada, but I never saw him again. He went in for experimental parachute work in his own country. During an exhibition flight to prove the safety of parachutes he jumped from an aeroplane. The parachute failed to open.

After his departure, Johnny Speaks, Bill the acting-adjutant and I were the only ones left in the Mess to dine in state – three where there had been twenty-three! – beneath that scroll of honour which in a small measure we had helped to lengthen ...

A few transport drivers still remained, and the orderly-room clerk whom I had so distressed by my late returns from patrols and ground-*strafes* sat faithfully by his records in the deserted office.

Three motor-bicycles, once furiously ridden by despatch riders with urgent news, had been retained until the end, and on these we toured the neighbourhood, visiting the graves of those who had been killed from the squadron, taking a last look at the places above which we had fought. In Cambrai I found the gateway where I had caught a company of sheltering Germans; bullet holes and scratches from my machine-gun fire showed up plainly – a mark that would not soon be erased.

One morning, when the snow lay thick upon the old battlefields and grey clouds hung low in a windless sky, I said goodbye to Johnny. A string of lorries waited outside the Mess; he was taking the remains of the squadron to the base depot and so back to England.

'Hope to see you in London in a few days,' he said. 'I shan't be sailing for America for a long time yet.'

'What are you going to do when you're demobilised?'

'Try to get a flying job somewhere, I suppose. It's about the only thing worth doing right now. You're staying on in the Air Force, aren't you?'

I nodded.

'Yes, for what it's worth – after all this.'

Johnny looked slowly over the whitened hills towards the village where his friend Larry now slept beneath the cross of his own propeller.

'Funny, after a rotten war like this, how hard it is to leave.' He sighed. And then smiled quickly to hide his feelings. 'War's all wrong, I guess, but – ah well, them *was* the happy days, them was! Goodbye, G.-M.'

The lorries rumbled away down the long straight road to Cambrai. I watched them go, I, the only one left of all the men in that once powerful squadron; for the acting-adjutant had been posted to England with the records, the last men had travelled down to the base, even the orderly-room clerk had gone. And with the final break-up of the squadron everything that had given zest to life seemed to have gone too. The deep rumble of the lorries died away, and in the wintry silence which then fell, the only sound I could hear was the faint humming of telegraph wires – feeble echo of past endeavour.

An Escaper's Log

I

In the autumn of 1915, when the excitement caused by the unsuccessful battle of Loos had subsided, and the conditions under which we were living in France had again become normal – when, in the words of a certain Staff Officer, "we had returned to the piping times of peace" – flying was by no means an unpleasant occupation. The risks in those days were, of course, greater than they are now, and the work was periodically arduous, but on the whole we lived in far greater comfort than did the unfortunate men in the trenches, and those of us who had come from the infantry had no real cause to regret our choice.

From one cause or another we suffered a good many losses and in the course of about three months the flying personnel of the squadron to which I belonged had been almost completely replaced. I began to count myself among the lucky ones, since not only had I successfully completed a number of more or less important flights, but I had come unscathed through no less than four aerial combats – quite a large number at the time.

It all seems such a long time ago that I find it difficult to remember my feelings when first I flew in France, but sometimes when day-dreaming I manage to recapture some of the thrill of those early days of war-flying, when the average speed of our primitive machines rarely exceeded sixty miles an hour, and the art of aerial fighting was almost unknown. There were no "specialist" squadrons then, and pilots in the Royal Flying Corps were ready to start at a moment's notice on bombing raids, long or short reconnaissances, photographic expeditions or artillery-observation flights. Fighting in the air was regarded as a "side-show". Occasionally, it is true, machines were sent up to attack and pursue some of the more daring German aircraft which had ventured to cross our lines, but it was a rare occurrence for an enemy to be brought down.

One day, towards the end of November 1915, some twenty-five of our aeroplanes sallied forth to bomb a railway junction on the German side of the lines. How much damage we did was difficult to estimate, but it is certain that one of the results of this raid was to spur the German airmen into greater activity than they had shown of late.

On 28 November a German machine appeared over our aerodrome and I was sent up in pursuit, accompanied by my observer, a Captain Strong [referred to by his nickname 'Dante' in *Wind in the Wires*]. For nearly an hour we climbed slowly towards the enemy, who pursued a leisurely course to the northward. At last we reached his height – about 6,000 feet – and at the same time he must have caught sight of us, for he turned back towards the lines. His course now brought him close alongside, and as he passed my observer opened fire with the Lewis gun. Just then I caught sight of three other German machines coming towards us; it looked as though we were trapped and I at once endeavoured to manoeuvre for a better position. The first aeroplane on the approach of his friends returned on our starboard side, fired at us and received a broadside at the hands of my observer. The enemy then turned slowly away, and a second or two later dived down steeply. I felt certain that he had been hit, but I was unable to watch him for long as the other three Germans were now closing in on us. For the next few minutes I was kept busy dodging and swerving in every direction in an attempt to avoid the enemy's fire. In 1915 aerial gunners were poorly trained and it must have been to this fact that we owed our preservation more than to any skill upon our own part. The enemy flew in no particular formation, and by getting in each other's way hindered their own fire considerably. Nevertheless the crack of passing bullets was almost continuous, and every now and then a slight jar and a flying splinter told that a shot had got home on our machine.

The fight lasted quite a long time, and after a short period of nervousness I began to enjoy myself thoroughly. I remember waving at one of the Germans as he came up close alongside and then emptying my automatic pistol in the vain hope of hitting the pilot, while my observer blazed away with his Lewis gun. After what seemed like half an hour but in reality was only some ten minutes, yet another German joined in the scrap. This time we were glad to note that he was himself being pursued by a small British monoplane, and the British machine was evidently getting the better of him. Very shortly this latest German machine turned away and started gliding for home. One of the other Germans, who had apparently been slightly damaged by my observer's fire, also turned and made off in the direction of Lille. Whereupon the remaining two aeroplanes, finding their superiority reduced, separated and broke off the fight. We pursued one of them for some distance, but he was faster than we were and eventually eluded us by dodging behind a cloud.

At intervals during the fight I had watched our first enemy circling slowly downwards. He did not appear to be out of control, but I fancied that the pilot was wounded. This was probably the case, for towards the end of the fight I saw him land and capsize in a field almost immediately beneath us – unfortunately in the territory occupied by the Germans.

We returned to the squadron overjoyed with our success, although as a matter of fact the achievement was to lead indirectly to our undoing. Headquarters were very interested in our account of the fight and wanted to have definite confirmation of the crashed German aeroplane. Consequently next day a great friend of mine, Herbert Ward, was sent over with his observer, Buckley, to try and take a photograph of the wreck. They reached the spot and almost immediately disaster overtook them. They were attacked by a Fokker monoplane (then quite a new machine just beginning to make a name for itself) and after a short fight Ward was wounded in the knee and forced to land his aeroplane in the German trenches.

Two days later two machines of the squadron were due to carry out the periodical "long reconnaissance" to Valenciennes. This reconnaissance, whatever its military value may have been, was undoubtedly productive of more casualties than any other job we were required to do. For one thing, although our engines were remarkably good they were not built to stand the strain of a long-distance flight at high speed. Secondly, the Germans – knowing of course all about our "long reconnaissance" flight – were in the habit of lying in wait at Douai aerodrome, rising to attack on our return journey when, short of petrol, we were generally beating against a strong wind.

Now it had been Ward's turn to undertake this flight, but Fate having seen him safely captured decided that it was my turn and that I too should be a prisoner.

The morning of 1 December was wild and blustering with half a gale of wind blowing from the north-west, but in the absence of the Squadron-Commander, who was away on duty, there was no one to stop us from going. Not that we were unwilling to start; personally I had a ridiculous idea that the reconnaissance might be productive of further fighting, from which we would return covered with eternal glory!

Strong and I left the ground at 9 a.m., followed a few minutes later by the second machine which was to act as escort. We steered south while gaining height and crossed the lines in the neighbourhood of Arras. At this point we lost sight of the escorting machine, whose pilot evidently thought that the weather was too bad.[1] Thence we passed over Douai, Denain and Valenciennes. I circled round each of these places while my observer counted the rolling-stock in the railway sidings, and then after going a mile or two beyond Valenciennes we turned to make for home. I had barely set the machine on its westerly course when I began to hear an ominous "knock" in the engine. At first I imagined that it was some little sound which I might have been hearing for a long time without noticing, but within a few minutes it had grown so loud that I realized we were going to have serious trouble. Suddenly there was a loud explosion; pieces of metal flew past my head and the machine was enveloped in a cloud of blue smoke. For one horrible moment I thought we had caught fire, and, switching off the engine and closing the petrol supply, I pushed the control-stick forward and dived the machine towards the earth. It was almost immediately obvious that the machine was not on fire and I gradually brought her back on to an even keel. I switched on the engine and cautiously opened the throttle, whereupon the engine started to run again, although it was now vibrating in a really astounding manner. I peered forward and noticed that with the explosion the greater part of one of the cylinders had disappeared. In spite of this I accelerated the engine as much as I dared, and the awful vibration notwithstanding we managed to make some headway. At this time our height was about 13,000 feet, and our speed between fifty-five and sixty miles an hour. I knew that we were over fifty miles from the lines and, judging from the rate at which the cloud-shadows on the ground were moving, we must have a wind of more than forty miles an hour dead against us. We were slowly losing height and the only thing to be done was to keep a steady course more or less due west. The cold that day, particularly at that height, was intense and, the top of my compass having frosted over, it was with the greatest difficulty that I could steer with any accuracy. I find it almost impossible to describe my feelings as it gradually dawned on me that we were certain to come down within

---

1. See pp. 117–18 for a fuller description of the early stage of this flight.

the enemy lines. I had a sensation of misery, depression and hopelessness, which grew so strong as time went on that I felt almost physically sick. I suppose it was a form of nostalgia – or was it just cowardice? At any rate, I felt unbearably sad at the idea that in all probability I would have to spend that night in a German prison.

At an altitude of about 8,000 feet we saw ahead of us a huge bank of clouds stretching for miles in every direction. There was no means of avoiding these clouds as they lay right on our course, but once inside, with no sight of the earth, the suspense became even worse. We were descending more rapidly now, the engine fast running itself to pieces, still heading due west in the vain hope that we might yet reach the British lines before we were forced to land. Presently we became involved in a series of snow, hail and rain storms, and, what with the shaking of the engine and the tossing and bumping occasioned by the storm, I wondered whether we should ever reach the ground in safety.

We went down in the clouds to within (by the aneroid) 300 feet of the earth and then, just as I was beginning to consider the possibility of hitting tree-tops if we were in hilly country, the clouds broke and we saw the ground not 200 feet beneath us. We were passing over a small village, which I was quite unable to recognize and which, with the exception of one man in civilian clothes, appeared to be deserted. The fields round about were also devoid of people, but it was still pouring with rain which probably accounted for the lack of inhabitants. Of trenches there was not a sign. I had a sickening presentiment that we could not possibly have crossed the war zone during our long flight in the clouds, but there was just a faint chance that we had. In a few minutes' time we were to find out.

The machine could hold the air no longer. Her engine had settled down to a gentle rumble and barely sufficed to drag her along. Two miles past the village we barely cleared the tops of trees standing on a piece of rising ground. Ahead of us there were more trees; we would be unable to cross them and the end of the flight had obviously come. Turning into the wind, I landed in a ploughed field.

Strong and I immediately jumped out and held a hurried consultation. Neither of us really believed that we had crossed the trenches, although we tried to pretend to each other that there was nothing to worry about. I asked Strong to go to the edge of the field and look over the brow of the hill, towards the village, to see if anyone was coming. He had been gone barely a few seconds when I heard a yell; turning round, I saw him rushing back shouting that the Germans were coming. The last glimmer of hope disappeared and there was only one more thing to be done. I went round to the front of the machine, pulled off a rubber connection and set fire to the petrol. By the time the foremost German breasted the hill there was little to be seen of our unfortunate craft but a cloud of smoke and a blaze of flame. Strong rejoined me and we deliberated as to what our next move should be. It was no use running away; the Germans were coming up on two sides, about two-hundred strong, and there was no cover near in which we could take refuge. And so, standing by our burning machine, we awaited their arrival.

They came up at the double, headed by a N.C.O. on a horse. All at once, when they were still some ten yards away, they came to a full stop, checked by a series of loud explosions which suddenly occurred in the aeroplane; the ammunition for the machine gun had evidently reached boiling-point and was beginning to go off. The effect on the Germans was quite extraordinary. Half their number threw themselves flat on their faces while the remainder took refuge in flight. On those who were lying down I tried a few phrases of my choicest German, informing them that we were quite harmless and would like to surrender. To this they made no reply, merely staring at us wide-eyed. It was a strange position to be in; we begged to be allowed to surrender and our enemies either lay flat on the ground in front of us or ran away. I felt like shrugging my shoulders and walking away in disgust, but presently, when our ammunition had burnt itself out, they plucked up courage and started to return. We were soon surrounded by a large crowd of harmless enough individuals, who stood gaping at us as though we had dropped from Mars. Then some German flying officers arrived and introduced themselves to us with much bowing and saluting as if the war had never existed.

It turned out that there was a German aerodrome not far from the village we had passed and that all these men were members of a squadron, which accounted for our chivalrous reception. Apart from this we had committed no particularly war-like act that day, having been forced down by engine trouble far from the heat of battle, the Germans were by no means unfriendly. The only man who was at all nasty was a member of the German field police who, arriving late and very much out of breath to search us for arms, was furious at finding that everything of importance or interest had been burnt in our machine. The German flying officers tried to engage us in an interesting discussion on aero-dynamics, about which we knew nothing, and we took a last look at our ill-fated craft. A few minutes later we walked away with several German officers and reaching a road where a large Mercédès touring car was waiting we were bowed into the most comfortable seats and driven off at a great speed for the village.

The officers' mess was situated in a large and moderately comfortable French château not far from the aerodrome, and here we were entertained to a most excellent lunch, accompanied by numerous wines and liqueurs. After lunch the senior German officers tried to pump us for information. But since we were junior officers in a Flying Corps squadron and the questions they asked us mainly concerned the disposition of corps and divisions, there was little enough we could have told them even if we had wished. As a matter of fact I believe that, generally speaking, Flying Corps officers knew even less of the situation of the armies in France than, say, the average junior Infantry officer. As an instance of this I remember a story about my brother, who while flying in France was forced to land, owing to petrol shortage, in a French army zone. French soldiers immediately rushed up and seeing a machine with strange markings, and a man in unusual clothing, took him to be a German spy and hustled him off to the nearest prison, where he was questioned by a French Intelligence officer. My brother was first asked to what squadron he belonged and this he was able to answer; but having only recently joined his unit, he was quite unable to tell the Frenchman to what brigade, division or corps he was attached. He was even uncertain as to what sector of the front he came from except that his aerodrome was "somewhere near" Béthune. The Frenchman thought all this was most suspicious and kept him in prison for two whole days before a British liaison officer, who happened to know my brother, came and cleared up the mystery.

To return to my own troubles – we stayed in the German mess until four in the afternoon, spending the time chatting with the German pilots. We ascertained that the aerodrome was situated not far south of Bapaume; the wind had blown us slightly off our course, but we had actually headed for the nearest point of our lines, from which we were only about eight miles distant.

When we had said good-bye, bowed and saluted to each member of the officers' mess, where we had been very well treated, we were ushered into another car in which we were driven off to St. Quentin. The journey took nearly two hours and it was dark before we got there. We were taken first of all to the Army Headquarters, where we were again examined and pumped for information, all kinds of tricks being played on us in an attempt to extract important news which, perhaps fortunately, we did not in reality possess. The Headquarters seemed to be full of Jews, and as a matter of fact I believe that, as far as Germany was concerned, a safe distance behind the lines was throughout the war considered essential by large numbers of this race. Towards eight o'clock in the evening we left the Headquarters accompanied by a German officer who said that he was taking us to an excellent hotel. We embarked in a cab and after a few minutes' drive we arrived at the "hotel", which much to our disgust turned out to be the French civil prison. It was a large building, capable of accommodating several hundred malefactors, and I suppose that as far as such places go it was all one could desire. But at that time, still unaccustomed to prisons, the whole place struck me as being very gloomy and our reception by the head warder distinctly chilly. We were locked into separate cells, each containing a wooden bed, table, stool, and a most unpleasant smell; but I was too tired to worry much and soon fell asleep.

Next morning I awaited the coming of the Germans with impatience, thinking that we would naturally be sent into Germany at once. No one came near my cell, except to push in a tray of food, until late in the afternoon when I was informed that I could go for an hour's exercise in the courtyard. Here I met Strong, a British Infantry officer named Hunter who had just been captured in a trench raid, and two French officers. The general impression among these prisoners was that we should be kept in St. Quentin for some days more. I asked one of the Frenchmen what he thought of our chances of escape if we tried from jail or from the train going to Germany. He seemed quite positive that it would be better to wait until we were settled in Germany, where we would be able to obtain the necessary maps and civilian clothing. The prison was certainly very strongly guarded and, as I could think of no method of getting out with any degree of safety, I gave up the idea.

The next few days dragged slowly by, punctuated by occasional visits from a German officer who again tried to elicit information. I found my existence in solitary confinement inexpressibly boring, although on the whole we were not badly treated and the commandant of the prison, a German Major, did his best for us and made sure that fairly good food was sent in from a small restaurant in the town. One day during the exercise hour, the commandant suggested that the prisoners of war should all have their photographs taken. We had no particular objection to make and a day or two later he presented each of us with a copy of the photograph as a memento of our stay at St. Quentin.

At the end of a week I was informed that I should be leaving for Germany at once. For some reason or other, Strong was not to travel with me, but I found that Hunter, the other British prisoner, was going in his place. Just after the midday meal we were taken out of our cells and, escorted by a German officer and two or three other men, we travelled down to the station in a cab. On arrival we found that there was about half an hour's wait before the train was due and we were made to spend the time in walking up and down the platform in the company of our German officer. The station was crowded with troops going on leave and we were the object of considerable attention. It was practically my first appearance in public as a prisoner of war and I felt rather wretched at being stared at by such a mass of Germans, but they were for the most part quite friendly. At last our train came in and we were put into a second-class carriage, accompanied by a new German officer and three armed guards. The journey was really very comfortable and, as no one else was allowed in our carriage, there was plenty of room for us all. I was very surprised at our travelling second class as I had imagined that we should be consigned to a goods waggon or a cattle-truck, but I found out later that, when only one or two prisoners were travelling accompanied by a German officer, it was usual for them to get somewhat better treatment.

In spite of this comparative comfort I was very depressed as I watched the country-side slip past the windows, and realized that this would be the last glimpse of France I should get for probably many months to come. Late in the afternoon we passed Le Cateau, where we could see on the sky-line some of the old British trenches. At dusk we crossed the Belgian–French frontier and after that there was little to do except sleep. During the evening we were served with quite a respectable meal, sent in from the dining-car. We were allowed to have whatever we liked on the menu, the German officer paying for us. The German leave-train was certainly very well organized and could not be compared to the awful trains behind the British front. I was told that the train was run with very few stops, right through to Berlin with sleeping-cars going on to Warsaw and even as far as Brest-Litovsk.

Just after passing Liége, the train came to a standstill and, knowing how close we were to the Belgian–Dutch frontier, I felt that it was essential to find out if there were any means of leaving the train unobserved. The only possible way seemed to be through the lavatory window, but after a visit of inspection – accompanied by one of the guards – I found that for many reasons this was out of the question. I am sure that even if I had succeeded in getting away it would have been of no avail, dressed as I was in British uniform and without maps or money, but it was most discouraging to pass so close to Holland without having a chance to make an attempt. A little later our train crossed the German frontier and ran into the station of Herbesthal. At this place there were crowds of cheering civilians on the platform to welcome the men coming home on leave. Every one was in the best of spirits and I thought rather bitterly of my own leave which had been due this very month; in fact I had foolishly hoped to spend Christmas in England.

After leaving Herbesthal there were no more stops till we got to Cologne at about half-past ten. Here we learned that there were no trains to Mainz, which turned out to be our destination, until two o'clock in the morning. Our German officer naturally preferred not to wait and, having handed us over to the station guard, he said good-bye to us and disappeared. Our guards took us down a subway running beneath the station and locked us up in a small waiting-room. The place was devoid of furniture and, having nothing to eat or drink and nowhere to sleep, the time passed very slowly. We spent the greater part of our three hours' wait in studying the inscriptions on the whitewashed walls. The waiting-room was evidently reserved for the use of prisoners of war, as countless names, generally with the regiment and date, were scribbled from the floor to the ceiling. It was curious to note that in some cases a prisoner had written a message to a friend in the hope that he would pass that way, and that very often the message had been replied to, sometimes many months later. All nationalities were represented, and

I added my own name with the number of my squadron and the date. At length our guards returned to fetch us and just before one o'clock we got into a slow train for Mainz. This time conditions were not as comfortable, as the train was packed and we travelled third class, being without a German officer.

It was nearly four o'clock before we reached Mainz, hungry and tired out. We were at once marched up to the camp in the old citadel situated on high ground just above the railway station of "Mainz South". As we approached the entrance two or three sentries appeared from shadowy corners of the gateway and, after interrogating our guards, the main gates were slowly opened and we were led in through the gloomy portals. We passed beneath a tall archway and came to a deserted barrack square surrounded by a few trees, through the branches of which shone the rays of a dozen arc-lamps. At that hour of the night, the silence only broken by the soft sound of our footsteps on sandy soil and the whispering of a cold wind, the camp presented a weird and uncanny appearance. As we walked across to the guard-room a police dog came and sniffed at our heels and growled, doubtful as to whether he should attack or let us pass. A little way off, in the shadow of one of the trees, a sentry stood motionless; in the distance, a glint of steel came from the bayonets of men patrolling the boundaries of the camp.

On reaching the guard-room, we were handed over to the sergeant in charge who, after consultation with some other authority in a room next door, led us into one of the tall buildings which surrounded the barrack square. Following our guide, we wandered about in a series of dark, cold passages where, on the stone floors, our footsteps rang out bravely with a metallic sound, like the clash of steel; we were at length shown into a large room containing at least a dozen empty beds. And the German having gone out, locking the door behind him, we at once lay down and forgetting our troubles were almost immediately asleep.

II

It was broad daylight and the whole camp was astir when we were awakened by a German orderly and given some much-needed food. We remained locked up in our room until the evening, when we were taken down into the basement and given a bath, while our clothes were removed for fumigation – a procedure intended to prevent the spread of any disease which might have been brought back from the war zone. Our disinfection completed, we were conducted to the *Kommandantur* and once again questioned for information concerning the British forces. The German officer who examined me pretended to be extremely interested in aeronautical developments, asking me numberless questions concerning different types of aeroplanes, about most of which I confess I knew less than nothing. We conversed in German – I had not realized the value of concealing my knowledge of the language – and in the middle of one of his sentences I recognized a familiar English name. On my asking him to repeat the question he said:

"Do you know anything about the new giant Crosse and Blackwell aeroplane?"

For a moment I was taken aback and could only stare at him.

"Surely you must have heard about it," he said. "One of the new prisoners told me all about it the other day; he said that it was well known in England. I understand that it is to be fitted with two wonderful new engines of great power made by Huntley something – I forget the exact name."

"Huntley and Palmer," I suggested timidly, suddenly tumbling to the hoax of which this poor man was the victim.

"Yes, yes," he said, at once very keen, "that's it. Can you tell me anything about it? I am always so interested in new aeroplanes!"

I am afraid that I was not quick-witted enough to pitch him a really perfect yarn, but by the time I had finished with him I think he was convinced that Berlin was going to be bombed that night. At any rate he was delighted with my answers and presented me with a handful of cigarettes, of which I was in great need. Soon afterwards I was dismissed and permitted to go and join the other prisoners in the camp. I was never able to find out for certain who was the inventor of the marvellous aeroplane, but I have an idea that it was a British prisoner named Medlicott.

Hunter and I were allotted beds in a room of French officers with whom, personally, I got on well. The camp, I learned, contained about six-hundred prisoners, the majority of whom were French or Russian. Of the British, who numbered about a hundred, the greater part had been captured just after Mons. One or two of them were old acquaintances of mine and I heard at first hand many tales of German brutality at the beginning of the war. Most of these stories have been told and retold until they seem quite common-place events, but some of them still retain their original horror. I was told of the cruelty to British wounded; how, with their wounds untended, they were herded into cattle-trucks where the floor was many inches deep in filth and left there for days while the train banged its way back to Germany. There was no medical attention, practically no food. At the stations where the train stopped, the wounded, many of whom were positively at their last gasp, would beg for water which the Germans almost invariably refused. German women – women, mark you! – wearing the uniform and badges of the Red Cross, brought bowls of water or boiling soup from the station buffets, spat into them, and threw the contents into the faces of the unfortunate men, whom they hated above all their enemies, because England was the country they feared.

The treatment of the unwounded officers was also pretty bad. Occasionally beaten with rifle butts by their guards on their way to the first camp allotted to prisoners of war, they were frequently rushed by mobs of infuriated civilians, who shouted curses at them accompanied, more often than not, by much spitting and throwing of stones. Conditions in this camp, near Torgau, were awful. Prisoners were crowded together in the meanest of huts, without bedding and with the minimum quantity of food necessary to keep them alive. They were at all times exposed to the brutality of the German guards, and the first prisoner ever to attempt an escape was brought back next day with his throat cut.

These events occurred while the Germans thought they were certain to win the war, but as soon as the wild enthusiasm waned, and they began to have doubts about the result, their treatment of prisoners improved considerably. At the time I reached Mainz, the authorities, except for occasional bursts of ill-temper, were really quite docile and the majority of prison camps were comparatively pleasant places in which to live. When later in the war the Germans once more had cause to hope for victory, their treatment of prisoners deteriorated, until in the spring of 1918 it was once again almost as bad as in the early days.

Among the older prisoners were very few who had any intention of trying to escape. This was partly due to their ill-treatment, which lowered both their morale and their physique, and partly to the advice given them by the senior British officers, whose opinion naturally carried great weight. There were two or three of these senior officers who honestly believed that it was almost impossible for anyone to succeed in getting away from a camp, and quite impossible to cross a neutral frontier. The Germans had informed them that, in the event of any prisoner escaping, very severe reprisals would be taken on those remaining. This made British officers very chary of attempting to escape; it also meant that those who did try took great trouble to see that their schemes were as nearly perfect in every detail as was humanly possible.

Shortly after my arrival, on Christmas Eve, an Irishman, Lieutenant Breen of the Intelligence Corps, and Lieutenant du Baudiez of the French army, succeeded in escaping. Disguised as French orderlies, they had followed a working party into the coal store under a disused gateway in some old ramparts forming one side of the camp, and had forced open the gate leading out. There was no sentry at this point and they were able to walk away unobserved. As they had good civilian clothes with them and Breen talked excellent German, they went straight to Mainz station, where they took a train to Wiesbaden. Here they changed trains and went on to Frankfurt. They had to break the journey at this latter town, having arrived too late to catch the last train out. They decided to wait in the town till next morning and put up at a small hotel. It may seem rather a risky thing to do, but in this case it was quite successful, and I have heard of it being done without difficulty on at least two other occasions. Next morning they unfortunately missed the first train, owing I believe to the inaccuracy of their time-table, and consequently they had to wait an hour or two in the station waiting-room. Eventually they were arrested, just as the next train was due to leave, by police who had traced them from Mainz. They were sent to prison for a short time and subsequently Breen was transferred to Fort Zorndorf, Cüstrin. This was the only escape made while I was at Mainz, and, as far as I know, the only occasion on which anyone succeeded in getting out, although of course there were many attempts.

A week after this really brilliant attempt a meeting was called by the senior British officer, at which the subject of escaping was talked over. It seems extraordinary now, but the question whether it was right for a prisoner to attempt to escape and get home to fight again was actually discussed. There were even those who, oblivious of the fact that we had not given our parole and that escape has always been officially recognized, firmly believed that a prisoner, having once surrendered, had no right to make an attempt if he was forbidden by his captors to do so. These men qualified all attempted escapes as undignified and as showing a complete lack of discipline, but their strongest argument, the expected punishment of the remaining prisoners, was no longer valid, the Germans having taken no reprisals since Breen's attempt. On the whole the advocates of prison-breaking won the day, and from this time on escaping began to gain in popularity. Personally, I detested being a prisoner and I disliked the camp at Mainz intensely. And after all, escaping from captivity must have been one of man's earliest adventures. Surely anyone deprived of his freedom tries to regain it. At all events it was not long before – with Breen's example to guide me – I began to turn my thoughts in the right direction.

For anyone completely inexperienced and having yet to learn all the tricks of the trade, Mainz was undoubtedly a difficult camp from which to escape. I racked my brains to think of some safe way out, and I seized every possible occasion on which to talk over various schemes with other prisoners. I soon found several others who were equally determined to break out. Chief among these was Medlicott, a well-known Royal Flying Corps pilot, who had then just been captured and later on became one of the most daring and successful of all prison-breakers. Many were the wild schemes we discussed, most of them either impracticable or far too risky. At length we decided to try tunnelling, although in Mainz of all camps the difficulties were well nigh insuperable. The point from which we were to start caused endless argument, but eventually we fixed on a small disused cellar in a passage close to the main bathroom in the basement of one of the buildings.

There was a serious disadvantage to this scheme: the baths were only open on three days a week and then only at certain stated times. Moreover, a sentry was always on guard at the bathroom door and consequently it was only very rarely that we were able to work. We carried towels very ostentatiously and slipped past the sentry when his back was turned, but often he was too watchful and many days were wasted. Nevertheless digging was started early in January and by the end of the month we had not only sunk a shaft some four feet deep in the floor of the cellar, but we had also driven a tunnel some two or three feet in the direction of the ramparts. By this time a small gang of workmen had been formed, comprising Mulcahy-Morgan, Medlicott, Beverley Robinson and myself, all of us pilots in the Royal Flying Corps. Herbert Ward came on from hospital at about this time and also joined the party.

As soon as the work had got well under way, we became so keen on the job that, as often happens, we rather neglected taking sufficient precautions, with the result that on several occasions one or another of the Germans must undoubtedly have caught sight of us entering the cellar. One day when two of us went down to put in an afternoon's work, we found the door of the cellar not only locked, but fitted with an extra padlock. A few days later it became evident that the Germans were aware of the identity of some of the members of the gang, for at a moment's notice Medlicott and I, in company with several of our room mates, were transferred to another camp. Mulcahy-Morgan, who was being treated at the Mainz hospital for a broken jaw and several other wounds received at the time of his capture, was not moved till some time later, but Beverley Robinson and Ward were sent elsewhere soon after us.

At 8.30 on the morning of 4 February (1916) Medlicott and I were suddenly warned that we were to leave the camp in two hours' time. This caused us considerable consternation and a great deal of hurried packing, for although we had very little real baggage, yet we had some vague notion of escaping en route, and we devoted the short time left to us in endeavouring to collect and hide the rudiments of an escaping kit. It was obvious that good maps and a compass were the first essentials, but these articles were almost unobtainable at Mainz. Next in order of importance were civilian clothes and money. I was well provided with the latter commodity, which I had purchased from some French officers. Many of the French captured at Maubeuge had brought with them almost all the possessions they owned, including a large amount of French gold. I got into touch with one or two of these men and in exchange for English cheques I obtained some fifty Louis in gold coin. As far as civilian clothes were concerned, a battered old felt hat purchased by Medlicott from a German workman was the only article in our possession. Being so ill-equipped, it was evident that we should have to abandon any idea of escaping during the journey. The prospect of a change, however, and the possibilities for getting away which a new camp might offer, made us feel quite reconciled to the idea of leaving in such a hurry and so unprepared.

When at about ten o'clock we were marched out of the camp, we found that the party consisted of a dozen French officers and half a dozen British, including Medlicott and myself. At Mainz station we embarked in a train bound for Wiesbaden. Here we changed into a slow train – so delightfully slow that it was difficult to restrain oneself from jumping off – and after winding about through some really lovely hill-country and forest we came, four hours later, to the little town of Weilburg.

III

Weilburg lies in a very picturesque country in the northern part of the Taunus forest, about forty miles east of the Rhine, and the camp itself was certainly the most beautifully situated of those in which I was confined. At the time of our arrival it was already occupied by one-hundred-and-fifty Russian and twenty French officers; also four elderly Belgian Generals, dressed, to our inexpressible delight, in civilian clothes. There were no other British officers, for which fact we were rather thankful, as we felt it gave us more chance of working out our schemes for escape undisturbed by ethical discussions on the why and wherefore.

Medlicott and I at once started to make a thorough examination of the camp and its defences. The place had originally been a school for German N.C.O.s – which accounted for a gymnasium – but new barracks had recently been built for them on a hill overlooking the town. We inhabited a three-storied brick building, some sixty yards long by twenty yards wide, surrounded by about an acre and a half of ground. The building stood on a flat sandy ledge at the bottom of a ravine through which ran the River Lahn. Behind the building was a stone wall, from which the ground rose steeply in terraces for a distance of a hundred yards to the outskirts of the town. The river curved round in front of the camp and formed the boundary for nearly half the perimeter. On the river bank was a wire-netting fence ten feet high and a raised boardwalk for the sentries. The remainder of the camp was enclosed by wooden palisades, surmounted by barbed wire, and patrolled on the outside by sentries.

Facing the river on the ground floor of our building was an archway, which had originally formed the main entrance. This archway led to a large vaulted hall with several doors, leading on one side to the canteen and to the stairs up to the first floor, and on the other side to the dining-hall. At the back of this main hall was a small green door, partly concealed behind a pile of wood and nailed up. This door at once aroused our curiosity and we determined to discover on the first possible opportunity what lay behind it. We did not have to wait long; on the second night after our arrival we were invited by some of the Russian officers to join them after dinner and discuss a few bottles of beer. After several bottles had been got rid of, the Russians asked us guardedly if we intended to escape and, on our replying in the affirmative, invited us to join forces with them. They expounded their plans and it turned out that a tunnel had actually been started behind the mysterious green door. We listened eagerly to the details and came to the conclusion that the scheme was very likely to be successful. The tunnel had been commenced by seven or eight Russians, who had prized open the green door and found that it led into an underground passage running nearly the whole length of the building. It had evidently been used as a store-room or cellar at one time, but, the door now being nailed up, it was to be supposed that the Germans did not intend using it any more. Work was impossible by day owing to the number of Germans constantly in the building. On the other hand, at night, although the staff of the *Kommandantur* slept in a room on the first floor, there was nobody at all in the basement. The doors leading down to the dining-room and the canteen were locked after nine, but one of the Russians very skilfully moulded some pass-keys out of soft white-metal spoons. Once the doors had ceased to be an obstruction, there was nothing to prevent work in the cellar being carried on all night. When Medlicott and I joined the gang, not very much progress had been made owing to the difficulty of breaking through the foundation wall. But at length the large stones used in its construction were removed with the help of a short iron crowbar, which one of the prisoners had managed to purloin from the canteen. After breaking through the wall we struck soft earth and the digging became comparatively easy.

It was found that the handiest instrument for digging in the very confined space at our disposal was an ordinary table-knife, and the soil as it was scraped out of the mouth of the tunnel was spread along the floor of the cellar, where it would be less noticeable in the unlikely event of a German inspection. The shaft was aimed to bring us eventually to a point some little distance outside one of the wooden palisades surrounding the camp. It was estimated that the total length of the completed tunnel would not be more than fifteen yards; working for the greater part of each night, we should be ready to leave the camp in just over a month from the time of piercing the foundation wall. Our progress was greatly delayed, however, by the looseness of the soil, forcing us to prop up the sides and roof of the tunnel with pieces of board, which were obtained either from old packing-cases in the canteen or sometimes from the firewood supplied to us. After we had been working for a week or more, eight more British officers arrived from another camp. They were none of them averse to escaping; three were particularly keen. These were Campbell (Norfolk Regiment), Elliot (Cheshire Regiment) and Stewart (Gordon Highlanders). We at once got them to join the tunnel gang, and with two of those who had come from Mainz, Kemp and Grantham (both R.F.C.), we formed a strong party of British workers. We were able to insist on working almost every night, from 11 p.m. to 4 a.m., thus getting rid of one or two useless Russians who, now that the scheme had got fairly under way, seemed to have lost all enthusiasm in the actual work. Of the remaining Russians one was a Colonel in the Engineers, and we frequently sought his advice on the construction of the tunnel. The propping up of the sides and roof became, as we advanced, more than ever necessary, and we were afraid that we were getting too near the surface. The Russian engineer thought differently, assured us that all was well and that we need have no fear. Unfortunately we relied far too much on this view and disaster followed.

Early in March we had reached a point almost beneath the palisade and we had hopes of completing the tunnel within a fortnight. For nearly a month we had experienced a succession of sharp frosts, accompanied by a certain amount of snow. But now a thaw set in and, on going to work one night, we found water trickling in through every crack and crevice, bringing down miniature avalanches of earth and stones; the tunnel roof was rapidly subsiding. We worked hard all night to prevent a catastrophe, using all the available boards and supports. It was of no avail; the end came next morning. Early in the day, two Germans happened to be passing the end of the building carrying a heavy ladder. One of them stumbled and, in recovering his balance, stamped on a spot immediately above the tunnel. The earth gave way beneath him and started to crumble all round. It was raining heavily at the time and within half an hour the water had washed away a large amount of soil, leaving a gaping hole in the ground. A party of Germans was immediately sent to examine the spot and, after an hour or two's work, they had dug up the greater part of the tunnel and unearthed a number of props and planks. One of these – the lid of a box of provisions – unfortunately bore Stewart's name in large letters and all the British were immediately sent for by the commandant. We were closely questioned but naturally we denied all knowledge of the matter. The Germans were fortunately unable to prove that we had taken active part in the digging and, beyond telling us that if we made another attempt we should all immediately be shot, the commandant took no action.

We were horribly upset at our failure, especially when all seemed to be going so well. The Russians on the other hand, being mostly confirmed pessimists, told us they had long ago foreseen the end and, while assuring us of their conviction that any attempt must end in failure, immediately started digging elsewhere. This time they began to work in a corner of the gymnasium. We helped them for a period; but the attempt was quite hopeless: the shaft was directed straight at the side of the steep hill overlooking the camp, and after the first few feet the workers struck solid rock, against which nothing short of dynamite would have been of any use. This did not deter them in the least and they went on, without hope and therefore content, for several months.

I am convinced that very few Russians ever undertook the organizing and planning of an escape with any hope of getting out of Germany, but were solely impelled by the necessity of having some sort of a conspiracy or intrigue which would give them that delightful feeling of mystery and depression characteristic of the Russian mind.

But, if the Russians were keen on conspiracies and became cheerfully miserable when a scheme failed, they were also invariably anxious to find some scapegoat who could be accused of having betrayed their plans to the Germans. And concerning this side of the Russian character, an extraordinary, but none the less true, story was told me by several of the older prisoners. A Russian officer was supposed to have sold his knowledge of a prisoners' tunnel to the German commandant. On hearing of this the other Russians in the camp convened a court-martial, before which the alleged traitor was summarily arraigned. After a short trial he was found guilty and sentenced to death. The president of the court then gave the victim the choice of three deaths: by hanging – and here a suitable piece of rope was produced – by cutting his throat, for which purpose a razor was laid before him, or by shooting. For the last alternative a rusty old pistol and two cartridges had been unearthed from Heaven knows where. Faced with these gruesome objects, the terrified captive broke away from his guards and, taking a header through several panes of glass, jumped out of the window. The room from which he jumped was three stories from the ground and the unfortunate man crashed to earth, breaking both arms and a leg. All this happened in the dead of night and the German guards hearing the fall and thinking no doubt that a prisoner was trying to escape, dashed up and finished him off with their bayonets. The Russians in the windows above, on seeing the end of their one-time brother-officer, merely shrugged their shoulders, exclaiming "*Nitchevo*", and returned to their strong drinks.

An inordinate desire for large quantities of the strongest of spirits seems to be another characteristic of the Russian nation and, at times when they were unable to obtain a sufficient supply of ordinary beverages, they would descend to almost anything. This was not, of course, the case with the better class of educated officers, but for those who had risen rapidly during the war, or had perhaps been promoted from the ranks – those in fact who represented the masses – gin, methylated spirits, eau-de-Cologne or even turpentine were positive necessities. A certain amount of bad wine and a large quantity of weak beer were obtainable in the canteen, but no Russian dinner, given to celebrate a birthday, a saint's day, or an imaginary victory, was ever complete unless some sort of neat alcohol was served as a liqueur.

On the other hand, the Russians are excellent singers.

As far as traitors are concerned, after the failure of the first tunnel at Weilburg, the Russians became extremely suspicious of the head of the French orderlies. This man, known as Joseph, was certainly a most peculiar character. He wore the uniform of a sailor in the French navy, although he was reported to have been captured in a cavalry regiment. His own stories of his exploits and amazing bravery on the western front were a continual source of amusement to us, and he asserted that he had been awarded the cross of the Legion of Honour and the Military Medal several times over. The Russians, as was to be expected, took a serious view of his peculiarities, and accused him of being a German agent. A court of inquiry was assembled and, late one night, Joseph was seized and brought, struggling violently, into the room where it was to be held. The whole thing was a perfect farce; Joseph emotionally protesting his innocence while the self-appointed president of the court, a ridiculous little Cossack, shouted at him in Russian and made various gestures expressive of hanging. The court finally broke up in confusion, everybody wanting to talk at once, and Joseph was let off with a caution.

In spite of their futility, we managed to make use of some of the Russians who had corrupted one or two of the German guards. Through them I managed to exchange half of the French gold which I had purchased at Mainz for German money, and with some of the remaining gold I bought various odds and ends of civilian clothing from Russians and Frenchmen. One of the Cossacks also succeeded in getting us some maps and a couple of compasses, doubtless obtained, at an exorbitant cost, from one of the Germans. Good civilian clothes were always difficult to procure, but some sort of kit was fairly easy to contrive, certain portions of the Allied uniforms lending themselves to conversion. Prisoners whose uniforms had worn out were generally permitted by the Germans to buy rough civilian coats of a semi-military pattern, which were embroidered by the camp tailor with shoulder straps and red stripes; when the clothes were required for escaping purposes, the stripes and other military badges were removed without any trouble. Trousers could generally be made from any dark cloth, and at a pinch our own khaki trousers would do. It was not so easy to obtain headgear, and this difficulty was present in all camps throughout Germany. After one or two trials we discovered that a soft felt hat, such as the Germans almost invariably wore, was terribly hard to manufacture. On very rare occasions one would be smuggled out in a prisoner's parcel from England, but generally we had to content ourselves with rather poor quality caps, made out of dark cloth or government blankets.

It was nearly impossible to obtain articles of civilian clothing by bribery, German soldiers being unable to purchase them. In practically every camp there was at least one German whom one could bribe with such luxuries as chocolate or white bread, but there was, of course, great risk attached to this proceeding and, beyond getting a few maps, there was very little these men could do.

While thinking over various methods of journeying to the frontier, apart from the immediate problem of how to break out of the camp, we were struck by the idea of making forged passports or permits to travel. At first we had no very clear knowledge of the appearance of these passes as made in Germany, but soon a stroke of good luck put us in possession of the necessary information.

An English parson who had lived in Berlin before the war was occasionally permitted to go round the various camps to look after the spiritual welfare of the British. Some of us, I am afraid, needed personal freedom more than the consolations of the Church and, when the parson came to Weilburg, we turned his visit to a more practical end. While he was holding a short service in the basement, Medlicott and I examined a small black bag he had incautiously left in our room. The first thing we saw was a brand-new railway time-table, containing a small-scale map of Germany and the various frontiers. Furthermore, on looking through a bundle of papers, we found a large number of passes signed by various highly placed German military officers. These passes, authorizing the holder to travel from one end of Germany to the other, were just what we needed. We had obviously no right to touch any of the parson's belongings, but, after debating the matter for some minutes, we decided that for once the end would justify the means. Replacing the majority of the passes, we retained three or four as well as the time-table. The parson left shortly afterwards without noticing anything, although I believe he was very perturbed on discovering his loss some hours later.

I still feel that I owe him an apology, but as a matter of fact his papers were of inestimable value to us and formed the basis of a large number of forged passes, many of which were successfully used by escaping prisoners.

Later on in the war prisoners were forbidden to possess typewriters, but at this time Stewart was the proud owner of one of these machines and for the next few days we were busy banging out a variety of permits, containing, as well as the usual wording, a description of the particular prisoner to whom the pass was to be issued. The only real difficulty we experienced was the making of the rubber stamp, consisting of the name of the town and a German eagle or some other emblem. After a lot of practice we were able, with a safety razor blade, to carve very passable imitations on a slab of india-rubber taken from the sole of a tennis shoe.

We had heard rumours from time to time that arrangements were being made, through various neutral governments, for prisoners to be taken for walks outside of their camps. These rumours eventually materialized and twice a week we were allowed out for two hours, on parole and escorted by numerous guards. These walks gave us some much-needed exercise and towards the end of March we had, not only collected an excellent assortment of escaping kit, but we were also comparatively fit physically.

We still had no very definite plans, but, should we succeed in finding a sure way out, Medlicott and I intended to travel by train together in the direction of Holland. At about this time, however, Elliot asked me to join him in a scheme of his own devising, and after some hesitation I agreed. It turned out that there was only room for two of us in this plan, and Elliot was forced to leave Medlicott and Stewart out of it. This somehow led to a violent quarrel – a common enough thing in prison where, after months of close confinement, tempers were generally short – and almost complete estrangement followed between Medlicott and Stewart on the one side and Elliot and myself on the other. For weeks we rarely spoke to each other and we remained stupidly in ignorance of each other's plans.

Elliot's idea was to get into the *Kommandantur* on a Wednesday night, when we would find four or five baskets containing the camp's dirty washing. Two of these, each of which was large enough to hold a man, would be partially emptied and we would be shut in by one of our friends. According to the usual routine the baskets would be carried out early next morning by French orderlies, put on a cart and taken to the station. A railway journey of twenty miles in a closed truck would give us an opportunity of getting out. It sounded most promising, but there were two main objections. First, the German staff slept in a room next to the *Kommandantur* and we should have to be careful not to wake them while removing the unnecessary washing;

secondly, the baskets were on the small side and therefore, we should be horribly cramped, possibly suffocated.

I had the good fortune to get hold of the *Kommandantur* key one day when no one was looking, and provided with this Elliot and I made a midnight excursion to see what the baskets were like. Except for the fact that we should have to break the padlocks off in order to get in – and to replace them we bought later some similar locks in the canteen – the scheme appeared sound.

I shall never forget Elliot on this occasion. He wore a sort of tweed cloak with numerous pockets for the various tools we needed and for any loot we might acquire; it also served as a shade for his electric torch. Creeping round the office, inspecting the baskets and examining the papers on the office desk, he looked for all the world like an old time conspirator, oblivious of the fact that whenever he stooped down a beam of light shone backwards from between his legs, generally striking the windows. I had several bad scares, but fortunately nobody saw the light and, our inspection completed, we crept back to bed.

After a few more preparations we arranged to carry out the attempt during the following week. A day or so later I was in the canteen and noticing a bottle of black hair dye, I waited for a moment when I was unobserved and put it in my pocket. I thought it would be an excellent idea to add to my disguise when escaping by dyeing my hair, which is normally red. Accordingly, on the day before we were due to go, I applied it in large quantities. The effect, so the directions said, was instantaneous and I was very annoyed when several hours later I could still notice no difference. That night we went to the *Kommandantur* in our civilian kit, accompanied by assistants – Kemp and Grantham. To our great disappointment we found that only the three smallest baskets were being sent; there was apparently not enough washing to fill the other baskets. The small ones were useless and we had to postpone our plans for another week.

Next day my head itched horribly, and in the afternoon I was sitting outside reading a book, when I noticed that people were staring at me in rather a strange way. Presently some British came along and burst out roaring with laughter. I asked what the matter was and for answer one of them produced a looking-glass. I caught sight of my head and nearly fainted. The dye had worked – my hair was a bright purple!

Washing, scrubbing and brushing wouldn't get that wretched stuff off; at last I had to get my head cropped before I dared appear in public again. Even then it was weeks before all traces of the dye, which had caused my hair to fall out in handfulls, had finally disappeared. The worst of it was that the Germans noticed that something was up and used to laugh every time they saw me. It was very fortunate that our plans had not succeeded when we intended, as a man with purple hair would have aroused an unpleasant amount of interest.

IV

Medlicott and Stewart had meanwhile almost completed their preparations, and asked us to delay our scheme until they had tried theirs so as to avoid giving the Germans any grounds for suspicion. We agreed to this proposal and offered our help, which, owing to the absurd quarrel we had had, they did not seem to want, and we even had difficulty in discovering the details of their plan before it was carried out.

Roughly described, the idea was to push a plank out of a certain window at the back of our building, where at one point the wall opposite jutted out to within twelve feet of the building, forming a buttress to the terraces. On top of this part of the wall there was a small piece of level ground, and from it a path led up through the terraced gardens towards the town. As soon as the plank forming a temporary bridge was in position, the lights were to be fused – a comparatively easy matter, the uninsulated wires being attached to the wall of our building at a point close to one of the windows. Medlicott and Stewart would then cross the plank, jump on to the buttress and make their way up the path to a road leading out of the town. If the alarm were raised, an attempt was to be made to haul in the board at once, but if the first two got clear it would be left in position and those of us who were ready could follow fifteen minutes later. We all thought it rather a risky business, but at any rate it would soon be over once the plank was ready. Nearly all the British were enlisted as accomplices, and Stewart typed out elaborate instructions for each one of them. The top of a bench in the dining-hall was to serve as the plank, and pieces of rope were manufactured from sheets.

The attempt was made on 18 March. The room from which the plank was to be lowered was inhabited by one of the four Belgian generals, whom I have already mentioned.[2] At half-past ten at night Medlicott went in and informed the officer in question of their intention to escape from his window. The general at first did not understand and, when he did, refused to permit anything of the sort. Stewart then tried to explain matters more clearly, although his French was almost as bad as Medlicott's, but the result was the same. At this point, a little tact and the help of an interpreter might possibly have pacified the old man, who was terrified of what the Germans might do to him if he was brought up afterwards as an accomplice; but Medlicott was determined to get out that night and refused to waste time in arguing. The general thereupon threatened to inform the Germans, and when Stewart told him they would use force if necessary the general started to yell for help. There was no alternative. They fell upon him, gagged him and tied him down to his bed. For the remainder of the night he was guarded by one of the accomplices.

The plank and the other gear were now made ready, but Medlicott did not intend to start work on the final stage till about three o'clock in the morning when the sentries would be less watchful, and when, from the appearance of the sky, it would probably be raining. Meanwhile the accomplices were posted at various points and sent in half-hourly reports on the weather, the behaviour of the sentries, and the condition of the general. Eventually Stewart asked me to go in and see if I could do anything for the captive. I made my way to his bedside and explained everything very politely, promising him immediate release if he would be good enough to permit the other two to escape. His gag was then removed to allow him to give his answer, but as he merely bawled out *Assassin*, it was quickly replaced. After this he struggled so violently that a fresh accomplice had to be detailed to sit on his chest.

Just after two o'clock it began to drizzle; by three o'clock it was raining hard, and operations started. The plank – which, by the way, could not

2. These officers had been living in retirement in Brussels, were over military age and had not taken up arms at the outbreak of the war. There was therefore no military reason why they should be held prisoners, but the Germans probably wished to swell their list of important captives.

be seen by the sentry as it had been carefully blackened on its under side – was now lowered from the general's window to the window of a room immediately below. This lower window was heavily barred, and the plank was jammed into position at the top of the bars; here Elliot and Campbell were stationed and fixed the plank securely with the help of two stout wooden pegs. Directly this was done, they signalled up that all was ready. To the outer end of the plank were attached two ropes which were now made fast to the upper window. Word was then passed down the corridor to put out the lights, which was done by touching the two live wires just outside the building with a third piece of wire. This caused a short-circuit and every light in the camp went out. At the same moment Medlicott and Stewart crossed the improvised bridge, jumped over on to the terrace, and started crawling up the slope.

So far none of the sentries had noticed anything, and all would have been well if the plank had been left in position. But, in his excitement, one of the men in the upper room let go of the supporting ropes and the pegs in the lower window being unable to take the whole weight, the plank crashed to the ground twenty feet below. To me, at the other end of the corridor, the crash sounded like a rifle shot, and it was followed by the blowing of whistles and shouts from the guards. From my window I could just make out two figures crawling up the opposite bank; below the sentries running about getting ready to shoot. It seemed certain that they had not yet seen anything, but any moment they might glance up the bank. To distract their attention, I started smashing the windows with a poker taken from the stove in our room. After I had broken two or three, I snatched at the nearest thing I could find and hurled it out. The sentry below yelled for assistance to the rapidly assembling guards; "a prisoner to escape trying was," he shrieked, "already his luggage out-thrown had been". That man had a funny idea of escaping kit; the object I had just thrown out happened to be a brass spittoon!

I ran back to our room where all the accomplices had gathered, and we quickly undressed and got into bed. The expected visit from the Germans did not occur for some time, however, and Elliot and I went back to see the general. We loosened his bonds, removed the gag and asked him how he felt. As he expressed a strong desire to be left to die in peace, we hurried back to bed again and a few minutes later the Germans arrived. They went into the general's room and found him lying on his bed with various cords around him. He told a pitiful tale of how the British officers had all assaulted him, and how some of them escaped from his window. The Germans were not very sympathetic listeners; they laughed at him and pointed out that the cords were so loosely tied that he must have done them up himself. In answer to his protests they put him under arrest and locked him in his room. Our room was visited next and the absence of Medlicott and Stewart duly noticed. The Germans spent the rest of the night making a thorough search of the camp, refusing to believe that anyone had actually got out. I went back again to the general's room once during the night to retrieve some kit we had left behind. This time one of the Germans saw me and thenceforth they marked me down as an accomplice.

Next day the local newspapers were full of the story. They stated that the escaped men spoke German fluently, and were travelling by train to Holland disguised as Americans. Why this was published remains a mystery as Medlicott spoke no German, Stewart only a few words, and neither of them intended to travel by train.

In reality their plan was to walk some eighty miles to Darmstadt, near which place there was an aerodrome (at Griesheim). Close to this aerodrome there was a hospital from which a wounded prisoner, whom we had met at Mainz, had seen instructional flying being carried out. He had noticed that during the midday interval several aeroplanes were often left standing unguarded, a couple of hundred yards from the sheds. Medlicott's idea was to camp on the edge of the aerodrome and watch for an opportunity to dash out, get into a machine, start up and fly away. It was rather a wild scheme though not entirely impossible, but whatever its chances they were completely spoilt by bad weather, which stopped any flying being carried out for many days in that part of Germany.

They reached the aerodrome on the fourth night out from Weilburg, and stayed there in excellent cover for thirty-six hours; although, at the end of this time, they were short of food and worn out by the cold and damp. They were unable to wait for a change in the weather, and decided to make for the nearest main line, hoping to get on a goods train and so work their way south to Switzerland. But the very next day their luck deserted them. They ran into some guards near an internment camp who stopped them and, finding that they could not speak German, arrested them. A day later the Weilburg authorities claimed them, and they were brought back.

They were closely questioned as to their method of escape, and the Germans soon found that they could not have committed all the various offences by themselves, such as fusing the lights and breaking windows. The British were accused of being concerned and threatened with all kinds of penalties. Suspicion had rested upon me ever since I had been seen in the passage on the night of the crime, and, to avoid further unpleasantness, I confessed my guilt and was removed to jail, where I stayed ten or twelve days.

On about 10 April I was taken to Frankfurt, for a court-martial, by one of the camp officers, Captain von Gölpen, generally known as "John Gilpin". He was one of the most charming Germans I have ever met and invariably treated us well. He was very kind to me that day in Frankfurt, and I felt sufficiently grateful not to make use of an opportunity to escape which he accidentally gave me. It was after the court-martial that the chance occurred. We were to catch a train back to Weilburg at about three o'clock and, as there was over an hour to wait, "John Gilpin" suggested lunch at the station. When we got to the restaurant, I asked to be allowed to wash my hands. I was shown into the lavatory unescorted, and found that not only was it deserted, but provided with a second door leading straight on to the station platform. Some time previously I had got the Weilburg tailor to line my uniform coat and trousers with black cloth and, as I had a very German-civilian-looking leather coat with a fur collar and a dark soft khaki cap, I had only to turn my uniform inside out to appear as a civilian. I should have had plenty of time to disappear from the lavatory, take a ticket and board a train before being missed, but the one thing I lacked was a map of the frontier. This and the thought of "John Gilpin's" kindness made me abandon the idea and I returned a few minutes later to an excellent lunch.

The court-martial itself was quite amusing, and Medlicott, Stewart and I had great fun laughing at the officials. We paid very little attention to the trial and missed a good deal of the usual procedure, although occasionally I had to do some translating, the interpreter being of no use. The whole business lasted about two hours, and the judge evidently took a sensible view of the case as Medlicott and Stewart merely got a month's imprisonment apiece and I only ten days. In the afternoon I was taken back to Weilburg jail and the other two went to Friedberg to serve their sentence.

I found jail life very dull, but, at Weilburg, not too unpleasant and on the whole I was well treated. If I had been serving a longer sentence I think I should have succeeded in cutting the bars of my cell window with a fair chance of being able to get away.

On my return to the camp, towards the end of April, I went into partnership with Elliot again, but we very soon realized that the basket scheme had been impracticable, a sentry now being posted inside the building itself at night. It was a great disappointment, but the inevitable result of the recent successful attempt.

The next idea that occurred to us was to dress up as German officers and bluff our way past the sentries in broad daylight. Something like this had been tried elsewhere and had only failed, owing to some slight miscalculation. We planned it out and started to collect the necessary uniforms, a matter of very considerable difficulty. A few minor articles such as cap badges and buttons we had already collected at various times – chiefly during midnight visits to the *Kommandantur* – but the main part of the disguise, especially the caps and shoulder-straps, required a lot of time to prepare. The dark-blue caps, we thought, could be sent out from England as they resembled in some particulars the caps worn in peace time by many British regiments. I managed to make quite a passable wooden sword-scabbard, painted black with a tin ferrule, and a French officer named de Blois, of the Spahis Marocains, with whom I had made great friends at Mainz, manufactured some shoulder-straps (which in the German army are made of twisted gold or silver cord) out of cleverly painted string. The long coats were not so difficult to obtain, since the pre-war Russian overcoat was almost identical in colour and only needed slight alterations in cut and facings to be indistinguishable from that worn by the Germans. After a lot of bargaining, one of these coats was handed over to me by a Russian officer, and given to the tailor for the necessary changes. But these preparations took a long time, more than a month, and before the kit was ready we were shifted to another camp.

In the meantime, an attempt had been made which nearly ended in a tragedy. Early in May, Pearson, a R.F.C. pilot, was sent with a small party of French and British to interview the dentist in a town some thirty miles away. On the return journey he managed successfully to jump out of the train. Unfortunately a guard in another carriage saw him and stopped the train, which was travelling slowly, within three hundred yards. A party of German soldiers were also on board and these men gave chase immediately. Pearson made for the nearest wood, but, finding his way barred by some farm labourers, he got into a ditch and tried to crawl away. He soon saw that the Germans had found his tracks and were searching the ditch he was in. Further escape was impossible, so he stood up and put his hands above his head. Three of the Germans immediately took aim and fired. The first shot missed, the second hit his right hand, damaging his thumb and blowing off the top joint of his forefinger, and the third hit him just below the heart. Fortunately the bullet was turned by a tin of food and passed between the skin and the ribs, coming out at the shoulder He was then seized, knocked about with rifle-butts and dragged back to the train, where he was again manhandled. Had it not been for the intervention of the other prisoners who contrived to get near him, he would very likely have been finished off.

He was brought back to the camp without further misadventure and on examination his wounds proved not to be dangerous, although extremely painful. We were all very sorry for him; as his attempt, in broad daylight, was most daring and might easily have been successful but for bad luck.

Not long after this, towards the end of May, we heard that some of the British were to be moved to Mainz and others, including myself, to Friedberg. We decided to put off further attempts until we reached the new camp, and began to make special double-bottomed and double-sided boxes to convey our carefully collected escaping kits. I was able to take most of the completed portions of the German uniform and a rough suit of civilian clothes, in addition to some tools, maps and a compass. Eventually the secret receptacles in our luggage threatened to become so large that I was forced to leave the German overcoat behind.

Shortly before we left I heard a rumour that my brother (also in the R.F.C.) had been shot down in France and was also a prisoner. I could scarcely believe it at first, but I at once wrote a letter to the commandant asking that he should be sent to the same camp that I was in. I was told that this would probably be done when they had ascertained if he had indeed been captured.

I was sorry in some ways to be leaving Weilburg, for not only was it quite a charming camp – as camps go – but I had had great hopes of escaping from it. So far I had spent over six months in Germany, and all the schemes in which I had been directly concerned had been failures. But for all that I knew escape was not impossible, for at the end of April I had heard from England that Ward had crossed the frontier. Details were at first unobtainable, but the news came through later. During a journey from one camp to another, the train had stopped at a station close to the Swiss frontier. There were very few guards and four prisoners succeeded in escaping. Two were recaught, but Ward and another eluded the pursuit and crossed the frontier without any trouble.

On 1 June six of us left for Friedberg. The train journey was only about four hours long, and there was no chance of jumping off as the guards were numerous and forewarned by Pearson's attempt. During the journey we bought some newspapers and read the first reports of the Jutland battle. I shall never forget the look of surprise on the German faces when they saw that there had been a great naval engagement and that some of their ships were still afloat.

V

Friedberg proved to be close to the once-famous Bad-Nauheim and about twenty-five miles north of Frankfurt. The camp lay outside the village in open country and, at the time of our arrival, contained six-hundred prisoners of all nationalities, only twelve of whom were British. Some of the latter were keen to escape and with their help we managed to get our illicit possessions stowed away in good hiding-places.

We soon heard that all the British from Mainz – about one-hundred-and-fifty – were due in a few weeks, and a day or two later a Frenchman arrived bringing me a note from my brother, who said he expected to come with them.

Friedberg was not an easy camp from which to escape, the lack of cover afforded by the surrounding country, and the fact that several abortive attempts by French and Russians had made the Germans very wary, adding considerably to the usual difficulties.

The camp was roughly square, bounded by double fences (barbed-wire and a wooden palisade) and guarded by two rows of sentries. It contained two large three-storied buildings and a gymnasium, all of which had been completed just before the war and were to have been used as infantry barracks. In the centre of the camp there was a large parade ground about eighty yards square, and on one side of this lay a piece of ground one-hundred yards long by twenty yards wide where prisoners were allowed to make themselves small gardens, which ran down to within a few feet of the wire fence surrounding the camp. Plots of ground were allotted by a garden committee, or they could be purchased direct from their "owners". A few days after our arrival I obtained one of these plots from a Frenchman, paying him in camp money for the plants and material on the estate.

A week later, the party of British from Mainz arrived and I met my brother whom I had last seen on leave in England a year previously. Elliot and Campbell were also among the party and we at once assembled to consider possible means of escape. *Faute de mieux*, a tunnel seemed to offer many chances of success; it was always a good way out, since one could take a large quantity of kit and choose the best time of the day for the actual escape. We explored the whole camp for a suitable spot from which to start, the main requirements being soft soil, a short distance to dig, and cover from the Germans. The basements of the buildings we lived in were useless as the floors were of concrete, and the gymnasium was out of the question, an unsuccessful attempt having already been made there. At first sight the gardens seemed impossible as there was no cover, except a few small bushes and a row or two of sunflowers planted by the prisoners, but some of the French had started building summer-houses and we obtained permission from the Germans to do likewise.

Most of these summer-houses consisted of a rough framework of wood, with canvas nailed round the sides, and the roof covered with tarred paper, all the necessary materials being on sale at the canteen. We thought that screened by a shack of this description, we might somehow be able to fool the Germans long enough to dig the tunnel.

The piece of ground I had secured measured fifteen feet from back to front and twenty-four feet from the next garden to the barbed-wire fence. We divided the ground into two equal parts; the part nearest the barbed wire we planted, and the other became the site for the shack, which was to be about ten feet square and just over six feet in height. While the building was going on, we managed to cut away the earth in the centre to a depth of nearly six inches without arousing undue suspicion, and later on this extra floor-space gave us room to dispose of about ten cubic feet of soil from the tunnel. Two sides and the back of the hut were covered with black and white striped canvas, the stripes running vertically, the fourth side, which was the entrance, being provided with a movable hanging curtain of the same material, supported by a horizontal pole whose ends rested on the top of the two sides. The ceiling was also canvas, with the stripes running from back to front, and the structure was surmounted by a sloping roof. It looked like a hideous bathing-tent when finished, but it served its purpose splendidly.

We tried to make it appear that we were designing a rock garden, and to this end all the earth had to be dug up and shifted round, being finally piled in several bounds. Many prisoners of all nationalities were thoroughly interested in their gardens by now, and the Germans, only too glad to keep us quiet, willingly sold us a large quantity of plants, many sacks of grey granite chips for the paths and all the other materials which we required. A mass of flowers were planted around the shack, preference being shown for the tall quick-growing varieties, which quite soon began to hide the sides. The floor, the entrance and the small path outside were covered with several sackfuls of granite chips, and the tunnel itself was at last started.

At first it was very tricky work, as a shaft had to be sunk to a depth of six feet before the person digging could work out of sight. The front of the tent was kept open all the time and the sentry on the other side of the barbed-wire fence, less than five yards away, or any of the numerous Germans who walked round the camp, could look straight in. This disarmed suspicion, but it made it impossible to dig in the middle of the tent, as we should have liked to do. The real object of our fourth curtain and the arrangement of stripes now became apparent. When work started, the fourth curtain was pushed back till there was a space of little more than a foot between it and the back of the tent. In this space the digging was commenced and, as soon as the shaft was a few feet deep, a trapdoor, roughly made out of an old packing-case, was fitted. Every day when work was over, two feet of earth were filled in on top of the trap and the whole floor re-covered with granite chips. Looking into the tent while work was going on, it was impossible to realize that there was a false back, partly because of the smallness of the double space, but chiefly owing to the vertical black and white stripes acting as camouflage. The outside of the tent, of course, appeared quite normal.

For the first few days the earth, as it came up from the shaft, was filled into empty granite-chip sacks, and these were temporarily piled up in the space at the back. Then when the coast was clear and the sentry had his back turned, the loose curtain was quickly removed, the sacks emptied evenly all over the floor and the contents stamped down. The curtain was replaced and a fresh man started digging, while granite-chips were hurriedly scattered over the new floor. It was rather nerve-racking work, particularly as one of the German officers and a *Feldwebel*[3] took it into their heads to walk round the gardens every morning, watching the amateur gardeners and looking into the summer-houses. But the camouflage worked well and no one noticed anything.

In five days the shaft was deep enough for us to be able to work completely underground, and the entrance was hidden during working hours with a piece of board thinly covered with earth and granite. The double curtain still had to be used, as the sacks of earth accumulated with such rapidity that there was no room to stow them underground, and we had to continue stacking behind the curtain till the end of the shift.

It took us well over a week to complete the shaft and make the first foot or two of the actual tunnel, and meanwhile we had to get rid of the earth by some new method since it was obviously impossible to go on raising the level of the floor indefinitely. At one time we thought of filling the space between the ceiling and the roof, but this would have necessitated putting in a large amount of planking which we could not obtain. The new rock garden offered certain possibilities, although of course it was under the eye of the sentry, but we might be able to dispose of some of the loose earth by piling it on the various mounds we had already made, the only obstacle to this being the difficulty of bringing the sacks out of the tent unnoticed. To add to our troubles the subsoil turned out to be almost yellow, whereas the earth

---

3. Sergeant.

at the surface was nearly black, so that every sackful we emptied outside had to be mixed with, or hidden by, a considerable amount of the top soil. To remedy this and to account for the increasing quantity of loose earth in our garden, we began wheeling barrow-loads of soil of various colours from the other end of the camp, and thus made it appear that our rock garden was going to be on a really large scale. But we could not afford to bring many such loads, and they were only brought when we were certain that some of the Germans were looking and likely to be duly impressed. To lessen the distance in the open across which the sacks had to be carried, a big mound was piled up alongside the entrance to the tent. From now on the sacks were whisked out from behind the curtain and emptied on this mound, which was immediately covered with shovelfuls of dark earth. It was found that the best opportunity for this operation occurred when the guard was being changed and the sentry nearest to us was down at the end of the beat, waiting for his relief. Practically the whole of the morning's excavation of earth would be disposed of during these two or three minutes and by the time the new sentry was in a position to look into the tent, everything was quiet again.

My brother, a R.F.C. pilot named Mansell-Moullin and I built the shack and planned the original lay-out of the garden. To prevent the Germans thinking that there were many people interested, we allowed practically no one else to help us, but as soon as the tunnel was under way our old friends Elliot and Campbell – and later on Fairweather (Cheshire Regiment) and Walker (R.F.C.) – were brought in.

The morning *Appell*[4] was at nine o'clock, and it was inadvisable to work earlier than this owing to the scarcity of people in the gardens which made us too conspicuous. A certain amount of work was done in the garden itself before breakfast, and with Moullin's and Walker's help it began to look more like a garden and less like a rubbish heap. Digging was commenced at half-past nine and continued generally without a break until midday, when the guard was changed and the sacks emptied. At first we had an interval for lunch, starting work again at about half-past one, but to speed up the job we made work continuous by sending a new gang down at noon. The third

---

4. Roll-call.

shift usually began at half-past two and knocked off just before five. During a portion of the summer, *Appell* was put off till after six; in spite of this it was safer to stop work in plenty of time and we continued closing down at five.

This routine went on day after day, although occasionally when the Germans were unusually troublesome in walking round the gardens, we closed down for a day or two so as to make certain that their suspicions were not genuinely aroused. Sometimes, of course, the weather was so bad that it was absurd to be seen sitting in the pouring rain. But, on the whole, we made good progress and the digging was fairly easy.

Each gang consisted of two men; one of them worked at the face of the tunnel, while the other filled sacks and piled them at the bottom of the shaft. As at Weilburg, we found that ordinary table knives were the most suitable tools for digging and, in the very small space available, the shortest and handiest instruments were obviously the best.

We kept the tunnel as small as possible – about two feet in diameter – thereby making sure that the minimum quantity of earth was taken out. The work would have gone a great deal more quickly had we been able to make the tunnel twice the height, and broad enough for two men to work abreast in a sitting position. As it was, the man digging had to work lying flat on his chest with just enough room to raise himself on one elbow. The actual digging was not very difficult, the soil being clay with a very few stones; but it is surprising how slowly a job of this sort progresses. The opening and shutting of the trap-door took quite a lot of time; the working parties had to change into their digging clothes down below before starting work, and the filling and hoisting up of heavy sacks was a lengthy and tiresome business. Moreover, as the tunnel got longer the air – always a difficulty in tunnelling – became rapidly worse, until it was not possible to work at the face of the tunnel for more than five or ten minutes at a stretch. This meant that the two men inside had to change positions frequently and yet more time was wasted. Nevertheless the average distance we progressed each day was from eighteen inches to two feet, the maximum three feet. We had started building the tent in the middle of June, and the shaft was driven down at about the beginning of July; allowing for the days on which we could not work, some fourteen yards had been completed by 1 August.

At about this time we brought in another worker, a Frenchman named Geerts, who had started a tunnel from his own garden. It was evident that this second tunnel would take much longer to finish than ours and was more likely to be discovered, consequently we suggested that he should stop work and come and join us. He agreed immediately and proved himself to be extremely useful, having done a good deal of mining in the trenches in France. He gave us some valuable advice on the ventilation, on the strength of which we altered the section of the tunnel slightly, making it more in the shape of a Gothic arch with a much larger entrance from the vertical shaft. We also tried, without success, some experiments with air pumps and bellows, but after Geerts's alterations the air improved slightly and we were able to work rather faster.

Every day at the end of the last shift, the gang in the tunnel measured the total length with a piece of cord, and a compass bearing of its direction was also taken. Then from a window in our building, overlooking the field in which the tunnel would eventually come up, we were able to make a rough estimate of the point we had reached. By the middle of August the tunnel was twenty-three yards long, and we believed that we had gone at least twelve yards beyond the edge of the outer sentry's path.

The question of the exact point at which we should come up had now to be discussed. There was no real cover on any side of the camp, but on the tunnel side, there were a few fruit trees standing in a field of tall corn and we hoped to finish digging before the crops (which were very late that year) were cut. If we could make the exit on the far side of one of the trees, we felt sure of being able to crawl away through the corn, but the greatest disadvantage of our tunnel lay in the fact, that it was almost impossible to reach at night, because after dark we were locked in our buildings. Some one suggested that we should be shut in the tunnel during the last few feet and get out during the night. This idea was quite feasible, but we should be missed on the evening *Appell*, and the Germans would therefore be searching for us before we had got away; if they had any vague suspicions of the tunnel they might even catch us in it. It was very annoying, but the only alternative appeared to be to do it in daylight, and the success of the whole scheme depended on whether we could get out while the corn was still there to hide us. Even so, we estimated that we should have to crawl nearly a hundred yards before we were effectively hidden from the sentries by a small fold in the ground.

The work was pushed on, and we put the finishing touches to our escaping kits, replenished and amplified with articles from the canteen. Now that we had got so near the end, we took double precautions. We kept the side curtains, which had never been completely nailed down, hanging half-way up the poles during the greater part of the day, and so allowed any suspicious observer to see right through the tent. More barrow-loads of earth were brought, quantities of cement and stone were arranged on the rock garden and the minimum amount of soil was brought out from the tunnel. Success seemed almost a certainty.

In the corner of the camp nearest to our garden, stood the small three-storied *Kommandantur* building. From its roof some three or four telephone and electric-light wires ran down to a post outside the camp. A certain British officer conceived the idea of concealing himself on the roof by day, and sliding out during the night on the wires. The idea itself was good, and it has been carried out many times elsewhere in the world; but in this instance it was out of the question. The wires ran down at too steep an angle – from twenty-five to thirty degrees; there were far too few of them, and their attachments to the poles were not secure enough The scheme required a good deal of nerve and plain courage, and the officer in question undoubtedly deserves credit for ever having thought of it, but he did not get very far, as he was caught with all his kit on him soon after he had got into the *Kommandantur*.

The unfortunate part of it all was that this officer was one of the number who intended to make use of the tunnel and the Germans knew him for a friend of ours. The incident of his capture may seem unimportant, but it was sufficient to fan the spark of German suspicion into flame, and the immediate result was a surprise *Appell* and a search of the camp. We had warning of this from some one who had overheard the Germans speaking of it, and we managed to close down the tunnel and get everything tidied up in plenty of time. After the *Appell* we were all ordered into our respective buildings, and a small party of German soldiers proceeded to search the camp. Practically nothing was found in the buildings and the authorities then decided to examine and dig up the various gardens. This procedure was rather disturbing, but it caused us no real anxiety. There was nothing suspicious in our tent or garden, and the trap-door was two feet below the surface. Only the day before one of the Germans had come right into our tent on some pretext or another and had looked around for a minute or two; although the double curtain was in position at the time and I was behind it, he had noticed nothing, and we felt confident that the search party would not find the trap-door.

The digging and searching in the garden continued for about an hour, during which time Geerts's abandoned tunnel was discovered and some civilian kit belonging to various other prisoners brought to light. We could see from the top-story of the building that our garden had been almost completely dug up – in some places to a considerable depth – and we wondered for how much longer they were going to continue.

At last the signal to stop work was given, and we saw parties of Germans pick up their tools and come back to the N.C.O. in charge. But in our garden they apparently did not hear the order to stop;[5] for fifteen seconds more we could see two men wielding picks at the back of the tent. Some one shouted to them to stop, but the next moment it was too late. One of them called out something and a crowd gathered round him; a man was sent off running to fetch an officer. Soon several men started again frantically digging up our garden and then, by the orders of the officer, the tent was pulled down and smashed up. At that, we finally realized that our poor tunnel was done for.

VI

The Germans only dug up a small portion of the tunnel and then sent a man down to measure it. Another man was made to go outside the camp and mark the exact spot where the tunnel ended. We could see him pace out the distance and then stand under one of the trees; we had done even better than we had thought and another two or three days would certainly have seen us out of the camp.

To say that we were disappointed would be putting it mildly. Digging the tunnel had not been very amusing work and the continuous anxiety,

---

5. We were told later that this was actually the case.

combined with the fact that the whole of each day had to be spent either in the tent or in the tunnel, had proved most irksome. The result had been to make us keener on finishing the job and getting away, and now that we saw all our labours brought to naught, captivity seemed even more unbearable than before. For the next few days the tunnel gang wandered about like lost sheep, for we had all been so concentrated on the work that we had taken no part in ordinary camp life and we found that we had nothing to do, it was but a small consolation to think that we had made a tunnel twenty-five yards long, and that thanks to the trapdoor and the camouflage of the double curtain we had kept the Germans in ignorance of our plans for a month and a half. The only remedy was to try again.

After one or two representatives of the tunnel gang had spent a few days in arrest, we reassembled and talked over half a dozen suggested schemes, eventually deciding to look more closely into three of them. First, there was the washing-basket scheme, but the baskets in this camp were far too small to be of any use and the only hope was to get smuggled into the closed van which came into the camp to collect them. For many reasons this was very difficult and before we could try it at all another party of British had made the attempt without any success.

A thorough inspection of both main buildings was then made to see if there was any chance of breaking through the basement walls, and digging a short tunnel. The advantages of this idea were that we should be able to work and escape by night. One of the basement rooms in our building offered some possibilities; it was used as a store-room and the Germans seldom entered it. A wooden paling, through which we were able to force our way, shut it off from the corridor. Having settled on the corner in which we should start work, we began by loosening the bricks with the help of a short crowbar – a relic of Weilburg days. After a few days' work it became obvious that it would be too long a business and the difficulty of disposing of the earth would be almost insuperable. In the other building, mainly inhabited by Russians, there was considerably more chance of success as there was no concrete in the basement and the Germans rarely visited any of the rooms. But a tunnel had already been started there by some Russians who were rather naturally averse to having any suspected characters in the scheme, for after the digging up of our garden the Germans had developed the unpleasant habit of following us round the camp all day long.

The next plan we worked at was one which I still believe had the least chance of complete success – and offered more prospect of getting those who tried it seriously injured – than any other scheme in Germany. Roughly described, the idea was to try and swing out from our window on the first floor to beyond the second line of sentries. This was to be done by means of a rope attached to the top of a pole holding one of the powerful electric lamps illuminating the camp. A rod twelve feet long was to be pushed out of our window, which was exactly opposite an electric lamp, and a noose slipped over the top of the lamp pole. From this noose two ropes ran back into our room. Hanging on to one of these two ropes, one of us would then be lowered from the window, carrying the second rope coiled up. As soon as this man reached the electric-light pole, he would uncoil the rope he was carrying and slide down it to the ground. As the pole stood on the outside of the wooden paling, once we were on the ground we had no more obstructions to face and only a possible chase in the dark by one of the outside sentries.

It was essential that the moment the noose was in position the lights should be fused. This was a difficult business as we were not sure whether the electric wires, twelve feet away from the building, were insulated or not. If they were uninsulated, the fights could be put out by means of another long rod carrying a piece of wire, with which both electric wires would be touched simultaneously, thus causing a short circuit. All that would then be needed was wind and rain to drown what noise we made. My brother and I were to try it together, and of course any of the old gang could follow on if our escape was successful, but it was difficult to believe that the two of us alone would not attract some attention and alarm the guard. We set to work to make the necessary ropes, for which we used the old canvas from our tent (which was still lying wrecked in the garden) cut into strips and plaited with four strands. The ends were spliced together and bound tightly with string. About fifty feet of this rope was made and carefully tested to carry the weight of four men. The rods were made of bits of the framework of the old tent. It was suggested that one rod would be sufficient, but as the lights had to go out the very instant the noose was fixed on the lamp standard, two were considered essential. It was not an easy matter to make these rods as they had to be rigid and at the same time very light and narrow, but after many trials we were at last satisfied with them.

Our kit, having been completed and made ready for the tunnel, was still intact and nothing else was needed before we made the attempt. When my brother came out of arrest, where he had spent a week in connection with the tunnel episode, it was voted we should try at once, the weather being suitably bad. At the same time it was rumoured in the camp that our rooms were again to be searched. How the various camp rumours started we seldom knew, but they were very often correct. In any case there was no time to be lost, and on 3 September we tried to put our plans into execution.

Unfortunately the weather improved rapidly at the last moment and we were faced with the awful prospect of a fine night. After ten o'clock, when the Germans had gone the customary rounds in the building, we warned the necessary assistants – Elliot, Campbell, Fairweather and Kemp – and started the final rigging-up of the poles and ropes. The pole which was to fuse the lights was taken to a room immediately above ours, where one could get a better view of the wires, and the man who was to do the job was told to put out the lights the moment he saw the noose in position.

As in Medlicott's scheme at Weilburg, we were to try between two and three o'clock in the morning, when the sentries were likely to be fairly sleepy and less watchful, but we badly needed wind and rain. As the night wore on the weather became finer, until it was one of the calmest, quietest nights imaginable. Then just after midnight a slight breeze sprang up and we began to have hopes. We started pushing the pole out of our window, but almost immediately we had to withdraw it; the sentries were too alert, and I am almost certain one of them actually caught sight of us. There were four of them who were dangerously near and could easily see or hear us, not to mention several others two hundred yards away who might possibly give trouble. The breeze instead of improving died down again, and by two o'clock there was once more complete silence. We waited until well after three, and then as it began to get light we packed up the gear and went to bed, intending to try on the next night and on every night until we got suitable weather.

But next morning came the rumoured search. We had been unable to find a suitable hiding-place for the ropes and one of the poles, which were rather poorly hidden behind some boxes in a corner. The Germans seized them with great jubilation (although they had no idea what they were for) and carried them off in triumph. Fortunately they did not get our civilian kit, and we felt that we had been let off rather lightly.

While the Germans were searching, the officer who accompanied them – a bespectacled young bounder, nicknamed "Gig-lamps" – suddenly asked us:

"Do you vant for to go out, jetzt?"

We looked at him blankly, and understanding him to mean did we want to leave the room while he carried on with the search, naturally answered yes. At this he almost exploded and screamed at the top of his voice:

"You cannot esgape, your are brisoners of var!" A statement which caused us much mirth.

This search ended the "rope scheme" and I may as well admit that I was heartily glad to have finished with it, for it seemed almost certain that one of the four sentries on that side of the camp would manage to get a shot in at close quarters while we were halfway out.

The old tunnel gang held a council of war on the day after the search to talk over further methods of escape. Whatever we did would have to be done quickly, for the month was now September. We were not well equipped against cold and it was a long way to the frontier. A trek in late autumn or early winter was therefore to be avoided if possible, but the more we looked round the camp the more convinced were we that the schemes most likely to succeed were either those which allowed one person to get away, or else were of the same dangerous type as the "rope scheme".

On the whole the best plan was for me to go out dressed as a German officer. It had often been suggested, but I had not wished to try completely alone, and, in addition, it had always seemed impossible as there were only three or four German officers in the camp, all of whom were well-known to the sentries. It was given a trial because we were short of other ideas, and we started on the uniform.

I had still got the odds and ends from the uniform begun at Weilburg, the principal things lacking being a cap and a pale grey overcoat. A Russian friend of ours was persuaded to ask for a new overcoat through the French tailor, who had to get permission from the Germans to procure the necessary material. But the authorities made a lot of bother, pointing out that the only cloth resembling the Russian stuff in any way was that out of which the German officers' uniform was made. This, of course, was just what I wanted, but eventually it was refused and I had to start again negotiating with the Russians. I obtained one at last and gave it to the French tailor for the necessary alterations. He had to work in secret and consequently took a very long time, besides which the coat was old and shabby and I was not sure whether it would pass muster when it was finally ready. The cap, too, proved almost impossible to procure and we were beginning to despair of getting the kit ready for months, when a great stroke of luck put us in touch with everything we wanted.

Walker and Fairweather had been working on this same scheme for many months at Mainz, where there was a distinct probability of success. They had gradually obtained almost all the necessary kit for German officers: dark blue mess-caps from England, grey overcoats from the Russians, tin sword-scabbards and badges (home-made). They had succeeded in smuggling all this gear into Friedberg, although the overcoats, which had not yet been altered, were actually seen and passed by the Germans who probably thought they were presents or souvenirs from the Russians. And this splendid kit was lying idle. Walker had other plans just then and did not fancy the chance of using the German uniform at Friedberg, while Fairweather – who thought the scheme was possible – could not speak German.

Walker, by the way, intended to get into a rubbish tub, and be carried out and dumped into a heap of refuse just outside the camp. More rubbish was then to be tipped over him by the French orderlies, who were employed on this job, and he was to remain hidden until the sentries had moved off when he would be able to make a dash for freedom. Unluckily, in this particular camp it was no good; the sentries were too watchful. He tried the plan one Sunday morning and was successfully tipped out, but before he could be covered up he was spotted by one of the guards and hauled back to camp. He was given the usual fourteen days' imprisonment and, on leaving the camp for jail, handed over to us the whole of his German kit, saying that we were to make whatever use of it we could.

Fairweather and I now had almost complete sets of uniform which, with the help of the tailor, could be made perfect. I began to think that it might be possible to rig up a third person either as an officer or a soldier, but as yet we had no very definite scheme as to how we were to get out.

The details of our uniforms still needed a good deal of care and thought. Such things as buttons and cap badges took a lot of time either to collect or to make satisfactorily. Fairweather's cap badges were made out of metal trouser buttons, filed flat and painted with the German colours, whereas mine were real ones, captured in the *Kommandantur* at Weilburg.[6] Plain brass buttons for the overcoats we bought in the canteen; they answered the purpose quite well as many of the Germans were wearing them. The shoulder-straps on Walker's coat were somewhat better than the ones made at Weilburg and, covered very neatly with silver paper, looked most realistic. For footwear, we purchased in the canteen[7] some very yellow and expensive boots with leggings to match.

With our kit thus nearing completion we commenced mapping out a more detailed plan of escape, and towards the middle of September a series of events occurred which greatly increased our chances.

The first of these events was the arrival of two new German officers in the camp. Then there was an inspection of the place by a Red Cross Commission, followed by a party from the American Embassy. Next came another Red Cross Commission from some other neutral country, and finally a visit by various German officers and civilians. All of these different parties came to see the sanitary conditions and the regime under which the prisoners lived at Friedberg, the camp being one of the cleanest and healthiest in Germany at the time.

Obviously, one result of these visits was that the sentries no longer knew by sight each person who entered and left the camp. We noticed too that none of these strangers had to show passes and, as far as we could make out, there was no password to be given. Most of the visitors came and left by the main gate between the two principal buildings, but once or twice some were seen to leave by a small door near the *Kommandantur*. We watched this door

---

6. The German cap badge was a small round disc about half an inch in diameter, having on its surface three concentric circles of red, white and black.
7. At this period of the war, the camp canteens sold, at exorbitant prices, almost every commodity except civilian clothing and food.

on several occasions and soon became convinced that it would be possible for us to get the sentry to open it, if our disguise was sufficiently perfect.

VII

A few days later we got an inspiration for the general idea of our scheme from another small party which visited the camp. It consisted of an officer, a N.C.O. and a civilian. They apparently made a rough survey of the camp, inspected the covers of the drains, and left by the side door near the *Kommandantur*. We decided that our own party should be arranged on much the same lines – Fairweather and I as German officers, my brother as a civilian – and from that time on we styled ourselves "The Drainage Commission".

The first question was how we were to get across the camp from our building to the gate. We could not risk leaving our room and walking the whole way in German uniform, there were too many Germans about who might know us by sight. Possibly it would be best to transfer our kits to one of the gardens, dress there, and then walk straight to the gate. But even this was not good enough as the Germans still wandered round the gardens each morning, and it would be particularly unwise for us to be seen in that part of the camp.

A better plan seemed to be to dress in our quarters, concealing our German uniforms with khaki overcoats and covering our legs with ordinary khaki trousers. We would then be sure of getting safely to the far side of the camp where the gate was, although we still had to find some means of getting rid of our khaki kit without being observed. Eventually we hit on the idea of using the *Kommandantur* itself as a changing-room.

The *Kommandantur* was a small, square three-storied building, standing in a corner of the camp not far from our late garden. It contained the usual clerks' rooms and commandant's office, and in addition the censor's office and the pay department. It was quite usual for prisoners to go to these two latter rooms in the mornings, to see about letters or to obtain camp money. The building was surrounded by a little garden enclosure of its own through which ran a gravel path, bringing one to a short flight of steps leading into the house. At the top of these steps was a hall from which doors and passages led off in different directions. On the left there was a short passage and then the pay-office door. This passage was very dark and had two swing-doors at its entrance, making it an ideal changing-room. There was little chance of our being surprised there, it would only take a moment to throw off our overcoats, and then two German officers and a civilian coming from the *Kommandantur* would seem the most natural thing in the world.

To accelerate our quick change, we decided not to wear complete khaki trousers, but only small pieces of trousers from just above the knees downwards. We cut up some pairs of old slacks, tacked the short lower halves to our real trousers just above our German leggings, and found that with a long overcoat they looked perfectly natural, while only a sharp tug was necessary to remove them. It was arranged that Elliot, Campbell, and a new-comer named Collis would act as assistants, precede us to the *Kommandantur* and help us off with our coats and trousers. Further to improve my appearance, I was to have my hair cropped short on the morning of the attempt and while passing the guard, I was going to wear spectacles. Fair-weather's appearance did not need alteration as he had no very noticeable characteristics – in my case, red hair – and my brother was sufficiently disguised by his civilian clothes with a felt hat pulled down over his eyes. It was unlikely that the sentry would have seen any of us before and, the other two would be walking close behind me so the sentry's gaze would chiefly fall upon me; we therefore concentrated on my disguise.

We went over all the details carefully and held several rehearsals in our room. The difficulty of stowing away sufficient food for the journey was evident, and to overcome this we made a set of flat body-belts fastened at the waist. Into these belts we carefully packed various concentrated foods, every tin of meat lozenges, every packet of chocolate, and every biscuit, being sown in place to prevent them slipping down and forming an unnatural bulge.

We disposed of most of our food in this manner, although we realized we were going to look very fat with all these things underneath our civilian clothes, which themselves had to be worn under the uniform. Nevertheless we fancied that we would not be going beyond the usual standard of German corpulence. But even so, we had maps, compasses, haversacks and water-bottles and extra food for which no place had yet been found. We put these, as well as a spare pair of boots and a small flask of brandy, in a tin box the size of an attaché case, wrapped in brown paper and tied up with string. My brother, who was supposed to be a sort of clerk, or perhaps an "Assistant Drainage Commissioner", was to carry it. As soon as we had finished these preparations and the uniforms were ready, we had a final dress rehearsal in our room, watched by some of the old tunnel gang. Every one agreed that the affair ought to be a complete success. It was now time to discuss our plans for getting away once we were out of the camp. I had originally intended to go by train, but my brother and Fairweather insisted on walking and, against my better judgment, I was eventually persuaded to give up the train idea. The nearest frontier from Friedberg was the Dutch (about one-hundred-and-fifty miles as the crow flies), but as the journey involved crossing the Rhine and making many detours round thickly populated districts, we thought it best to make for Switzerland – a distance of over two-hundred-and-fifty miles; Fairweather, however, resolved to go alone and to Holland. We obtained an excellent set of maps to Switzerland from Geerts – the Frenchman in our tunnel gang – who had somehow managed to get them sent out from France. I also received some maps and a compass from Ward (who, it will be remembered, had escaped in the spring) concealed in a tin of biscuits which I contrived to smuggle out of the parcels office; but these maps being for the Holland route, I passed them on to Fairweather.

At last everything was ready and we arranged to make the attempt on 25 September. Early that morning I had my hair cropped, and then all our kit was brought out from various hiding-places up in the roof of our building. Just as we were beginning to change our clothes an orderly came in to say that one of the German officers wanted to see me. We were much perturbed and I wondered if rumours of our plans had somehow got round to the Germans. I dressed again and went down to the office, where I was told that I was on the fist of prisoners to be inoculated against cholera and typhoid that morning. Fortunately the camp doctor had not yet arrived and I managed to get away almost at once, although of course my German-looking hair-cut was noticed. I heard afterwards that the German officer in question remarked to one of his subordinates, that he wondered why my hair had been clipped and that he felt sure I was going to try to escape. Luckily he took no steps to prevent us.

We hurried on with our dressing and by ten o'clock we were ready, with our khaki overcoats and half-trousers over the German kit. We looked remarkably stout, but, as it was a cold, misty morning and every one was wearing thick clothes and heavy overcoats, we were not very noticeable. Our three assistants preceded us to the *Kommandantur* carrying our German caps hidden under raincoats. Then, as soon as they signalled that the camp was more or less clear of Germans, we sallied forth one by one. Each of us went through the gardens by a different path and entered the *Kommandantur* enclosure at short intervals. There were a few prisoners going in or coming out of the building and the usual sentry on the gate, but otherwise there were no Germans about and everything seemed favourable.

We walked in up the steps and turned into the dark passage. Campbell and the other two at once took our overcoats, wrenched off the half-trousers and gave us our German caps. We made a hurried examination of each other's kit to see that everything was still correct and walked out of the sheltering passage.

As we reached the steps, I seemed to realize for the first time the utter absurdity of our position. Here we were, British prisoners of war, dressed in ill-fitting German uniform, about to demand an exit from the camp in broad daylight. Now that it was too late to turn back, the whole scheme seemed ridiculous. We were certain to be caught and made to look thoroughly foolish; possibly we might even be shot at. Why on earth had we ever thought of anything so stupid?

I went on walking more or less mechanically, and we went down the steps and turned to the right out of the building. I was positively trembling with nervousness, when just at that moment several British officers passed us. They glanced up, obviously without recognizing us, saluted and went on. This steadied me a bit and I fancied the other two felt the same. The gate was twenty yards off and the sentry on duty was talking to a N.C.O., while a third man was only a few yards away. We walked quite slowly towards them and, as arranged, I began talking loudly to my brother in German. I talked about various alterations to camp buildings and improvements to the drains, while my brother took down my observations in a notebook and occasionally murmured "Ja wohl, Herr Leutnant!" – generally at the wrong moment.

Our progress was a veritable triumph. The Germans near the gate sprang to attention; the man in charge jumped for the key, rattled it in the lock and threw open the gate. Some workmen doing a job on the *Kommandantur* building stood up and took off their caps. I nodded and answered the salutes, still talking nonsense to my brother, and we strolled on with Fairweather just behind us. The gap in the barbed-wire fence was reached; the sentries, still standing stiffly to attention, were passed and the next moment we were outside. At that very instant I heard a strange gurgling noise coming from my brother and I looked round in alarm, thinking he might be on the verge of collapse. To my surprise I found that he was merely shaking with laughter! I was glad somebody could see the joke; personally I felt extremely uncomfortable and by no means safe.

A path with a few steps down brought us to the road and on reaching it we turned to the left. There was a considerable distance to be gone before we could reach cover and the only way was to follow the high road between Friedberg and Frankfurt-am-Main. Although we were now completely below the level of the camp, we were still under the observation of the outer sentries and we had to continue to go carefully. I went on jabbering German, in case anyone should be watching us, and occasionally we managed to whisper a few remarks in English. Fairweather was lagging behind and we found it necessary to slow down considerably to allow him to keep up, his kit being so tightly fastened that he had great difficulty in walking at all. Fifty yards from the gate we had left, there was a track on the right leading directly away from the camp. We had hoped to be able to follow it, for it was evidently a short cut to the woods, at this point only two or three miles away. But just as we were about to turn off we noticed some soldiers coming out of a building used as a guard house and lying close to the track. It was too risky to walk past all these men, some of whom might know us by sight, and we were forced to continue along the main road.

The next three or four hours were agony to us both mental and physical. The morning mist cleared away, the sun came out, and in our double kit of uniform and civilian clothes we suffered greatly from the heat. The tightness with which our food belts were tied on prevented us from going fast, and Fairweather, in particular, was impeded by a string which cut into his chest and shoulders. Apart from this we were seriously worried about our position, for we could find no branch roads or even tracks leading towards the distant woods and the high road was absolutely straight and devoid of any cover. We felt extraordinarily obvious in our German garb and it seemed certain that the few passers-by must guess what we were and raise the alarm. We could hardly believe that we had left the camp without attracting any attention, and every few yards we looked furtively around expecting to see the pursuit in full cry. At the end of two hours, however, we had covered about five miles and there was still no one in sight.

Just as we were about to enter a small village we found a track leading west in the direction of the woods. We took it at once as it was now essential to get off the main road. At first the track was good and led us straight through the open fields towards the hills, but at length to avoid some farm buildings we were forced to abandon it and take to the fields themselves.

The worst part of the morning's ordeal, we soon found, was yet to come. We had already seen a few scattered peasants working in the fields, but on breasting a slight rise in the ground we suddenly came in sight of several lines of men, women and children, stretching right across the way we had to go. It was impossible to get round them without wasting valuable time and there was still absolutely no cover that could afford us a safe refuge. The only thing possible was to brazen it out and walk straight through the middle of them, following the shortest and best tracks to the woods now only a mile away.

The next half hour proved finally how excellent was our disguise and general appearance, for from all sides we became the objects of an intense scrutiny by what seemed like the entire population of that part of Germany. In every direction we could hear people call to one another, pointing at us; labourers two or three hundred yards away would catch sight of us, shade their eyes with their hands to make sure of what they saw, then turn and shout to others to look. Whole groups would stop work and stare while we passed within a few feet of them. One thing is certain: no German officer had ever taken a stroll over these fields before. The people were amazed, they could not imagine what brought us there – especially on foot. That, I think, was the most difficult thing for them to understand. If we had been mounted, or escorted by a body of men, it would not have been so bad, but we had obviously come many miles across country in a region where there was nothing of any possible military interest, and – well, the whole thing was absurd.

We managed to keep going somehow, and I talked a steady stream of nonsense in German about the war, politics, the latest Zeppelin raid on hated England, and the possibility of buying up the land we were walking over and turning it into new parade grounds, artillery schools, etc. Fairweather and my brother nodded wisely at my brilliant remarks, although of course they understood not one word of what I said. When we were a little way off any particular group my brother would wave his arms, tap his notebook and make strange cackling noises that at a distance might easily be mistaken for German. Then when we were getting near again, I would start contradicting all he might be supposed to have said, thus apparently keeping up a lively conversation. The short distance we had to go seemed unending, but at long last we reached an orchard screened by a low hedge from the open fields. A hundred yards further on the path we followed turned sharply, bringing us to a gate leading into another orchard. We climbed the gate hurriedly, hoping we were not being watched, and found ourselves in a delightfully secluded spot shut in by trees and bushes, and finally out of sight of the crowd.

But we did not know whether some of the more curious of the people we had just passed might not follow us, and I considered that we ought not to stop just yet. If only we kept on going, the excellent cover we now had would make it easy to throw off any pursuers. Fairweather, however, was completely worn out by the strings that held his food belt in place. The strings, very irritating at the start, had slipped during the long walk so that now they were tight around his neck, nearly strangling him at every step. He told us that he must get rid of the string and have a short rest before continuing, pointing out that there was no need for us to wait, now we had reached the outskirts of the Taunus forest, for we had come to the parting of our ways; his route lay north-west towards Holland, and ours south to Switzerland. There was no time to argue and we said a hurried good-bye. My brother and I watched him crawl – a strangely pathetic figure in spite of the brave uniform – into the centre of a dense patch of Indian corn growing alongside the path, and then we made off at our best pace. A few minutes later we reached the fringe of the woods and headed straight up a steep slope, aiming for the thickest part of the forest. We saw nobody and, after making one or two detours round small farms and foresters' cabins, we met with no further obstructions and rapidly put a lot of ground between us and those awful fields.

About half an hour afterwards we were apparently some two hundred feet above the level of the plain and well into the dense forest. There was no sound of anything resembling pursuit and we were right off the beaten track, so calling a halt I proceeded to get rid of my German uniform. My overcoat, leggings, dummy sword, cap and uniform collar were soon buried under a pile of branches and leaves. Then the food belts were ripped open and the contents put into two small canvas haversacks, which my brother had carried in his tin box. A muffler and an old black cap completed my shabby civilian outfit. My brother also made a few slight alterations to his kit, making him look more like a workman and less like the smart official he had been on leaving the camp.

After thus completely transforming our general appearance, we got out the maps and talked over the proposed route during a meal of biscuits and chocolate. We felt pleased with our progress so far, and the way we had fooled the Boches caused us a good deal of laughter.

The day was fine and warm; the woods were very still, and we thoroughly enjoyed lying on our backs gazing up at the sky through the trees, and realizing that we were free – at any rate temporarily.

Somewhere to the west we could hear a low rumbling, like a tired thunderstorm, and with quite a thrill of excitement we realized that it was gunfire on the Western Front. The sound was like the call of a trumpet to us. A big battle was being fought on the Somme; a great victory was perhaps already won. We too had won a victory; soon we would be back in the war zone. That day it seemed as though nothing could stop us, and the face of Fortune wore a broad smile.

VIII

The stillness of the forest air was suddenly rent by two loud reports, which brought us instantly to our feet, our hearts in our mouths. The same thought crossed both our minds – Fairweather was being fired at. The guards from Friedberg must have been warned and put on to our trail by those peasants.

We listened intently and heard far away the sound of voices; then one or two shouts, followed by another shot.

We waited no more and, gathering up our few belongings, made off at a run. The path we followed took us slightly downhill, adding to our speed, so that, when we paused to listen at the end of some twenty minutes, we found we could hear nothing more. If what we heard had been a pursuit at all, then we had certainly outdistanced it, and perhaps, after all, it was only an unfortunate rabbit being peppered by a local sportsman.

Looking at our map we made out that we should be heading further south again, as we wanted to make sure of leaving the woods and hills and striking the plain as soon as night fell. A grass track took us in the right direction for two or three miles, after which we had to branch off to the left to avoid a quarry where some men were working. We passed two men with a horse and cart coming from the quarry just then and exchanged "Good afternoon". We noticed that they merely glanced at us, without the long stare to which we had become accustomed in the morning, and we concluded that our present disguise was quite passable.

At about four in the afternoon we felt sure of being clear of the vicinity where we had last been seen in German uniform and we decided to stop and wait until night. There was still plenty of cover and we found a good place on a kind of promontory, giving us an excellent view of the country over which we were to walk that night. The chief landmarks fitted in with some of those shown on our map, and we passed the time trying to work out a course that would take us clear of the rather numerous villages. After that we slept till eight, when it began to be reasonably dark, and after a short meal we started off again.

The first two miles were very easy as we were following downhill paths and there was nobody in the woods, but soon we came to a long string of farms and cottages at the bottom of the hill, where people were still about, compelling us to go very carefully. Caution was particularly necessary, for by now the Germans must have discovered our absence, and the whole district had probably been warned. Any of the roads might be watched and we might meet men on bicycles, or with dogs, in almost any of the villages. Wide detours round any place capable of giving trouble seemed essential.

It was slow and heavy going almost the whole of the night, for apart from having to avoid roads and cut across country, we were also going "across the grain", by which I mean we were going at right angles to the main roads and railways and principal streams. This forced us to stop every now and then and make a careful survey in all directions, before coming out into the open to cross one of these obstacles. As bad luck would have it on almost every road we came to, we either saw or heard some one passing and were forced to wait. On one occasion a cyclist passed us while we were actually on the road; he gave us a bad scare, for we were certain that any cyclist at that time of the night would turn out to be a soldier on our trail. To add to our difficulties we soon found that our map of this district was quite inaccurate and therefore of less than no use. The excellent maps Geerts had given us did not start till south of Hanau, and we had been unable to obtain anything further north other than an enlarged railway map. Fortunately we knew the exact point we had started from at nightfall, and taking a compass course – roughly south-east – we followed it as closely as possible all night.

Towards midnight we crossed the main road to Frankfurt, and a few yards further on we found the embankment of the main line, an express roaring by just as we got there. I remember wishing that I was on it, rather regretting that I had changed my mind about travelling by train. As soon as it had passed, we cautiously climbed the embankment and crossed the double tracks. We noticed some signal wires on the near side and stepped over them with great care, but foolishly enough we forgot that there might be some more on the far side. Those infernal signal wires always make a considerable noise at any time, but on that night it was simply terrible the way the clattering din seemed to echo and re-echo up and down the line for miles. Half a mile to the north was a signal cabin and, as we slid rapidly down the embankment, a small light detached itself from the glow coming from the doorway, and a few seconds later we heard footsteps hurrying down the track towards us. We took to our heels and ran as hard as we could, impeded by ditches and ploughed field, and dived into a dark mass of trees which suddenly loomed up. Looking round, we could see the figure of a man, lit up by the lamp he was carrying, pausing at the very spot we had just crossed. He searched about for a minute or two and then moved on down the line. As soon as he was out of sight we breathed a sigh of relief, and registered a vow never to cross a railway line again without searching not one but *both* sides for possible obstructions.

The next obstacle, encountered half an hour later, was a canal about fifteen yards wide and apparently fairly deep. Like most other things, it was not marked on our map. We skirted a large farm on its bank, hoping to find some means of crossing, but after wasting a lot of time and getting very frightened at an old white cow we retraced our steps and followed the canal bank southwards. Shortly afterwards we passed through a small village and, much to our relief, found a bridge. We crossed the canal and got out of the village again without incident, except that a score of dogs started barking and kept it up until we were a good two miles away, when another pack from a group of farms on our right took up the chorus. This barking nuisance always used to occur in Germany and escaping prisoners invariably complained of it. It did not generally cause any trouble, but it was very alarming when it started in the middle of a village.

For the next few miles we followed a road across open downs, practically devoid of houses of any sort. To the south we could see a faint glow in the sky which we fancied must come from Frankfurt. Since crossing the main railway we had seen no landmarks that were marked on our map, and we had no idea how far we had gone. The few signposts, carefully inspected by match light, showed only the names of small villages which were unknown to us. We felt sure, however, of having kept a fairly straight course and we estimated the distance covered by 3 a.m., at over fifteen miles, although a lot of mileage had been wasted in making detours.

Towards dawn we left the open country behind and began to find fields, hedges and coppices again. It was time to look for cover for the day and, after trying various small woods in vain, we saw a fair-sized clump on the top of a hill. After walking right through it we managed to find a thicket on the far side with some dense undergrowth. We crawled in and a few minutes after lying down we both fell asleep.

We woke up about an hour later, feeling very cold and wretched. We ate some biscuits and, as we still had some water, with the help of a small stove and solidified spirit, we made a sort of soup out of dried sausage, hard biscuit and Oxo cubes. This strange mixture was extraordinarily good and quite filling, and, as our small supply of food had to last us for probably over a fortnight, it provided an economical means of nourishment. We hoped later on to be able to supplement it with vegetables from the fields.

After this meal we smoked our last cigarette. Quite a lot of things had been sacrificed to make our kit smaller when we escaped, and cigarettes had been amongst them. We regretted it now for, with nothing to smoke, time passed very slowly. After making ourselves as comfortable as possible, we spent the day in sleeping and in trying to puzzle from our wretched map exactly where we were so as to plot out the night's march.

During the night we had just gone through we both had a most peculiar feeling that a *third person* was with us. This feeling was especially strong towards dawn, in fact I found myself on several occasions looking round to see where this mysterious third person had got to. Medlicott and Stewart had both told me of the same feeling, and so had various other prisoners who had escaped. Hundreds of people have experienced the same sensations and have generally explained them by saying that it was a Divine Presence leading and helping them on. As far as we were concerned I do not think that the Almighty had anything to do with the course we steered on that night or on any of the subsequent nights – unless, of course, His maps of Germany were as poor as ours. But whatever my brother found himself on two occasions that morning dividing our rations and making sure that there was enough water for three persons. We compared notes on our feelings and came to the conclusion that, since we believed that Fairweather had been shot at on the previous day, he must have been killed and this must be his ghost haunting us. We found out later that Fairweather at this time was thinking the same thing about us.

At midday three or four shots were fired in the distance. This time we were not alarmed, as we supposed that they probably came from a shooting party. It turned out that we were right but much to our annoyance we realized that the party was coming in our direction. Game seemed to be plentiful, the shooting gradually becoming almost continuous, and, after occasional intervals, the next shots sounded appreciably nearer. It took several hours for this party to get really close to the wood we were in, but between four and five o'clock we commenced to be seriously worried. The shots sounded less than a hundred yards off and several times we heard pellets spattering through the branches. Our corner of the wood was thick enough to prevent us being seen more than ten yards away, but it was obviously no protection against shot guns and we had no mind to be peppered at this stage of our journey. We lay low as long as we could, then at last, when we could see figures approaching twenty or thirty yards away, we were compelled to move on. Fortunately the course we took lay, for the first hundred yards or so, through fairly dense bushes and we were not seen, although we had an unpleasant feeling of being hunted, accompanied as we were by several rabbits and hares, and even a small deer, also running from those wretched sportsmen.

The main part of the wood consisted of tall trees with no undergrowth, and it was traversed by a track. As we felt we were being watched from all sides we slowed down to a walk and it was lucky that we did so for, on crossing the track, we caught sight of a German soldier with a rifle slung over his shoulder. He was some way off and did not see us so we walked on to a part of the wood where we could make out a patch of dense bushes near the limit of the trees. When we got there it was merely to find that not only was there insufficient cover, but that another German soldier – or perhaps a forester, but in uniform and with a rifle – was standing just outside the wood only fifty yards away. Behind us were the guns; on our right we could hear two men shouting to one another; in front were armed men – it was like "The Charge of the Light Brigade!" On the left only did the wood seem to be clear, otherwise it looked as though we were completely surrounded. We turned off and went on quickly, trying to look as unconcerned as possible and expecting at every step to hear a staccato *"Halt!"* and the click of a rifle bolt. Fortune favoured us and we reached the far side of the wood in safety. There was no one here and, a ditch affording some protection, we sat down and waited. In front of us was open country, with a village half a mile away. We thought of going into the open and chancing our luck by walking straight through the village, but it seemed too risky. At any rate we were still under cover and darkness was only some two-and-a-half hours off.

After an hour or so the shooting gradually died down and presently, to our left, we saw a small cart and a party of men in uniform, going down a track to the village. We gave them half an hour to get clear, and then got up and went back to our original place. There was a small pool of clean though rather stagnant water near and from it we refilled our water-bottles, empty since noon. Thirsty though we were, we only intended to use this water in an emergency and even then we hoped to be able to boil it first, but water was often difficult to find during an escape and we had to take what we could get. We tried to rest for another hour till it was quite dark, but we were dreadfully bored with waiting and anxious to get further.

At about 7.30 we could stand it no longer and started off. From our map we made our course to be approximately S.S.E. for ten miles, which would bring us just to the north of Hanau where we would turn almost due south. A track leading out of the wood started us on the right compass course and seemed to be deserted. We met two men a short time later, but beyond saying "Good evening" they took no notice of us. Our track eventually joined up with a road and led us into a village which we reached about eight o'clock. It was obviously dangerous to walk through so early in the evening and we decided to go round it to the south. The ground quickly became very marshy and intersected with irrigation ditches. Presently after climbing a fence and crawling through somebody's back garden, we came to the road we wanted. We walked down it for a few yards and then as we saw lights and people ahead we left it and were forced to take a path through an orchard, which ended in a swamp. After struggling out of this, we reached yet another road, but had gone barely twenty yards along it when we realized that this was the same highway we had originally followed into the village. We retraced our steps and this time boldly walked right through the village. On the far side we found a bridge over a broad stream. We crossed it, fortunately without seeing anyone, and took to the fields again on the far side.

The country now became thickly wooded – much more so than our map led us to imagine – and paths and tracks began to get scarce. There were a good many fences and enclosed woods, round which we had to make detours and into which we were continually blundering owing to the darkness of the night. To add to our confusion we were working on the extreme edge of our strip of bad map, and we were about to come into the country shown on our better map. As might be expected, the edges of the two maps did not fit and we found it impossible to make out our position; in fact, at this stage we might just as well have been without a map. A rough compass course across country was the only thing we could go by, helped by the lights of Frankfurt showing dimly to the south. The night seemed very long, our tempers exceedingly short, and the wind, bringing with it a fine rain, unpleasantly cold. The only signpost we passed for miles showed various names, none of them on our map, and we were more than ever puzzled.

At about midnight we were on some high ground and the distant lights showed up more clearly. Frankfurt seemed to be well behind us to the south-west, and almost due south were what we took to be the lights of Hanau. To keep well clear of the latter place, we made our course due east and pretty soon entered a dense strip of forest through which, owing to the undergrowth and lack of paths, we wandered interminably. The forest having effectively shut out the lights of Hanau and there being no other landmarks, we again relied solely on our compass.

After an hour we imagined that we had gone far enough to avoid Hanau with safety, and we therefore turned south. Sure enough on reaching a clearing we made out the lights of a town to the southwest, and it appeared from our map that we now had a clear course ahead of us.

IX

Dawn found us in a little thicket, providing good cover and apparently an excellent place in which to rest and pass a part of the coming day. We lit the spirit lamp, and made a hot drink with beef tablets and water. There was only enough water for one small drink each and our first care was to find a stream. We had passed one shortly before coming to our camping-ground, and we expected to find it again about a hundred yards or so to our right. Leaving my brother in the thicket, I went out into the more open woods. I had gone barely fifty yards when I saw that the forest ended a short distance further on, and on reaching the edge of the trees I looked out over a wide expanse of open country. Much to my astonishment I noticed a main road just in front of me and, as I watched, a large touring car roared past. The road ran roughly east and west and I felt certain was not marked on our map; furthermore, the forest ought not to have ended there – on our map it continued for another twenty miles or more.

I went back to my brother with an uneasy feeling that something was very wrong. As we went over the maps and tried to follow our movements during the night, it gradually dawned on us, instinctively more than by any process of reasoning, that we had not passed round Hanau as we had hoped to do but that we were now just north of the river Main, between Frankfurt and Hanau. The lights we had seen and avoided on our night's march must have been those of some intermediate town – probably Offenbach. We argued the matter and looked at the maps from every conceivable angle. At last, thoroughly disturbed at being more or less lost, we decided to move on through the wood and explore. We had just started to repack our small stock of provisions, when we saw a man coming towards us, dodging behind the trees and carrying what looked like a rifle. Something resembling panic seized us, and snatching up our kit we once again made off at a run.

It was evidently a false alarm and we soon slowed down to a walk. For two miles we retraced our steps and then turned north-east. We were now well inside the forest away from any habitation and therefore safe for the time being, but with only the vaguest idea of our position. Presently we found a road which seemed to correspond with one marked on our map and to take us in the desired direction. Still further on, the road led us into some sort of private estate and then past the front door of a large house. The grounds were literally swarming with gardeners and gamekeepers and we had several bad scares, although nobody seemed to take much notice of us. The only two men who passed close by, contented themselves with a good stare in answer to our "Good morning".

But we had barely got clear of this place and, into the thicker woods again, when we were brought to a stop by a high brick wall of the type we generally have round kitchen-gardens in England. It was no good climbing over it with the chance of being caught by a gardener for trespassing and we felt safer in the woods. We bore to the left, keeping the wall on our right and using it as a guide. We had not gone very far when through the trees we saw a man in uniform with a gun over his shoulder. We moved forward cautiously and suddenly caught sight of another man a hundred yards away to our left. At the same moment several shots rang out, and it became evident that we had run into another of those accursed shooting parties. The worst of it was that there was comparatively little undergrowth to hide in. We tried lying in a shallow ditch, but hearing the voices of people coming in our direction, we quickly changed to the only bush near. This, we discovered to our horror, was surrounded by a bed of nettles and wild garlic, and we got severely stung while the smell of garlic was almost unbearable. Nevertheless, as the cover was quite good, we stayed there for about half an hour until the sounds around us had died down. We looked around cautiously and seeing that the German soldier previously noticed had disappeared we walked on.

Towards noon, we reached a gap in the forest, shown on our new map, apparently about three miles wide. As far as we could see the whole of this area was cultivated and large numbers of German peasants were at work. A detour to avoid crossing this space would have added many miles to our route and after a few minutes' hesitation we walked straight across the fields, following a rough cart track. As on the first day, we felt very nervous when passing the German peasants, but by loudly talking German and greeting them with an occasional "*Guten Tag*", we managed to get through without arousing any undue suspicion. When at last we reached the far side of the gap, we hurried into the woods again and sat down to rest by a small stream.

We had been on the move now for nearly twenty-four hours on end and naturally felt very tired. I think my brother was more exhausted than I, as the very uncomfortable pair of boots he was wearing had made large blisters on his heels. The only remedy he could suggest was to cut large holes in the backs of the boots so as to prevent them from rubbing any more. The result looked quite ridiculous, and for the rest of the journey we were particularly careful to avoid all habitations and villages, for my brother's heels showing through the backs of his boots would probably have caused a lot of curiosity.

After resting by the stream for two or three hours we continued our march through the forest in the late afternoon. Presently we came to a main road and then a double line of railway, both of which we crossed with great caution, although this did not prevent us from being seen by quite a large number of people. In fact whenever we reached roads or railways, all the local inhabitants seemed to have forgathered at the very point at which we had chosen to cross. The crossing of this particular road and railway was most encouraging as it helped us to find our whereabouts and to show us definitely that we were now on the new and accurate strip of map. Every now and then we passed large clearings in the forest and at the end of one of these we could see, half a mile to the south of us, a cluster of houses and, on comparing their position with the details on our map, we agreed that we must at last be on the outskirts of Hanau. Another two or three miles further to the east and we turned practically due south, estimating that we had rounded the bend of the river Main. Another encouraging sign was the river Kinzig, which we forded at about this time although it was some twenty-five yards wide and about five feet deep. As luck would have it, just as we were right in the middle of the river and struggling against the rapid current, we saw a middle-aged man, wearing a top hat and dressed like a typical German professor, walking along the bank a little way off. Anything more out of place than his appearance in the middle of this forest it would have been difficult to imagine. He gave us no trouble, but on seeing us he seemed much perturbed and hurried off in the direction of Hanau. We wondered if he was also a prisoner escaping, who had solved the difficulty of obtaining headgear.

On the other side of the river we took off most of our clothes, squeezed out as much water as we could, and then hurried on as fast as possible, endeavouring to get warm again. At sunset just as we were walking down a very easy track in the middle of the pine forest, feeling thoroughly secure, we very narrowly escaped running into a barbed-wire entanglement and three or four men in German uniform, only a hundred yards ahead of us. This sudden appearance brought us to a full stop and we disappeared into the undergrowth as quickly as we could. After crawling on our hands and knees for about fifty yards, and peering through the trees, we made out the place to be some sort of a heavily guarded fortress, with barbed-wire fencing stretching out around it for a considerable distance. There was nothing on our map corresponding to this, and we fancied that it might be a prisoner-of-war camp. Later on with the help of another map we discovered that it was a powder factory. Crawling back through the woods, we made a tremendous detour and eventually got round it in safety.

Just after dusk we had reached approximately the position we would have attained early that morning, had we not lost our way on the previous night. After a short rest we decided to walk straight on, hoping to make up for lost time during the coming night. The weather was still very fine, but it soon became bitterly cold, and somehow or other we could not manage to keep warm however fast we walked, probably because we were getting very tired. At about two o'clock in the morning, after walking steadily for several hours, we felt that we must have at least a couple of hours' rest. We found a safe place, a long way from any paths or tracks and well screened in by trees, where we sat down and tried to get some sleep. One of us, of course, staying awake while the other slept. But thinly clad as we were it was far too cold to sleep, and after a while we lit the spirit lamp and made some hot soup. This did us a certain amount of good, but the contrast after the drink was finished seemed almost worse. Consequently the next step we took, a very unwise one, was to light a fire. Being in the middle of a large forest and miles from any habitation, it was probably perfectly safe, and if anybody had approached we could certainly have got a start by running away into the surrounding darkness. We agreed that my brother should sleep first for about an hour whilst I kept up the fire. But the inevitable happened, and after about twenty minutes I felt myself quite unable to keep awake any more and fell asleep too.

Half an hour later we both woke up shivering; the fire had gone out and we were colder than ever. My brother was naturally furious with me for having gone to sleep and we proceeded then and there to make the forest ring with the echoes of a family row. If there had been any German onlooker, I am sure he would have been highly amused at the strange spectacle of two English officers, dressed in the filthiest of civilian clothing, cursing each other roundly at two o'clock in the morning! But fortunately no one heard us and our arguments continued unchallenged. By the time we were more or less worn out with shouting at each other, we felt that it was quite impossible for us to go on together any more, and quite inconsequently decided that my brother should keep the maps and I the compass, and that we should each find our own way to the frontier. After this we got up from our camping-ground and walked on, side by side, without speaking a word.

We sulked on in this manner for about an hour, at the end of which time my brother disappeared. When I say "disappeared" I do not mean that I just lost him in the darkness, but that the ground actually seemed to swallow him up. I stopped and looked around in amazement, for where a few seconds ago there had been a large and very indignant man there now appeared to be no one at all. Then, from almost beneath my feet, I heard his voice. He had fallen into some kind of a swamp or mudhole and wished to be pulled out. I caught hold of a slimy hand and dragged out a horrible muddy object, only faintly reminiscent of the brother I had just lost. The odour of the mud was like the peppermints – "curiously strong", and, laughter overcoming us, our late quarrel was soon forgotten.

Dawn was now approaching once again and we had to find the usual place in which to lie up for the day. As we had emptied our water-bottle and, during the latter part of the night, crossed no streams, it was important to find water and we were compelled to go on. It was broad daylight and people were beginning to stir before we finally found a suitable coppice close to a small stream. After having eaten a few biscuits and cooked our morning soup, we lay down and slept for the greater part of the day. We were not disturbed by shooting parties, and we had a thorough good rest. By the time the sun went down, we were once more impatient to be moving.

This time we started walking between eight and nine o'clock in the evening and, after passing one or two farmhouses and skirting round a village, we came into the forest again. Here the going was comparatively easy, and we had only to follow our compasses due south. Before starting we had debated the question as to whether we should cross the Main on that or the following night. The sooner we crossed and got into less-populated country, the better it would be, but by waiting two nights we stood a better chance of crossing where the stream was narrow. There were also more bridges farther south and we therefore remained on the eastern bank. We must have covered over fifteen miles that night and we began to feel that we were making good progress at last, and that our prospects were undoubtedly brightening. We found several fields of vegetables, and reinforced our slender stock of provisions with a few potatoes, a cabbage and a turnip.

An hour before dawn, the forest thinned out again, and we had the same trouble as before in discovering good cover where we could hide during the day and which, at the same time, was reasonably close to water. We hurried on and it was still dark when at length we crossed a brook and filled our water-bottles. On the far side of the stream we saw a dense thicket into which we pushed our way about twenty yards, finally stopping at the foot of a steep slope up which I thought it useless to climb. The position seemed be perfect for a daytime hiding-place and, being very tired, we did not trouble to look any further.

We slept for about an hour and when we woke it was broad daylight. We lit the spirit lamp and commenced cooking our usual soup composed of

Oxo cubes and dried sausage, to which we added a few of the vegetables gathered during the night. As the cooker was heating very slowly, we put a few twigs underneath to speed it up and finally made a small fire. While this was going on, we heard to our surprise the noise of a distant train. The noise grew louder and louder, until we realized that the train was actually coming through the middle of the forest, and then all at once we saw that the slope against which we were sitting – we had only faintly perceived it in the dark – was the bottom of a railway embankment. The train passed above us, so that we could see the engine-driver and stoker looking down through the trees. It did not seem to matter much that they had seen us and we did not worry about it; after we had finished our meal, we could move back from the embankment into some other part of the wood.

About twenty minutes later, just as we were going to move, we saw two men coming along the track. As soon as they caught sight of our camping-ground they climbed down the embankment and came towards us. We still did not think there was any necessity to bolt; our clothes were good and we appeared to be doing nothing wrong by being in the wood. I could talk German if necessary, and I would be able to explain to them what we were doing and where we were going. Besides, if we were to run away, we would have to leave some of our much-needed food, and the men would give the alarm.

When they reached us, the two men were quite polite and unsuspicious. One of them explained that the driver of the recent train had reported at the next-station that he had seen a small fire in the wood. As forest fires in that locality had been frequent during the summer months, the station-master had sent these two employés to investigate. I quickly made things clear and told them our story – previously invented – to the effect that we were munition workers on a holiday from Hanau, enjoying a few days' walking tour. I also said that we had lost our way during the night, and that we did not think there was any harm in cooking food near the railway embankment. To bear this story out, I produced my forged pass, a relic of Weilburg days, duly describing me as a munition worker and bearing my photograph upon it. In addition I pitched them a long yarn about my brother being deaf and dumb, owing to a bicycle accident of a few years ago when he had been run over by a tram in Frankfurt. This piece of embroidery was necessary to explain my brother's ignorance of the German language. Both the men expressed much sympathy – in fact they were almost moved to tears by my sad tale and seemed inclined to let us go without any further trouble. I am quite sure that if at this time I had offered them a couple of hundred marks, they would have been only too glad to see the last of us. But I foolishly refrained, thinking that I might arouse their suspicions by any attempt at bribery.

We were about to move on when another man came along the embankment and down to where we were standing. He announced himself as the station-master, and turned out to be a much more inflammable type of German than either of the other two. He told us we were offending against all kinds of by-laws and regulations and threatened us with arrest. At one moment in his excitement he even pulled out a little bayonet from a scabbard at his side and waved it about in front of us in a most ridiculous manner. By dint of much argument I managed to quiet him a bit, my brother standing by looking as much like an idiot as possible, and occasionally giving vent to piteous mumbles. The worthy station-master was at length sufficiently appeased to say we should be allowed to go, if we promised further good behaviour. At the last moment he changed his mind and said that, first of all, we should have to go to the station, and make an official report to the effect that it was we who had lit the fire in the wood, and not the forest that had caught fire of itself. Of course I protested, but it was of no avail, and two other German workmen having come up by this time, we could only submit and go to the railway station, thinking that we could probably get away afterwards. We climbed up the embankment, surrounded by a strange collection of railway officials, and marched down the line.

When we got to the station we were taken into an office where we found that the village firemen had arrived, complete with side-arms and walking-sticks, but with apparently no other appliances for dealing with forest fires. We were questioned and cross-questioned, and I had to tell my story over and over again, and show my forged pass to each of the officials in turn. Finally a policeman arrived and the whole matter had then to be re-explained for his benefit. The strange thing was that, during this time, not one of them suspected us of being escaped prisoners.

Finally, when we were beginning to think that the whole affair had been talked out and that we would be allowed to go, the policeman made a brilliant suggestion. In order to check our statements it would be advisable, he said, to telephone to the munition factory at Hanau where I had stated that we worked. This he immediately proceeded to do, much to our annoyance, with the unfortunate result that he not only discovered that nobody knew us, but that the munition factory did not even exist! This succeeded in arousing the whole party to a somewhat belated sense of suspicion and every one present became duly agitated. The policeman telephoned to H.Q. for more policemen; the station-master telephoned to the nearest garrison for a strong guard, and the remainder of the gang contented themselves with shouting at one another and at us. About a quarter of an hour later two corpulent, red-faced Landsturm soldiers, very much out of breath with the unaccustomed exercise of walking, arrived in the office and we were formally arrested.

There was now no hope of our being liberated and, realizing that the game was up, my brother immediately ceased being dumb and started an animated conversation with me, asking what it was all about. I really think this surprised them more than anything else, and when later on I informed them that we were British officers and prisoners of war attempting to escape, they were completely astounded. Funnily enough, in this strange little out-of-the-way station they did not become infuriated at finding that we were two of the hated English. Usually at the arrest of a British prisoner, Germans of all ranks and classes used to fly into a terrible rage, cursing and shouting at the shameless audacity the English "pig-dogs" had shown in daring to escape. On this occasion, however, I must admit that they were extremely nice and, beyond warning us that if we attempted to bolt we should be immediately shot dead, they did not molest us in any way. In fact they were only too interested to hear our story and to find out from which camp we had come.

After a short interval masses of German policemen began to arrive, and a great discussion took place as to what should be done with us. Instructions eventually arrived from Army H.Q. that we were to be taken back to Friedberg as soon as possible. At midday a train came in, and accompanied by four guards we began the return journey.

X

An hour's journey in the train brought us to Hanau, where we got out and marched through the streets to the headquarters of a local infantry regiment. We were closely questioned on our method of escape and then locked up in the military prison. Up to this time no one had searched us and we still had our compass and maps concealed about us. We realized that immediately on reaching Friedberg we would be searched and, as further concealment would then be impossible, we tore up our maps and threw the pieces, with our compass, down a drain.

In the afternoon a new escort arrived and marched us down to the station, where we took train for Friedberg. The journey passed off uneventfully and most of the way back we slept. Upon our arrival at Friedberg Station we found that the news of our recapture had evidently been well advertised, for there was a large crowd of civilians, soldiers and officers from the camp to watch us. We must have been filthy-looking objects as we marched out of the station and down the main street. Our guards took us to the civil prison in the centre of the town, and there we were locked into separate cells. I heard from the jailer, just before he shut my door for the night, that Fairweather had been recaptured the day before and was somewhere in the same jail.

The next day various German officers came down from the camp to cross-question each of us in turn, and I soon realized that our method of escape had been discovered on the afternoon of the day on which we had got out, owing apparently to several rather excited prisoners talking about it in front of one of the German officers.

What chiefly puzzled the Germans was the way we had managed to get so excellent a set of disguises, and when I told them that we had made the German uniform ourselves, they refused to believe me. I found out from one of the German officers – a particularly good fellow named Dubois, who had been with us at Weilburg – that the sentry on duty at the gate at the time of our escape was in prison on a charge of having accepted a bribe. I believe I ended by convincing Dubois that we had bribed no one, and the man was released.

We were kept in jail for fourteen days pending further investigations into our case, after which we were sentenced to a further fourteen days, and we considered ourselves extremely lucky in getting off with so light a sentence.

Generally the Germans managed to trump up extraordinary charges of damage to German property, or of offences against some obscure sections of German military law. A court-martial generally followed and prisoners were often sentenced to terms of many months' duration.

But even the mere four weeks spent in solitary confinement in that particular jail were exceedingly boring. At the outset no books were allowed, no parcels of food, no change of clothing and no smoking. During the whole month I was only taken for exercise twice, and then only for half an hour each time, and I was only once allowed to have a bath. I realize that all this does not amount to any particular hardship, but at the same time it made an already unpleasant existence as a prisoner almost mentally unendurable. Not being allowed to smoke was perhaps, in this and in similar prisons, the hardest thing of all, and when one day Dubois was good enough to leave me two cigarettes, I smoked them with absolute relish by fractions of an inch at a time, treasuring up the "fag ends" for many days. Dubois forgot to leave me any matches and I could not get them from the jailer, who was a most unpleasant man, and Dubois had told me not to let him know that I had anything to smoke. Fortunately I remembered an old expedient. One of the few objects of furniture in my cell was a large glass water-bottle, and by putting this bottle in front of the small window early in the morning when for a few minutes the sun shone in, I managed to focus a certain amount of heat on the end of a cigarette and by degrees I got it to burn. Towards the end of October I was told that my brother and Fairweather were soon going to leave for some new camp, and that I would be leaving a few days later for yet another destination. It was most annoying to be separated from my brother and from Fairweather, but of course inevitable. Why the Germans had decided to move the other two first and leave me for another couple of days, I could not imagine, and I naturally felt rather depressed at being the only remaining prisoner of war in the jail.

Prison-life was not entirely without its diversions, for every morning one of the German civilian prisoners used to be sent into my cell to clean the place up. These prisoners were generally of the lesser criminal type, most of them being in prison for some minor offence such as theft. They were most interesting companions and, generally speaking, thoroughly anti-Prussian. They expressed an intense hatred for anything connected with the war, unless a British success had been reported in the papers that morning, in which case they pretended to be very pleased. I spent many amusing minutes with one of these fellows listening to his ideas on Socialism, Communism and Red Revolution, ideas which should by now have won him a high position in the Russian government. At times, indeed, I wondered whether I had not been shut up in a lunatic asylum by mistake. But at any rate this sort of conversation was better than no conversation at all, and it helped to pass the time.

I was allowed to write one letter home from jail, a portion of which I reprint here as it shows how little of my experiences I was able to tell.

Friedberg Jail,
27 October, 1916

My dear —

Whilst sojourning pleasantly – neither toiling nor spinning – in my old haunt the local jug, I have at last found occasion to write you the much desired line. How exactly to begin and how to explain my presence here are matters which require tact and forethought – to avoid erasure by the censor. All I can say is that the well-known genius of the family has at last come to the fore, and that on the 25th of September – date of glorious and happy memory – the cobbler of Köpenick[8] was completely outdone by the brothers Milne and a third party. More I am unable to say, save that by the evening of the 29th we had again hung up our metaphorical harps, and sat down to weep by the waters of Bad Nauheim. Well, that should be enough to worry that mighty god, the censor, and I expect he is more or less bound to cut it out since it is the only news I have.

After many demands both in writing and verbally to be allowed to have some books, some extra food and some clothes, I managed to obtain permission for most of my kit to be sent down from the camp. I had never had very much in the way of luggage; it was too great a nuisance to be hampered by

---

8. It will be remembered that a few years before the war, a cobbler from the town of Köpenick, near Berlin, masqueraded as a German officer and successfully fooled the Imperial Guard at Potsdam.

an enormous quantity of trunks and suit-cases when travelling from camp to camp. This was in contrast to the ideas of some of the other prisoners who, when they arrived at Friedberg, had as much luggage as a party of American tourists arriving at a fashionable hotel for the season. I remember one officer in particular who came from Mainz with no less than twenty-five trunks, suit-cases and packing-cases!

When my kit was finally sent down to the prison, all that remained of it appeared to be one pair of boots and two or three small bundles of under-clothing. Who had managed to get away with the rest I could not imagine, but I very much suspected the German N.C.O.'s in charge of the building I had inhabited. The only thing I was really very sorry to lose was my shaving-brush, in the handle of which I had managed to secrete about twelve pieces of the French gold obtained at Mainz, which would have been very useful for future attempts.

A few books were sent down with my kit and these helped to pass the time, but somehow or other very little food arrived, and I spent most of each day pacing up and down my cell planning out what I should like to eat if, by the grace of God, I ever managed to get back to the Carlton or the Berkeley.

The rather severe restrictions imposed on us at this prison were largely due to the fact that Medlicott and Stewart, who had been sent here after the Frankfurt court-martial, had succeeded in scaling the outside wall one afternoon while taking exercise in the yard. At that time only one sentry was on duty and his beat extended round all four sides of the prison. Taking advantage of a moment when the sentry was round the corner, they had managed to put an old ladder – carefully left in a tool shed – up against the wall. On dropping into the road outside, they made off down the main street at a run. Very few people were about that day and no one seems to have given chase. Turning down a side street, they came out almost immediately into open country and for some minutes it really looked as though they would get clean away. But as their escape had been discovered a few seconds after it had taken place, a party of armed men were sent after them on bicycles and caught them up, only a few hundred yards from a large wood where they would probably have been safe for the night. After this attempt, the Germans were very naturally more prudent, and escape from the jail was almost impossible.

XI

On Friday, October 27th, I was told to pack up my kit and at about three o'clock in the afternoon, in charge of a German officer and a party of four men, I left the prison. We marched down to the station, where we boarded a train going north. I had no idea of our final destination, but I vaguely imagined that after my various attempts to escape I would be sent to some more remote camp in the interior of Germany. At Giessen we changed trains and this time we got into an express labelled "Berlin", but I did not know yet whether we would go right on to Berlin, or whether we were to get out at some intermediate station.

As was generally the case when one or two officers were being moved from one camp to another, we travelled second class, and I must admit that travelling under these conditions was extremely pleasant. To anybody who would enjoy long railway journeys without the anxiety of looking after luggage, tickets or other worries, I must thoroughly recommend these trips made as a prisoner of war. For one thing, the problem of keeping annoying people out of one's compartment was entirely solved. One did not have to put one's luggage on the seat, or stand at the window making faces when the train reached a station; all this was done by the guards. Positively no one was ever allowed into the compartment during the journey, the German idea probably being that a prisoner would contaminate an ordinary German civilian, or perhaps infect him with unpatriotic ideas. If there was a restaurant car on the train, food was sent down from it, and on other occasions meals were bought at buffets in convenient stations. One's slightest personal want was attended to willingly by one of the ever-present guards. If, for instance, the carriage became stuffy and one desired to have the window open, a German at once jumped up and helped; at the same time he would take the seat beside the window, nominally to prevent the all-important prisoner from catching cold, but in reality of course to stop him from jumping out.

This particular trip was one of the pleasantest that I was ever to perform whilst in Germany. Not only was I seeing country a great deal of which was new to me, but there was a certain fascination in the thought that I was going to a new camp, should meet old friends whom I had last seen in France, and where there would undoubtedly be new possibilities of escape. The only objection I had to find with a journey of so great a length was the lack of sleeping-cars: a total of six men in a compartment left very little room for lying down. But if I was uncomfortable the Germans were equally so, and there was also consolation in the thought that one prisoner of war was keeping an officer and four men away from the front.

It was interesting to note the large numbers of Russians – numerous parties of fifty to a hundred, each guarded by only one German – employed on railway repair work throughout the country. Germany's prolonged stand in the war must have been made largely possible by the millions of prisoners she could use on important work such as this, while her own men were at the front.

The journey was uneventful; I had an excellent book to read and the time passed quickly. We reached Berlin at about ten o'clock on the following morning and had to go across the city to get to another station, where apparently we were again to take a train and go still further east. The German officer accompanying me was as pleasant as could be expected under the circumstances, and decided that this would be a good opportunity to show me the wonders of Berlin. Consequently, on coming out of the Potsdam Station, we got into a one-horse victoria, and with a guard on the small seat in front of me and another one on the box with the driver, we drove solemnly through the main thoroughfares of the capital. Berlin in wartime struck me as being particularly depressing. There was very little traffic on the streets and the shop windows were almost entirely devoid of any articles worth buying. We ended our rather dull drive at the Friedrichstrasse Station, where we had lunch.

At one o'clock we embarked once more in an express train, the carriages being marked "Warsaw" and "Brest-Litovsk". This seemed encouraging, but somehow I could not bring myself to believe that I was actually going to be taken to the Russian front. I again questioned the German officer about our destination, and as he evidently thought we were now far enough away from any frontier to prevent my trying to escape, he told me: Cüstrin [Kostrzyn nad Odrą]. The name seemed vaguely familiar, but I could not think why, nor could I imagine what sort of a camp I should find myself in. It took us two or three hours to get there, and I spent much of the time puzzling over the name. I remembered vaguely that it was the place in which the young Crown Prince, later Frederick the Great, had been imprisoned as a deserter, and it was from a window of his prison that he had seen his best friend shot. This alone was a depressing thought, but, try as I might, I could not recall in what other connection I had heard the name mentioned.

Presently the train slowed down and steamed across a bridge over a great river, which I recalled must be the Oder. A few minutes afterwards we got out at Cüstrin Station and marched through the town. The main road led to the north and presently we left the town behind and came into open country. I asked how far it was to the camp and was told that it was a very short distance, but I began to doubt the truth of this estimate when the German officer, after much saluting and bowing, left the party and said he was going no further. Soon we passed some kind of an old fort with a short steep road leading down to its gloomy-looking entrance. I ascertained that this was a prison-camp for Russians, which made me feel more than ever glad that I was not a soldier of the Czar. Another four miles, mostly uphill and rather tiring, then, just as we were coming to the fringe of what appeared to be a big forest, we turned off sharply and two-hundred yards farther on came to the camp.

With something of a shock I remembered all at once what I had heard about Cüstrin. It was of the existence of this camp – Fort Zorndorf [Sarbinowo] – notorious as the worst camp in Germany. For one thing, it was the place to which various batches of French prisoners had been sent as a reprisal for supposed atrocities committed in prison-camps in France. Secondly, the Germans believed that no prisoner could ever hope to escape from such a place and all kinds of dark rumours were current about those who had attempted to do so – one man had been shot, another had been murdered, yet another had gone off his head in solitary confinement. It was not a pleasant outlook, and on the top of all this I remembered hearing that like most fortresses its main buildings were underground, damp and dark even on the warmest day, so that prisoners rapidly became ill through lack of fresh air and exercise.

I had a good look at it as we approached and tried, from the little I could see, to get some idea of its general shape and size. It was built apparently on the same plan as were most forts of thirty or forty years ago. The highest point of it was scarcely above the level of the surrounding country. It was five-sided and surrounded by a dry ditch some fifteen yards wide and at least thirty feet deep. Nothing else was visible from the exterior save a few trenches and traverses near the summit. The road at the entrance sloped steeply downwards to the bottom of the ditch, where heavy iron gates guarded by two sentries barred the way. Just outside was a brick blockhouse, evidently used by the guards, with embrasures for small guns. As we came to the gates, one of them swung slowly open and we were admitted into the ditch. No passwords, no questions asked. It seemed easy enough to get in; would it really prove to be impossible to get out? A narrow cobblestone road led across the ditch to the main entrance of the great mound which now towered above us. We passed under a high stone arch, gloomy and weather-worn, on which was carved the date of the fortress, but where it would have been more fitting to have seen as on the gates of Hell: "Lasciate ogni speranza—" I must confess that as we walked up the long vaulted passage – smelling of damp earth and Germans – towards the centre of the fort, I felt almost excited at being at last inside this formidable place.

On reaching the German office I was formally handed over to the authorities by my guards, who then withdrew. An officer with eyes set dangerously close together welcomed me with a crafty smile, and a *Feldwebel*, with whom later on I became unpleasantly well acquainted as the central figure in many a search, went over my pockets and clothing for contraband without success. The usual particulars as to my name, profession and career were taken down in a large ledger, and after a few more formalities I was shown the door which led into the prisoners' section of the camp and set "free".

The place in which I now found myself seemed, for the moment, to be considerably worse than even my gloomiest anticipations had led me to believe. A peculiarly evil-smelling passage, badly lit by a single oil lamp, led away on either hand. In the unaccustomed darkness I was quite unable at first to make out in which direction I was supposed to go. After a moment's hesitation I perceived a small circle of daylight some distance off to the right and I turned towards it, feeling my way. Presently I came out of this tunnel and saw in front of me a long two-storied building apparently containing the rooms inhabited by the prisoners. To my left, and behind me, the ground rose almost perpendicularly to the level of the flat, earth-covered top of the building, which seemed to be the summit of the fort. To the right a wide path led past the front of the building, disappearing some twenty yards off under an archway. Just then a man came out of a door in the building in front of me, and to my joy I recognized Stewart, my friend and enemy – and therefore doubly my friend – of Weilburg days.

XII

Stewart at once took charge of me, piloting me round the camp, showing me the different rooms and telling me the names of the other British prisoners. It was most amusing meeting him again and being able to talk over old times at Weilburg. He had been sent straight on to Zorndorf from Freidberg and had been unable to escape so far, but he was evidently very keen to try. He gave me news of Medlicott, who had been transferred to some camp in Hanover, whence he had broken out twice in rapid succession, unfortunately without success, although on one occasion he got to within a mile of the Dutch frontier.

There were only five British officers at Zorndorf when I arrived, and two of these were serving a short period of imprisonment for an attempted escape. There were, in addition, six Belgians, thirty French and one-hundred-and-fifty Russian officers. All the Belgians and half of the French had been sent there for attempted escapes and the remainder of the French for reprisals. The Russians were there partly for escaping and partly for reprisals; a few because they were a general nuisance or drunkards.

Stewart was in a room with Fraser of the Gordon Highlanders, who had also recently succeeded in getting out of a camp. My room, normally containing four, was at present only occupied by one Darcy Levy. He was at times subject to fits of the most violent depression when he would either fly into a rage about nothing or else sit for hours without saying a word, but generally he was a most amusing man, having done almost everything from second-rate music-hall turns to sailing "before the mast". He had been captured while flying in the Naval Air Service, and came to Zorndorf after a very clever attempt at escape from Münden in Hanover. He and Stewart soon put me wise as to the various methods which had been employed, or were still untried, in attempting to escape from Zorndorf.

The other two in my room, at the moment in jail, were Breen, the man who had escaped from Mainz, and Hardy of the Connaught Rangers. In their

recent attempt they had been within an ace of getting away. Their scheme
had consisted in cutting through a wooden grating near the *Kommandantur*
and then forcing their way into a passage leading to the German section
of the fort. This passage went past the kitchen, and they chose the dinner
hour for the attempt. Dressed as German orderlies and armed with soup
bowls, they marched boldly down the main gallery, arriving at the main gate
without being challenged. Here they explained to the sentry that they were
new-comers to the camp and that, as there had not been enough rations to go
round, they were returning to the outer guard-house. The sentry was duly
sympathetic and was just on the point of opening the gate to let them out,
when a German N.C.O. approached and, taking pity on the new-comers,
insisted on escorting them back to the kitchen and obtaining the necessary
food. On the way back this man became suspicious, and, after putting one or
two questions, realized that something was very wrong and gave the alarm.
Whereupon, amid scenes of great excitement and with much triumphant
shouting, they were arrested and led off to jail.

I had never met Hardy, but I had heard a great deal about him. His
reputation as a prison-breaker was, I suppose, the most widely known
throughout the camps of Germany. He had been captured just after Mons,
where he had gained a D.S.O., and on coming to Germany he was amongst
the first to try to escape. Some of his adventures were really quite astounding.

On one occasion he broke out of the camp at Halle, situated in an old
factory in the middle of the town. The camp was very heavily guarded,
and some of the many prisoners who had been there told me that escape
was almost impossible. Hardy made light of the difficulties and by skilfully
picking the locks of several disused sheds, climbing over roofs of various
houses and bluffing his way past the outside sentries, finally managed to
get clear. Dressed in the most wretched of civilian clothing and speaking
very little German, he made straight for the railway station and took train
for Leipzig. On arriving at that town he had to wait for several hours before
finding another train; then, doubling back on his tracks, he made for Berlin.
He crossed the capital on foot, bought food and drink at a small restaurant
and, finding the station he wanted, caught a train going in the direction of
Holland. At Bremen he had to change again and finally left the railway at
Delmenhorst.

It had been his intention to walk the rest of the way to the Dutch frontier; but when he left Delmenhorst it was midnight, in the depth of winter, with many degrees of frost. Not only had he been travelling by train for twenty-four hours almost continually – most of the time standing up in a fourth-class compartment – but also he had had very little food and his clothing was extremely thin. It is easy then to understand how rapidly he became exhausted. After walking for a mile or two in what he thought must be the right direction, he lost his way, went round in a circle and eventually found himself approaching the station he had recently left. More or less worn out, he decided that the only course open to him was to get into some kind of shelter and wait for the morning. On one of the deserted sidings he found a small shanty quite empty except for a braiser. It was too inviting to be resisted and he went inside and sat down. He must have fallen asleep, for the next thing he remembered was a railway guard standing over him tapping him on the shoulder. His first rather hazy explanations, probably made in bad German, aroused the man's suspicions and, calling one of his mates, he marched Hardy off to the local prison.

Hardy's next attempt was even more astounding, and much more nearly successful. He and a Belgian named Basschewitz escaped from Magdeburg. I am quite unable to remember the method of the actual escape, save that it was in some way particularly daring. On getting clear of the camp they made for the town and immediately took train to Berlin. Here they changed trains and went on to Stettin [Szczecin], thence to Stralsund, crossing by ferry to the Island of Rügen. They then headed, on foot, for the small port of Sassnitz and, on arriving there, began to make inquiries amongst the seamen working on the dockside for information about ships crossing to Sweden or Denmark. There happened to be several neutral ships in the harbour and the captain of a Swedish steamer, chancing to hear of them, offered for a comparatively small sum of money to engage them as deck hands. The arrangement was made in the morning and the ship was to sail in the afternoon. They went on board at midday and tried to find odd jobs to do, so as to give the appearance of being busy to any inquisitive onlookers.

But there must have been some one in the town who suspected them, because less then half an hour before the steamer was due to sail a party of police marched down to the dock and demanded that the ship's company should be assembled. Hardy and his companion were at once spotted as not being members of the original crew. They were dragged off to prison, and the next day a party of guards arrived to take them back to Magdeburg.

I forget if they were marched back across Rügen or not, but at any rate at some point on the island the N.C.O. in charge of the party decided that they were to pass the night at a small wayside inn. The guards slept in the same room as their prisoners, two on either side of them, and thinking apparently that this made everything safe they all fell asleep. In the middle of the night Hardy and Basschewitz managed to crawl to the window, open it and climb out without giving the alarm. They made for the coast at their best speed, but a day later, the whole country-side having been alarmed and it being more or less impossible to get off the island, they were both recaptured. This time they were very badly treated, thrown into jail and, to their amazement accused of murder! After many inquiries as to the identity of the person they were supposed to have killed, they were told that it was the N.C.O. in charge of the guard from whom they had escaped. He had, it appeared later, been so terrified of the consequences of his carelessness that he had committed suicide by blowing out his brains. After many weeks in prison, the charge was dropped, owing I believe to the admission made by one of the guards that he had actually seen the N.C.O. in question shoot himself. It was then that Hardy had been sent to Zorndorf.

I very soon realized that the story of the utter impossibility of escape from Zorndorf was not strictly accurate, and as a matter of fact two Russian officers who had recently escaped were still at large. They had succeeded in getting out by means of the old washing-basket trick, a familiar feature in every camp. Strangely enough the working of this scheme at Zorndorf, where one would have expected the Germans to be very wise, was very easy.

The camp washing was sent away once a week in a huge box measuring about five feet square. This box was packed in the afternoon and stood for a whole night just outside the window of the Russian orderlies' room on the ground floor of the building. The two Russians had cut a panel from the back of the box and crawled in after taking out some of the washing. They then screwed the panel up on the inside, and the next morning they were hoisted upon a cart and driven out of the camp in triumph. It was some time before we had news of their further adventures. One of them was recaptured, after a fortnight of freedom, wandering about in Poland. The other, of whose success we were convinced, was found no less than seven months later, staying with some German relations in Berlin.

I was unfortunately just too late in coming to Zorndorf to take part in the digging of the famous tunnel. This tunnel, certainly the longest ever constructed in Germany, would, if it had been completed, have measured approximately one-hundred-and-fifty metres. Even so, it was over one-hundred-and-ten metres long when discovered by the Germans. Tremendous difficulties had been encountered in the course of the digging, and wonderful ingenuity had been displayed by the prisoners. The entrance was concealed in a corner of one of the French rooms, and for the first few yards a channel had been cut through some soft concrete. After this the shaft had wound about along the various foundation walls, passing right underneath them at points where the earth was softest, or breaking through them where the cement was fairly brittle. The earth was carried away from the tunnel mouth in sacks made by the prisoners. It was then disposed of under the floors in the various rooms, where there was a space of about a foot between the boards and the concrete foundations.

After clearing the foundations the tunnel sloped downwards for about sixty metres in a straight line towards the ditch, but, on arriving beneath one of the concrete gun positions – known as *Caponnières* in the ditch, the diggers struck water and the tunnel became completely flooded for many yards. Another passage was then commenced at right angles, and after some ten yards was again turned towards the ditch. This time no water was encountered and the shaft was pushed on, to beneath the foundations of the outer wall. The question of how to bring the tunnel as quickly as possible to the surface, forty feet above, was still being discussed when suddenly the Germans made a move. Up to that time they had not seemed to have even the vaguest suspicion, but one morning they raided the French room and without any hesitation pulled up the floor boards and discovered the entrance.

The prisoners were astounded at the abruptness of the disaster since the work had been carried on for many months with the greatest care and secrecy, and nothing had been done which could possibly have alarmed the Germans. Almost every prisoner in the camp had been engaged in some way or other in the making of the tunnel, the very few exceptions being prisoners who were either too ill to escape or inebriate Russians. Every one racked his brains to try and discover how on earth the Germans had got wind of the affair and, after much roundabout questioning, one of the Germans admitted that it was a Russian who had betrayed the scheme. Apparently a confirmed drunkard, this Russian had one day run short of alcoholic refreshment and being seized with a craving for drink of any kind had gone to the Germans and offered to sell them the secret for a bottle of gin. The bottle was immediately produced, and the Russian, having told his story, was clapped into jail.

Overjoyed with their discovery, the Germans did little more than close down the tunnel and make a thorough search of the camp. Very unwisely they permitted the Russian to whom they owed so much to return to the camp a few weeks later. Feeling was naturally so strong against him that three of his compatriots were told off to watch him day and night lest he should be murdered. I am quite uncertain as to his ultimate fate, but I have a strong suspicion that he did not live very long.

Amongst those who had given themselves wholeheartedly to the tunnel construction was the celebrated French aviator, Garros, who was still in the camp when I arrived. Some of his devices, particularly for the ventilation in the shaft, were really brilliant. I never saw the ventilating apparatus, but I believe it consisted of a long pipe, made entirely out of circular food tins cleverly soldered together, leading from the entrance to the end of the shaft. At the mouth of the tunnel a fan worked by a gramophone motor drew out the bad air, whilst a bellows pumped fresh air down a second pipe.

Garros was an extremely nice fellow who had had a very hard time as a prisoner, having been in Zorndorf ever since his capture in 1914. Unlike many prisoners, he did not take to escaping from a love of adventure or as a relief to the tedium of captivity, but solely from the point of view that it was his duty to return to France again. At the time of my arrival he and some other French officers were secretly at work on a scheme, the details of which were unknown to us.

In spite of the tunnel failure, the inhabitants of Zorndorf remained optimistic and countless new schemes were soon on foot. I started to collect the elements of a new escaping kit and made inquiries with a view to obtaining a compass and maps. I discovered that Zorndorf possessed one great advantage over the majority of camps in Germany: ordinary German money was allowed to the prisoners. The Germans probably thought that none of them would be able to get very far from the camp even if they succeeded in breaking out, and that there was therefore no need to supply the usual valueless "token" currency. This was a great advantage to us since it did away with the necessity of buying real money at a high rate of exchange from one of the more corrupt Germans.

At the beginning of November, just as I was beginning to get settled in my new abode, Hardy and Breen returned from jail. I at once got in touch with them and asked if I might join up in any future attempt. They agreed and we started to look around for ways and means. Another confederate of theirs was Captain Bacquet, of the French cavalry, and we decided that, in the event of our getting out, we would divide into two parties – Hardy and Breen, and Bacquet and myself.

I do not remember what our first scheme was, but I feel sure that it was something wild and very unlikely to succeed from the fact that I can recollect nothing of the method of escaping, but a great deal about the route we were to follow afterwards. It was always a bad sign when a tremendous amount of talk was expended on such details as the trains to be taken, towns to be passed through, and the exact point at which the frontier was to be crossed, as this generally implied that not very much was being said about the actual plan of escape – possibly because those attempting it had little or no confidence in its success.

In this particular case, Bacquet and I worked out a marvellous and complicated system for eluding pursuit. It consisted principally in travelling by train in every direction possible except the right one, and in taking about a month to reach the frontier. But we never got any further than collecting a lot of kit, and eventually the whole arrangement died a natural death.

Towards the middle of December, Hardy and I realized that we were actually without a single good plan for breaking out. Something had to be done, and we examined and re-examined every possible scheme that had ever been suggested. The various plans for walking out dressed as Germans were more or less out of the question, not only since Hardy and Breen's recent abortive attempt, but also because a month or two previously one of the Russian officers had attempted it. Dressed as a German officer and speaking perfect German, he had managed to bluff his way past all the sentries, in spite of the fact that he had no pass of any sort. But like so many Russian schemes his plan contained an element of eccentricity, for he carried with him a home-made saddle and bridle intending, as he afterwards told us, to catch a horse and ride back to Russia. A German N.C.O. outside the camp noticing this strange equipment and having observed that the sentry on the gate had not asked the supposed German officer to produce a pass, followed him and eventually brought him back to the camp – saddle, bridle and all. After this, of course, the Germans were much more on the look-out for schemes of this type. As a matter of fact, we seriously considered for a short time the possibility of dressing up one of the French officers, who closely resembled the camp commandant both in face and figure, and strolling out with him in our ordinary uniform as though we were going on one of the weekly afternoon walks which had recently been authorized at Fort Zorndorf. Somehow the idea did not appeal to the Frenchman, and this delightful scheme also fizzled out.

At length Hardy and I came to the conclusion that there were just two plans in which success was at all likely. One of these had been originated by the French and was not likely to mature for several months, and in any case it would only be after the French had succeeded that we would be able to try it. The other scheme was very much more desperate and offered, in the opinion of most people, very little prospect of success.

XIII

The commandant, a fat benevolent-looking Prussian of over forty, lived just outside the fort in a cottage lying on the fringe of the woods, which grew close to the camp on the north-eastern side. Being not only corpulent but lazy, he seldom troubled to come inside the fort, so that, if he wished to see any of the prisoners, they were usually brought under guard to his house. The guard never consisted of more than two men with rifles, and lately we had noticed that there was only one man. When the prisoners who were to see the commandant reached his house, the escort knocked at the door and went in to announce his arrival, leaving the prisoners outside. The position was more or less screened by trees, although less then a hundred yards away from the sentries on the fort, and the woods were scarcely fifteen yards off. Barely ten seconds were necessary to dash round the corner of the house and jump over the fence into the woods. A sprint for several yards, and steady running for a few miles, would take one clear from all immediate pursuit. With food, money, maps and a compass, there was just a chance of getting clean away.

After much discussion three of us eventually decided to try it, the party consisting of Hardy, Breen and myself. There were only three main obstacles to be overcome: we had to make sure that all three of us were taken over to see the commandant at the same time; secondly it was necessary to carry sufficient food for several days, and lastly we had to wear our civilian clothes underneath our uniforms as far as the commandant's house. To avoid appearing unnaturally bulky we could only take the absolute minimum of food and clothing, but this had the advantage of enabling us to travel faster once we were away. We determined to start on 1 January (1917), but we were delayed by bad weather until the 3rd.

At about half-past two in the afternoon of that day, I went into the German office and asked one of the clerks to telephone to the commandant asking him whether he could see us about a cinema, which we wanted to start in the camp. A few moments later the commandant sent a message to say that he wished to interview us at once – little knowing what kind of a movie show we were going to enact near his picturesque cottage.

I hurried back to the room where we lived and told the other two of the news, and we hurriedly put on our civilian clothes, then uniform overcoats, and crammed our pockets with biscuits, chocolate and malted-milk tablets. By this time we all had nervous misgivings and the prospects of success seemed remarkably small. As soon as we were ready we went back to the office and asked for the escort.

One man, unarmed save for his bayonet, took us out. Everything went as well as could be desired, and none of the many Germans we passed seemed to notice how fat we looked. But as we got near to the house we saw that the sentry, whose duty it was to inspect the outside of the fort once every hour, was just behind us. This made matters extremely awkward as the man was armed and would be able to give chase immediately we started running.

There was no question of turning back and we simply had to take the risk, although personally, I must confess, I felt by no means keen about it.

We reached the house and our escort went inside according to plan. There was not a moment to be lost, as he would be out again in less than a minute. We tiptoed away from the door, rounded the corner of the house, and broke into a run.

I had the luck to be first. Closely followed by Hardy, I jumped over the fence into the woods and sprinted away as hard as I could. There was scarcely any undergrowth, and running was easy and silent. Two-hundred yards from our starting-point lay the main road from Cüstrin to Stettin; I crossed this, glancing to either side to see if anyone could tell which way we went, scrambled up the bank opposite and plunged into the woods again. I ran on for another hundred yards or so, and then slowed down and looked around. I had not heard a sound except my own footsteps and was surprised to see that Hardy was close behind me. He had thrown away his khaki overcoat and cap, and was now arrayed completely in a villainous black civilian suit with a dirty black cap on his head. Breen was nowhere to be seen. Hardy came up, apparently astonished that I was already slowing down, and shouted to me:

"Take off your coat and come on. They are after us!"

I pulled off my overcoat and the khaki collar and tie I was wearing, re-arranged my civilian clothes and put on an old workman's cap. By this time Hardy had got some way ahead and I started off to try and catch him up. There were still no sounds of pursuit, and a little farther on I looked round once more. Through the trees I caught sight of Breen about three-hundred yards back, walking slowly and apparently out of breath. I turned again and ran on, but Hardy had disappeared somewhere in the bushes ahead and I was unable to find him. We were fortunately quite prepared to be separated from the outset, and each of us was independent of the others, having a map, a compass, money and food of his own. I was very sorry to get out of touch with the other two, but in a wild scramble like this each man had to fend for himself.

I jogged on for some time, thoroughly pleased at being temporarily free again. Suddenly from some distance behind I heard faint shouts and the sound of rifle shots; the Germans had evidently overtaken Breen. I wondered if they had already got him and were firing as a signal, or if they were actually shooting at him. The thought that they might get on to my tracks next, made me redouble my efforts to get clear of the danger zone.

The route we had chosen was a fairly simple one. About three miles to the east of Zorndorf lies the railway to Stettin. The line runs nearly due north through large tracks of forest, and we intended to follow the course of this line for about twenty miles, then branch off in a north-westerly direction.

Little over half an hour's running through the woods brought me to the railway, and after some difficulty in getting round a few houses and avoiding farm labourers, I found a path running parallel to the line and about twenty yards from it, which I proceeded to follow. The pursuit did not give any further trouble and, getting very blown with continuous running, I slowed down to a walk. The short winter's afternoon was drawing to a close and with darkness came increased safety. I had no very definite plan of action, except that it was necessary to put as much distance as possible between myself and the camp during the night, and next day I would take the train, if possible, straight to Berlin. Once in Berlin, it would be time to think again.

I walked on for several hours, avoiding all houses along the line and keeping a careful watch at the level crossings I came to. Occasionally, when passing an isolated house, the usual dog would start barking furiously and I made wide circuits of these places in case the owners should come out. Once I thought I was caught. A particularly annoying dog had been barking for a good ten minutes at me, when I heard voices and saw lights approaching along a track crossing the railway. They seemed a fairly numerous party, and just when I was turning round to take cover I heard footsteps coming down the track from the opposite direction. I turned and ran back into the woods, and almost instantly, as though I had been heard, a whistle was blown and another dog began to bark close at hand. I went on running for a few seconds and then, pushing my way into the thickest part of the undergrowth, stopped to listen for any further signs of pursuit. I could still hear a dog barking in the distance, and not very far off I could hear the cracking of twigs and approaching footsteps. Presently I fancied I could hear voices coming from yet another direction. I seemed to be completely surrounded and I believed that a large party of Germans must be closing in on me. I felt thoroughly unnerved. I have never been particularly brave in the dark, and I naturally imagined every bush was a man and every branch a rifle.

After about ten minutes, as the various sounds died down, I began to retrace my steps cautiously and on reaching the track found it deserted. I crossed it at once and went on. I neither heard nor saw anyone else, and I never found out whether there was really a search party out, or whether it was not largely my imagination.

I found the railway again and walked beside it until I came to a stream which I had been expecting to find for some time. According to the map, it should have been very small – barely ten yards across – but actually it was in flood, a hundred yards wide at some points and with a very strong current running. I did not like the idea of swimming it, and, moreover, I wanted to keep my clothes respectable for the train journey next day. On the far side were the first houses of a village and a railway station, making swimming even more inadvisable. The alternative was to cross by the railway bridge, which was in all probability guarded. We had heard in Zorndorf that if anyone escaped all bridges and railway stations, and many of the larger villages in the neighbourhood, would be watched by sentries within a very short space of time. It seemed likely therefore that this bridge would be guarded as well as others. In the dark, and from the side of the railway embankment, it was impossible to see whether this was so or not, and to approach close enough to find out appeared risky.

Something had to be done, however, so climbing up the embankment to the railway track I crawled to the bridge. It was unguarded. I crossed it and got down from the embankment as quickly as possible on the far side. The lights of the station were barely fifty yards off; there seemed to be nobody about; but I was afraid that I might be seen and, making a wide detour of station and village, I got quickly back into the woods.

It was now about half-past eight, and I had been on the move since about half-past three in the afternoon. At a rough estimate I had covered about fifteen to eighteen miles in a northerly direction. I was beginning to feel rather tired and a small stream in a quiet corner of the forest decided me to call a halt. I sat down, ate some chocolate and drank some water. Ten minutes later, feeling quite fresh again, I got up to go on. I was just lighting a cigarette when I heard footsteps coming towards me. This time it was useless to run and if I stood still the man might have no suspicions. I waited. He passed by without looking in my direction, and I watched him go with considerable relief. Then, in spite of the darkness, something about him struck me as familiar. A moment's hesitation, and I called out in German. He answered and I realized that I was not mistaken; it was Hardy!

We had been separated for over five hours in the forest, so it was a remarkable piece of luck which brought us together again, and for several minutes we must have been in real danger of being recaught while the forest echoed with our laughter – it was such a relief to have a companion again.

Hardy told me what had happened to him since he left Zorndorf. He had lost his compass and had had much difficulty in finding his way. We discussed the best route to follow, what point we should make for, and then went on again. For some time we followed the path alongside the railway line where it ran through the woods. It was easy going and we kept up a good pace, but after about four or five miles the railway came out into the open country and we could see in front of us the lights of a station.

We had decided to leave the line at this point and strike off roughly north-west across country. The first half-hour or so was terribly hard work over ploughed fields, made particularly soft and muddy by recently melted snow. After this we reached a fairly good track, skirting the edge of the woods. We followed it for some distance and it eventually brought us to a small village – Klossow, our map called it. It was fairly late, the chances of our meeting anyone were slight, and we made up our minds to walk straight through it. The lamps in practically all the houses were out as we went down the road and we only passed one cottage with a light. Through the window, we caught sight of a man comfortably reading in front of a large fire of logs.

At about this time it began to rain. The sky had been overcast the whole day, and occasionally a few flakes of snow had fallen. It had cleared up slightly at the time we started and we had been in hopes of a fine night; but now it commenced to pour, and in a short time we were wet through. It was very dark and in spite of map and compass we had great trouble in finding our way. Occasionally we followed cart tracks, and when we lost them we would walk across country till we found a path or a road going in the right direction. It was heavy going all the time and just about as cold as it could be, though not actually freezing. The wind seemed to take all the life out of one.

At last we found a passable road which we followed for several miles, still in a north-westerly direction, to a large village not far from the bank of the River Oder. We walked through the village – it turned out to be Zellin [Zielina] – without any trouble, but it was a maze of winding streets and lanes and we had a lot of bother finding our way out of it. We tried the doors of some barns on the outskirts to see if we could get shelter from the rain for at least a few hours, but it was useless; they were all either locked or else dangerously close to houses.

After leaving the village behind we pushed on as hard as we could to the north, with the rain beating in our faces. We passed through another village without stopping and, at about one o'clock, came to yet another, standing on the banks of the Oder. This time we went down to the water's edge and found a boat. We managed to undo the chain securing it and then saw that there were no paddles or oars. We hunted round for some time, found a couple of poles and pushed off. Unfortunately the river was in flood and what we had imagined to be the banks were in reality flooded fields with the hedges just above water. It meant that we would have to steer through innumerable small gaps in order to get to the main stream. At this point – near Güstebiese – we estimated the river to be over a mile, and it was pitch dark. Walking fast over rough ground had kept a certain amount of warmth in us, but sitting in an open boat with a cutting wind and heavy rain beating through our scanty clothing was wearing us out much more quickly. To make matters worse, the small sack containing our slender stock of food and cigarettes fell into the bottom of the boat which was full of water; finally both our punt-poles broke off short. This ended our river trip. We must have looked remarkably comic, but we were without doubt the two coldest and most miserable men in Germany. We made for the shore again as quickly as we could, with only our hands to propel the horrible craft, and "abandoned ship".

We started walking again at once and soon reached the comparative shelter of the woods. It was positively warm after our boating experience and we went along at a good pace. But it was not long before we began again to feel the effects of our hard cross-country tramp, for Zorndorf had not made either of us too fit, and once or twice I went to sleep while we were walking, to dream of hot drinks or a warm bed.

The woods through which we were now going were much more dense and also marshy, and we could only follow paths that often took us miles out of our way. Several times we walked into impassable swamps and had to retrace our steps, and more than once we seemed completely lost. The map was not of much assistance and a northerly compass course was our only guide. Somewhere between two and five o'clock in the morning we each went through a period of utter exhaustion, fortunately not both at the same time as otherwise we should have been entirely off the track. As it was, our course was rather erratic and we wasted a lot of time. But we made considerable headway through this wilderness in spite of our exhaustion. We were so tired and sleepy that at times we thought we could see lights in the distance or houses in the forest, and once we felt certain we were alongside a railway line which we knew was many miles away.

I cannot remember exactly when and how things happened, but at length, just before six o'clock in the morning, we got clear of the forest and marshes and suddenly found ourselves near a large farm. Several houses were lit up and work was just starting in the farm buildings. We managed to slip right through the centre of the farmyard without raising the alarm, although there were one or two people about and the place was bright with lights. Fortunately, the customary dogs were silent – tired out, we supposed, after a night of barking. We could find no tracks and were forced to take to ploughed fields again, heavier than ever after the night's rain. Then suddenly we heard a most welcome sound: the noise of an engine shunting, not far off. We were about to strike the branch line towards which we had been heading all night.

This line runs roughly from north-east to south-west, crossing the River Oder not far from where we now found ourselves, and then going south-west to Berlin. We intended to make for a station on the line and travel straight to Berlin. But it was not so easy to find the station. We walked a long way through the ploughed fields and at last found a road leading to the village of Selchow where people were just beginning to stir. We could see no signs of the railway, and we realized that the station must lie some way out. We tried one of the roads starting from the centre of the village, but it seemed to go in the wrong direction and we halted to discuss our next move.

It was just beginning to get light and everywhere men were starting out to work. It was bitterly cold and the wind was as keen and strong as ever. We were feeling stiff and footsore from our long march, and we decided to go into a shop or a public-house to ask the way and if possible get something warm to drink. The local blacksmith's shop was horribly tempting. There was a bright fire burning in the forge and the man was already at work shoeing a horse. We hesitated. The place looked warm, and blacksmiths are honest folk – too honest for us perhaps. It seemed unwise to go in, and we passed on.

In the main street of the village we saw a lighted window; coming closer we found it to be a small shop. We hastily repeated the main points of the story we were to tell if any question were asked, and walked in. The shop was empty and seemed to be the sort of place we wanted. A girl came out of the back room and we asked her for something hot to drink. In a short time she produced some excellent hot coffee and biscuits. We swallowed the coffee at a gulp and asked for more. While waiting we sat down and rested, overjoyed at the short spell of comparative comfort. Presently an unpleasant-looking individual, sallow-faced and with a "Kaiser" moustache, came from the back of the store. I think he mistrusted us from the first, for he at once began to ask questions. We certainly looked rather suspicious objects. Our clothes were saturated with rain and plastered with mud. Hardy's coat was badly torn by barbed wire, our faces were dirty and unshaven. Luckily we could both speak German.

"Have you come a long way?" said the man eyeing our clothing.

"A fair distance."

"You seem to have been out all night; you are very wet."

"Yes, we had to start last night to catch the train here this morning."

"Are you travelling a long way? "

"As far as Berlin. This is my cousin," I said, pointing to Hardy, "who is going with me. You see my mother has just died and we are going to the funeral."

This silenced him for a time. The story of the "dead mother" is always useful, and, if told with proper pathos, generally most effective.

Presently our friend got inquisitive again and asked where we had come from. I hurriedly thought of the name of some village which we had passed in the night:

"Güstebiese."

"Who is your employer there?"

"Herr Ebenstein," I answered.

He could not say much to that, as he obviously did not know the village, and could not possibly know Herr Ebenstein because he did not exist. This about ended our cross-examination, and we went on with our coffee, while the man retired to the back of the shop to think things over. We borrowed a needle and thread and mended Hardy's coat; then, having paid our bill, we set out again.

The station we discovered lay about a mile and a half from the village. It was now broad daylight, and labourers, including parties of Russian prisoners, were at work in the fields. The country around was bleak and bare, for we had left all the woods and forests behind when we passed through the farm before dawn. There was nowhere to hide if we were pursued, but we had little fear of that, as we were well off the route the Germans would expect us to take.

We reached the station at last; it consisted of only one building, but outside the yard there was a sort of restaurant. The place was completely deserted and there were no signs of a train coming, although we had hoped and expected to catch one almost at once. We did not like the look of it in the least – it was so deserted. It seemed strange for two bedraggled tramps to go up and ask when the next train left for Berlin, but we pulled ourselves together and walked in. After searching around a bit we found the waiting-room, and, inside, a couple of railway officials who were busy cleaning and sweeping. We asked them for the next train and were told that it did not leave until half-past eleven. We were at a loss what to do. It was only seven, so that we had over four hours to wait. There was no cover in the surrounding country, and it was out of the question to sit in the empty waiting-room with inquisitive officials about. The restaurant close to the station appeared to be shut and it would have been risky to try and get in. Meanwhile, we were still in the station, stiff with cold in our damp clothes. We had to discuss the situation and decide on our best course. As we could not very well argue on the platform, we made for a little wooden shed, some way from the main building. This happened to be the station lavatory and, as far as such places go, it was the most unsanitary I have ever seen. But it was at least a shelter from the freezing wind, and we were out of sight.

There seemed to be no alternative except to walk back to the village, and if possible get some more coffee, as we realized it might be many hours before we could get any other food. We left the station, followed the road back and returned to the store. There were several other customers in there this time, and our suspicious friend was still behind the counter. A large, unpleasant-looking farmer, with a little pointed beard and small vicious eyes, looked hard at us as we came in. After saying the customary "Good morning", he at once asked me:

"Why aren't you in the army?"

In tones of injured innocence I answered that I was unfit – in fact, that I had been ill for years. The man put the same question to Hardy who said something about the terrible condition of his heart, or his lungs, I forget which. After this, the man contented himself with having a good stare at us. We certainly looked pretty sick that morning, and apparently satisfied him, for he soon left the shop. The rest of the customers also left and we were alone with the owner. We had some more coffee, successfully negotiated a few more questions, and then sitting down we settled ourselves to wait for a couple of hours.

Tired as we were, it was only natural that we should fall asleep, but the owner of the place would not have this at any price, and abruptly woke us up again. He said it was against the rules of the establishment to allow people to sleep there, and if we wanted to do so we must go outside. After this either he or the girl who had been in the shop when we first came in was constantly behind the counter, and whenever we started dozing we were immediately shouted at. Nevertheless we were fairly comfortable and stayed in the place for about two hours, after which we walked slowly back to the station, feeling much better.

Even then we had a good half an hour to wait for the train, but the waiting-room was no longer empty. About a dozen other people had also arrived early, and nobody took much notice of us. We sat down near the booking-office, which was not yet open, and discussed our plans when no one was listening. Once Hardy dozed for a few moments, woke up with a great start and began talking in English! Fortunately there was a good deal of conversation going on and it passed unnoticed.

Presently the booking-office was opened, and when our turn came we each bought a fourth-class ticket to Berlin, and made our way to the platform. When the train came in we found it was extraordinarily crowded, owing,

I suppose, to the reduced war-time service. All the carriages were full and there was only standing room in the fourth-class. This was rather in our favour, as it prevented us from being too conspicuous.

The journey started well, and after the conductor had paid us a visit, clipped our tickets and inspected our passes, we felt that our chances were increasing. We passed a station, and the next one, as we knew, was at the bridge across the Oder. Once beyond the river, we felt we should be out of the zone watched by the Zorndorf authorities.

But our luck had deserted us. At this very next station, Zäckerick, the train stopped an unusually long time, and, just as every one was beginning to wonder why, the door of our compartment was thrown open and a man came in who instantly recognized Hardy, drew a revolver and shouted "Hands up" at the top of his voice. Then seeing me next to Hardy, he repeated his yell with various epithets of abuse. Several women in the carriage shrieked, the men got up and waved their arms at us, and some officials outside joined in the chorus. It was awe-inspiring, but I think we would have been more impressed if we had not noticed that the aged revolver levelled at us was unloaded and did not even possess a breach.

We were bundled out upon the platform and marched in triumph to the station-master's office, where they proceeded to search us, without very much result, as we tore up our maps, swallowing most of the larger pieces, and Hardy managed to put our passes into a stove. The man who had arrested us turned out to be a N.C.O. from Zorndorf; I had never seen him before, but Hardy knew him well and had been caught by him before when filing through some bars in one of the passages leading out of the fort. Both he and a sergeant-major amused themselves at our expense by being noisily rude, but they did not actually knock us about.

The search over, we were taken to a small guardroom at the end of the station, and four men and a corporal were set to watch us. We sat on a bench opposite these men, each of them with a loaded rifle and his finger on the trigger, for something like two hours till the train which was to take us back arrived. The return journey took five hours, and we slept practically all the way; but we woke up just enough at the stations to notice that at each place a man from Zorndorf joined the train, showing that the elaborate precautions we had heard of had actually been taken. By the time we got to Cüstrin, the Germans with us numbered over a dozen. Five of them marched us to the military prison in the old Citadel, and we were locked up for the night. Breen was already there, although naturally we were not allowed to see him. Next morning, 5 January, the general commanding the Cüstrin area – a dear old very white-haired man with a Polish name, who was always very kind – came to see us. He said he disapproved of our method of escape as it involved the commandant, whom he had been compelled to punish. I am afraid we were rather pleased at this, the more so when it was rumoured later that he had been given seven days' arrest. The general sentenced us to a week's solitary confinement, about the most lenient punishment any of us ever received in Germany, and far less than we had expected. The week passed uneventfully and we returned to Zorndorf on the evening of the 12th, where we met Breen, who had been released the day before. He had a lot to tell about his capture and his return to the camp immediately afterwards; he had been quite badly knocked about with rifle butts by several of the guards. Considering that he was caught so soon after starting, when his pursuers' blood was probably near boiling-point, we thought he was lucky not to have been seriously injured. He had been able to destroy his map and papers before being caught, but we learned from one of the more friendly guards that the Germans had found the remains of the map, and piecing it together had discovered the route we were likely to follow, as this and the railway to Berlin were the only things shown. They had just time to send to Zäckerick during the night the man who was able to catch us next morning. It was unfortunate, but of course Breen was not to blame. We had made a fatal mistake in taking the train at all on that day. If we had waited till nightfall we might have stolen a ride on a goods train, or if we had remained in cover for another twenty-four hours it would probably have been safe by then to take the train openly. We thought we had marched farther than the Germans could possibly expect – allowing for detours, we had walked a good forty miles in fifteen hours. But, for the decision to board a train, I must accept all responsibility; Hardy by himself would never have done anything so foolish.

XIV

For about a week after coming back from jail. Hardy and I gave up all thoughts of escaping and enjoyed what we considered to be a well-earned rest.

Heavy snow had been falling for some time and the whole camp was covered to a depth of several inches, providing the chance of a limited amount of winter sports. We built a toboggan run on quite a good course from the top of our building, down a steep path ending up just outside one of the rooms. The path was very narrow, and towards the bottom passed through a wooden gateway only about two-and-a-half-feet wide. After a few days of frost the whole track, almost one-hundred yards long, was covered with ice, and we used to get up a really considerable speed. The negotiation of the small gateway was thrilling and fraught with danger – particularly as the gateposts were covered with barbed-wire. Several men ran into the posts, but the casualties only amounted to a few cuts and a black eye. The Russian orderlies made us two very good toboggans out of old packing-cases and, during the week or so of hard frost, it became an all-day habit among the British. Towards the end of January, a thaw set in and nearly all the snow melted, putting an end to our childish amusements and making us turn our thoughts to escaping once again.

Our first step was to unearth fresh suits of civilian clothing, and in Zorndorf it was difficult to obtain a good kit, largely owing to the fact that there were so few prisoners and so many who wanted to escape. But, one article, a pair of black trousers, was always obtainable. As at Weilburg the Russians, many of whom had been captured in rags and were unable to procure fresh clothing from home, received permission from the Germans to have trousers made out of dark civilian cloth, provided that a red stripe was inserted in the seam. A hint to the Russian tailor, coupled with a few German marks, was sufficient to ensure that the red stripe was only lightly sewn on and therefore easily detached. In the same way many of the Russians had been able to purchase from the German authorities cheap civilian coats, rather resembling Norfolk jackets in shape, from which the regulation badges and buttons were soon removed if they were needed for escaping. As far as overcoats were concerned, either the Belgians or the French could generally be relied upon in an emergency to part with one of their old-style, dark blue service overcoats, which only needed slight alteration. The new-style Russian overcoat, dark reddish-brown in colour, was also a possibility and, if the worst came to the worst, a rather rough-looking coat could be manufactured out of a German blanket.

The hat question was, as ever, much more difficult. A cap could sometimes be made by a tailor out of a blanket, the peak reinforced with cardboard; but the Germans, like other Europeans, generally wear soft felt hats, for which there is no good substitute. Unless you are an experienced hat-maker it is practically impossible to make one. In one or two cases hats were smuggled out in parcels, although in Fort Zorndorf this was rare as the parcel supervision was very strictly carried out. Occasionally, perhaps, a prisoner might be able to snatch – as did Medlicott – such a hat off the head of a German civilian workman, who had been unwise enough to bring his headgear with him into the camp. But in Zorndorf practically the only way to procure this most necessary part of our kit was by bribery.

The Russians discovered that several of the sentries in the camp were Poles sympathetic to the cause of the Allies. On getting into conversation with one or two of them it was soon found that a few hundred marks would buy not only felt hats, but also compasses and maps. The Russians, who received very few parcels from home, were then only too willing to exchange them with us for a few tins of food.

The collecting of our new kit took time, but by the beginning of February Hardy and I had succeeded in scraping together all the necessaries for a long journey. Since our return from jail, I had no very clear idea of what our next scheme would be. In response to my almost ceaseless inquiries Hardy had told me that I must be patient and presently something really good would be forthcoming. I tried to find out from him what plans he had in mind, but he had been sworn to secrecy and I could obtain none save the most meagre details. I was only able to gather that we were to get on to the top of the fort at night, crawl down into the ditch, and there await a favourable moment for crossing the ditch and scaling the outer wall. The plan had been worked out in all its details by some French officers, who were about to put it into execution. Just then the strangest rumours began to float around the camp. A man, it appeared, had been arrested in Cüstrin and had admitted that he was employed by a French firm as an agent in an attempt to rescue Garros.

We soon had confirmation of these rumours from the Germans, who in a great state of excitement seized upon Garros and his friends, and bundled them all off to a camp in Silesia. These precautions were of little use, for only a few months later Garros succeeded in escaping, crossing the Dutch frontier and returning to fight in France.

In the fort the discovery of this plot caused several severe searches of the camp and an even stricter supervision of the parcels. Henceforth every tin of food was opened by the Germans in front of each prisoner, and every bit of the contents was cut up into the smallest pieces.

Quite another effect was caused by the removal of the French: they left their excellent and well-thought-out scheme in the hands of a Belgian cavalry officer named Bastin, who, being great friends with Hardy, asked us both to join him.

Bastin, I must relate *en passant*, had already escaped from two camps, and on one occasion had experienced the most remarkable adventures. He had broken out of Magdeburg, from which place he took the train to Bremen. He had some previous knowledge of this port and felt certain that he could manage to stow away on a tramp steamer sailing for a neutral country. On arriving at Bremen he made inquiries and found that there was no steamer leaving for a week, whereupon he put up at a small hotel. Now Bastin had no proper passports, no luggage and could not at that time speak very good German, yet for one whole week he stayed at that hotel and succeeded in convincing the authorities of his respectability. He had quite a lot of money with him and on the day of his arrival he bought himself a trunk and several suit-cases to represent his " luggage" and had it sent first to the station and then to his hotel, as though it had just come on by a later train. He used to spend most of his days sitting in small out-of-the-way cafés, drinking beer, and writing himself letters which he would then post and receive at the hotel.

At the beginning of his week's stay, he got in touch with a Swede – or a Dane, I forget which – the captain of a small steamer. This man was willing for a certain sum to take Bastin on board as a passenger. But, as the week went on and the time for sailing drew near, the captain's price went up, until finally, either alarmed or suspicious of Bastin, he refused point-blank to have anything more to do with the arrangement. Bastin had a final and stormy interview with him on board the ship in Bremen harbour, ending in the captain putting him under arrest and sending for the police. By jumping over the ship's side into a small boat and rowing for dear life to the quay, Bastin managed to get away; but Bremen had become too hot for him and he was forced to leave the same night. He then took train to as near the Dutch frontier as he dared, and got out to do the last few miles on foot. He had nearly crossed the frontier, when an inaccurate strip of map led him astray and he was recaptured.

Bastin was of course thoroughly acquainted with all the details of the scheme, which he explained to us carefully, asking for our help or criticism.

The main idea, as I had thought, was to get out on to the top of the fort at night and crawl to the ditch. This idea was naturally the starting-point of many of the schemes of escape from Zorndorf, but the great problem was how to do it. According to the French plans, it was almost easy. At the back of our semi-subterranean building ran a long corridor with, on the one side, doors giving access into our rooms, and on the other a blank wall. In the centre of the fort this blank wall was pierced by a small iron gateway, from which a corridor ran back fifty yards to a brick dug-out, or *caponnière*, divided into two rooms. One of these was used by some of the prisoners during the daytime as a kitchen, and the other was rigged up as a Roman Catholic Chapel. Although both the passage and the compartment were underground, each room had a small barred window looking out into the deep trench, which ran round the fort near its summit. In the chapel room there was also a wooden door leading into the trench. This door was made of stout planks, and was nailed shut and reinforced on the outside with heavy beams of timber. Sentries on the top of the fort could see down into the trench both by day and by night, and they had this door and the two windows under observation, apparently making any attempt at forcing them out of the question. In spite of this, after weary weeks of work, the French had managed to cut away a small section of the door right at its foot where the planks happened to be thinnest. This had been done so carefully that it was impossible to see the cut, even at close quarters.

How to get into the chapel at night was another of the questions to be solved. The iron grille at the bottom of the passage leading to the chapel was closed every night by the Germans, after they had made sure that no prisoners were left in the chapel or in the other room. The French priest who officiated was allowed, however, to keep his vestments and other religious equipment in two small cupboards standing in the chapel; and of these two cupboards he kept the key. By hiding in one of these while the Germans went their evening round, it would be possible, so the French said, for one to stay in the chapel in perfect safety all night. The small panel having been cut from the bottom of the door, it would be equally possible to get into the trench and crawl down the side of the fort into the ditch. Permission to make use of the cupboards was given by the priest and having got thus far with the scheme, a French officer, for whose courage I have the most intense admiration, carried out a reconnaissance. He hid in one of the cupboards, and in the middle of the night crawled out of the chapel door into the trench. Worming his way round through the various trenches and fortifications, he was able to see exactly where all the sentries were placed.

Every prisoner in Zorndorf knew that during the night a dozen sentries patrolled the ditch, which was lighted at intervals of about forty yards by petrol lamps. In addition there were on the top of the fort some six or seven sentries, but what no prisoner had known hitherto was that at reveille – about 6.30 a.m. – the sentries in the ditch and the sentries on the top of the fort all went to the guard-room. The ditch sentries then came up to the top of the fort to complete their period of duty, and during the day there were no sentries in the ditch. As all the sentries came off their beats and went to the guard-room together, there was an interval of about ten minutes during which no sentries whatever were watching the ditch or the outer wall. During these ten minutes it would be possible for prisoners in hiding near the ditch to climb out with the help of a ladder or some other contrivance.

The next step was the construction of a ladder. When Hardy and I were brought into the scheme, the ladder had been completed with the exception of a few small details which we helped to provide, and the credit for its design lies entirely with the French. The height of the wall surrounding the fort had been estimated at thirty feet, and, as a ladder of this length was obviously too bulky to be carried in safety around the fort in the middle of the night, it was divided into two portions. It was built up in the most ingenious manner with pieces of wood taken from the frames of ordinary deck chairs, and reinforced on the sides and at the joints with small strips of iron. These iron strips were taken from our beds and were destined to be the cause of much trouble with the Germans.

It was thought at first that we should wait until the snow had been completely melted before making the attempt, but towards the middle of February snow fell again in great quantities and Bastin suggested that we might profit by it by making the attempt disguised in white clothing. This seemed to be an excellent idea which might well succeed in baffling the Germans, and, as events turned out, it probably saved Hardy's life.

At length everything was ready, the ladder completed and our kits prepared. We had only to wait for Bastin's word to go. We were quite secure against any searches by the Germans, since the ladder was hidden under the floor of Bastin's room and our civilian clothes and other kit were likewise stowed away in thoroughly reliable hiding-places.

We all three felt absolutely certain of success. During what we believed to be the last few nights we were ever to spend in Zorndorf, we were in the highest of spirits. I shall never forget some of the extraordinary concerts we used to hold in our room at about this time. We had made great friends with some of the French and with one or two of the Russians, and we used to have the most amusing dinner-parties, generally followed by a game of roulette in one of the Russian rooms, and ending up with a medley of songs.

For some absurd reason we conceived the idea that we could intensely annoy the German sentries posted outside our windows by singing German patriotic songs. Therefore after listening to some really wonderful Russian song, sung in perfect harmony by three or four Russian officers, we would break into the strains of "Die Wacht am Rhein". This noble Teutonic marching-song was rendered amazingly hideous by the banging of tin cans and the discordant shouting of the British. The party usually broke up accompanied by loud cheering and a jazzed-up version of "Die Lorelei". Peering through the windows we watched the effect it was having on the German sentries, clustered outside in the cold, muttering to one another and wondering what was going to happen next. They must have imagined that we were all quite mad, but at any rate our behaviour probably persuaded them that we were incapable of any serious attempt to escape.

XV

On 15 February, the snow being about four inches deep, we decided to make the attempt. Late in the afternoon we transferred our kit from the various hiding-places to the cupboards in the *caponnière*. Bastin meanwhile brought out the sections of the ladder and deposited them under the altar. The last *Appell* was at about half-past five or six o'clock, and immediately after this we all three went up to the chapel. We unlocked the cupboards at once and got inside. Bastin being the bulkiest of the three had a cupboard to himself, whereas Hardy and I with the greatest difficulty managed to squeeze into the other one. As soon as we were inside, Bastin locked our door and then proceeded to fasten himself into his own receptacle by means of a special iron clamp which he had made.

In a state of semi-suffocation we waited in those coffin-like cupboards for about twenty minutes and then, almost on the point of bursting out to get air, we heard the steps of the German guard coming up the passage. He paused at the door of the room opposite and then walked into the chapel. After stamping around for a few seconds, he was evidently satisfied and went out, walking briskly down the passage. A moment or two later we heard the iron grille clang to and the rattle of a key in the lock.

The first stage of the game was successfully accomplished and we were now free to do as we liked for the rest of the night. As quickly as he could, Bastin climbed out of his cupboard and released us from our terribly cramped position. It was still quite light and we crept cautiously past the chapel window into which a sentry might be looking. It was not yet seven o'clock and we did not intend to get out into the trench until three o'clock in the morning. We had a long and weary wait ahead of us, but Bastin had provided a kettle and a small spirit lamp to make coffee, Hardy had brought some sandwiches, and I some blankets so the time passed fairly quickly. One of us was continually on guard by the window watching the nearest sentry pass and repass only a few yards away, on his beat at the top of the fort.

At half-past two we began to get ready. Bastin attended to the screwing up of the various parts of the ladder, while Hardy and I packed all the heavy kit into two large bags made out of white sheets. When these preparations were finished, we took off our uniforms and donned our civilian clothing with the exception of our hats and overcoats, already packed into the bags.

Over our civilian clothes we put on the white camouflage dress. It consisted of a white shirt, white trousers, white socks pulled on over our boots, and a close-fitting cap of the type known as a "Balaclava helmet", which covered everything except our eyes. By three o'clock we were ready to sally forth.

But now an unforeseen obstacle suddenly presented itself. A new sentry had come on duty and, unlike the previous one who had gone at least a hundred yards along his beat in each direction, this man elected to stand almost immediately opposite the chapel window, continually looking in our direction and only moving a few yards every now and then to stamp his feet. It was obviously quite impossible to do anything whilst the man was in that position, and we were forced to wait. At least a dozen times he started to move off in one direction or another and each time, just as Bastin was about to open the panel in the door, the brute would return again to stamp his feet directly in front of us. A couple of hours passed and we began to be seriously worried as to whether he had not seen something of our movements through the chapel window. Shortly after five o'clock we realized that, although the sentry would now be relieved, it was no use trying any more that night. It would soon begin to get light and there would then be no chance of concealment. Very reluctantly we took off our clothing, unfastened the ladder and hid the sections again under the altar. At eight o'clock we knew that the iron grille would be opened again, but we were not sure whether the German guard would take the trouble to come up the passage or not, and we hid ourselves once more in the cupboards. Shortly after eight o'clock, we heard the distant footsteps of the guard and sounds of the iron grille being thrown open. Nothing further happened and a few minutes later we collected our kit and went back to our rooms, announcing ourselves, somewhat crestfallen, for breakfast.

During the following two or three days the Germans made no sign of having discovered anything and, on going over the details of our night's adventure, we felt certain that we had given the Germans no grounds for suspicion. The sentry's position in front of the window of the chapel had evidently been purely accidental. We waited three days, improving slightly on our kit and watching the sentries for any signs of activity in the neighbourhood of the chapel. The only thing that in any way disturbed us was the presence of two Alsatian police dogs. They were led around the camp at night, and fortunately appeared to be only half-trained.

A great deal of snow fell during these days and the camp was now covered everywhere with at least five inches, making us feel more than ever sure that the snow clothing would be invaluable. During the evening of 18 February, we again transferred our kit to the chapel and by seven o'clock we had locked ourselves in our respective cupboards. Once again we heard the German guard come up the passage to the chapel, and once again he noticed nothing and we heard him lock the iron grille on his way out. We felt much more confident than we had been on the previous occasion and after some sandwiches and a cup of tea we settled down to sleep – in pairs, the third man being on watch – from about ten o'clock until nearly two in the morning. Bastin reassembled his ladder, while Hardy and I packed away the kit and distributed white clothing. At half-past two we started a more intensive watch on the sentry patrolling the ramparts. Unlike the troublesome sentry of a few days before, the man on duty did his job properly, marching along his beat from end to end and only repassing the window about once in every five minutes.

At last the time came for us to go and Bastin cautiously opened the small panel at the bottom of the door. We had previously settled on the exact load to be carried by each man, the route to be followed and in what order we were to proceed. Under this arrangement Hardy was the first out. With great difficulty he was squeezed through the minute opening, helped by Bastin, whilst I stood just alongside at the window, ready to give the alarm if the sentry reappeared. As soon as Hardy was in the trench, the first and longest section of the ladder, which he was to carry, was slowly and quietly pushed out to him. Watching from the window, I could see him barely three feet away from me, The snow clothing was excellent and so was the white wood of which the greater part of the ladder was made. But certain parts of his face, his hands and the metal parts of the ladder seemed to show up with painful clearness.

While getting through the hole in the door, Hardy lay flat on his chest and, as we pushed the ladder out to him, he naturally kept this position, which was the least conspicuous. Now, having got the ladder, he was just rising to his feet – one hand still on the ground, grasping the ladder with the other –

when, like the villain in a melodrama, the black figure of the sentry suddenly became outlined against the grey sky. His appearance at that moment was terribly awkward and I positively gasped from the shock, but I managed to whistle softly to Bastin, who hissed out a warning to Hardy through the trap-door. On the top of the parapet, not twelve feet away, the sentry stopped and peered down into the ditch. Then taking a step forward he began to unsling his rifle. The suspense of the next few seconds was almost unbearable, and a catastrophe of some sort seemed absolutely imminent. I felt sure, seeing Hardy as clearly as I could, that the sentry could see him too and was about to take aim and shoot. But, having unslung his rifle, the sentry held it for a few seconds in his hands – and then slowly slung it over the other shoulder. He was not going to shoot, but how much had he seen? He stood quite still for at least half a minute, and I was positive that Hardy would be unable to remain immovable for much longer. Hardy, who had been about to rise when the sentry appeared, still had one hand on the ground. Hence he was supporting himself, and the weight of a fifteen-feet ladder, on one hand and one knee. At the moment of warning, he had screwed his head round so as to watch the sentry: it was about the most uncomfortable position in which I can imagine an unarmed man to be.

But Hardy was admirable. For the better part of two minutes he remained in that strained posture gazing at the sentry, while I could see that wretched German looking straight down into the trench. Neither Bastin nor I could move or do anything lest we should be heard. And then suddenly the tension was relaxed; the sentry turned his back and walked away. The relief was extraordinary, and now that the immediate danger was over the whole scheme seemed to be easy of execution.

Hardy waited a second or two, turned round to get an "all clear" signal from us, and walked off along the trench carrying the ladder. We gave him three minutes, and then I began to worm my way through the trap-door. Somewhat bulkier than Hardy, I had a struggle to get through, but fortunately no sentry appeared while I was jammed half-way and eventually I scrambled into the trench. The other section of the ladder and a small bag of kit was passed out to me, and I helped Bastin push out the large bag containing the greater part of our civilian clothes and equipment. Before leaving I also made sure that Bastin himself was able to get through that incredibly small opening. Then, the sentry being out of sight, I tip-toed off.

In front of me I knew Hardy was safe, since no sound of any alarm had reached us, and, behind, Bastin was closing up the trap-door, leaving no trace of our departure. Fifty yards down the trench there was a sharp turn to the right and then a further fifty yards to go before coming out of the trench on to a flat triangular piece of ground sloping down towards the ditch. I negotiated the two lengths of trench successfully and then with much fear and trepidation I crept out into the open. From now on, the ground was a great deal more difficult to cross. For nearly a hundred yards there was a gradual slope from the top of the fort, and in full view of any sentry who might happen to be there. Part of it was just in sight of the sentries in the ditch whose voices I could plainly hear, and the slope itself was faintly illuminated by the lamps whose rays, reflected by the big wall against which they were placed, threw a glow over the greater part of the fortress. For one hair-raising moment I fancied I could see in the dim light, the shadowy form of a police dog, but after a few seconds it – whatever it was – disappeared.

Dragging my ladder through the snow and keeping as flat as possible, I slowly covered the distance and reached a point where the ground sloped sharply away, at an angle of forty-five degrees, into the ditch. At the foot of this steep slope there was a low, loop-holed wall, designed to act partly as a buttress to the mound above and partly as a means of defending the ditch. It was behind this wall that we were to hide until daylight.

I had almost crossed the flat open ground when, pausing to search once more for the sentry before making the descent to the wall, I suddenly heard some one running. For a moment I felt sure that we had been discovered and were being pursued by the Germans. As the footsteps came nearer, I began to realize that the figure gradually taking shape in the semi-darkness was anything but German and, intensely relieved, I found it was Bastin. But Bastin so comically disguised that I had the greatest difficulty in restraining the noisiest of laughter. A huge white shirt flapped about well below his knees, big white trousers trailed on the ground, and his boots seemed enormous, covered as they were with thick woollen socks. Under his arm was tucked the huge white bundle, representing our entire luggage and grasped firmly in one hand was a small, yellow leather hand-bag of which he was inordinately proud – was just the thing, he said, to complete his disguise as a commercial traveller. The white helmets made us all look like polar explorers, but, making a serious situation utterly ludicrous, on the top of Bastin's head was perched a little black felt hat. And here he came, actually running across the ground over which I had so laboriously crawled. But in spite of his strange appearance he was justified in running, for no sentries were visible on the top of the fort, although one of them might show up at any moment, making speed advisable.

Throwing himself on the ground in front of me, Bastin slid rapidly down the slope towards the buttress wall. I was handicapped by my ladder and scrambled down more slowly behind him. It must have been solely due to our snow clothing that we were not seen on this portion of our route; it was in full view of the sentries in the ditch and well lighted by the lamps. Luckily no untoward incident occurred and we were soon assembled in the narrow trench at the bottom.

It had taken us nearly an hour to get round the fort, and the time was now well after half-past three. According to our information, the relief of the sentries was at 6.30 and we should be able to scale the wall at about 6.35. We had a wait of rather less than three hours in front of us. The time was spent in joining and securing the two sections of the ladder and in fixing a small support half-way along its length to prevent the ladder from sagging when against the wall. A little later we took off our white clothing, arrayed ourselves in complete civilian clothes with the help of the kit from the big white bag, and made ourselves look as ridiculously German as possible. The camouflage clothing was put into the kit bag and carefully hidden in a snow drift.

It was exceedingly cold and, after finishing our various jobs, there was nothing to do but sit on the ground and freeze. Through the loopholes in the wall we could see some of the sentries, one of whom was only a few feet away. We naturally kept absolutely silent, although this was an almost needless precaution; the sentries were talking to one another all the time. Moreover, one of the men close to us had a hacking cough which he kept up for the remainder of the night, effectively drowning any slight sounds we may have made. At six o'clock we were standing by with the ladder in position, waiting to haul it over the sloping end of the trench and down a short path into the ditch. At half-past six an order was passed down the ditch and the sentries immediately began to move off.

The last man was just passing in front of our loophole, when there was a sound of footsteps approaching from the opposite direction and we heard a sentry exchange "Good morning" with some one else. Looking cautiously through a loophole, we saw to our astonishment two Germans coming down the ditch. Why on earth they were there we had not the slightest idea, but we were not long left in doubt.

In the ditch, just beyond the end of the loopholed wall where the trench sloped upwards, right across the path we had to follow, were two small sheds. In these sheds, constructed by order of the commandant, were kept a small herd of swine. These pigs were being specially fattened, either for sale or else for the corpulent commandant's own table. When the two men who had just passed us reached the corner they stopped, and we could hear them open the doors of the sheds. Presently a joyful grunting sound was borne to us on the morning air and we realized that the pigs were being fed. According to our information – gathered by the French officer who had made the original reconnaissance – these pigs were invariably fed half an hour later, when we hoped to be away. In working out our scheme we had naturally completely forgotten their existence. It now came as a terrible blow to realize how precious time was being wasted by a change in the hour of the pigs' breakfast.

Minute after minute passed and still we could hear the voices of the two swineherds and the happy grunting of numerous small pigs. At last, when we were beginning to despair, we heard the shed doors being shut, and a minute or two later the men repassed, us going down the ditch. We waited until they had got to a safe distance, and then we decided that the time had come. With Bastin at the head, Hardy in the middle and myself at the extreme end of the ladder, we formed a strange procession as we clambered out of the trench and went over the top of the mound bordering the ditch.

As we came once more into the open, we realized that another unpleasant surprise lay in store for us: the sentries were already out on the top of the fort!

There was nothing to be done now, for it was too late to go back to our quarters. Stumbling about in the deep snow we reached the ditch. As we passed the pig sheds, a small dog – fortunately chained up – started to yap and kicked up a terrific row. A glance up at the top of the fort showed us that the nearest of the sentries was looking directly at us. He made no move, but he would probably shoot when we were on the ladder; perhaps he had already warned the others. It had been our intention to put the ladder up against the wall immediately alongside one of the sheds where the ditch was shallower by a few inches. Now that the sentries on the top of the fort were watching us and could see exactly what we were about, we hurriedly decided that this was too unsafe and turning the corner in the ditch found ourselves temporarily screened by the wall behind which we had lately been hiding. Our fingers were numbed with cold and the miscarriage of our plans was beginning to make us lose confidence. Somehow or other we heaved the ladder up against the wall and Hardy and I held on to the bottom of it to prevent it from swaying and slipping, while Bastin slowly climbed up.

He reached the top and paused. Hardy and I were having trouble in holding the ladder steady at the bottom and for a few seconds we were unable to look up to see what was happening. After what seemed a very long time we glanced up expecting to see Bastin disappearing over the wall, but instead we saw that he was still standing on the top rung of the ladder and we realized that for some reason or other he was unable to get any farther. In a few seconds, he came down the ladder again and explained the situation. Apparently on this side of the fort the ditch was a few inches deeper than the calculations for the ladder had allowed. This under ordinary conditions would not have stopped us. But the top of the wall was covered with several inches of snow, which had melted a few days previously and then had frozen again forming a curved ledge of ice, upon which it was utterly impossible to get a grip. Unfortunately we had nothing with us with which to break the ice and no hooks or other instruments which would have enabled us to obtain a foothold upon the top. We discussed our position in agitated undertones and finally persuaded Bastin to go up and try again. He was the tallest of the three and probably the strongest in the arms, so that if he could not reach the top we felt certain that neither Hardy nor I could do so. Bastin again went up and struggled hard to get to the top of the wall. At one moment he had practically succeeded, only to slip back just as our hopes were beginning to rise. It was maddening. We had broken through all the German defences;

we were, to all intents and purposes, outside the camp, there was no one to stop us, and yet we could not go a step farther.

By this time we were really alarmed, and our position was critical. The dog near the sheds was still barking furiously causing two or three sentries to look down from the top of the fort at Bastin whom they could see at the top of the ladder, and about sixty yards away on our right, a crowd of German soldiers was beginning to assemble in the ditch for their morning inspection and roll-call.

Once more Bastin came down. It was quite impossible, he said, to get to the top of the wall and, even if we succeeded in doing so, there now appeared to be Germans on the outside of the camp, who would make it impossible for us to get away. We thought of carrying the ladder back to the shed where we knew we could reach the top of the wall, but this seemed to be quite useless, as several of the sentries could not help seeing what we were doing. Bastin thought that any further attempt was out of the question and that we might as well give ourselves up at once before we were shot at. At this point, Hardy suggested that there was just one more chance of our being able to get away. He proposed that we should walk boldly down to the right, through the group of German soldiers and out of the main gate of the fortress, which we could see was open to admit some of the Germans billeted outside the camp. It seemed our only hope and we immediately put it to the test. Extraordinary as it may seem, we marched straight down the ditch without attracting any particular attention, and passed right through the mob of some sixty or seventy German soldiers, who scarcely glanced at us. We made for the open gate and for a few moments I began to think that we were really going to get away, when suddenly we came face to face with a German N.C.O. who knew all three of us by sight. For a moment he was completely taken aback and his face was a picture of amazement. Then suddenly the realization of what was happening dawned upon him and he screamed loudly for guards. We were immediately surrounded by armed men, fortunately too astonished to do us any bodily harm. The main gate was slammed shut and we were hurried back through the gloomy archway into the guard-room. Yet another of the best laid plans had gone "agley".

XVI

We were not ill-treated in the guard-room. Every one seemed to have something to say and we understood at last why the sentries on the fort had taken so little notice. They had apparently mistaken us for contractors who had come to inspect and repair the outer wall. Presently the guards began to realize that possibly some of them would get into trouble over the night's work, and their feelings towards us underwent a noticeable change.

Half an hour later one of the German officers, furious at having been turned out of bed so early and with very much of an early-morning face, dashed into the guard-room. He immediately ordered us to be searched, a precaution hitherto neglected. Luckily we had had time to get rid of the more important of our belongings such as false passes and maps, but most of the kit, including compasses, money, and of course all our civilian clothing, fell into the hands of the enemy. A guard of twelve men was then told off to watch us and we sat down and waited for some two hours, while the Germans telephoned frantically to headquarters for instructions.

At ten o'clock, without further warning, a N.C.O. and a fresh guard arrived and we were marched out of the camp down the main road to Cüstrin bound for jail. It was a marvellous day, the country glistening white in the rays of a brilliant sun, almost as warm as in summer, and we raged inwardly to think that we should by now have been safely on board the Berlin train had our attempt met with success. But notwithstanding our failure Bastin refused to be discouraged. To him the road to jail would lead some day to freedom; the morning sun would prove to be the sun of victory: "*Le soleil d'Austerlitz*"; our recent reverse, the incentive to further efforts. His optimism was infectious and made us forget the prospect of many days to be spent in solitary confinement.

On arriving at the Citadel we were greeted by our old friends, the N.C.O.'s. in charge of the prison. We were searched once again and then locked into separate cells in different parts of the building. At midday I was given a bowl of soup, which was very welcome as we had had no breakfast that morning, but nothing else happened for the rest of the day, and the reaction after the previous night's excitement made us pass most of the time asleep. Next day I began to inquire whether we were likely to be in prison very long, and if in the meanwhile some of my kit could be sent to me from Zorndorf. The

Feldwebel, who was really a very decent sort of man, said that he had no idea how long we were to be kept in solitary confinement, and that as far as kit was concerned he had instructions to allow us absolutely nothing for the time being.

During the following week I had plenty of time to realize again how bored one can get with one's own company. I had no kit of any sort except the clothes I stood in, and nothing wherewith to wash or shave. Smoking was, of course, forbidden in the prison and in any case I had no cigarettes with me. We were allowed no books or newspapers, no bath, no exercise, no lights after dark and no food parcels from the camp. The cold weather continued and the heating in the prison was almost totally lacking. There was positively nothing to do but pace up and down the cell for hour after hour in the daytime, and go to bed, to try to keep warm, as early as possible in the evening. Not that the beds were by any means comfortable. They consisted of a wooden framework, with planks instead of springs, a thin straw mattress, and the roughest of army blankets.

At half-past seven each morning a bowl of tepid, *Ersatz* coffee was pushed into my cell, representing breakfast. At midday a bowl of soup and a small piece of potato-and-sawdust bread served the purpose of lunch and the menu for dinner consisted of a scrap of rather disgusting German sausage and another small piece of bad bread. It was evident that on this diet one could not get very fat, nor could one accumulate many provisions for escaping purposes.

The heavily barred window of my cell looked out on to a courtyard, guarded by three or four sentries. In the mornings, by standing on tiptoe on the head of my bed I could watch the more fortunate German prisoners; more fortunate since practically none of them were in solitary confinement and they were all given plenty of exercise and some sort of work. For us prisoners of war there was nothing but emptiness during each successive day. Truly, we could sleep or think; but it is remarkable, if one cannot sleep much, how tired one can get of thinking.

After ten days of this life, a German officer from Zorndorf was sent down to interview us. We were each subjected separately to a severe cross-examination with the evident intention of confusing us and forcing us to incriminate ourselves with some offence against German civil or military

law. At the end of my cross-examination, I asked on what charge we were
being held and how long we were to remain in jail. I was astounded to hear
that, failing other and more serious charges, we were to be tried for theft
and that we should be kept in solitary confinement until the trial took place.
On my asking what we were supposed to have stolen, I was told that the
Germans had found that the metal strips which had reinforced the sides
of our ladder had been taken from several of His Majesty the Kaiser's
beds. The obvious answer to this was that we had left the ladder within the
precincts of the camp, we had not stolen, but merely borrowed the imperial
strips of iron. I argued the point for some time with the German officer until
he became furious and ordered me back to my cell. I heard from one of the
jailers that Hardy and Bastin had also been complaining vigorously against
their treatment; it was of no avail and life continued in exactly the same way.
In the course of the next few weeks we had two or three visits from the old
general in command of the Cüstrin area whom we had met on our previous
stay at the jail. He was very sympathetic, but he could do nothing for us
without direct orders from Berlin. Finally he obtained permission for us to
have one hour's exercise each afternoon, but even for this short period we
were not allowed to be together. In spite of this continued separation from
the other two, I was able to find out from one of the jailers more or less what
they were doing and how they were faring.

One day I got a small note from Bastin, in which he told me that he had
managed, using a broken safety-razor blade as a saw, to cut through one of
the bars of bis cell window. The note added that, if he could get sufficient
bread and any other useful articles of equipment, he intended to try and get
out of the prison in a few days' time. Bastin was fortunate in having a cell
which did not overlook the main courtyard as did both Hardy's and mine.
His window faced a small strip of garden, with a path leading round to the
front of the prison and to the main road through the town. His equipment
was by no means perfect, but it seemed as though he stood a good chance of
success.

By dint of eating more or less nothing for two or three days, Hardy and
I managed to send him a small quantity of food and also some articles of
clothing. Our friend, the jailer, acted as intermediary, apparently thinking
that Bastin was very weak or ill and not that we were helping him to escape.

At length I got a note from Bastin saying that he was to try at nine o'clock that night, and that if we could we were to attempt to draw off the only sentry who was likely to give trouble. I had found out a few days previously that, when the sentries were at the far end of their beats, I could talk to Hardy, who was only a few cells away on an upper floor, by shouting through the bars of my window. We concerted a rough plan for helping Bastin, and kept up a lively conversation in spite of the sentry's protests till half-past nine, when, no alarm having been given, we felt sure that he must have been able to get away. But a few minutes later a tremendous uproar from the front of the building told us that something untoward had occurred. Presently we heard much stamping of feet in the passage, accompanied by a lot of yelling and the noise of cell doors being slammed. The next minute the *Feldwebel* and several jailers burst into my cell, expecting to find that I too had been trying to escape. They were all very angry; and, as far as I could gather from their confused shouting, Bastin had succeeded in getting out of his window but had been chased and caught while in the street going through the town. I heard a few days later that the real cause of his capture was that a German soldier in the next cell had seen him getting out and had informed the Germans of his discovery on condition that some portion of his sentence should be remitted.

Bastin was ill-treated immediately after his recapture and badly knocked about by the infuriated jailers. As a result of his attempt a very much closer supervision of our cells was maintained, and every morning the *Feldwebel* came and tapped our window-bars with a heavy hammer.

Day after day passed slowly and drearily by, the monotony only relieved by such exciting events as a visit of inspection by a German officer or the arrival of a small parcel of clothing from the camp. Eventually after many complaints we were allowed such luxuries as safety-razors and one or two German newspapers. With much trouble I persuaded the friendly jailer to supply me with about three cigarettes each week. The supply was not very regular, but such as it was it helped considerably to relieve the utter boredom of my existence. When each cigarette had been smoked down to the end, I carefully concealed the short stub under my mattress and in two or three weeks' time, having collected about half a dozen or so fragments, I was able to roll one or two extra cigarettes. Smoking a portion of a cigarette, washing, shaving and rereading an old German newspaper formed the daily routine. With the exception of marking upon the wall the passage of each day, there was still nothing to do but pace up and down the ten feet of my cell floor.

For the first month of our confinement, we were not allowed to receive or send any letters, but eventually, after an appeal to the old general, I obtained permission to write two. The first one was sent off and got home, but as I did not write the second one until several more weeks had passed, and I was getting really thoroughly "fed up" with prison life, I put into it more than was advisable in the way of bad language about the Germans and the injustice of our prolonged detention: a week later the letter was returned to me, having failed to pass the censor. This discouraged me and, being unable to tell anything approaching the truth, I wrote no more.

Over two months passed by without the Germans breaking their silence upon our ultimate fate, and I was beginning to despair of our ever being liberated until the end of the war, when one day the general paid us a visit. The old man seemed quite pleased with the good news he had to bring. He told us that a decision regarding us would soon be made and that if we chose to give him personally our word of honour not to try and escape from the jail, he would allow us to be moved into another cell where we should all three be together. He would then issue orders for our parcels of food to be sent down from the camp and for our daily exercise to be extended. Since we had each of us long ago come to the conclusion that any attempt at escape from the jail was foredoomed to failure, we readily accepted this arrangement. The general was, of course, going quite beyond his powers in accepting our word of honour, for not only was it a point of German military law that prisoners of war were not to be put on parole, but our own regulations also forbade it. In this particular case the general was evidently moved by a feeling of common decency, and we on our part felt there was nothing to be gained by prolonging for a week or two our misery in solitary confinement.

A few days later we were moved into a large cell on the other side of the prison. To be able to talk to some one again after months of solitide was incredibly pleasant and for the first few days we were positively happy in our new abode. But at the end of ten days, when the newness had begun to wear off, we wondered how much longer we would have to endure even this form of confinement. Bastin suggested that if the Germans did not soon bring us to trial or send us back to the camp, we should ask the general to release us from our parole and that we would then make a bold attempt to break out of the prison. He had worked out a scheme with a German corporal in prison for desertion. The corporal was to let us out of our cells and out of the prison with the help of a set of keys. He then intended to provide us all with bicycles on which we were to ride to the frontier. The whole scheme sounded rather quaint, and before we had been driven to this extreme the welcome news came that we were to be released within the next few days. At about the same time, permission came through from Berlin for us to have a real, full-sized bath. Strangely enough the prison had no facilities for washing, other than a few buckets of cold water. In order to get a bath therefore we were marched, twice in the last few days, under a heavy escort right through the town to a military hospital where we enjoyed the luxury of hot water.

On a certain Sunday in May, a German officer from Zorndorf came and informed us that proceedings against us were being dropped; that Hardy and I were to pack up our kit immediately and return to camp. Bastin was to be detained for the present and would probably be court-martialled in a few days' time for having damaged the prison by cutting a bar of his cell window.

Hardy and I left the jail that same afternoon, escorted by the usual armed guard, and were marched back to Zorndorf.

Bastin was court-martialled a few days later and sent to a fortress at Königsberg [Kaliningrad] in East Prussia, whence a few months later he succeeded in escaping. This time he justified his most optimistic hopes, crossed the Dutch frontier near Aachen and returned to fight in Belgium.

XVII

We found many changes in the camp when we got back to Zorndorf. Not the least of these was the change in the official reputation of the camp. After numerous complaints and under pressure of neutral opinion, Zorndorf was no longer to be designated as a "black hole" for the taking of reprisals, nor was it to be looked on as a prison for miscreants. It was to be just an ordinary camp situated quite by accident in an old-fashioned fortress, where the treatment of prisoners was to be as good as anywhere else in Germany.

To heighten this impression several British prisoners had recently been brought straight from the scenes of their capture, on the Somme or Arras battlefields. From them we got detailed and first-hand news of the progress of the war. In spite of all their optimism, it was obvious that things were not going too well, and that the great struggle was likely to continue for a long time. This was very discouraging, but it certainly made us realize that we would have to continue trying to escape and that we should have plenty of time in which to execute our plans.

The difficulty of finding a good plan of escape from Zorndorf was now really very great. One of the greatest drawbacks was at the same time the great consolation for the failure of our last scheme: the guards had been almost doubled. Sentries were on duty in the ditch all day long and extra men guarded the top of the fort. The number of German soldiers in Zorndorf at this time actually outnumbered the prisoners by more than two to one. In addition a company was held in reserve at Cüstrin periodically to relieve the men at the fort.

It was in February that the ladder scheme failed, and we were now in the middle of May. Snow schemes were out of the question, and the nights were growing shorter, making it more difficult for lengthy operations to be carried out under the cover of darkness. Most of the usual schemes had already been tried, and had either failed or had been discovered by the Germans after having succeeded. It required a considerable amount of imagination to plan anything sufficiently original to baffle the Germans. Hardy and I thought that an attempt to scale the wall by night should still be feasible, but, since the discovery of the hole in the chapel door, it was almost impossible to reach the top of the fort without being observed by one of the sentries.

We eventually decided that from a certain window at one end of our quarters it might be possible to climb up to the top of the fort, especially if heavy rain were to fall, or a thunderstorm kept the sentries away. We were to carry with us a long pole in sections, thirty feet of rope – knotted for quick climbing – and a specially constructed grapnel. Having reached the ditch, where again we counted on a storm to distract the attention of the sentries, the pole, with the grapnel secured at its upper end, was to be pushed up and an attempt made to hook it over the projecting ledge at the top of the wall. If this succeeded we were then to scale the rope hanging down from the lower end. It was an absurdly risky scheme and quite hopeless in fine weather, but one night during a heavy thunderstorm we had proof that it might have worked. Had we been ready on that particular night I have no doubt that we should have succeeded, for at the height of the storm Hardy and I actually got out of the window in question, and noticed that the sentries were far away from their beats, taking shelter either in sentry-boxes or under the lee of the many mounds on the summit of the fort. Unfortunately, or perhaps fortunately for us, we never had another heavy storm during the whole summer, and although we got ready to try we never had the chance.

For a short time most of the British and the Belgians and some of the French, became extremely enthusiastic over a new tunnel scheme. The idea originated with a Belgian colonel who had commanded one of the Liége forts at the beginning of the war, and consisted in digging a series of short tunnels in various parts of the fort in an attempt to discover a secret subterranean passage leading out into the open country. Those who had had any previous experiences of fortresses stated that there was generally some such passage, used in wartime either for the reprovisioning or for evacuating the garrison. Personally I have not the slightest idea whether such passages do in reality exist, or whether there had ever been one beneath Fort Zorndorf; but like searching for hidden treasure the idea appealed to us all tremendously, and we started work with the conviction that we were going to find something.

The tunnel was commenced by the Belgians, and was provided with a cleverly concealed entrance beneath a doorway in their room. The shaft wound about in a most amazingly intricate way underneath the floors of the various rooms and eventually dived down beneath the foundations of the fort. Various branch shafts were then driven in different directions in the endeavour to find the secret passage. These attempts meeting with no success, we finally struck out straight towards the ditch. Whether we should come out in the ditch and make an attempt at scaling the wall, or whether we should tunnel right underneath and come up outside the camp, were questions which we never definitely decided, for after a couple of months of hard work the ever watchful Germans became so suspicious that we were compelled to abandon the attempt for the time being. Searches of various rooms in the camp were of daily occurrence at this time. On one occasion a party of us – including Hardy, Beverley Robinson, who had been at Mainz and had just arrived at Zorndorf, and myself – were just about to emerge from the tunnel, when the prearranged alarm signal was tapped on the floor above our heads and we realized that the Germans were actually searching the room belonging to the Belgians. We held our breath in an agony of suspense, but they were unable to find the entrance to the tunnel and we were able to get away unobserved.

Somewhere towards the beginning of June a party of British arrived from Ingolstadt. They had come from the famous Fort 9, the counterpart of Fort Zorndorf. They had all escaped at least once before and were determined to renew their attempts. Amongst them was Medlicott, who by now had escaped from four or five camps, and one named Wilkin whom I was to know in the future as an expert at lock picking.

It was from this party that we first heard of the escape of Evans and Buckley, who had jumped off the train near Nuremberg. We heard nothing further about these two for several weeks and then a vague rumour came through from England that they had succeeded in crossing the Swiss frontier. This turned out to be the case and the story of their wonderful eighteen days' march across Bavaria to Switzerland has been told in that excellent book *The Escaping Club*. Buckley, by the way, had been captured with Ward, and it was remarkable to think that both pilot and observer had been able to get away.

Medlicott and Wilkin brought with them an extraordinary assortment of escaping kit and a large collection of tools for picking locks, forcing doors and cutting bars. With their help we at once set to work to pick the various padlocks, securing the door of the parcels room, and night after night we entered this place to secure the maps and compasses occasionally sent out from England. We were more than glad to have the assistance of fresh brains in Zorndorf for devising some new scheme for escaping, and we thought that Medlicott, with the reputation of having got out of almost every camp he had been in, might be able to suggest something really clever. But, although it was disappointing, it was at the same time a relief to find that there was nothing we had overlooked. The idea of being able to find the secret passage leading out of the camp still lured us on and we dug holes in almost every corner of the fort, but it was all in vain. Hardy had an idea that there might be an entrance to the mysterious passage in the German part of the fort and that we might be able to get through by forcing two small iron grilles in one of the corridors. We set to work to cut through the bars of one of these grilles, but the Germans were too watchful. Several times we were nearly caught and the experiment was given up.

The time dragged slowly on and, as scheme after scheme was abandoned as useless, we gradually found ourselves with more or less nothing to do except to carry on a sort of guerrilla warfare against the Germans. Life in the close confinement of Zorndorf during the beautiful summer months became terribly dull. At that time I think that we should even have welcomed the sudden end of war. One by one, many of the British prisoners were shipped away to other camps and Hardy and I began to feel that we were permanent inhabitants. One day, Medlicott while running down a corridor tripped up over some obstruction or other and got water on the knee. He was sent to hospital for a few weeks and was then transferred to another camp. I did not know it, but it was the last I was ever to see of him.

At last in August, having exhausted all other possibilities of leaving Zorndorf, I suggested to Hardy that we should each write a personal letter to the general, saying that as we had been in Zorndorf for almost a year we were beginning to suffer in health and requested to be moved to some other camp. I was able to make the additional plea that I wished to be allowed to rejoin my brother who had until recently been at Fort 9, Ingoldstadt. It was now over three months since we had returned from jail, six months since our last definite attempt to escape, and it was an unwritten, but officially recognized, law in Zorndorf that prisoners who had been there for over four months without attempting to escape had a chance of being transferred to some better camp. There was no answer to our requests for several days and then, suddenly, I was told to pack up my kit and be ready to move off with several recently taken prisoners. Hardy, on the other hand, was told that his transfer would not be considered for the present. It was a bitter blow to be separated, for we knew all the ropes of prison breaking by now, and we had felt convinced that we would cross the frontier together. It seemed certain that Hardy would be moved in the near future, but if we were to escape before the war ended we had to get away from the neighbourhood of Zorndorf as quickly as possible.

For all that, it seemed very sad to leave the accursed fort without one final and successful escape, and I spent my remaining days in vainly planning various futile ideas for last minute escapes. Had Hardy and I stayed many months longer in Zorndorf it is possible that we should have found a sure way out, but, as a matter of fact, in spite of one or two attempts no one ever escaped from the place that had seen the birth and death of so many fair schemes.

XVIII

In the afternoon of 17 August four other British prisoners and I were for the last time marched down the evil-smelling passage to the *Kommandantur*. Here we were subjected to a search of the utmost severity, being stripped stark naked while every article of our clothing was carefully gone over by German N.C.O.'s. In spite of this I managed to conceal two compasses, a set of maps of the Dutch frontier, two forged passes and several hundred marks of German money. I do not propose to reveal the various methods by which these things were concealed as it is conceivable that the information might be useful to me in the next war, but I must say that I heaved a sigh of relief when the search was over. We had the usual long and dreary walk down to Cüstrin and an hour's wait at the station before the train came in. Finally, we were packed into a second-class compartment, with four armed guards and an officer. Just before the train started, the guards carefully and very ostentatiously loaded their rifles in front of us. On arriving at Berlin, we were marched through the town to the Friedrichstrasse Station. While waiting for the train we were put into a small restaurant and allowed to purchase some light refreshments. At about six o'clock we were bundled into a train bound for Hanover and stations farther west. I began to have a pretty shrewd idea of our destination. Various rumours had recently been current in Zorndorf about a new all-British camp at Ströhen, somewhere to the north-west of Hanover. The camp itself was not much more than a hundred miles from the Dutch frontier, and some Russian officers who had been there a year previously said that escape from it should be easy. After many months at Zorndorf, where the nearest neutral frontier was over three-hundred miles distant, this sounded most encouraging. The sight of familiar names, on the coaches of the train, of German stations reasonably near the Dutch frontier gave me a thrill of excitement. On leaving Zorndorf I had taken steps to be ready in case there should be a chance of jumping off the train. But unfortunately there was no originality in the idea, and the Zorndorf Germans travelling with us were quite prepared for the event. A guard was placed in each corner of the carriage, with the German officer in the middle, and the windows were kept almost shut the whole time. The Germans told us that we were to travel all night and I decided to keep quiet and give as little trouble as possible so as to allay their suspicions. Next day there might be some chance of jumping off and at any rate we should be more than a hundred miles nearer the Dutch frontier. The night passed off peacefully enough and next morning, after going through Hanover and Minden, we reached the small town of Bünde. Here we waited for a couple of hours until the branch-line train came in. The journey from Bünde to Ströhen took about four hours, through hilly country for the most part where the speed of the train seldom if ever exceeded thirty miles an hour. It was one of the most uncomfortable journeys I have ever made. I was in an agony of suspense the whole time, wondering whether the next minute or two would not bring the chance of a lifetime for a sudden jump out of the window. Again and again I edged cautiously towards the window and collected myself for a spring, but each time one of the guards or else the German officer was watching me. It may have been that I was not bold enough, but somehow I felt that one of those five Germans would either grab me or shoot at me before I could get out. Had it been night time I think I should have tried it, hoping to succeed as did Evans and Buckley, but it was broad daylight, the train was packed with German soldiers and I remembered only too well the ending of Pearson's attempt near Weilburg, when the train was stopped almost immediately after he had got out and he was chased by a score of soldiers. When at length we reached Ströhen and there was no more hope of escape from the train I began to feel rather ashamed at not having made a more determined effort, but I consoled myself with the thought that had I tried I should in all probability have gone straight to a hospital.

The camp lay two miles west of the station in open moorland devoid of houses and with only occasional clumps of trees. It was obvious that in breaking out of the camp it might be extremely difficult to find cover quickly, but the very flatness of the country made it seem nearer to Holland and encouraged one in spite of other drawbacks. As we got close to the camp, which was surrounded by numerous sentries but only a single barbed-wire fence, I began to recognize several prisoners whom I knew by sight. In spite of the protests of the camp sentries and our own guard, they managed to shout out a warning that we would be searched before being allowed into the camp. We asked them what the place was like and, judging by the strength of the language they employed, the camp appeared to be somewhat below the average. I also asked for news of my brother and half a dozen prisoners at once volunteered the answer, accompanied with much laughter, that he was in prison under sentence of death! This seemed most encouraging, and with a feeling that new adventures were about to begin we marched in to the *Kommandantur*. The search proved to be a very tame affair after all, and with the exception of one of my two compasses the Germans got nothing. This particular compass, a very small one, I had concealed in one of my boots. During the journey I had found that it got rather in my way when walking, I thought it best to remove it in case I succeeded in jumping off the train. I had no time to replace it in the hiding-place in my boot before arriving at the camp, with the result that as soon as the search started I more or less allowed the Germans to find it. They were so delighted at having captured something, however small, that they practically forgot to search us any further. We were then taken into another office where we were solemnly introduced to the commandant of the camp. He was a doddering old idiot of about seventy years of age, quite "gaga" and weak at the knees. He mumbled a few sentences about German military law and discipline which I had to translate to my companions, who had much difficulty in restraining their laughter. We also met the second in command of the camp, an odious person of the name of Niemeyer. This man and his twin brother, at that time in charge of Claustahl, were two of the most infamous of the German officers who had dealings with prisoners during the war. They had both lived in America before 1914, and it was said that one of them had been a billiard marker in New York and the other one a bar-tender in Milwaukee. Whatever truth there may have been in this, they were both despicable cads. I believe that the one who was at Ströhen died soon after the war, at any rate I hope so. He was very proud of his knowledge of English which caused us endless laughter. None of his phrases ever had the meaning he had intended them to convey and each one terminated with the ludicrous remark: "I guess, you know!" and "I-guess-you-know" he was nicknamed.

I noticed as we were ushered into the camp through the small barbed-wire gate that the prisoners who had gathered to watch us on our arrival hurriedly withdrew to a distance of over fifty yards from the entrance and kept on retreating until the gate was finally closed and the guards who had accompanied us were outside the camp. I asked one of the prisoners why they did this and I was told that only a few days previously some fresh prisoners had arrived, and the old prisoners having assembled at the gate to watch them come in they were suddenly charged by about half a dozen sentries. For some unexplained reason the old commandant, who was standing close by, had told the guards to go in and clear the place and not to be afraid of hurting anybody. The guard were only too pleased and rushed upon the prisoners who were quietly walking away, and before anything could be done they had bayoneted two or three in the back! Two of the prisoners were severely wounded and one of them, I believe, died afterwards, although of this I cannot be sure. At any rate it was a most disgraceful and unprovoked attack upon unarmed men, who not only were behaving quite normally, but were actually walking away in obedience to orders.

I was told that this sort of treatment was by no means uncommon in the camp and that, since one or two recent attempts at escape, parties of German soldiers were often sent into the camp to charge at prisoners who appeared to the authorities to be acting in a suspicious manner. Sentries had also been given orders to shoot any prisoner who was seen loitering near the barbed-wire fence, with the natural result that not only was the local jail full to overflowing with suspicious characters, but the interior of the camp was at times quite dangerous from stray shots and charging Germans.

The camp was about three-hundred yards long and a hundred yards wide. It contained four large wooden huts, where the bulk of the prisoners lived, and several smaller huts where, mixed with the British, were several Indian native officers. A barbed-wire fence ten feet high surrounded the camp, with a line of sentries at intervals of about fifty yards on the outside. Ten yards inside of this main fence was a smaller wire fence some two and a half feet high – the space between the two fences being known as the "neutral zone", but where the "neutrality" came in is hard to understand, as although the Germans could walk in it with impunity any prisoner seen inside it was immediately shot.

On the east side of the camp there were two small extensions outside the wire, each extension surrounded by barbed-wire and provided with one gate into the camp and another gate leading out into the open country. In one of these extensions there were several small huts with separate cells comprising the jail, and in the other extension there was one large hut where some fifty British orderlies were housed. These men were variously employed either in fetching parcels or the German rations from the station, or else in cleaning the camp. Several small buildings, serving as guard-rooms and living quarters for about two-hundred German soldiers, were on the west side of the camp. On this side there was also a small wired enclosure containing a very primitive shower-bath establishment for the use of the prisoners.

The camp had originally been used for Russian soldiers, but there was very little work for Russian soldiers to do in the neighbourhood and eventually the camp was condemned as unhealthy. It was therefore only natural that in the autumn of 1917, when German hopes of victory were rapidly rising, this camp should be chosen for the hated British.

The cooking arrangements were very primitive, the sanitary conditions appalling, and at the end of a hot summer disease of some sort, encouraged by the presence of numerous flies, was almost unavoidable. At the time of my arrival out of about five-hundred prisoners two-hundred were laid up with what must have been a mild form of dysentery. A small hut in the camp, set aside as a hospital, was full, but as it only contained eight beds and there were practically no medical supplies it was almost entirely useless. A German doctor was, I believe, supposed to come to the camp twice a week, but very frequently he did not put in an appearance for a much longer period. Among the prisoners there was a pre-war medical student and one of the orderlies had been a stretcher bearer. Although both certainly did their best for us, it was little enough they could do. Fortunately the disease was not very serious; out of hundreds of cases only one man actually died. But many of the prisoners after a few days illness became so weak that they were unable to leave their beds and it must have been largely due to great care and cleanliness – and the use of cod liver oil – that considerable numbers of British officers did not end their days at Ströhen. I had been there scarcely a fortnight when I was laid up with this horrible illness, but not before I had made one rather ridiculous attempt at escape. On the first day of my arrival a friend of mine, hearing that I came from Zorndorf and that I had a fairly complete kit, suggested that I should join him in a scheme to be tried within the next two or three days. I readily agreed, although I scarcely hoped to be able to shake the unhealthy dust of Ströhen from my feet so quickly. The scheme I soon learned was known as the "Battering-ram", the idea being that a heavy iron bar normally a gymnastic horizontal bar which the Germans for some unknown reason had put up in the camp, was to be manned by six men who were to charge a small gate facing the *Kommandantur*. If the blunt end of the iron bar was aimed so as to hit the lock, the authors of the scheme felt sure that the gate would give way and the six men carrying the bar would rush straight on and out of the camp. Once the gate was open there was really nothing to stop them, for their course lay between the two *Kommandantur* buildings which would effectively screen them from the sentries until they were nearly a hundred yards away from the camp. There were a number of trees not far away, and it was hoped that the cover they provided combined with the darkness – the attempt was to be made just after nightfall – would ensure every one getting away.

The idea had the merit of being extremely simple and it certainly contained an element of surprise, but if the gate failed to fall at the first blow there was a very real danger of being shot. I was allotted a place at the tail end of the bar, until it was found that there were too many claimants for this honourable position. Another job was soon found for me. It was necessary to have some one standing near the gate not only to give the signal when both the nearest sentries were at the far end of their beats with their backs turned, but also to open the small gate in the inner fence giving access to the neutral zone. Unless this gate was open the party with the battering-ram would be unable to have a clear run at the main gate; on the other hand if it was opened too soon, or when the sentries were looking, the alarm would naturally be given.

On the second day after my arrival I was told to be in readiness for that very night. I had been unable to obtain any civilian clothes, but with the Dutch frontier only a hundred miles away, this was not a matter of great importance if one was willing to make the journey on foot and by night. As the time drew near I became very worried about my particular job, especially after hearing all the stories about people being shot or bayoneted if they loitered too near the barbed-wire fence. But when the time came all seemed to be well and the sentries on duty hardly noticed me as I walked up and down near the gate.

At last just as it was getting really dark, I noticed the gang assembling. The iron bar had been brought up earlier in the afternoon and hidden in a corner of one of the huts near. Presently one of the gang strolled by, muttering as he passed that all was ready and that they were only waiting for my signal to begin. I waited a few minutes more and then gave the first signal to show that the coast was clear; the gang could now pick up the battering-ram and get into position. I gave them a few moments and took another look at the sentries who were nearly a hundred yards apart and could dimly be seen in the growing darkness. Strolling towards the small gate I cautiously opened it. It squeaked loudly and I noticed that I would have to hold it open as it showed a tendency to swing shut again. So far the sentries had seen nothing and I whistled twice softly to the other conspirators. From about thirty yards away there was a vague scuffling sound as the gang got into motion, and a few seconds later with much pounding of feet it came hurtling past complete with battering-ram. I have a distinct impression of feeling at that moment much like an old man at a level-crossing holding open the gates for the express to go by, and the next moment in my imagination the express was derailed and I was left looking stupidly at the accident.

There was a tremendous crash as the front man of the party hit the gate. In the darkness he had missed the lock with the end of the ram and it was with his face that he charged the wooden framework. In spite of the five strong men behind him, however, his face was not hard enough to push down the obstruction, and he let forth a yell that must have curdled the blood of all the sentries round the camp. The iron bar was immediately dropped with a loud clang, and the party having picked itself up made off at top speed in the direction of the huts. Somewhat dazed at the rapidity of these happenings I stood for a moment still holding the little gate open, gaping at the battering-ram on the ground. A loud report close behind brought me suddenly to my senses and I took to my heels as quickly as I could, much encouraged by the chorus of police whistles now being blown in every direction.

As I ran towards my hut I could hear some one thudding behind me and, passing the lighted windows of one of the other huts, some of the inmates leaned out and screamed abuse at the man behind me, who turned out to be Niemeyer. Brandishing a couple of automatic pistols, he shouted to me to stop, and I have not the least doubt that had I done so he would have had the greatest pleasure in shooting me on the spot. The yells of the other prisoners, leaning out of their windows throwing things at him, and hurling insults such as: "Get out of the camp, you filthy Hun"; "I'll wring your neck, I-guess-you-know"; "Stop running, you dirty son-of-a-gun." This had the effect of turning him aside and while he stopped to deal with the others I managed to dodge into my hut. Next morning we had the inevitable search, but the Germans found nothing except the iron bar abandoned near the gate. A few days later I developed the camp disease and for a fortnight I was confined to my room, unable even to think of escape.

Not very long afterwards, when numerous attempts had driven "I-guess-you-know" to the verge of insanity, a properly organized search was made with the help of detectives from Berlin. From the time they entered the camp to the time they left, these unfortunate men were given no peace. Impeded at every turn, they were harried from one room to another. Contraband captured in one was but recaptured by the prisoners in the next. On leaving, surrounded by a band of cheering prisoners, several of them complained that their pockets had been picked and their identity cards and police papers stolen. And the very next day several more prisoners escaped.

XIX

On arrival at Ströhen I had heard that my brother was in jail, supposedly under sentence of death. This turned out to be almost literally true as, a day later, I heard from his own lips. One of the small huts overlooked the exercise yard of the camp prison and one could easily communicate with any of the prisoners who were out walking. The Germans seemed to have no objection to this proceeding and I spent several hours talking to my brother.

I had not seen him for nearly a year, since Friedberg, and he had a lot to tell me. He had been taken first of all to Fort 9, Ingoldstadt, where he had spent many months without being able to escape. He had then been moved up to Crefeld with a party of British, several of whom had managed to jump off the train on the way. Four or five of them had actually succeeded in crossing the Dutch frontier. My brother had only been a few days at Crefeld when the camp was broken up and all the British transferred to other camps. For two or three days the whole place was in absolute turmoil and several prisoners made attempts to escape in the confusion. Some of them succeeded in getting away, but my brother, who had hidden himself in a cupboard in an abandoned outhouse, was discovered at the last moment and duly despatched with the rest. He was sent to Schwarmstedt, a camp very similar to Ströhen, but from which it was infinitely easier to escape. For the first few days, as far as I could make out from my brother and other prisoners who had been there, it was simply a case of walking straight out of the camp. My brother escaped about a week after his arrival with a man named Grossman, and made for the Dutch frontier. They covered the distance at quite a good rate and, after eleven days' walking, they were beginning to get close to the danger zone of the frontier. On the twelfth day some children found them in a wood, gave the alarm and eventually the whole of a neighbouring village turned out in pursuit. After dodging about for the better part of a day, they were caught and brought back to the nearest police station.

On the way while passing through some fields my brother and his companion threw away some malted-milk tablets, which had got damp during the journey and were consequently of no further use. One of the Germans escorting them back noticed the discarded tablets and picked them all up. On arrival at the police station he reported this to the authorities and, the story being duly embroidered, the fatal tablets were despatched to headquarters at Hanover, where an idiotic chemist declared that they contained anthrax germs. The German authorities naturally decided that this was an act of sabotage and consequently my brother and Crossman were punishable with death. They were hurried from jail to jail, finally ending up at Ströhen, where they were kept in solitary confinement for five weeks. During this period they made continued complaints to the Germans, who answered with apparent indifference that their case was being decided in Hanover and that they would probably be shot. Subsequently they were allowed to engage a German lawyer to act on their behalf. This man evidently did his business very ably, for at the end of another fortnight they were suddenly released from prison and turned loose in the camp without any further reason or explanation being given them.

On the occasion when I had talked with my brother whilst he was still in jail, he had begged me not to escape until he was back in the camp and able to join me. As a matter of fact, although I nearly took part in one successful scheme, I was much too ill most of the time to think of leaving.

During the time that I was laid up a party of six prisoners managed to escape one night by hiding themselves under the wooden flooring of the bath hut. This hut was situated just outside the wire and every evening after dusk the gate leading to it was closed. At night time therefore the hut itself was beyond the line of sentries and there was nothing to prevent anyone in the bathroom from getting away. The scheme worked very well the first time, and although some of the party were recaptured later four of them, I believe, succeeded in crossing the frontier. The Germans were, of course, furious but quite unable to discover how the prisoners had got out. A few days later another batch of six tried the same thing, but this time the Germans had some vague suspicion as to what was taking place and whilst we were all assembled for roll-call on the parade ground a thorough search of the camp was made, ending in the bathroom floor being torn up and the prisoners dragged off to jail. The scheme which appealed to me particularly consisted in crawling down an open drain leading from underneath one of the huts to the barbed-wire fence. At this point where the drain ran under the fence, the wire had been extended downwards for a distance of about two feet and firmly picketed into the ground, but there were several pairs of wire-cutters in the camp, some of them home-made, others smuggled out from England in food tins. Armed with a pair of these it would not be very difficult to cut one's way out, provided that some one was on guard to give notice of the sentry's approach. The camp was rather badly lighted at this point and there was a deep shadow in the ditch, making it practically impossible for anyone to see a motionless figure lying at the bottom of it. Before I was well enough to try it myself, it was successfully attempted by a prisoner named Somerville, who cut the wire and crawled away without being seen by any of the Germans. He was followed by Collier, a friend of Mainz days, and Beverley Robinson, just arrived from Zorndorf. Somerville and Collier met again outside the camp and travelled together as far as the frontier. Here they separated and whereas Somerville succeeded in crossing the frontier, Collier sprained his ankle, was recaptured and brought back to Ströhen. Beverley Robinson, after a series of misfortunes, including the loss of his compass, was caught while sleeping in a barn by a farmer who had been disturbed by the clucking of his hens.

These various attempts, in addition to several others made before my arrival, put the Germans much more on their guard, and by the time my brother came out of prison escaping from Ströhen was beginning to be a more difficult problem. For several days we thoroughly explored the camp and discussed ways and means of escape. I had obtained a pair of wire-cutters, and we thought first of all that some sort of scheme involving wire-cutting by night would be the most suitable. But by now the majority of the possible places for this kind of operation were closely watched by special sentries. The German guard had recently been increased, and several additional electric lamps were being placed round the camp. The sentries were encouraged by the promise of a twenty marks reward for each prisoner they caught, and the alternatives of fourteen days' leave if they succeeded in catching us or fourteen days' jail if they failed. Moreover, those who failed in their duty were packed off to the front – the one place in the world that no German soldier ever wanted to see again.

In spite of these precautions it was rumoured that one or two of the sentries were open to bribery, and although personally I did not care to investigate the truth of this, being afraid that it might only be a trap prepared by the Germans, yet one or two other prisoners managed to find their man and to make good use of him. One night two prisoners got out through a hole they had cut in the wire under the very nose of a sentry, who could not have helped seeing them. They got away in the darkness, unnoticed, and the bribed sentry was wise enough not to report the hole in the fence. The escape occurred early in the evening and it was not until next morning – by which time several other sentries had been on duty on the same beat – that the prisoners were missed. The Germans were consequently unable to accuse any one man and the sentry in question, evidently finding this a pleasant way of making money, allowed himself to be bribed again a few nights later. This time he was on duty near the bathroom gate and when during the evening a young Australian came up armed with a false key, opened the gate and walked out, the sentry resolutely kept his back turned. A few minutes after the Australian had got away, one of his friends passed me in the passage of our hut. He was on his way to collect his kit and walk through the gate, which was still open, and gave me this hint in case I wanted to follow on after him. I was not at all ready, most of my kit being dispersed and the important articles, such as maps and compasses, stowed away in rather inaccessible hiding-places. These hiding-places, either in the roof or under the floor of the hut, were difficult to get at quickly and by the time I had everything ready nearly a quarter of an hour had passed. I rushed down to the gate, still in uniform and without a hat. About twenty yards away I slowed down and sauntered past as nonchalantly as possible with my small bundle under my arm. The gate was still open and I turned and walked towards it. Provided one of the other sentries did not spot me, I was as good as out of the camp. But at that moment the bribed sentry turned round and came towards me. I did not see him at first and we both reached the gate at about the same time. I hurriedly reached for a handful of mark notes, which were among my treasured possessions, hoping that a little extra money would tempt him to let me pass. But he was probably getting scared and the time limit was up. Before I could say a word to him he had quietly shut the gate, locked it and then walked quickly down his beat. There was nothing more to be done and I went disconsolately back to my quarters.

The next day the Germans kicked up a tremendous row, but again they were quite unable to find out from what part of the camp the escape had taken place. Again no sentries were caught or punished and I began to have hopes of being able to make use of the man after all. It was not so easy, for by now many other prisoners had got wind of the scheme, and whenever that particular sentry was on duty, a crowd of suspicious-looking prisoners would be seen loitering near his beat with twenty mark notes sticking ostentatiously out of their pockets. As a natural result the sentry became more wary and told one of the prisoners that he could not possibly do anything more, or else his comrades would begin to be suspicious. For all that, I believe that, if at this time we had been able to raise a moderately large sum of money in the camp, every single sentry would have grounded arms and we should have been allowed to walk out at any time of day or night.

The stock of simpler plans was becoming exhausted, something more elaborately audacious was required. After days of reflection we developed a scheme which was in many ways the most ambitious either my brother or I tried during the time we were in Germany. We originally thought of dressing as Germans and marching out of the camp in broad daylight. This was reminiscent of Friedberg days, but in the entire camp at Ströhen there were only three German officers, each of whom was well known by sight to all the sentries. To make matters worse we knew for certain that passes were required for any individual leaving the camp. Among the guards, on the other hand, changes were very frequent and a new face would surprise nobody. We would therefore have to be disguised as N.C.O.'s or private soldiers, and at this point the difficulty of procuring the necessary uniform arose. At Friedberg we had the great advantage of having French and Russians with us, who could supply various important parts of the equipment, especially the Russian–German overcoat. At Ströhen not a stitch of German uniform was to be found, and it was obvious from the first that we would have to make it ourselves. As this became more apparent, we realized that it would only be possible to make one uniform, and it seemed that only one person would be able to get away. We did not see how my brother could be disguised as a civilian, for practically none ever came into the camp, and if, during the attempt, my brother remained in British uniform he would certainly have to be escorted by something more than a single private soldier.

The only prisoners taken out of the camp by a single German soldier were the British orderlies, a party of whom generally left the camp each morning. This gave us an idea and after studying it carefully we came to the conclusion that one of us, dressed as a sentry, would take out the other, dressed as an orderly. We elaborated the details and decided it would be even better if there were two or three orderlies in the party, this being the more usual number to leave the camp.

We started at once to search for anything that could possibly be useful for the German kit. Our first piece of luck was the discovery that a recently taken prisoner had been provided, when in hospital, with a pair of German soldier's boots of the type that are pulled on over uniform trousers and reach half-way up the calf. The German Landsturm soldiers on guard round the camp wore similar boots over old grey trousers, and for our purpose a pair of ordinary dark flannel trousers would do just as well. There were a few pairs of these in the camp, and the lower part of the sham German sentry was therefore complete.

The upper part was not so easy. It was forced on us that we should have to make the service-dress coat either out of a dark blue blanket or else out of an old blue cricket blazer, of which there were several in the camp. The cap was a big problem, that worn by the sentries being rather tall and flat on top with a black peak and black waterproof cover. We hoped that we might be able to obtain one by bribery, or perhaps one of the prisoners at that moment in jail would be able to steal one from the warders. Meanwhile two main difficulties remained: the forged pass, and the rifle. We noticed that no party, however small, ever left the camp without a sentry with a rifle. We had not taken this into our calculations at first, but now it became evident that some sort of gun would be essential. Naturally enough all rifles were kept outside the camp and there seemed to be absolutely no chance of stealing one. The only solution was to make a dummy. It seemed almost a hopeless task to undertake, but it had to be done somehow. Leaving the other problems to be solved later, we settled down to study the construction of German small arms.

XX

My brother and I knew very little about rifles, particularly of the old-fashioned type generally carried by the camp sentries. But by dint of following any armed man who came into the camp and watching his rifle closely, we picked up the details and immediately made rough sketches of the important parts. We were neither of us much good at wood-carving, or at hammering out small pieces of metal, but we soon found a willing worker in a Royal Naval Air Service observer, named Hoblin. We showed him our sketches and explained to him what had to be done and on his agreeing to help us we took him into the scheme as "second orderly", my brother being "first orderly", and I, as the only German-speaking member of the party, the German escort.

The material for making the rifle gave us much trouble and we searched the camp fruitlessly for many days trying to find bits of scrap iron which would serve the purpose. At length we came across the remains of an old wooden picket, about two feet long by four inches square. The wood seemed to be quite seasoned and hard and just the thing out of which to make the stock. A few days later one of us was in the camp cook-house and found that an iron hand-rail in front of the range was not only loose and easily removable, but also was just about the length of the German rifle barrel. We carried this off in triumph one evening when no one was about, and hid it with our other possessions beneath the floor of our hut. We soon unearthed another good piece of wood to form the support under the barrel, together with several bits of iron which might come in handy. Having secured these few trifles, we made a rough design of the gun and work on it started in earnest. We began by carving the stock out of the larger piece of wood. This was done mainly with table knives and later on we obtained a few small wood-carving tools, which the Germans had allowed one of the prisoners to retain. When the stock had taken shape, we finished it off with bits of razor blades, finally polishing it up with bits of broken glass.

We worked next on the dummy barrel, filing and smoothing the muzzle and scraping and polishing the whole tube. It was extremely difficult to get the right kind of blue appearance on the barrel, as we had neither sufficient heat nor the right kind of oil for the required treatment. It was not a matter of very great importance, German rifles being very old and worn. The breech proved very troublesome, for in the real rifle the barrel swelled suddenly to almost twice its average thickness, and in order to get this appearance we had to drive a short piece of thicker piping on to the dummy barrel, and then file down the edges so as to give an appearance of tapering. The stock and the extension under the barrel were screwed together and wired to the barrel. The skeleton of the rifle was now complete, but the most intricate parts such as breech mechanism, sights, trigger and trigger-guard still had to be made. Again we searched the camp in vain for bits of useful scrap metal, and for several days work was suspended for lack of material.

Endless suggestions were made, put into practice and failed. Then Hoblin suggested that the breech mechanism could be made out of tin. He proposed to do this by first of all making wooden models of the various parts, copying them from the rifles we occasionally saw in the camp. None of us being skilled draughtsmen, it took us days of close observation to make sure of the various details, and many were the sentries in Ströhen at that time who must have been quite anxious about the way their footsteps were dogged round the camp. Eventually Hoblin completed the mechanism in wood and started to cover each piece over with thin sheets of metal taken from food tins. It was essential that each piece of tin should be bent absolutely smoothly, and that no dents or kinks should appear on the surface; each strip of tin being secured to its piece of wood by small French nails, driven in underneath where they could not be seen. When the complete breech mechanism was assembled, after many days of hard work, the bright tin was filed off each piece leaving the metal underneath exposed. I had at first been extremely sceptical of the result of this method of construction, but I must admit that when it was completed, polished and slightly oiled, it was quite impossible to tell the tin dummy from the real thing. The appearance of the rounded and sand-papered pieces of tinplate was exactly similar to that of heavy pieces of solid steel, and the remaining details of the rifle were soon made from wood or tin.

Meanwhile my brother had been set to work on the task of collecting suitable material with which to complete the German uniform. He was also to try and find out details of the pass carried by every German leaving the camp. I think it was Darcy Levy, recently arrived from Zorndorf, who discovered what the pass looked like. While in prison he had become acquainted with a German corporal willing to accept a bribe. This man had first of all supplied him with various articles of minor importance, such as electric flash lamps, and after more money had been given him he had consented to supply maps and compasses. Darcy Levy found that in exchange for a loaf or two of white bread, a packet of chocolate and a cake of soap, he could purchase an excellent set of maps of the country between Ströhen and the Dutch frontier. One day he asked to see the official camp permit and the corporal showed it readily enough. It consisted of a small piece of pink paper, about four inches long by three inches wide, bearing the name of the camp, the soldier's company, regimental number and name, and words to the effect that the bearer could enter and leave the camp when on duty. It was signed by the commandant and bore the usual rubber stamp.

We thought this piece of paper would be quite easy to duplicate, until we found that there were no typewriters of any description in the camp. After a closer examination we even discovered that the passes were not printed upon pink paper at all, but upon a sort of oiled fabric, rather similar to the stuff out of which a linen envelope is made only thinner and with a very smooth shiny surface. How on earth we were to manufacture this indispensable piece of our outfit was more than we could imagine, but, hoping that we should eventually be able to procure one by bribery or by theft from our friend the German corporal, we cheerfully left this difficulty to be dealt with last.

The information about the pass and the purchase of a complete set of maps led us to offer Darcy Levy a place as "third orderly" in the scheme. He accepted at once, and was most useful in supplying us with various articles of kit and in helping with the work on the rifle.

With the exception of the sling the rifle was now completed and, when we had assembled all the different parts, we showed it to my brother and Darcy Levy. They had been engaged on other business for several days and had not seen the progress made, so now when they first caught sight of it they were absolutely astounded, and for a few seconds I believe they thought that we had managed to get possession of a real rifle. The last detail – the sling – was made out of an old leather belt and the rifle was then carefully wrapped up in several old shirts and buried under three feet of sand beneath the floor of our hut.

By this time my brother and Darcy Levy, assisted by one of the orderlies, had finished the sentry's uniform. Only two things gave much trouble in this connection, one being the cap for which a black waterproof cover could not be found, and the other the bayonet and scabbard; we could scarcely trust the German corporal to supply either of these articles.

The actual cap did not matter much provided the peak was black leather, but the cover was unobtainable. We tried in vain various bits of oil-cloth and even pieces taken from an old Burberry; none of the material was stiff enough to answer the purpose. We persevered and after many experiments it was found that several thicknesses of brown paper, glued together and painted black, made a cover which would deceive even the sharpest eye at close range. The large brass "Iron Cross", affixed to the front of the cap, was the only thing which we purchased from our German, and he let us have it without any fuss, having no suspicion of our intentions.

A bayonet scabbard was made out of wood covered with leather which was sewn on and carefully darkened, but the guard of the bayonet hilt was quite another matter. In the real article the hilt consisted of a bar of steel, about four inches long, curving down at one end and up at the other, curling at each end into a sort of spiral knob. We tried at first to make this with the usual wood model covered with tin, but it was quite impossible to make the tin conform to the sharp spiral curves without dents appearing at the bends. We were unable to find a piece of iron which would answer the purpose, and in any case we had no suitable tools for making the curves. The only way was to cast it out of soft white metal. The required material was always at hand in the shape of white-metal spoons. We melted down a sufficient quantity of these and made a sand mould, into which we poured the molten metal. The result, although not an astonishing work of art, was quite satisfactory.

At the last moment we found that one other article had been forgotten, namely the ammunition pouch. This was hurriedly made, a block of wood taking the place of the ammunition and the leather covering being cut from an old flying coat. Some three weeks' work saw the German uniform completed and stowed away underground.

The disguise for the other members of the party was easily obtained from the orderlies, exchanged for some of our clothing, and we turned our attention once again to the question of the pass. We could get no help from our German friend on this score; he was quite willing to show us his own pass, but nothing would tempt him to part with it, as it was impossible for him to obtain another. There was no alternative but to manufacture one ourselves.

We made discreet inquiries in the camp, and at length found a prisoner, an excellent draughtsman, who thought he might be able to imitate the print on the pink pass. He made a few samples for us to see if the imitation was sufficiently good. These were passed as satisfactory by the members of the "gang", and we took him into our confidence and managed to show him the pass belonging to the corporal. But before he could start work we had to procure some sort of material which would closely resemble the peculiar pink linen previously described. Various methods of manufacturing this stuff out of pocket handkerchiefs painted pink, or with coloured paper, met with no success and we were beginning to despair, when one bright member of the "gang" suggested the red linen cover of an ordinary cloth bound volume. The colour was much too bright, but after sponging it over with water it toned down to the right shade of pink. The linen was very thin and in consequence the small piece we needed was far too flabby. We could not get hold of any starch, which I think would have been the correct thing to use, but we found that a thin coating of varnish had the desired effect, and by ironing it out while it was still damp we got a dead smooth surface. The pink square was then handed over to the draughtsman who at once got to work and in a few days produced an almost perfect forgery. He had written all the print with indelible pencil which, when slightly steamed, turned to a faint violet tone imitating perfectly the colour of typed ink.

During this time we had been endeavouring to cut out a good rubber stamp. I had never been very good at this, Hardy having done most of this work at Cüstrin, and it would have taken me weeks of practice to become perfect, but the draughtsman again came to our rescue and drew a stamp, complete with eagle, on the pass itself. This again he did with indelible pencil, well rubbed in and steamed rather longer so as to make the colour deeper than the type. The whole thing when finished could not have been done better, and we felt confident that no sentry would turn it down.

Our preparations were now almost complete, but one important question still remained to be settled: how to get our civilian clothes and food out of the camp. At Friedberg we had got over the difficulty by wearing our clothes under the German uniform and sewing packets of concentrated food into specially made belts. At Ströhen this method was impossible, for the orderlies never wore heavy overcoats and not one of them was particularly fat. There was therefore no room under our scanty disguise to conceal provisions. We knew, however, that parties of orderlies were often sent down to the station with parcels or luggage belonging to prisoners who were leaving the camp, and that there would be nothing strange in our taking out some fairly bulky package. We decided that it would be best for all of us to put our kit and provisions into one large canvas kit-bag, and have this carried out by one of the sham orderlies. If questions were asked, we could say that this kit belonged to an officer transferred to another camp, and that the other orderlies were going down to the station to unload prisoners' parcels, which arrived in large quantities two or three times a week.

A few days before the attempt Darcy Levy suggested bringing in another man, named Parish, who had helped us in collecting indispensable articles of equipment. We agreed and he was allotted the place of "fourth orderly". The kit-bag, which now contained complete sets of equipment for five people, became almost too heavy to be carried by one man, and we were much relieved on hearing from the orderlies that, when luggage was taken to the station, either a handcart or wheelbarrow was generally used for the purpose. Accordingly we arranged with one of the orderlies that he should try to get the wheelbarrow left in front of the orderlies' hut on the day of our escape.

By the time our preparations were complete September was drawing to a close, and although my brother and I were anxious to delay the attempt a bit longer, in order to perfect our disguises and improve on some of the details of the scheme, it was decided that we should carry out our plan as soon as possible. One of the reasons for not delaying was that the weather might be expected to break up soon and make walking to the frontier very uncomfortable. There were also rumours that the camp might shortly close down owing to its impossible living conditions, and we were anxious to get away before being sent to some possibly remote part of Germany.

One day we heard that several new men had been drafted into the guard stationed at Ströhen, and it was obvious that we would stand a better chance if we made the attempt before these men became well known.

Immediately after the nine o'clock *Appell* on a certain morning in October, Hoblin and I crept underneath our hut and dug up the German equipment. It was then carried piece by piece, covered up with overcoats, to another hut not far from the entrance to the orderlies' quarters. Darcy Levy's room was in this hut, so that we were perfectly secure from outside observation. The rifle was given a final touch-up, and I donned the kit for the last inspection by the other confederates. An accomplice stood on guard to give me warning of the approach of any Germans, while my brother and the other three went back to their huts and put on their orderlies' clothes.

At this time of the morning various orderlies were continually passing from their section of the camp into ours, and, although there was a sentry on the gate whose duty it was to see that none of the officers got through into the orderlies' section of the camp, discipline was rather lax and he usually handed the key of the gate to one of the orderlies. On this day the orderly who got hold of the key gave it to one of the confederates, who opened the gate and went in. The key was then returned to the camp by means of another orderly, who gave it to the next one of the party, and so on until all four were inside. The kit was a more difficult affair, but with the help of the orderlies we had managed to smuggle part of it out on the previous day and the remainder was taken into the orderlies' hut that morning.

As soon as all the members of the "gang" were inside the orderlies' compound, I was warned by the accomplice who was keeping watch. It was now my business to wait until the camp was more or less clear of one or two Germans who had either been superintending the *Appell*, or who were now watching the fatigue parties of orderlies clean up the camp. When these parties had finished work, the orderlies would again be locked up in their compound and the sentry would move away from the gate. Work in the camp went on for longer than usual that morning and I found that time was slipping by and I dared not wait any more. The sentry on the gate had walked off a little way into the camp and it looked as though I should be able to pass him without any difficulty. I put the finishing touches to my uniform and the moment the "all clear" signal had been given by one of the watchers I walked out into the camp. I was immediately assailed with an almost overwhelming fear of discovery and for the first few seconds I could hardly tell in which direction I was walking. Then as no shots went off, no shouts came from the sentries and no whistles were blown, I gained courage and went on to the gate. The sentry who should have been there was still standing about twenty yards off and greeted me with a smile and a "Good morning." A little farther off I could see our old friend the German corporal, possibly enjoying what he may have guessed were partly the fruits of his corruption.

Just before starting I had been handed the gate key, which had been brought back once more, and I had no difficulty in getting inside the orderlies' compound. I left the key in the lock in case we had to beat a hurried retreat, and marched up to the hut. On looking in at the door I found the whole "gang" assembled, peering out and laughing at me. There was no sentry in sight for the moment and I gave them an answering grin. The first and in some ways the most difficult part of the scheme had worked out most excellently. We had broken through the first line of defences; we were practically out of the camp. There was only one sentry between us and freedom.

XXI

Out of the corner of my eye I caught sight of the sentry at the gate through which we were to pass, glancing in my direction and it struck me that it was time to carry on with the details of the scheme. Adopting what I considered to be my most Teutonic tone, I called for four orderlies to fall in in front of me. The four confederates trooped out of the hut and slouched up as slowly as real orderlies would have done had I been a genuine guard. As soon as they had fallen in I pointed to the large canvas bag of kit, telling them to load it on to the wheelbarrow, which was standing conveniently near, and accompanying my commands with suitable gestures to make the "English pigs" understand.

When this had been done, I waved them towards the gate and gave the order to march. The procession started off in good style, taking care not to go too fast, and we soon covered the thirty yards separating us from the gate. On seeing us approach the sentry came up and peered through the wire. When we were close enough I produced a cloth-covered card case, opened it and showed him my pass. He glanced at it muttering something about "going out to work I suppose", and then slowly produced the key and unlocked the gate. I stood aside while the confederates trooped out, my brother coming last with the wheelbarrow. The moment we were all clear, the sentry turned and closed the gate behind us. We were now right outside the camp and everything seemed to be going well. In another two or three minutes we would reach the cover of the trees on the main road, when we would be safe from pursuit for a considerable time.

And then I noticed that the sentry had started to follow us. Going as slowly as we were he had no difficulty in catching up and keeping pace with us. We had gone barely thirty yards when he came up to me and said in a low voice:

"You ought to be careful of that party of orderlies, I can recognize an officer amongst them."

"An officer?" I said. "Impossible! I know all these men by sight."

"You are wrong," he answered; "that man pushing the wheelbarrow is Hauptmann Milne. I used to be on guard in the camp prison and I know him well by sight."

"Anyway," I retorted, "I shall keep my eyes open; he won't be able to escape from me."

"But there may be other officers in the party," he insisted; "they may all be trying to escape. I don't think you should go any farther with them."

I tried to laugh off my embarrassment and said:

"That's all right, you leave this to me."

But by this time the man was beginning to get thoroughly alarmed.

"No, no! you *must not* go any farther," he said. "I know that one with the wheelbarrow is an officer and I think I recognize one of the others. You must take them back into the camp at once."

I did my best to pacify him; I argued with him:

"Oh, but, come now, these men are all right, and we have to get down to the station at once and send off this luggage and then unload some wagons that have just arrived."

"I can't help that; you had better take them back into the camp at once and have them searched – or else I shall have to alarm the guard. Hi! come back," he shouted, as the two farthermost of the confederates, Darcy Levy and Parish, impatient of the delay, started to wander off, hoping no doubt to get away unobserved.

"It's no good," said the sentry, "I must alarm the guard."

And he blew his whistle.

At this we all realized that the game was up. In broad daylight, with cover over a hundred yards away, and many armed sentries between us and safety, it was no use bolting. The best thing was to make an orderly retreat. With this end in view, I reassumed command of the party and ordered them to go back at once to the orderlies' enclosure. Fortunately our sentry fell in with this idea and accompanied us back to the gate which he opened. While the members of the "gang" filed reluctantly into the enclosure, I went on protesting to the sentry that everything was all right and that he was causing a lot of trouble for nothing. The man was now thoroughly exasperated and very suspicious, and as I stood there arguing with him he started to look me over in a most unpleasant way. Up to this time he had apparently had no idea that I could be anything but a German soldier, but now it seemed to dawn on him that something was wrong.

"Who are you, anyway?" he asked. "I have never seen you before." A slight pause, during which I tried to tell him my name. "And what sort of a bayonet have you got there?" striking at the weak point in the equipment. "And that ammunition pouch looks rather different to me."

He clenched the argument by slamming the gate in my face. As there was nothing more to be said I turned tail and hurried off after the others, who by this time had safely reached the shelter of the orderlies' hut.

Once inside the hut I got rid of my uniform and equipment in double quick time. There was not a moment to be lost if we wanted to save our kit and get away ourselves, for the sentry had started blowing his whistle again and we could hear the shouts and whistles of the guard, which had been turned out and was arriving at the double. The other confederates thought they could hide all their belongings in and under the hut we were in and then wait, dressed as orderlies, until all the excitement had blown over. But I had an idea that there was still a chance of getting back into the camp before the Germans arrived, which would give me time to put some of the more valuable articles of kit, such as maps, money and compasses, into really safe hiding-places. My German uniform and rifle were quickly hidden by the orderlies, either in their hut or down a drain, and immediately after seeing this done I left the hut by a window on the side farthest from the Germans and nearest the camp.

I made straight for the gate through which we had entered the orderlies' enclosure, but on reaching it I found to my dismay that it was locked and the key nowhere to be seen. A squad of Germans had already arrived and were ordering the orderlies back into their hut. I was unable to go back to get help and for the moment it seemed as though I should be caught with the "goods" on me. It was useless to try climbing over the gate; it was about ten feet high and had several rows of barbed-wire at the top. Luckily I noticed that there was a loose strip of wire at the foot of the right-hand gatepost. I knelt down and wrenched at it as hard as I could; it gave a little, but not quite enough to let me get through. I looked around, not knowing what to do, and caught sight of one of the prisoners inside the camp. I shouted to him, and he at once ran up and joined me in my struggles with the wire. But my shout for help had attracted the attention of the Germans round the orderlies' hut. Two or three detached themselves from the group and rushed towards me, unslinging their rifles and yelling at me to stop. Just in time the wire fence gave way and I managed to wriggle underneath it into the camp. With the man who had helped me, I sprinted across the camp and made a dash for the cover of the nearest hut. Fortunately the pursuing Germans had no key to the gate and, while struggling with it, they forgot to shoot. Once inside my own hut I lost no time in disposing safely of the gear I had brought away.

I was not yet out of the wood, for I felt certain that if the whole camp was assembled and the sentry on the gate brought in to identify me he would be able to do so. I at once changed my clothes, removed my moustache and had my head shaved by the camp barber – an English orderly. The "disguise" served its purpose for a few hours, but that evening I was sent for from the *Kommandantur* where, in spite of my protests of innocence, I was easily recognized by the sentry, placed under arrest and thrown into solitary confinement in the camp jail. The other confederates, caught more or less red-handed in the orderlies' enclosure, had preceded me and had already secured the most comfortable cells.

The jail was full to overflowing at the time I went into it and partly because of this, but mainly because the Germans looked upon me as the ring-leader of the "gang", I was put into a cell which, owing to its tumble-down condition, had been condemned as unfit for prisoners to inhabit. The whole of the prison was built of wood, as were all the buildings in the camp, and there were large chinks in the walls of my cell letting in the unpleasantly cold autumn winds. The glass of the little barred window was broken; the roof let in the rain. The details of prison life, the same here as in other jails, are hardly worth reiterating: no extra clothing; one worn-out blanket on my bed; no books; insufficient food; no exercise.

On being arrested I had refused to admit my share in the attempt, thereby annoying the Germans considerably, for the sentry's unsupported evidence would not be sufficient if we were brought to trial. Being quite convinced of my guilt, the commandant of the camp made it a condition that I should be allowed extra food and clothing if I would but confess. This seemed rather like torture and, hoping for an early release or a chance to escape, I prolonged the agony for about ten days. At last, recognizing that my attitude could serve no useful purpose, I summoned the jailer and asked him to tell the commandant that I had confessed, and that if an invitation to a court-martial were issued to me I would willingly attend could I but have an extra blanket on my bed at night. The commandant at once permitted me to have most of the things I wanted, with the exception of cigarettes.

I had thought that, after this, events would move fairly rapidly and that we should soon be sentenced to some short term of imprisonment. I was quickly disillusioned. For, as the days dragged into weeks and the weeks themselves began to mount up, I realized that the authorities were playing the same game with us as at Cüstrin, and that we might be kept there for many months before a decision was arrived at.

The weather during October was extremely bad, and after many days of continual rain my cell resembled a swimming bath. Walking up and down my cell – the only form of exercise – became almost out of the question, as once my boots were wet I could not get them dry again. The alternative was to sit on a damp bed all day long, covered with a blanket. After a week or two I caught a bad cold, and one night I woke up with a pain in my chest and the worst headache I have ever had. Next morning I felt very ill and asked to see the doctor. The German doctor was, of course, not available, but a British officer, ex-medical student, came to my rescue with a thermometer and some asperin. My temperature was 104 and, on hearing this, the German authorities kindly consented to put me in a drier cell. In a dry bed and with lots of asperin I felt better, but next day my temperature was still high and the authorities were compelled to admit me to the camp hospital.

As a hospital it was nothing very wonderful, but at least it was warm and dry. I stayed there for a fortnight, fed on asperin and cough mixture, and occasionally attended to by the German doctor. The majority of the cases were not very serious and after a few days, when I was beginning to get better, it was really quite pleasant. One of the occupants, a Tasmanian, had been shot through the leg while trying to escape. There was also an Indian native officer, off his head, who had tried to commit suicide by carving his stomach with a razor blade. He was recovering from his wounds but not from his madness, and, being convinced that he was already dead, looked upon us as the denizens of hell. He was quite a pleasant fellow in his saner moments and we were all very sorry for him. He was eventually moved by the Germans to an Indian camp, where, I believe, he died.

Many prisoners used to come to the hospital daily on the pretext of visiting the sick but in reality to plan some method of escape; the hospital being situated close to the fence, it was considered suitable as a jumping-off place for an attack on the wire. To visit me one day came Beverley Robinson with a pair of wire-cutters, a compass and a set of maps. He suggested that as soon as I was convalescent we should make an attempt at wire-cutting together. I naturally agreed and at the end of my second week in hospital we decided to start work.

The advantage of the hospital as a starting-point lay in the fact that it was placed in one of the worst lighted parts of the camp, there being no electric lamp for nearly a hundred yards on either side of it. The first night on which we tried all went well, but the sentry was a little too watchful and we could only cut a few strands in the first fence guarding the neutral zone. The next night I climbed out of the hospital window; working in the shadow, a complete section was cut out of the first fence, and we started work on the outer fence. I wore gloves and a dark woollen muffler round my face to make certain of not showing up against the darker ground. Nevertheless, the sentry was again too close for a final attempt to be made on the outer fence. We contrived to fasten up the flap we had cut out of the first fence with a single strand of wire so that it would not show during daylight, and then put off the attempt for another night. But in the course of the next day it became evident that in spite of our precautions the Germans had noticed something, as a party of men came along and inspected the wire. Shortly afterwards, on the same day, a new lamp was brought along and much to our dismay some workmen started to erect a pole immediately opposite the hospital. That night, although the new lamp was not yet in working order, an extra sentry was put on, effectually preventing us from making a further attempt. Worst of all, the German doctor visited the hospital two days later and passed me as fit; whereupon I was immediately sent back to the jail.

For a short time Robinson, arrested for some unsuccessful attempt elsewhere in the camp, was put in a cell next door to mine. We were both very fond of chess and, having obtained two sets, we spent the next few weeks in playing a most amusing series of games, shouting the moves to one another through the wooden wall which divided our cells. This method of playing had one great advantage; whenever it seemed likely that I was going to be beaten, which was more often than not, I was able to put matters right by pretending that the positions on my board were quite different to those of his, a state of affairs which must have arisen through my misunderstanding one of his calls.

There was still no news from the Germans as to our fate and when, in the middle of November, my brother and the rest of the "gang" were suddenly moved to another camp, I felt that I had probably been forgotten and was destined to stay in jail for ever. At last came the welcome news that I was to be tried by court-martial. Upon what charge and whether the rest of the "gang" were also implicated I did not know. In any case it was the end of the tedium of jail and implied the possibility of being sent to a new camp. On 21 November I was allowed into the camp for an hour to pack a few belongings into a suit-case and to get ready to leave for Hanover on the following day. I found that I would not be alone as there was another prisoner also going to Hanover for trial. My only regret was that, owing to a very strict search which I knew would take place before we left, I would not be able to take any escaping kit with me. It was perhaps just as well, for we had recently had a spell of very hard weather with a lot of snow, and I was not altogether fit after my recent illness.

At an early hour the next morning we left for Hanover which we reached at nightfall after an uneventful journey. We were marched through the town, unpleasantly cheerful with a foretaste of Christmas, to the civilian jail where we were lodged for the night in filthy cells. The next morning at ten o'clock, I was taken across to the army headquarters and shown into a waiting-room where I came face to face with my one-time confederates. We spent a most amusing morning, talking and laughing loudly the whole time, except during the actual proceedings of the trial, which lasted only a quarter of an hour. There being no interpreter present I had to act as spokesman for the party, causing us all a lot of quiet laughter. The other members of the "gang" refused to take the trial seriously and kept up a cross-fire of the most absurd questions, which fortunately were not understood by our judges. In the end we were sentenced to terms of imprisonment varying from four and a half months in my case down to three months in the case of one of the "gang" whom the judges evidently considered not to be responsible for his actions. Luckily they had heard of the long period we had already spent in jail, and showed sufficient appreciation of this fact to allow us the option of a fine. I forget the exact amount, but it worked out at something between five and ten pounds per man. We were getting very tired of jail and, stipulating that the money should be paid into Red Cross funds, we agreed to the fine. And somehow I have a feeling that very little of it was ever paid.

Just as we were leaving the court at about midday, thoroughly pleased to have no more prison time to serve, we were recalled and told that of course the invariable rule of fourteen days' disciplinary punishment would have to be observed. We protested loudly against this, but it was of no use and we were marched out. We had lunch at the buffet at Hanover Station, after which my brother and the other three were taken back to their camp at Holzminden, and I and my companion – who had also escaped with a small fine that morning – took the train for Ströhen.

All went well until we got to the small junction at Diepholz where we had to change into the slow local train stopping at Ströhen. Unfortunately our train from Hanover was about an hour late and we missed the last train that night. The station was very small and had no proper buffet or waiting-room in which to spend the night and our guards, anxious to get back to their own quarters, were naturally furious at being kept out in the snow. We had got on quite friendly terms during the journey back from Hanover, and I suggested half-seriously to the guards that I should order a special train. The *Feldwebel* in charge, who was what the Americans call a " dumb bell," thought this an excellent idea and took me up to the station-master to whom I repeated my request. He seemed rather surprised at first, but much impressed by the *Feldwebel*'s statement that all English prisoners were "*kolossal reich*", he allowed himself to be persuaded. The station staff were at once called up and various orders given with the result that a few minutes later, with a great deal of puffing, an engine and two carriages were shunted up alongside the platform. There were several other passengers who, like ourselves, had missed the last train and were only too ready to avail themselves of the invitation which we extended to them through the *Feldwebel*.

My companion and I were just beginning to chortle with delight at the idea of riding home in such unusual luxury when, as luck would have it, a bustling and interfering German officer turned up. After a short conversation with the station-master he told the bewildered officials that it was utterly impossible to allow prisoners of war to carry on in this high-handed manner. Very reluctantly the engine driver, to whom we had promised a substantial tip, shunted his little train out of the station into the siding again. Meanwhile we were hurriedly led out of the station by the *Feldwebel*, who thought it would be as well to keep clear of the German officer and avoid awkward questions. Some of our guards knew the town well and suggested going to a small inn a few hundred yards from the station. We reached it a few minutes later and found that although small it was old-fashioned enough to be clean and comfortable. We were given some food and then shown into a bedroom on the first floor. As we neither of us had any escaping kit with us, any attempt to escape during the night was out of the question. But, in order to make doubly sure, we were locked into our room and our boots were taken away. In addition a sentry was posted in the garden outside. We passed a rather restless night, being unaccustomed to the delights of a spring mattress and clean sheets. Next morning we caught an early train back to Ströhen, where we arrived without further incident.

As soon as I got into the camp, I was escorted back to prison to complete my sentence. I fancied that in accordance with the court-martial decision I should only have fourteen days in jail, but apparently the sentence had not yet been promulgated and it was nearly three weeks before I was told that I still had another fourteen days to serve. This time imprisonment was not quite so unpleasant. The jail was almost empty and, as a result, I had a cell to myself which generally served for two prisoners. I was also allowed all the books I wanted and most of my kit. Collier, recently recaptured, was in the cell next door and through our thin wooden partition we held long conversations on every imaginable topic. We discussed innumerable plans for escaping from Ströhen all of which were suddenly brought to naught by a rumour that we were to be among a number of prisoners shortly leaving for another camp.

As usual the idea of going to a new camp was quite exciting. There would probably be some chance of escaping *en route*, and one never knew if the

Germans in the new camp might not be entirely ignorant of the ways of prisoners, thus making escape easy. In the first week of December these rumours took definite shape, and we were informed by the authorities that more than eighty prisoners including ourselves were to be transferred to a camp somewhere near the Alsace-Lorraine border. We gathered that a number of small camps were being established in this neighbourhood, in the vicinity of important industrial centres, to hinder the bombing of these towns by Allied aircraft. On 6 December Collier and I were released from jail in order to pack up our kit and make ready for our departure which was to take place on the following day. My last night at Ströhen was really quite amusing. Not only were eighty of us leaving on the following day, but a number of prisoners of over three years' standing were due to be exchanged to Holland against an equivalent number of German officers from England, under an agreement recently made between the respective governments. The remainder of the prisoners were also to be moved to other camps shortly, for the Germans had at last admitted that Ströhen was impossible as a camp for prisoners of war. The evening was therefore rather in the nature of a farewell party celebrated with much beer and a small consignment of port, which had just arrived from England – by international agreement, labelled "medicine!"

Next morning, in spite of thick heads, we devoted our remaining moments to secreting about our persons and in our luggage the various valuable articles of our escaping kit. At midday, accompanied by a large party of armed guards, we were marched down to the station, followed by the cheers of the remaining prisoners.

XXII

Our journey lasted for nearly two complete days and during the first part of it we had good cause to wonder where on earth we were being taken. The train left Ströhen in the direction of Bremen and after a couple of hours' travelling, when we could almost smell the sea, it turned south-west. Then it wandered slowly around through all the points of the compass until eventually towards midnight we found ourselves in the Ruhr district.

Next day our train followed the course of the Rhine as far as Bingen. Collier and I and two others were in a carriage with two German sentries, and several times during the journey we fancied there were chances of jumping the train, but we were poorly provided with kit and the line we followed lay a good way from the frontier. Our guards, a couple of unpatriotic blackguardly communists, told us they were quite willing to allow us to escape if we would only give them a loaf of white bread, a cake of soap or a packet of chocolate. Apparently like other Germans of the same type they were not in need of these articles themselves but knew of individuals to whom they could sell them for a good price. On the whole we thought it best not to trust these men; they were quite capable of accepting a bribe and shooting afterwards.

Although we travelled for most of the way in the oldest of third-class carriages, our journey was not too uncomfortable, and every now and then the train would stop at a wayside station where, at exorbitant prices, we were able to purchase rather indifferent meals from the Red Cross canteens. At nine o'clock on the morning of the second day, we arrived at the station of Neunkirchen. I suppose most of us had never heard the name before and we were surprised to find that it was quite a large mining town, situated some ten miles from Saarbrücken.

We were marched through the town, loudly booed and jeered at by the populace who, not having seen British prisoners before, no doubt imagined that we were the fruit of the recent German counter-attack in the battle of Cambrai. Having crossed the greater part of the town, we were halted in front of a funny, drab little two-storied building. Across the front in faded letters of gold were the words "Catholic Friends Meeting House". As a prisoners' camp it was evidently brand-new, for the wooden palisade had, judging from the fresh sawdust on the ground, just been erected. After a few moments' delay the gate was opened and we filed into the house.

We were ushered into a small room labelled 'Billiards', and our guards left us. At the far end of this room there was what appeared to be a boarded platform about four feet high. Intent on finding as soon as possible some suitable places for hiding our compasses and maps, some of us set to work to pull up the planks and see what was underneath. One or two of the planks came up quite easily, and to our amazement we found that they concealed an ordinary public house bar. We also discovered that the back of the bar connected with a much larger room by means of a small door. Half an hour later when our names had been taken and a mild search had been finished with, we were allowed first of all upstairs where we discovered a long, narrow room, probably once used as a sort of banqueting hall, and two or three other smaller rooms on the top floor under the roof. The doors downstairs were then opened and we were allowed into the large chamber of which we had caught a glimpse from behind the bar in the "billiard" room. In all of these rooms, with the exception of the small rooms beneath the roof, we found concealed bars with all the mechanism for serving large quantities of beer. The "Catholic Friends" had evidently been pretty good fellows in their time!

The large room downstairs presented a most peculiar appearance. It contained a bar on each side of the entrance and had originally been a theatre or concert-hall, for at the far end there was a stage, the place of the curtain now being taken by stout planks. A gallery ran round three sides of the room, a few feet above our heads and on one side there were eight windows, four in the gallery and four underneath it. There were no windows in the other walls of the room, which was filled with sixty-four beds, one above the other in pairs like sleeping-car berths, leaving practically no open space anywhere. On the side where the windows were placed, a small glass door gave on to a courtyard surrounded by a brick wall and measuring only twenty yards long by ten yards wide. On the far side of this yard was what looked like a long shed, which we presently discovered was an old and much decayed bowling alley. A few melancholy soot-covered trees grew around the sides of the yard which was overlooked from above a brick wall surmounted by barbed-wire, and various tumble-down houses. It was not a very cheering spot and naturally gave an impression of overcrowding confinement, but the general aspect and contents of the building seemed so strange, and the innumerable beer bars so different to anything we had seen for years, that we were at first vastly amused.

The defects of the camp, and particularly of our dormitory, soon made themselves apparent. We had already had some experience of "double-deck" beds in various camps and had found them to be very unpleasant. The lower berth was probably the most comfortable, but the upper berth had more air and in a room where eighty were sleeping at the same time the lack of air was very noticeable. To make matters worse the windows were all permanently shut and bolted. Our demand to have these windows opened was met by an unqualified refusal, causing endless trouble between us and the authorities.

For the first few weeks we were not allowed to use the so-called billiard-room, which immediately after our arrival was handed over to the guards, about thirty of whom lived in the building. The two very small rooms at the top of the house were occupied by two or three of the senior officers, and as a result there were only two rooms which the majority of us could use: the theatre in which we slept, and the dining-room on the ground floor. We were only allowed into the exercise yard at certain stated times of the day, and as it was winter when we arrived at Neunkirchen we could not make much use of even this small space.

The lavatory and washing accommodation was totally insufficient. At first there was only one cold shower bath available in a small cellar beneath our dormitory. Eventually two baths with hot water apparatus were also installed, but even these were inadequate.

It was some time before our food parcels started to follow us on from Ströhen, and a small canteen, established at one end of the dining-room, was quite incapable of supplying our demands. As if purposely to annoy us the Germans issued a series of aggravating regulations which, while serving no useful purpose, made us even more uncomfortable. We were not allowed, for instance, to smoke in our dormitory at any hour of the day or night; we were only permitted to cook and eat our meals at certain hours, and all lights had to be out by nine o'clock.

During the first few days we were continually being assembled, either in the building or in the yard for some notice to be read out by the German officers or the camp commandant. On these occasions we were kept standing for as much as half an hour on end for no apparent reason and the only thing which in any way relieved the tedium of this procedure was the stupidity of the camp interpreter. This man, a fat little Jew from Berlin, was in mortal fear of being sent to the front and had wormed his way into the position of interpreter as a last desperate effort to save his skin.

One thing is certain; he knew no English other than what we chose to teach him, and, as soon as we had found this out, we proceeded to fill him up with a series of the most ridiculous and meaningless phrases we could think of. Some of the notices posted on the walls of the camp, for which he was responsible, were too ludicrous for words besides being quite unintelligible. One of these notices referred to the commander of the guard, whose official title was: "*Kommandant der Landsturm*". Our amazing interpreter rendered this phrase as 'Commander of the Storms on Land'. Whenever the general commanding the district came to inspect us, which later on was about twice a week, the unfortunate interpreter was reduced to a state of abject terror and used to beg those of us who knew any German to take his place and translate the general's speech – an invariable accompaniment to each of his visits. But to these entreaties we turned a deaf ear, being unwilling to miss the wonderful entertainment thus provided.

As soon as we had thoroughly grasped all the complicated regulations and the absurd conditions under which we were expected to live, we started to protest, at first politely and verbally and then more firmly, and in writing. This brought us our first visit from the general. He made a long speech, of which the majority of the prisoners understood nothing and which the interpreter was unable to explain. After one or two rude and very German remarks about the victorious German Army and the approaching defeat of the Allies, he tried to be very pleasant and answered most of our objections in a satisfactory manner. He quite realised, he said, that the yard was too small for us to be able to obtain sufficient exercise, but the usual bi-weekly walks on parole were soon to be started, and he was obtaining permission for us to make use of a football ground on the outskirts of the town. He also gave permission for the windows on the ground floor to be opened, but the upper row of windows opening from the gallery he insisted on keeping closed to prevent our communicating with the local inhabitants in the houses opposite.

Weeks passed by, however, and nothing further happened as far as the promised walks and the football ground were concerned. Another protest was written, bringing the general back very angry for what he termed our impudence, and rather apologetic for not having kept his word. He explained that the population was so hostile that he dared not let us out into the streets. Our answer, that not only did this not appear to be the case, but that the strong guard which had usually accompanied us on similar walks in other camps would provide ample protection, was not listened to; it took us many weeks of continual complaining before our requests were granted.

Our parcels gradually began to arrive in reasonable quantities and, with the help of watery beer and bad wine sold in the canteen, we were able to furnish ourselves with quite a respectable Christmas dinner. After Christmas – my third in captivity – many of us began to cast around for ways and means of escaping. All the usual schemes were discussed; but, owing to the smallness of the camp and the abnormal number of Germans living in the same building and continually mixing with us, there was not much scope for putting them into practice. In fact, in a very short time we realised that although the Germans in this camp were quite inexperienced it was undoubtedly a difficult camp to escape from. A tunnel was, of course, among the earliest of the schemes suggested, and it was obvious that while waiting for other chances to occur to us we might just as well be digging our way out. Among the eighty prisoners a large proportion had tried to escape before, and we were sure of finding plenty of people to do the work. In addition to Collier and myself, there were Wilkin, late of Fort Zorndorf, renowned as a picker of locks and an excellent all-round mechanic; Major McClean, Gordon Highlanders, who had already escaped from two camps; Blaine, who had nearly crossed the frontier on his first attempt, and a dozen others of the same type.

At first sight, there seemed to be plenty of places in the camp suitable for starting a tunnel. To begin with there were all the board covered bars, the majority of which had already been adapted to serve as excellent hiding-places for our kit. Beneath any of these it would be quite practicable, as far as the ground floor was concerned, to start a tunnel and there would be plenty of room for stowing away the earth. The exercise yard was also very tempting, as the distance required to reach the outside of the camp was extremely short. For instance, if we had been able to sink a shaft at one end of the bowling alley, we should only have had to dig under a brick wall in order to gain access to what the Germans told us was a disused gymnasium, from which we had reason to believe there was an exit leading into the street. But we were forced to give up the idea as there were two German sentries on permanent duty in the tiny yard and, moreover, we could never tell whether we were not being observed from the windows of the main building.

It was decided that the best place of all would be behind and underneath the stage, if only we could manage to gain access to it. Why on earth the Germans had ever thought of boarding up the stage, I cannot imagine. Not only would there have been more room for the prisoners if they had left it un-boarded, but also they could easily have seen everything that was going on, and, in addition, we should have had none of the incentive which invariably prompts one to investigate the mystery of a locked door.

There were four doors leading to these mysterious regions behind the boarded up stage. Two of these were on the ground floor, only a few feet from the nearest beds which completely screened them from view, the other two at either end of the gallery. All four of these doors opened inwards, that is towards the back of the stage, and, although Wilkin made short work of the locks, we soon found that there must be some obstruction on the far side, as three of these doors would not give an inch. The fourth door opened easily but we did not feel safe in using it, the Germans having decided to store the prisoners' luggage on the stage and this being the door through which they passed two or three times a week. It would be easy for Wilkin to cut a panel out of one of the other doors with his kit of tools, but meanwhile we found another entrance.

One day, when we had been up to have a talk with McClean who lived in one of the small rooms reserved for the senior officers, Wilkin thought it would be a good idea to examine a small door leading apparently out on to the roof from the top floor landing. After very little trouble with the lock Wilkin forced the door open and we found that it led into a large passage running the whole length of the eaves under the roof.

Closing the door behind us we crept along to the far end, where we discovered a rickety wooden staircase leading down into the wings of the stage. The place had evidently been disused for years and was covered with cobwebs. The staircase ended half-way down and we had to complete our journey to the stage itself by sliding down the tattered remains of an old drop curtain. Picking our way through the pile of trunks and suit-cases belonging to the prisoners, we reached the side of the stage and found a short staircase bringing us down to the ground level. To our great joy we noticed that we were now standing on bare earth, unprotected by concrete or even boards. But although we were now close to the end wall of the building, and therefore on the very edge of the camp, we considered it out of the question to start digging there since any German who came in to attend to the prisoners' luggage would see the results of our labours.

We prowled about in the dark and eventually discovered a little trap-door which we had no difficulty in forcing open. Creeping through it we found ourselves beneath the stage itself. Here again the floor was bare earth and it was quite evident, from the cobwebs which brushed our faces and from the lack of any articles connected either with the prisoners or the German authorities, that it had been a long time since anyone had pushed his way into this dark corner. We were not very far from the outside wall and there was plenty of space beneath the stage to stow all the earth from the tunnel.

Before actually beginning to dig we had to make sure of a quick and easy way in and out of the part of the building behind the stage. The passage under the roof was very good in some ways, but it meant using the main staircase a great deal, and this staircase, starting outside the dormitory, passed immediately in front of the door of the guard-room, which was generally open. Climbing down behind the stage was also a very noisy business, and it seemed essential therefore to open one of the doors leading from the gallery into the wings. The gallery contained tables and chairs and was used as a reading and writing room, so there was nothing suspicious in two or three prisoners seen loitering there. The backs of the doors had been boarded up, but an hour's work was sufficient to loosen a panel in one of them so that it was easily removable and yet when in place showed no sign of having been tampered with.

A few days later, having provided ourselves with the usual table knives and several suits of old clothes for digging purposes, work was commenced and a shaft was rapidly sunk beneath a corner of the front of the stage. Starting at this exact point would enable us to dig a short second tunnel beneath the floor of the theatre itself so as to have direct access to the tunnel from the floor of our dormitory, enabling us to do without the gallery door.

Unfortunately an immense amount of rain fell during the month of January and, as the drains were not sufficient to take away the water collected round the camp, most of it collected at the bottom of our shaft. The tunnel mouth which had just been commenced at a depth of six feet below the ground level was soon under water and we had to stop work and resort to baling. A few days of fine weather and much hard labour allowed us to get ahead of the infiltration and, as soon as the bottom of the shaft was uncovered, we proceeded to deepen it to about ten feet. There was thus a distance of some four feet from the lower lip of the tunnel mouth to the bottom of the shaft. This was boarded over to form a platform upon which the workers could stand. A hole was left in this platform, sufficiently large to allow buckets, lowered from the top of the shaft, to pass through and collect the water accumulated in the sump. The ground beneath the stage sloped down quite sharply towards the corner opposite that in which our shaft was sunk and we were able to empty the buckets outside the shaft with a certainty that the water would run away.

Digging in the tunnel was resumed, but we now found that the number of workers so far admitted into the "gang" were not sufficient to carry on the digging and cope with the drainage problem as well. Fresh workers were recruited from among the other members of the camp, and as time went on almost every able-bodied man who considered that he had a chance of escape and was willing to try was brought into the scheme. At one time there were thus about fifty prisoners employed on some job or other connected with the tunnel.

After a few yards of the tunnel had been dug and the entrance of the shaft reinforced and revetted with wooden props obtained largely from old boards found under the stage, we started work on the auxiliary tunnel which was to pass beneath the front of the stage and come up through the dormitory floor. In spite of the fact that a great many large stones had been used in the foundations of the stage, work in this direction was fairly easy as the cement was soft and the soil loosely packed. After ten days' work we reached a point estimated to be about two feet in front of the stage, and we then drove a shaft vertically to the surface. The last part was most unpleasant work, since the whole floor beneath the boards of the theatre was covered with six inches of clinker and ashes. One or two of the workers were almost blinded on first striking this layer, but, with the help of spectacles fitted with a protecting edge of blanket material, the work was soon completed.

The next and most difficult part of this branch tunnel was the cutting of a trap-door in the floor of our dormitory. We had imagined that this would be perfectly simple and would merely consist in cutting a piece about two feet square out of the boards, but if this had been done it would have been noticed at once. To make sure of it being invisible we were forced to cut through the dovetailing, joining the planks together, for the whole way around the proposed trapdoor. The planks were hard, well-seasoned wood, fitting very closely together, and only the finest of razor-blade saws could be used to prevent the saw marks being left along the upper edges of the planks. Even so the trap could not be cut square, for in a well-made floor the ends of all the planks are not in line, but only every third or fourth. This compelled us to cut out a very irregular section of the floor, and consequently the space to be allowed for a man coming through had to be considerably increased. It was also necessary to cut through two heavy supporting beams to which the planks were nailed and, to prevent the now weakened floor from giving way, the ends of these beams had to be supported by large blocks of stone taken from beneath the stage.

Wilkin very cleverly devised a complicated but successful system of fastenings, allowing the trap to move perfectly freely and at the same time ensuring that the hinges were invisible from above. A spring catch was fitted to each separate plank, which effectively secured the whole framework and prevented the planks from giving way if anyone stepped on them. These catches were all connected to a rod, from which a wire ran for several yards under the floor to a corner of the dormitory where it was hooked to the wall. A small, unnoticeable hole at the edge of the boards permitted one to reach the wire which, on being pulled, released the safety catches and the end of the trap-door was then pushed up by a strong spring. The whole arrangement – due almost entirely to Wilkin – was most ingenious, and when the trap was shut from the outside there was positively nothing to be seen.

The gallery door was now abandoned in favour of the new entrance. Later on, when the water in the shaft had subsided, we intended to close up the top of the shaft and fill it with earth, leaving no trace of digging in the space beneath the stage. Meanwhile, although considerable progress had been made with the main tunnel, the incessant rain had nearly filled up the shaft once again. It was extraordinary to see how quickly the shaft filled and many gallons must have been emptied into the far corner beneath the stage without making any noticeable impression. Eventually the ground where we emptied the water became water-logged and failed to soak up more than a small quantity of the huge amount we threw away.

Some other means had to be found of draining the shaft and, casting around for something that might help us, we came across an old iron cauldron among the rubbish at the back of the stage. We placed this cauldron close to the top of the shaft and emptied our buckets into it. A rubber tube was led from the cauldron, through the boards of the stage, over the footlights into the dormitory. The floor of the dormitory was on a lower level than the ground beneath the stage and consequently the water automatically siphoned from the cauldron into various buckets and basins outside. These again were emptied down the sink of one of the disused bars. If no Germans approached, the process was continued until all the water from the shaft had been got rid of. This system worked remarkably well, although it was naturally risky.

We had arranged a series of signals, consisting of taps with a hammer on the front of the stage, to serve as a warning to those digging when anyone approached. On one or two occasions we fancied that the Germans had noticed these sounds and we had to devise something new. Wilkin was again invaluable, and, with the help of an electric torch battery purchased from the German barber for a loaf of white bread and two eggs, he constructed an electric buzzer. This instrument gave the alarm or 'all clear' signal to the workers but was quite inaudible in the theatre. The wire was carried up into the gallery where an accomplice sat all day apparently reading a book, ready to press the button in case of necessity.

When the tunnel was fifteen yards long we began to have the usual trouble with the ventilation, but by widening the entrance and the first few yards, and using electric torches – supplied by the barber – instead of candles, we were able to improve matters considerably. A short period of frost and snow permitted some really rapid progress to be made and, from the only window overlooking the point aimed at, we took sights and calculated how far we had yet to go.

Outside the building on this side of the camp there was a path for the sentries not more than six feet in width. For half its length this path was bounded by a brick wall fifteen feet high, surrounding the civil prison. For the remainder of its length, it was separated by a wall eight feet high from a series of small allotments belonging to a row of houses, the backs of which could be seen from our window. A lane one-hundred yards distant passed between two of these houses and led to the centre of the town. To bring us to a point where we felt we should be safe in coming to the surface required a total tunnel length of about twenty-four yards, and as we gradually approached this point we thought it was now time to start to brush up our escaping kit and organise for the final exodus.

There were now so many prisoners engaged in completing the tunnel that it became obvious there would not be enough compasses and maps to go round. A number of prisoners were therefore grouped into a firm of escape outfitters comprising many branches. McClean opened a compass factory in his upstairs room. His compasses, although rather rough in appearance, were thoroughly reliable, being made for the most part out of magnetised needles supported on the jewelled bearings taken from watches, and enclosed either in a small wooden box or else actually in watch case with dummy face and hands. He did not take long to make each one, and I believe he manufactured more than a score of them. One or two prisoners, able to use needle and thread, volunteered to make civilian clothes out of old uniforms and blankets.

Blaine and I set up a passport department. I had several samples of home-made passes to go by and I remembered the details of many similar papers made out by prisoners at Zorndorf. Three or four nights running we broke into the German canteen in our dining-room after the Germans had gone for the night, and secured their typewriter. The machine was rushed down to the dormitory and a dozen different styles of passes and permits to travel were hurriedly thumped out. Later on a young Canadian, named Dodwell, made us some really beautiful passes, imitating printed Gothic characters with the skill of an expert. A photographer was allowed to visit the camp and we had our pictures taken in old uniforms, taking care that no badges showed. Cut to a suitable size and pasted on the pass these photographs were most effective.

The greater part of the prisoners, of course, could not speak a word of German and consequently would be forced to travel by night and on foot, avoiding all towns and villages. It was just possible that they might manage to board a train, in which case the passes would probably come in handy, and it was more or less certain that, however cautious they were, some of them would meet and perhaps be questioned by Germans. On such an occasion a word or two of German, spoken with a reasonably good accent and without nervousness, was very often all that was needed to allay suspicion and get one out of a tight corner. At the request of several prisoners, we therefore made out a typewritten list of the more common German expressions and forms of greeting, questions likely to be asked and the answers to be given. We also explained the pronunciation of the various phrases and tested the ability of those who had learnt a certain amount.

We made a list of all those intending to use the tunnel and found out their requirements. There had not been much escaping kit in the camp until we had started making it and several prisoners had to be furnished with a complete equipment. This consisted of a compass, a forged pass, a rough suit which would pass muster in the dark, and the list of German phrases. We were also short of maps, but we had some fairly good copies and certain sections of the Swiss and Dutch frontiers. We filled in the gaps fairly successfully with the help of a map taken from a railway time-table. Those who wanted maps were lent the originals and traced their own copies.

All those who were going to make the attempt were naturally anxious to know in what order they were to go out and at what time of night or day they were to be ready. Long before the tunnel approached completion we made out a list allotting a place and the probable time of exit for each prisoner. The first twelve places were reserved for those of us who had either escaped before or had originated the scheme. After these, there was a second batch of about fifteen who had taken an active part in the digging of the tunnel; a third party, consisting of those who had helped indirectly, was some twenty strong.

The first prisoners on the list would leave at about nine o'clock in the evening, which meant that if all went well the last prisoner would be clear of the tunnel mouth, allowing for safe intervals between each party, by about one o'clock in the morning. This gave even the last prisoner ample time to get clear of the town and into cover before daylight. Blaine and I, who were among the first, hoped to catch a train at 9.30 from Neunkirchen which, with two changes, would bring us to Düsseldorf or Crefeld in the afternoon of the following day. We were then to make straight for the frontier and

Blaine, who knew the district well, thought that we should be able to cross the Dutch frontier the same night.

At last, in spite of the troublesome drainage operations which we had frequently been forced to suspend to avoid attracting German attention, the tunnel reached a point where we could safely break surface, and at this moment, as in the case of so many tunnel schemes, Fate stepped in and swept away the whole of our deep laid plans. By a stroke of ill-luck a few days before the completion of the tunnel, the commandant of the camp was removed. We had little cause to like him and, when we found that the new commandant was a thoroughly good sportsman who intended to do the best he possibly could for us, we thought we had benefited by the change. But one of the first things he did was to have a thorough inspection of the camp with the idea of seeing how he could improve our quarters and remedy the inefficient sanitation and drainage. While this close inspection went on we stopped all work on the tunnel, but on the second day the commandant decided to have a look behind the stage doors. When first the Germans went in we had no fear of anything being discovered, as we knew that they had never looked beneath the stage before and the little door leading in had been securely fastened after the construction of the dormitory trap-door. But the commandant was inquisitive and, finding that the ground on either side of the stage was unpleasantly damp, he had the small door forced open and a man sent in to inspect the ground in the centre. When half an hour later the commandant and two Germans came out into the dormitory we knew at once that we had failed once again. I felt peculiarly foolish; it was the sixth unsuccessful tunnel in which I had taken part.

The guard was called out; sentries with fixed bayonets were posted at every conceivable angle of the stage and the dormitory, and a squad of Germans armed with spades and pickaxes were sent in to demolish the tunnel, and to secure any evidence they could find against individual prisoners. They discovered the trap-door, the working of which puzzled them completely. They were unable to find the means of releasing the safety catches and after much hammering and scratching they were eventually forced to break the floor in with sledge-hammers. The commandant himself was not particularly upset, but the entire German staff and the guards were almost frantic, and there was a terrible to-do in the *Kommandantur* where each prisoner was sent for separately and cross-examined as to his share in the proceedings. A deep cut on my hand caused a lot of suspicion to fall upon me, but fortunately I was not arrested.

The inevitable result of the discovery of the tunnel was a visit from the general. He arrived, purple in the face, the same afternoon and the prisoners were assembled in the yard to receive him. We were quite prepared for a speech, but we were not expecting the amazing harangue which he and the interpreter gave us. In tones of deep emotion the general said something like this:

"*Meine Herren,* I am grieved to hear that an attempt to escape has been made. After all I have done for you; after I had permitted you to have air in your bedroom at night; this is the way you reward me. I shall take steps to have you punished."

He then mumbled to the interpreter, who was also trembling with emotion, but from a different cause, to carry on with the translation, and this is what the interpreter said:

"Gentlemen, this morning in your camp an underground outgoing is found!"

There was a burst of laughter at this, whereupon the general mumbled something more to the interpreter, who went on: "The General is not satisfied with you already; he is quite angry, and why not?"

Again we roared with laughter and again the general mumbled something. This time the interpreter was quite unable to deal with the situation, but, doubtless feeling that he had to say something or else lose his post, he emitted a series of grunts and faint squeaks. He was greeted with loud cheers. The entertainment went on for nearly twenty minutes during which time the general delivered himself of a most impassioned oration reducing us all to a state of helpless giggling. When he had quite finished, the general gravely saluted us, a gesture which the interpreter imitated, and surrounding himself with a party of guards dashed out of the camp. We just had time to run upstairs to our dining-room and from the two windows overlooking the front of the camp we gave the unfortunate man one more hearty cheer as he drove off in a ramshackle little two-seater car. The comic side of the general's visit made us almost forget the tragedy of the tunnel and at the end of the day we felt quite ready to start again.

XXIII

A feeble attempt at a search was carried out a few days later, but little or nothing was found by the Germans. In spite of its failure therefore we could say that the tunnel had succeeded in forcing us to prepare and had made us keen to devise fresh plans.

As far as Neunkirchen was concerned it was obvious that we should never again have such a chance of getting so many prisoners out together. The regulations were now stricter than ever. There were extra sentries in the yard; an extra *Appell* was held in the evening, and a number of German N.C.O.'s and soldiers were told off to play the role of comic detectives. We were continually finding means of fooling these men and setting booby traps for them. One night after lights out a few of us were still sitting up smoking and drinking beer, when we noticed a man peering over the edge of the gallery. We tiptoed to the side of our dormitory and unhooked the fire hose. When next his head appeared we let fly, not only with the hose but with boots and any other hard object ready to hand. There was a muffled gasp, and then a patter of stockinged feet as the amateur detective rushed down the back stairs and took refuge in the guard-room.

At about this time air raids started again on manufacturing towns in the Saar basin. It was to prevent these that camps had been established at Neunkirchen, Saarbrücken and one or two other points. We were naturally very excited and all kinds of wild projects were discussed, to be put into operation if only the town and the walls of the camp were knocked flat by a salvo of bombs. The first raid we saw gave us all kinds of new ideas. Although the bombing aeroplanes were miles away in the direction of Saarbrücken, we could see the searchlights and bursting anti-aircraft shells. The moment the alarm was given we were all locked up in the dining-room, while the Germans took refuge in the cellars. All the lights in the town as well as those in the camp were put out and we began to think that with a few more raids we might be able to stage a successful escape.

Meanwhile we believed we could possibly be of some use to the Allied airmen, if they came over Neunkirchen, by showing them the position of our camp – its bearing in relation to the rest of the town being known to our Intelligence Service. Wilkin was consulted once again and was asked if he could install a signalling apparatus in the roof. As just before the failure of the tunnel he had succeeded in constructing a small but quite efficient telephone set to be used between the tunnel and the dormitory, this new task was comparatively easy. There was only gas installed in the camp and he had to rely entirely on the primitive electrical apparatus obtained from the German barber. With his usual ingenuity Wilkin soon overcame all difficulties and, as far as I remember, a lamp was fitted in the roof above McClean's room, and connected to a Morse tapping key in the dining-room below.

Not content with this, Wilkin went on with his experiments with the object not only of providing the camp with a complete telephone service, but also of setting up a wireless installation capable of communicating with the nearest Allied post some ninety miles distant. He had got far towards achieving this remarkable plan, and was only waiting for some of the essential material to be smuggled out from England, when we left the camp a month or so later.

In addition to these varied employments Wilkin was kept continually busy picking locks in different parts of the camp, partly with a view to finding some new places which might afford opportunities of escape and also to discover suitable hiding-places for the large amount of kit now at our disposal. Really sure methods of breaking out of camp were practically non-existent, although it seemed within the bounds of possibility to play the old washing-basket trick successfully. For weeks we tried to devise some scheme for bluffing our way out of the main gate, disguised either as German soldiers or civilians. At one time we even thought of disguising ourselves as the general and his staff and walking boldly out at the end of one of his frequent visits. As well as being decidedly humorous this scheme would have enabled us to make a quick get-away in the general's motor-car, but as it involved the temporary kidnapping of the general by the prisoners remaining behind, it was naturally difficult to find accomplices who were willing to lend a hand.

Some of the prisoners thought that the town prison adjoining the camp would be easier to escape from than the camp itself, and in this connection a rather amusing incident occurred at about this time. One morning at *Appell* the interpreter called out my name. He knew none of us by sight or by name, although it was his business to do so, and in a spirit of mischief Collier presented himself in my place. The interpreter informed him that the authorities at Ströhen had announced that I still had fourteen days of my sentence to serve. Personally I was sick to death of solitary confinement, but Collier seemed to be quite anxious to spend two weeks in the jail to investigate its possibilities and also to pass a few quiet nights 'far from the madding crowd's ignoble strife'. I agreed to his taking my place, the Germans were none the wiser, and Collier was duly transferred to prison under my name. He stayed there for about a week, during which time he read a lot of very interesting books and found that escape was out of the question. Then one of the German officers came back from leave and found me in the camp. He was astounded and said that he thought I was supposed to be in prison. I gave some rather lame excuse which did not satisfy him, and, Collier having confessed to his real name, he was brought out of prison and I was put in in his place. After a fortnight I returned to the camp, agreeing with Collier that escape from the jail – at any rate from the cell in which we had both been placed – was impossible.

We were now reluctantly forced to admit that failing a relaxation of the strict supervision maintained by the authorities, the best we could hope for was a transfer to another camp, which, rumour had it, would take place in the spring. Meanwhile we were able to improve our physical condition. The promised walks had at last started and, to our great joy, permission to use the football ground just outside the town was granted. There were just enough rugger players in the camp to make up two fifteens, and we had some very amusing games which did us all a great deal of good. The general's story about hostility of the inhabitants was complete nonsense; most of the inhabitants took no notice of us at all, and those few who did were extremely friendly.

At the beginning of March several of the older prisoners were told that their turn for exchange to Holland was drawing near. Most of them, being old prisoners of the retreat from Mons, were naturally very pleased at the prospect, but one or two who were keen on escaping wondered whether they had better not refuse to go. The conditions of the exchange were certainly very tempting, for within the limits of certain towns ex-prisoners were allowed to live in complete freedom and to do exactly as they pleased. The English prisoners were centred in The Hague; the German prisoners from England in Rotterdam or some other town. The great disadvantage lay in the fact that, by the terms of the agreement between England, Holland, and Germany, prisoners once in Holland would stay there until the end of the war, being expressly forbidden by their respective governments to make any attempt to escape. Some of the prisoners felt that they ought not to make this final and irrevocable surrender and that by staying in Germany they were at least preventing a certain number of Germans from taking an active part in the war. It was, however, obviously impossible for all of us to escape and after several years of imprisonment many began to despair of ever succeeding.

A farewell banquet was arranged as a send-off to the first party from Neunkirchen, and shortly afterwards the names of the second batch were announced. McClean found himself among these and made up his mind not to go. He informed the Germans of his decision, but he was told that his name being on the official list he would have to go as far as Aachen, the camp to which prisoners were taken on their way to Holland, in order to satisfy the authorities of his definite refusal. He still determined to escape some day and it was just possible that at Aachen he would find a chance. On leaving McClean took with him an excellent assortment of escaping necessaries and we watched his departure with interest, hoping that the next time a party left for Aachen one of us might be smuggled out in a large wicker basket such as some of the prisoners used for packing their belongings.

Three days later, like the dove to Mount Ararat, McClean returned to Neunkirchen. He reported that escape from the camp did not seem to be very difficult but that it would require time to work out the details. Owing to his having been sent back a day sooner than he had expected, he had been unable to accomplish his purpose, but he was able to give us a rough plan of the camp together with its exact position on the south-west side of the town of Aachen. He also brought us news of one or two other prisoners who had likewise refused to be exchanged to Holland.

A week or two elapsed and then the Germans published yet another list of prisoners who were to be prepared to leave for Aachen at a moment's notice. This time the list included Collier, Wilkin and myself. Collier was inclined to accept, but Wilkin and I were firm in our belief that we still stood a reasonable chance of escaping successfully and consequently refused. Thinking that the authorities would have benefited by McClean's case, we imagined that we should not be sent even as far as Aachen and put the matter completely out of our minds. Rumours that we were soon to be transferred to another camp were becoming more frequent, and to hasten this move we continued making a series of written protests to the Germans, dealing chiefly with the unhealthiness of the camp. I also put in my usual application to be allowed to rejoin my brother. I felt so certain I would not be sent to Aachen that I even wrote home asking for more escaping kit to be sent out, and for all parcels to be sent to Holzminden, my brother's camp.

* * *

One morning, to our surprise, the Germans announced that the authorities in Berlin had decided we must go as far as Aachen, so that there should be absolutely no doubt of our refusal to go to Holland. They were apparently worried lest they should be accused by the Allied governments of keeping prisoners back. This decision put the whole matter of escaping on a totally different footing and we accordingly revised our plans.

I was not to leave Neunkirchen, however, without once more getting into trouble with the authorities. A fortnight before our departure we were examined by a German doctor who had to certify that all prisoners were free from disease before entering Holland. The examination took a very long time and we were ordered to strip completely naked in front of the most unpleasant specimen of the German medical profession it has ever been my misfortune to set eyes on. I informed the doctor that as I was not going to Holland the examination was quite unnecessary in my case, and that I did not intend to strip. After a short argument he lost his temper, sent for some guards and had me arrested. The commandant, while expressing much sympathy, was forced to award me seven days in jail. This time instead of being sent out of the camp to the prison, I was locked in one of the empty rooms at the top of the house. I spent a pleasant week there, putting the finishing touches to a forged passport and practising picking and unpicking the lock of my room with a bent fork. Every evening, having picked the lock, I went downstairs, had a glass of beer and listened to the camp gossip. By ten o'clock when the Germans went on their rounds, I was upstairs again and had relocked my door for the night.

A week after my release the time came for our departure. We had arranged to take a large stock of escaping kit so that, should we be unable to escape from Aachen and not be sent back to Neunkirchen, we would be fully equipped in the next camp. It was by no means easy to hide so many things, and the news that we were to undergo a strict search before leaving the camp gave us cause for anxiety. On entering the *Kommandantur*, we found that our fears were justified when we were told to take off the greater part of our clothing and unpack our luggage. Wilkin and I made some excuse and hurried back to the dormitory where we got rid of the bulkier and least necessary of our possessions. After that the search passed off satisfactorily and nothing was found. I had with me a compass, a map of Aachen and the Dutch frontier, two or three-hundred marks of German money, a forged permit to travel, and a moderately good felt hat sewn into the lining of my coat in such a way as to be practically unnoticeable unless the coat was ripped open. Fortunately we were not completely stripped as the pass and some of the money were in a canvas belt tied tightly around my waist.

We got into the train at Neunkirchen at nine o'clock in the morning and, travelling all day long through the picturesque Rhineland, reached Cologne without incident at about eleven that night. We had to change trains here, and there was a wait of over an hour. Here again we were taken into the underground waiting-room where we found numerous other prisoners from different camps also on their way to Aachen. High up on the whitewashed wall of this temporary prison, I found my name with the date 'December 8th, 1915!' Beneath it I added 'April 16th, 1918'. Nearly two years and a half – perhaps I had a pre-monition of victory, but somehow those dates seemed to look like the beginning and the end.

The train for Aachen arrived just after midnight and our party, now nearly a hundred strong, was soon packed in. Wilkin and I had entertained high hopes of leaving the train before we reached our destination. But, notwithstanding a dark night and a scarcity of guards, the train maintained far too high a speed for any attempt to be made with safety.

XXIV

We reached Aachen at half-past one in the morning, and marched through the dark deserted streets towards the east side of the town. It was quite clear that we were not going to the camp described by McClean, and our hopes fell. Both Wilkin and I talked over the possibility of bolting down a side street during the march, but the guards were numerous enough to be able to give chase without weakening the main body, and we were also quite ignorant of the topography of the town.

Upon arriving at the camp we were all interviewed by the authorities, and particulars were taken down and compared with a list supplied from Berlin. When my turn came I told them of my determination to stop in Germany and not to be exchanged; Wilkin did the same. The Germans were much amused, as they fancied we preferred the delightful prison life we had been leading to the freedom of Holland. But they told us we should have to stay another night in Aachen before they could get permission from Berlin to send us back.

This only gave us the next day to decide on a plan of escape, and the next night to carry it out. It was difficult to believe that we should be able to find a sure method, but we began to investigate the camp at once. We were not allowed out of the building till the morning, and we had to content ourselves with making a rough survey from the inside before we went to bed.

We found that the place we were in was only one half of the whole building; the other half being used as a hospital for German wounded. There was apparently no communication between the two halves, for we could see several bricked-up doorways on the first and second floors. Moreover, when we had been brought in, we had come through the main entrance of the German hospital out into the courtyard at the back, then through a gateway into another yard, and finally by a side door into our own part of the building. One side of the camp was bounded by a main road, and the remaining two sides by the usual wooden palisade and barbed-wire, enclosing a small exercise yard. The hospital section possessed a similar yard for the use of the German wounded, and was surrounded by a tall barbed-wire fence. The two yards were separated by a wall, in which was the gateway we had recently passed through, and by an iron-roofed brick shed. Next day we discovered that this shed contained the camp lavatories, both for the prisoners and the hospital inmates.

From the top floor we counted the sentries and estimated how large an area the arc-lamps illuminated. We could see that the camp was well defended, particularly owing to the proximity of the hospital and the houses in the street. We were actually inside the town but near the outskirts, and there were fields in front of the camp. In the distance, a few miles to the north we could dimly make out a line of hills which we knew must overlook the Dutch frontier. The thought that we were so close made us doubly keen. I felt very excited and remember saying to Wilkin as we watched from the window:

"There, ahead of us, lies the frontier we have been trying to get a glimpse of since 1915. By hook or by crook we have *got* to get away tomorrow night!"

Next morning several batches of prisoners due for exchange came in; among them were Strong, my one-time observer, and Beverley Robinson, who had been at Holzminden since leaving Ströhen. Robinson had also refused the exchange to Holland, and hearing that Wilkin and I were doing likewise, offered his help if we attempted to escape. We gave him a rough idea of our plans and he asked if he might follow us if the scheme were successful. He had brought some sort of kit with him, including a compass and a felt hat, and we therefore agreed to his making a third.

The rest of the morning we spent in walking round the yard, examining the wire and the positions of the sentries, and searching for a safe way out. Our escape would have to be made without any preparation, owing to the short time at our disposal: it was useless to think of anything like bluffing our way out as German officers, or even workmen, for we had none of the necessary kit and no knowledge of the regular routine of the place. We had to make sure that we got away without being noticed, because once the alarm was raised it would be easy for the Germans, with the frontier only a few miles distant, to patrol every yard of the sector we were likely to cross. For the same reason, since we were certain to be missed early the next morning, it was essential to cross the frontier the same night, and therefore an early start was necessary.

Scheme after scheme was suggested and thrown aside as impracticable, and we were driven to the conclusion that the only possible way out was to get somehow into the hospital yard, which was not so well guarded and less brilliantly illuminated. With only one barbed-wire fence to cross, it seemed probable that once there we should be able to get safely into the open. The problem was how to cross the wall. It was fairly well lighted and several sentries would be able to see it clearly. The lavatories on our side had no communication with those on the German side – at least if there had ever been a door, it was bricked up now. The gate in the wall was of no use; it was locked and there was a sentry on duty near it.

Almost in despair we made another inspection of the lavatories, and this time we noticed something that had previously escaped our attention. Twelve feet from the ground there were two ventilation holes, each less than two feet square, piercing the wall and evidently leading into the hospital lavatories. Both these holes were wired up, but in one of them the strands were loose and widely spread leaving enough space for us to squeeze through The question as to what we should do on the other side was still unsettled, but at any rate we knew how to get there.

We went indoors and up to the top floor where we could watch the other yard, and notice how many Germans were using their lavatories. We found that, while there was only one exit from our lavatories, there were three on the hospital side and one of them close to the wire. The wire fence was about six feet high and fairly closely woven, but we thought we could climb it in the dark. We could only see two sentries, one outside the wire and one in the yard. They were probably meant to guard against possible deserters from the hospital, but they might easily give us trouble as well. We learnt from prisoners who had arrived before us, that the yard was closed for the night at a quarter to ten and it was not dark till 9.15 – so there would not be much margin of time for our escape.

We worked out our scheme again in the afternoon, and made another careful survey of the camp to see if we could find anything better, but there seemed to be nothing else. We collected the small amount of kit we had, and decided what to wear and what to take in the way of food.

I had still with me a moderately good map, some money, a forged pass, a small compass and a felt hat. I was wearing grey flannel trousers, and my khaki coat had ordinary bone buttons and no badges of any sort, so that in the dark I might well pass for a workman. Wilkin was similarly equipped, and we managed to get him a felt hat from another prisoner who was going to Holland. Chocolate and a few biscuits were all we needed for provisions; we intended to breakfast across the frontier on the following morning.

As soon as it began to get dark, we again posted ourselves at a window and watched the hospital yard. At first there seemed to be an awful crowd; but gradually it thinned out, and by half-past nine there were only a few men left in the whole place. We got ready and went out. There were still many prisoners about and it was fortunate that it was so, for a sentry was already standing near the shed telling every one it was time to go into the main building.

As soon as we got to the shed, I went straight in while Wilkin watched the sentry from the doorway. The ventilation hole was almost in line with the doorway and could be seen from it, as the partition screening the toilet was only some seven feet high. At that moment the sentry put his head in at the door and said something about making haste. We replied with unintentional humour that we would be out in a minute, and the instant he had his back turned I slipped into one of the toilets. With the aid of a wooden partition and some water pipes I climbed up to a small cistern, and standing on it reached the hole, pulled up and pushed through. I let myself down on the far side and found the corresponding cistern with my feet. Looking back through the hole I saw that Robinson had followed me and was already climbing up, while Wilkin was still near the door watching the sentry, and – as he told me afterwards – the sentry was watching him. I waited a few seconds, but there was no time to be lost; at any moment we might be discovered.

We let ourselves down cautiously from the cistern. On this side the lavatories were almost pitch dark, and not meeting any Germans we tiptoed to the doorway and looked out, no one was in sight. A few paces forward we reached the fence. We made a hasty inspection of the wire; there was a small open drain running out at this point, and we found just enough room to crawl through. As we scrambled out I spotted the sentry in the German yard barely fifteen yards away, and even closer on the other side I could see one of the camp sentries; fortunately both had their backs turned. We crawled slowly for twenty yards, and then, getting into the shadow of a low hedge leading away from the camp, stood up and ran, A hundred yards farther on we reached another field with a taller hedge screening us completely from the sentries. Looking back I could see the window from which, only five minutes ago, we had been watching the Germans and discussing our chances. Except that Wilkin was not with us, everything was going well, and there were no signs of pursuit.

But we nearly had trouble within the next two minutes. We had crossed the field diagonally, making for a road on the far side. To get there we had to climb over a barbed-wire fence and pass close to a lamp-post standing in front of a row of houses. As luck would have it I caught my trousers on the fence, and in my haste to get unhooked tore a strip six inches long out of the seat. A party of two men, a woman and a boy, who were passing the lamp at this moment, glanced round, then stopped and stared at us. For a minute it looked as though they were going to come and question us, which would have been very awkward as Robinson could not speak German. But by talking loudly in German I made it seem that we were perfectly ordinary, though rather rough, young men on our way home.

"*Donnerwetter*," I said, "it is most annoying to tear one's trousers; but no matter, we shall soon be home now."

Robinson mumbled a bit, and said "*Jawohl*" once or twice; the Germans stood still and did nothing. They were still staring when we turned the corner and disappeared from their gaze.

We passed between the houses and turned into a lane which we had just been able to see from the camp, and which appeared to lead clear of the town. For a quarter of an hour we followed this track, and then had again to dodge houses and factories. The country to the north-east of Aachen is thickly populated, and dotted with mines and blast-furnaces; in between the industrial patches it is hilly and wooded. To keep on a definite course by night with an inaccurate map was wellnigh impossible, and the difficulty of the situation was increased by the detours we were forced to make round all the numerous villages. At times we were scared by the glow from one of the furnaces, suddenly lighting up the whole countryside and giving us an unpleasant feeling of insecurity – as though we were being held in the beam of a searchlight.

For the first two hours we headed north-east, and then gradually turned until we were facing north. We came to better country and our pace increased, but we had wasted a lot of time getting clear of Aachen and its suburbs. Although it was a dark night and raining slightly, we soon noticed how clearly white houses or white posts showed up and wondered how much could be seen of us. Our faces were easy to cover up with our woollen mufflers, but we found that, through several bad tears in our trousers, our knees were showing and could be seen some way off; our hands were almost as bad. The only remedy seemed to be to rub earth on all the places that were noticeable, so we sat down in a corner of a ploughed field and plastered ourselves with mud. It was unpleasant and messy, but it rendered us almost invisible and we went on more confidently.

We got lost several times in a perfect maze of hills, rivers and woods, often made worse by the discovery of roads and railways not marked on our map. On these occasions we kept on a rough compass course, and the later it grew the straighter our course became, as there was less risk from villages and farms whose occupants had long since gone to bed. There seemed to be fewer dogs about than usual in Germany; we expected trouble with them as we came nearer to the frontier, but we had practically none. Our chief source of worry was the large number of small industrial settlements evidently constructed since the date of issue of our map. We were often forced to walk straight through such places and we were very fortunate in not meeting many people.

At half-past two we lost all confidence in the map, which after leading us to a correctly marked road suddenly brought us to a railway line, a brightly illuminated mine and then a river broad enough to make us look for a bridge. None of these features were shown on the map, and we wondered what we should do on the frontier. I began to lose confidence in our chances of success; in fact, when we had made an almost complete circle round the mine and its neighbouring buildings and found ourselves heading due south, I was on the verge of despair. But within half an hour, the country flattened out and we came across several landmarks which, with some lights we could see to the north, convinced us that we were close to the small town of Kohlscheid, itself only two miles from the nearest point of the frontier.

We blundered into the southern outskirts, and were only saved from passing right through the place by discovering a main road with tramlines and seeing the station lights just ahead. Had we missed Kohlscheid we might easily have continued due north and run into the thickly populated and probably strongly guarded area of Kohlberg. Turning due west we found a stream and followed it to the main railway line from Aachen. We waited while a goods train passed slowly by and then crossed the line, picking up the stream on the far side. The lights of Kohlscheid station shone not five-hundred yards to the right, and to our left a row of houses showed up faintly, indicating the position of the village of Bank.

From now on we were in the frontier zone and great caution was essential. Under normal circumstances it was an understood thing that one went dead slow in this zone, and for the last two miles it was considered best to crawl on hands and knees taking advantage of every scrap of cover. In our case this was out of the question; it was already half-past three and we estimated that to reach the point where we intended to cross the frontier, we had another four miles in front of us. Dawn would come between five and half-past and by that time we wanted to be more than a mile across the border; bearing in mind the uncertainty of its exact position, we had over five miles to do in less than two hours. Slow going was not to be thought of, and heading north-west we pushed on at a good three miles an hour.

Our route took us through open rolling country, with large ploughed fields, making concealment difficult but allowing us to see and avoid houses, villages and woods (which might contain guards) before getting dangerously near to them. We felt, too, that where we could not hide at any rate there was no chance of a sentry being concealed, and we made no noise in the open fields, whereas in a wood we should have been cracking twigs the whole time. Every now and then we stopped to listen for any sounds of voices or footsteps, and to take fresh bearings with the compass. Occasionally lying flat on the ground we scanned the dark grey skyline, hoping to see ahead of time any unusual movement that might betray the presence of a sentry. In this way we covered about two miles without any difficulty, and the only obstacles we encountered were the stream, which we recrossed, and a farmhouse. As we got nearer, we could see more lights some miles to the north, though whether this was another German village or actually one across the frontier we could not tell. One especially bright light shone out above the others and was very useful as a bearing-point. For a short time we headed towards these lights, but we were brought to a full stop by another farmhouse from which a sound of voices was coming, and what seemed to be the clicking of rifle bolts. Then we fancied we could discern the figure of a sentry near the house, and hurriedly turning back we made a wide detour to the west and lost sight of the place without raising the alarm. By this time it was past 4.30 and it seemed almost certain that we were within two miles of the frontier.

There was not much time to spare. Our map was very vague as to the precise line of the frontier in this neighbourhood, but there was one certain indication of having crossed it: about a mile and a half across the border and parallel to it, there ran a line of railway. To be quite sure of success, we had to reach this line before dawn. And already the eastern horizon was giving a pale warning of the approach of day. Within an hour it would be light.

A mile past the farmhouse where we had heard voices, we reached a small patch of wood bounded by barbed-wire, and beyond it what appeared to be a much larger wood. We skirted the former, not trying to enter it as it was apparently crossed by several wire fences. On reaching the second wood, we found it to be composed of widely-spaced tall trees, with the undergrowth cut away and a high closely-woven barbed-wire fence running round it. This might be either part of the frontier defences or it might be merely farmers' wire. In any case it would be most unwise to attempt to get into the wood.

The side we had reached ran roughly east and west. On the whole it seemed safer to follow it in the latter direction and after two or three hundred yards we came quite suddenly upon a road. It ran nearly north and south, and, from its size and good surface, we judged it to be the main road from Aachen to Holland. This gave us an excellent idea as to how far west we had come, but, owing to the lack of detail on our map, still no certain knowledge as to how far north. There was no one about; the road was straight and, with its white surface, easy to see. A low hedge bounded it on either side. If we were challenged we could separate and hide in the woods. We were taking a big risk, but there was no time for hesitation, and we walked along it boldly for a few hundred yards. Then, as it turned and we could not see clearly around the bend, we took to a track on the left-hand side. The troublesome woods flanking the road had given way to a series of fields and orchards from which we again caught sight of some lights. They now bore roughly east-north-east, showing that we had made good progress to the north-west.

We strode on as fast as we could, for the sky was rapidly getting grey; in less than half an hour it would be broad daylight. And then we almost tripped over a sentry! He was sitting in a little rough shelter down in a hollow; in front of him there was a fire in a bucket over which he was warming himself. I dimly perceived a *Landsturm* helmet on his head, and a rifle propped up beside him. Fortunately he gave no sign of having seen or heard us.

We retraced our steps on tiptoe for twenty yards, and then turned back towards the road. We reached it and found it deserted, but having just seen a sentry the danger of following it seemed too great and we contented ourselves with going straight across so as to avoid a house only a few yards ahead. By the time we had crawled through a hedge on the far side and crossed a small field, it was light enough for us to be seen nearly half a mile away. With a sense of having failed, we realised we could go no farther that day, and began looking around anxiously for cover. The only possible hiding-place in sight was a small, sparse wood some four hundred yards farther north. We walked hard for it and, screened by a hedge, even ran the last hundred yards. We reached the trees and searched for a spot where we could if necessary lie up for the whole day. There was much wire and very little undergrowth; the best cover available was a blackberry bush. As we crawled in some men passed along an unseen road lying ahead of us and evidently joining up with the one we had just crossed. They were talking and I listened attentively, but I was unable to make out what they were saying though the words sounded distinctly German. For the present we could do nothing but keep quiet and watch for sentries.

Now that it was daylight we were able to go over our map more carefully, and followed mentally, step by step, the course we had taken during the night. Very gradually I became convinced that we had actually crossed the frontier and were already in Holland. This was a dangerously optimistic view to take and Robinson disagreed entirely. He was sure we were still in Germany, rightly arguing that we had seen practically nothing of the frontier guards and that we had not yet reached the all-important railway. We talked it over for a long time, while Robinson produced a needle and thread and mended some of the worst tears in our clothing. For a short interval we took it in turns to sleep, and, during Robinson's watch he woke me up to point out two men in uniform going along the road. It was impossible to see at that distance whether they were Dutch or German since the two uniforms are very similar; yet they were going in the direction from which we had come and presently two more men came back. Supposing that they were sentries being relieved, this would seem to prove that the frontier was behind us.

Then a clock struck not very far from us. I counted six chimes, but by Robinson's watch it was now seven. Of course the clock might be wrong, but if not then the inference was obvious: the Germans had summer time, the Dutch had not – it was a Dutch clock. But a Dutch clock might well be heard in Germany. Were we a few yards inside Germany, or had we just crossed the border?

We were still anxious, but the evidence was turning in our favour, and Robinson was getting more optimistic when shortly after eight o'clock the unexpected happened. Some way off we heard the puffing of an engine and we listened intently trying to make out in what direction it was going. It must be on *the* railway; if we could reach it we should be safe. At times the sound seemed to die down, only to burst out again closer. There was something awe-inspiring about the slow rhythmical puffing. Like the beat of a war drum in an African forest. I felt almost frightened. It came nearer and nearer, and then to our amazement the engine steamed into sight a hundred yards ahead of our hiding-place, along what we had thought to be a road and which the trees had prevented us from seeing clearly. It was a goods train, and on the sides of the trucks were the Dutch colours and the word 'Nederland' in large letters.

We stood up and walked to the line; on the far side of it we saw a house with a Dutch advertisement on its side, and a signpost pointing to Spekholz … Holland! A thousand prison dreams of freedom faded into one reality: we were no longer prisoners.

XXV

Of my own adventures there is little more to be told. We were unable to find any of the Dutch frontier guards or other officials to whom, in the ordinary course of events, we ought to have reported. This proved to be a very fortunate occurrence, as escaping prisoners were usually locked up and kept in prison until it had been ascertained that they were in reality prisoners of war and not smugglers or spies. Even when their statements had been verified a further fortnight's confinement had to be spent in quarantine.

After walking for about a mile we came into the village of Spekholz and, uncertain of what we should do next, made our way into a small shop. I still felt the necessity for caution and spoke to the old lady behind the counter in German, asking her for some cigarettes. To my horror she not only answered me in German, but asked me whence we had come and whither we were going. Her questions and the setting of the scene reminded me forcibly of old times in Germany and I began to have an unpleasant feeling that we might have made an awful mistake and not have crossed the frontier after all. The old lady soon explained, however, that she was an Austrian who had taken refuge in Holland, though for what reason I was unable to make out. Her whole household seemed very strange, consisting as it did of her daughter married to a German, a Belgian girl refugee, a German deserter and a Dutchwoman. They treated us very hospitably, gave us food and helped mend our clothes. One of the customers who came into her shop during the morning happened to be the local photographer and he immediately insisted on taking our photographs.

In the course of the day the old lady communicated with the head office of a coal mine just outside the village, which was owned and operated by Belgian refugees. In the afternoon we got a message from the manager of the company, asking us to come up to the works and spend the night there. There we were made extremely comfortable and next day the manager lent us sufficient money to buy a few articles of clothing and tickets to Rotterdam.

While we were at Spekholz, we made inquiries to find out whether the local people knew anything of Hardy's escape. If it was true that he had crossed the Dutch frontier it would be somewhere in this neighbourhood, because in the days when we had worked together we had always agreed to make for Aachen. I did not have to push my inquiries very far, for the local inhabitants were full of the news that about six weeks previously two English officers – "generals" the Dutch called them – had crossed the frontier some two miles away near Simpelveld. Much later I heard that Hardy and Loder-Symonds had escaped from a camp at Schweidnitz [Swidnica] in Silesia and had travelled by train the whole way to Aachen. A remarkable performance considering that Loder-Symonds could talk no German and that the whole trip was accomplished with the help of two of Hardy's home-made passports.

On the afternoon of 19 April we drove to the railway station at Heerlen, and took the train for Rotterdam which we reached at ten o'clock that night. We noticed during the journey that we were under the continual observation of Dutch detectives. The police had evidently been warned of our arrival and were wondering what they should do with us for not having reported to the frontier authorities. We put up at a small hotel in Rotterdam for the night and next morning reported to the Consul-General. The Consulate people were extremely kind and provided us with all the money we required during our enforced stay in Holland. We were told that we should have to wait about ten days before a convoy of ships sailed for England. We bought some clothes in the town and then made for The Hague, where we spent the greater part of a week.

We met again large numbers of the prisoners we had known in Germany including the very batch who had been at Aachen only two or three days before. Wilkin was amongst them and was, of course, absolutely miserable at not having shared in our success. He told us how he had tried to follow a few minutes after our escape, but the sentry had been too watchful. Bitterly disappointed at his failure, he had consented to go to Holland. Stewart was there, and Elliot, Collier and many others. It took quite a lot off our own enjoyment to meet these old friends who had tried so hard to escape during the wretched years in captivity and who were now condemned to remain in Holland for the rest of the war.

We had been warned by the British authorities not to talk too much of escaping adventures while at The Hague, and on no account to mention the name of the ship or date of its sailing. The Hague was full of spies; in fact, many of the waiters in the best hotels were known to be German agents, and it was most amusing to watch them hovering round tables at which prisoners of war were seated, trying to pick up scraps of conversation and writing the secret notes on backs of menu cards.

We were notified secretly of the date on which our convoy was to sail, and at the appointed time we hurried back to Rotterdam and embarked. Next morning at dawn we steamed out into the North Sea. I had an unpleasant feeling that it would be just our luck to be recaptured at sea by a German submarine. Fortunately the blocking of Zeebrugge, which had been effected while we were still in Holland, had made this possibility much more remote.

Escorted by British destroyers we spent the better part of two days zigzagging through mine-fields and submarine-infested waters. In the early morning of 31 April we steamed up the Thames estuary, and at nine o'clock we anchored off Gravesend.

For the next few weeks I was kept frightfully busy giving information on every conceivable subject to officers in various departments of the War Office and the newly formed Air Ministry. I had also begun learning to fly again, but I found time to despatch a considerable quantity of escaping kit, carefully concealed in food tins to my friends in Germany. Later I had the satisfaction of knowing that many of these things had been received and had proved to be of value.

In August I returned to France. Just previously, in July, I had heard that a tunnel which had been in preparation for over a year at Holzminden had at last been completed and that twenty-nine prisoners had escaped. Many of these prisoners were ex-Neunkirchen tunnel workers, proving that our experience had been of some use. No less than ten of the party succeeded in crossing the Dutch frontier, and among them was Blaine. To my very great sorrow I never saw him again, for by the time he reached England I was back in France, and when I returned to England on leave after the Armistice the first news I heard was that he had been killed in an aeroplane accident.

Shortly after my return from Germany I got news of the death of Medlicott. He had escaped for, I think, the twelfth time, from a camp in the centre of Germany, but after a few days of freedom he and his companion had been recaptured. Guards were sent from the camp to bring them back, and it is to be supposed that these men had instructions to make sure, in case of any trouble, that the prisoners did not return alive. At all events, according to the German statement, Medlicott and his companion made a dash for freedom during the return journey. They were pursued by their guards, who headed them off and shot them both down. Strangely enough the old, inexperienced Landsturm soldiers succeeded in killing their victims with only one shot each, although they were some way off and running. The bodies were brought back to the camp and the senior British officers were allowed to inspect them. Both bodies were covered with sheets, reaching to their heads through which they had been shot, but one of the British officers, suspecting foul play, succeeded in snatching away the sheet covering Medlicott's body.

It was torn by more than a dozen bullet and bayonet wounds, There seems to be little doubt, both from this and from the conflicting statements issued by the Germans, that both these unfortunate men had been murdered in cold blood.

A very gallant fellow, was Medlicott; one of the most daring pilots in France. As brave a man as I have ever met, foolhardy almost. There was hardly a jail in Germany he could not escape from, but, although on at least one occasion he came close to success, his plans lacked caution. This alone would not have caused failure; it was purely bad luck that stopped him. And so it was with all of us. One might try and fail and try again. One might take all possible precautions and show the utmost determination, yet without luck there was no chance of success. Hundreds of prisoners must have tried seriously to escape; scores tried again and again, but fortune only favoured a few. Out of some eight-thousand officers in Germany, a mere handful – between forty and fifty – succeeded in regaining their freedom before the Armistice.

Many never returned; others returned to die. It is strange how many of those I knew in prison and whose friendship I valued have disappeared: Blaine and Medlicott, Stewart – killed after the war – Darcy Levy. … Poor Darcy Levy, perhaps his fits of depression at Zorndorf were a premonition of his fate. I saw him just after the war; he was learning to fly again. The next I heard was that he had rejoined the North Russian Expedition. Engine trouble brought his aeroplane down in the enemy lines and there the Russians – I will not call them Bolsheviks, Russians are nearly all the same – murdered him, brutally, in cold blood.

Loder-Symonds was killed learning to fly. Hardy returned to France with his infantry regiment and lost a leg at the last great battle of Ypres, and two other ex-prisoners whom I had known slightly were killed.

I must confess to feeling a desire for revenge when I returned to France. I had several scores to pay my ex-jailers and, in those days when the world was mad, I enjoyed doing it. But, in spite of the joy of flying and the ever new sense of freedom, I was wretchedly lonely. The friends and companions of 1915 were most of them dead, a few were still prisoners, and the remainder had reached exalted ranks. True, there were on the battlefields of France friends like Hardy, but they were in the infantry and I never saw them. It was sad to realize that of all those captured flying in France, I was the only one to return to fly and fight on the same front.

I often wondered what would happen if I were recaught, and I had made arrangements to pass under an assumed name. Fortunately I was not destined to languish again in a German jail. Several times during the last few months prison loomed unpleasantly near. Twice the wheels of my aeroplane actually touched the ground in enemy territory, and I could almost hear a hard Prussian voice shouting the familiar "*Kommen Sie mit.*" Largely due to a very good engine and a stable machine, I somehow managed to get home on each occasion.

And, looking back and taking my own adventures as a whole, there is one thing I can assert without fear of contradiction: ill luck may have caused my capture, it was good fortune that set me free.

THE END